Japan and the IISS

Connecting Western and Japanese Strategic Thought from the Cold War to the War on Ukraine

Edited by Robert Ward, Yuka Koshino and Matthieu Lebreton

IISS The International Institute for Strategic Studies

'This authoritative work is a must-read for anyone interested in the evolution of Japanese strategic thought and how Japan sees itself in the world. The careful curation of articles from each era, alongside excellent introductory chapters, results in an engaging and insightful work. With the signing of the Hiroshima Accord, the work of the IISS and the deep understanding and knowledge codified in this work have never been more vital.'

– Michael Rivera King, Chief Executive, The Japan Society

Japan and the IISS

Connecting Western and Japanese Strategic Thought from the Cold War to the War on Ukraine

Edited by Robert Ward, Yuka Koshino and Matthieu Lebreton

IISS The International Institute for Strategic Studies

The International Institute for Strategic Studies

Arundel House | 6 Temple Place | London | WC2R 2PG | UK

First published December 2023 by **Routledge**
4 Park Square, Milton Park, Abingdon, Oxon, OX14 4RN

for **The International Institute for Strategic Studies**
Arundel House, 6 Temple Place, London, WC2R 2PG, UK
www.iiss.org

Simultaneously published in the USA and Canada by **Routledge**
52 Vanderbilt Avenue, New York, NY 10017

Routledge is an imprint of Taylor & Francis, an Informa Business

© 2023 The International Institute for Strategic Studies

DIRECTOR-GENERAL AND CHIEF EXECUTIVE Dr Bastian Giegerich
SERIES EDITOR Dr Benjamin Rhode
ASSOCIATE EDITOR Alice Aveson
EDITORIAL Nick Fargher, Ben Ho Wan Beng, Grainne Lucey-Tremblay, Michael Marsden, Jack May, Adam Walters
PRODUCTION Alessandra Beluffi, Ravi Gopar, Jade Panganiban, James Parker, Kelly Verity, Loraine Winter
COVER ARTWORK James Parker

The International Institute for Strategic Studies is an independent centre for research, information and debate on the problems of conflict, however caused, that have, or potentially have, an important military content. The Council and Staff of the Institute are international and its membership is drawn from almost 100 countries. The Institute is independent and it alone decides what activities to conduct. It owes no allegiance to any government, any group of governments or any political or other organisation. The IISS stresses rigorous research with a forward-looking policy orientation and places particular emphasis on bringing new perspectives to the strategic debate.

The Institute's publications are designed to meet the needs of a wider audience than its own membership and are available on subscription, by mail order and in good bookshops. Further details at www.iiss.org.

British Library Cataloguing in Publication Data
A catalogue record for this book is available from the British Library

Library of Congress Cataloging in Publication Data

ADELPHI series
ISSN 1944-5571

ADELPHI AP498–501
ISBN 978-1-032-73478-1

Contents

Editors' Note   8

Contributors   9

Acknowledgements   14

Map: East Asia   16

Foreword   *Sir John Chipman KCMG*   17

Introduction   *Robert Ward*   21

Chapter One   **Japan's bridging role between Asia and the West**   37
                 Hosoya Yuichi

Chapter Two   **The role of the IISS in bridging Japanese and Western**   53
                 strategic thinking   *Yuka Koshino and Matthieu Lebreton*

1960s

Timeline of events (1945–1960s)   79

Chapter Three   **The Japanese attitude towards China**   *Ogata Sadako*   83
                 Survival 7-9, 1965 (originally published in *Asian Survey*,
                 August 1965)

Chapter Four   **American–Japanese relations**   *Matsumoto Shigeharu*   97
                 Survival 8-4, 1966 (originally published in *Japan Quarterly* and
                 Atlas, 1965)

Chapter Five   **The Asian balance of power: a comparison with European**   111
                 precedents   *Royama Michio*
                 From Adelphi Paper 42, 1967

Chapter Six   **The non-proliferation treaty and Japan**   *Imai Ryukichi*   149
                 Survival 11-9, 1969 (originally published in the *Bulletin of
                 the Atomic Scientists*, May 1969)

1970s

Timeline of events   165

Chapter Seven   **Japan's security in a multipolar world**   *Saeki Kiichi*   169
                 From Adelphi Paper 92, 1972

Chapter Eight   **Japan's non-nuclear policy**   *Kishida Junnosuke*   191
                 From Survival 15-1, 1973

Chapter Nine   **Options for Japan's foreign policy**   *Kosaka Masataka*   205
                 From Adelphi Paper 97, 1973
                 Introduction 205
                 VI Findings and policy suggestions 213

Chapter Ten   **The energy problem and alliance systems: Japan**   229
                 Momoi Makoto
                 From Adelphi Paper 115, 1975

Chapter Eleven	**Naval competition and security in East Asia** *Uchida Kazutomi* From Adelphi Paper 124, 1976	245

1980s

	Timeline of events	259
Chapter Twelve	**The changing security circumstances in the 1980s** *Satoh Yukio* From Adelphi Paper 178, 1982	263
Chapter Thirteen	**The 1984 Alastair Buchan Memorial Lecture** *Nakasone Yasuhiro* Survival 26-5, 1984	289
Chapter Fourteen	**Japanese security policy: address by Mr Tadashi Kuranari, foreign minister of Japan, 8 September 1986 (excerpts)** *Kuranari Tadashi* Survival 29-1, 1987	311
Chapter Fifteen	**East Asia, the Pacific and the West: strategic trends and implications: part II** *Kosaka Masataka* From Adelphi Paper 216, 1987	317
Chapter Sixteen	**The security of north-east Asia: part I** *Nishihara Masashi* From Adelphi Paper 218, 1987	333
Chapter Seventeen	**Prospects for security co-operation between East Asia and the West** *Okawara Yoshio* From Adelphi Paper 218, 1987	351

1990s

	Timeline of events	363
Chapter Eighteen	**Japan's role in international affairs** *Inoguchi Takashi* From Survival 34-2, 1992	367
Chapter Nineteen	**What role for Europe in Asian affairs?** *Takahashi Fumiaki* From Adelphi Paper 276, 1993	391
Chapter Twenty	**Rethinking Japan–US relations: security issues** *Sasae Kenichiro* From Adelphi Paper 292, 1994	411
Chapter Twenty-One	**Identities and security in East Asia** *Bessho Koro* From Adelphi Paper 325, 1999 Introduction 447 Chapter 1: Japan: reluctant leader? 448 Chapter 2: China: future leader? 463	447

2000–2020s

	Timeline of events	479

Chapter Twenty-Two   **China debates missile defence**   *Urayama Kori*   **485**
Survival 46-2, 2004

Chapter Twenty-Three   **Great-power relations in Asia: a Japanese perspective**   **513**
Okamoto Yukio
Survival 51-6, 2009–10

Chapter Twenty-Four   **The 13th IISS Asia Security Summit – the Shangri-La**   **521**
Dialogue: keynote address   *Abe Shinzo*

Chapter Twenty-Five   **'We are all small countries now': IISS 2019 Alastair**   **533**
Buchan Lecture   *Funabashi Yoichi*

Chapter Twenty-Six   **The 19th Regional Security Summit – the Shangri-La**   **541**
Dialogue: keynote address   *Kishida Fumio*

   Index   **561**

EDITORS' NOTE

All Japanese names featured in the republished material follow Western convention, with the given name followed by the surname, with the exception of the keynote address of Prime Minister Kishida Fumio at the 2022 Shangri-La Dialogue. All other Japanese names in the book, including in the cover, contents, contributor biographies, acknowledgements, timelines and original essays, follow the Japanese convention, with the surname followed by the given name.

With the exception of a few typographical and factual errors, none of the republished material has been edited, in order to preserve the authenticity of the analyses. As such, terminology no longer used has not been amended or updated.

CONTRIBUTORS

Abe Shinzo was Prime Minister of Japan from 2006 until 2007 and from 2012 until 2020. As of 2023, he was the longest-serving prime minister in Japanese history. Abe is regarded as one of the most influential prime ministers of post-war Japan for his security and economic policies.

Christoph Bertram was Director of the IISS from 1974 until 1982. Subsequently, he became Senior Editor of *Die Zeit* newspaper in Hamburg, contributing expertise on strategic and international affairs. He was Contributing Editor of *Foreign Policy* magazine from April 1998 and later headed the Foundation Science and Policy.

Bessho Koro is Grand Chamberlain of the Imperial Household Agency. Prior to this, he served as Permanent Representative to the United Nations in 2016–19, and Ambassador to the Republic of Korea in 2012–16. He received the Republic of Korea's highest award for his efforts to resolve bilateral tensions. He was also Executive Secretary to Prime Minister Koizumi Junichiro from 2001 until 2006. He joined the IISS as a secondee in 1997–98.

Sir John Chipman KCMG is Executive Chairman of the IISS. He was Director-General and Chief Executive of the IISS from 1 October 1993 to 1 October 2023. He has served on a variety of corporate international advisory boards and company boards of directors and consults widely for businesses with international interests.

Fujisaki Ichiro served as Ambassador of Japan to the United States in 2008–12. He is currently Chairman of International Strategies at Sophia University in Tokyo. He was previously Ambassador to the United Nations and to the World Trade Organization. Fujisaki joined the IISS as a secondee in 1987–88 and was interviewed for this project.

Dr Funabashi Yoichi is the Chairman of the Global Council of the International House of Japan and Founder of the Asia Pacific Initiative, and serves on the IISS Advisory Council. Dr Funabashi is an award-winning Japanese journalist, columnist and author. He has written extensively on foreign affairs, the US–Japan security alliance, geo-economics, and historical issues in the Asia-Pacific.

Dr Hosoya Yuichi is Professor of International Politics at Keio University in Tokyo. He is also Director of Research at the Asia Pacific Initiative and Group Head for Europe and the Americas at the Institute of Geoeconomics, both part of the International House of Japan, as well as Senior Researcher at the Nakasone Peace Institute (NPI), Senior Fellow at the Tokyo Foundation for Policy Research, and Senior Adjunct

Fellow at the Japan Institute of International Affairs (JIIA). Hosoya was a member of the Advisory Board at Japan's National Security Council in 2014–16, and a member of Prime Minister Abe Shinzo's Advisory Panel on Reconstruction of the Legal Basis for Security from 2013 to 2014. He was also a member of the Prime Minister's Advisory Panel on National Security and Defense Capabilities in 2013.

Imai Ryukichi served as Ambassador of Japan to the Conference on Disarmament in Geneva from 1982 until 1986 and chaired the Non-Proliferation Treaty Review Conference in 1985. Imai also served as Ambassador of Japan to Kuwait and Mexico. Prior to this he was Director of Engineering at the Japan Atomic Power Company, during which time he also served as a Special Assistant to the Ministry of Foreign Affairs of Japan on nuclear issues for negotiations with the US Carter administration.

Dr Inoguchi Takashi is Director and Distinguished Visiting Professor at the Institute of Asian Cultures at J. F. Oberlin University and Professor Emeritus at the University of Tokyo. He was Assistant Secretary-General of the United Nations from 1995 until 1997 and President of the University of Niigata Prefecture from 2009 until 2017.

Kishida Fumio has been Prime Minister of Japan and President of the Liberal Democratic Party since 2021. He is a member of the Japanese House of Representatives and served as Minister of Foreign Affairs from 2012 until 2017.

Kishida Junnosuke was the Editor-in-Chief of the *Asahi Shimbun* newspaper in 1977–83, Chairman of the Japan Research Institute from 1985 to 2001, and Chairman of the Japanese Association of Science and Technology Journalists from 1994 to 2001. Kishida was a science journalist who wrote extensively on Japanese nuclear policy, both for the *Asahi Shimbun* and the IISS.

Kosaka Masataka was a Japanese academic and strategist. He was Professor of International Politics at Kyoto University from 1971 until 1996, and Chairman of the Study Group on the Issue of Peace, an advisory body to Prime Minister Nakasone Yasuhiro. He also served as President of the Research Institute for Peace and Security (RIPS) from 1986 to 1992. Kosaka is widely regarded as one of the most influential figures in Japanese strategic and security studies. He served on the IISS Advisory Council from 1977 until 1986.

Yuka Koshino is a Research Fellow for Security and Technology Policy at the IISS, conducting independent research on security in the Indo-Pacific region and the impact of emerging technologies on security from defence and geo-economic perspectives. She was previously affiliated with the Asia Pacific Initiative in Tokyo as the inaugural Matsumoto–Samata Fellow (2020–21). She holds a Master's in Asian Studies from the Edmund A. Walsh School of Foreign Service at Georgetown University and a BA in Law from Keio University. She is the co-author of the *Adelphi* book *Japan's Effectiveness as a Geo-economic Actor: Navigating Great-power Competition* with Robert Ward.

Kuranari Tadashi was a Japanese member of parliament with the Liberal Democratic Party of Japan and served as the foreign minister of Japan from 1986 to 1987 under the Nakasone Yasuhiro administration. He also served as Director-General of the Economic Planning Agency between 1976 and 1977 under the Fukuda Takeo administration.

Matthieu Lebreton worked as a Research Assistant for the Japan Chair Programme at the IISS between January 2022 and June 2023. Matthieu holds a Bachelor of Science in Foreign Service from the Edmund A. Walsh School of Foreign Service at Georgetown University, where he majored in Regional Studies of Asia with a minor in Japanese. He studied at Waseda University in Tokyo under the Global Leadership Fellows Program for his year abroad.

Matsumoto Shigeharu was a journalist and a commentator on foreign affairs. He founded the Japanese Association for American Studies in 1947 with Takagi Yasaka and served as its President from 1952 until 1970. He also contributed to the establishment of the International House of Japan, serving as its Executive Director from 1952 until 1965 and Chairman of the Board from 1965 until his death in 1989.

Momoi Makoto joined the National Defense College (now the National Institute for Defense Studies–NIDS) of the Defense Agency in Tokyo in 1954 and later became its Research Director until 1982. He then worked as a freelance political and military analyst, studying defence issues from the perspective of international strategy and resource constraints.

Nakasone Yasuhiro served as Prime Minister of Japan from 1982 until 1987. He is best known for his pro-US, security-oriented foreign and security policy, and for pushing through the privatisation of Japanese state-owned companies in the 1980s. Prime Minister Nakasone's interests in strategy and security policy laid a strong foundation on which the IISS could expand its relationship with Japan.

Professor Nishihara Masashi was president of Japan's National Defense Academy from 2000 until 2006 and a member of Japanese Prime Minister Koizumi Junichiro's Task Force on Foreign Relations from 2000 until 2002. After his time at the Defense Academy, he became President of the Research Institute for Peace and Security (RIPS). Nishihara served on the IISS Advisory Council from 1987 to 1994 and was interviewed for this project.

Dr Ogata Sadako was the first woman, Japanese citizen and academic to be the United Nations High Commissioner for Refugees (UNHCR), a post she held from 1991 to 2000.

Ogata was also President of the Japan International Cooperation Agency in 2003–12. She was Professor of International Politics at Sophia University in Tokyo from 1980 to 1989, and Dean of the Faculty of Foreign Studies from 1989 to 1991. At the time of writing her contribution (1965) she was a Lecturer at the International Christian University in Tokyo.

Okamoto Yukio was Special Adviser to Prime Minister Hashimoto Ryutaro from 1996 to 1998, Special Adviser on Iraq to Koizumi Junichiro from 2003 until 2004, and Special Adviser to the Japanese cabinet in 2001–03. During these last two posts, he was Chair of the Prime Minister's Task Force on Foreign Relations. After retiring from the Ministry of Foreign Affairs in 1991, he established Okamoto Associates, an economic and political consultancy firm.

Okawara Yoshio was Ambassador of Japan to the US from 1980 until 1985. He played a key role in the restoration of US–Japan post-war relations, particularly during their intense period of trade friction in the 1980s, and was labelled a 'pragmatist' who saw the need to overcome the 'perception gap' between the two countries. Following his public service, he became President of the America–Japan Society. Okawara served on the IISS Advisory Council from 1989 until 1998.

Dr Robert O'Neill was Director of the IISS from 1982 until 1987, after which he became Chichele Professor of the History of War and Fellow at All Souls College at the University of Oxford from 1987 until 2001. He was Chairman of the IISS Advisory Council from 1996 to 2001. Prior to his time at the IISS, Dr O'Neill was head of the Strategic and Defence Studies Centre of the Australian National University (ANU).

Royama Michio was a scholar of international politics and Professor Emeritus at Sophia University in Tokyo. In the late 1960s, he was part of a group of scholars commissioned by the Cabinet Research Office to study the possibility of developing nuclear weapons in Japan. From 1970, he was part of the National Council for the Normalisation of Diplomatic Relations between Japan and China.

Saeki Kiichi was President of the Nomura Research Institute in Tokyo from 1971 until 1983 and President of the Japan Defense Association from 1973 to 1993. Prior to this, he was Director of the Defense Training Institute (now the National Institute for Defense Studies–NIDS) of the Defense Agency from 1961 until 1964. Saeki served on the IISS Advisory Council from 1968 to 1977, and later as one of the Institute's Vice-Presidents.

Sasae Kenichiro is President of the Japan Institute of International Affairs (JIIA) and was Ambassador of Japan to the US from 2012 until 2018. He was also Executive Assistant to the Prime Minister for Foreign Affairs from 2000 to 2002, and Vice Minister for Foreign Affairs from 2010 to 2012. He joined the IISS as a secondee in 1993–94 and was interviewed for this project.

Satoh Yukio is a member of the Global Zero Commission. He served as Ambassador of Japan to the Netherlands from 1994 until 1996, to Australia from 1996 to 1998, and as Permanent Representative of Japan to the United Nations from 1998 to 2002. He was President of the Japan Institute of International Affairs (JIIA) from 2003 to 2009. He was an instrumental friend of the IISS and a champion of the Institute's relationship with Japan during the 1980s and 1990s. Satoh was interviewed for this project.

Takahashi Fumiaki is President of the Japan–Cambodia Association. He served as Ambassador of Japan to UNESCO from 2001 until 2003, Ambassador to the Republic of Cambodia from 2003 to 2007 and Ambassador to Spain from 2009 until 2011. He joined the IISS as a secondee in 1992–93.

Admiral Uchida Kazutomi served as the eighth Chief of Staff of the Japan Maritime Self-Defense Force (JMSDF) from 1969 until 1972. He subsequently worked as an investigator in the Military History Department of the National Defense Research Institute, while also serving as the seventh President of the Suikokai Foundation. His experience during the Second World War as an officer in the Imperial Japanese Navy led Admiral Uchida to become a key promoter of stable and prosperous US–Japan relations, notably in the area of maritime security. He formulated the 'Uchida Doctrine'.

Dr Urayama Kori is the Manager of the Postdoctoral Fellowship Program for Engineering Excellence at the Dean's Office of the MIT School of Engineering. She was the Executive Officer at the Harvard Academy for International and Area Studies from 2021 until 2023. Formerly, she was a contracted foreign-policy analyst at the US Office of the Director of National Intelligence (ODNI) from 2008 to 2011. She has also held research positions at the *Asahi Shimbun* newspaper, the Tokyo Foundation for Policy Research and the Shanghai Institute for International Studies (SIIS).

Robert Ward holds the Japan Chair at the IISS, conducting independent research and writing extensively on strategic issues related to Japan. He is also the IISS Director of Geo-economics and Strategy, focusing on a range of issues including global economic governance, rules and standards setting, and how economic coercion affects policy at a national and corporate level. Prior to joining the IISS, he was Editorial Director at the Economist Intelligence Unit. Robert lived and worked in Japan from 1989 to 1996, latterly holding a position in Japan's largest credit-rating agency, the Japan Bond Research Institute. Robert holds Bachelor's and Master's degrees from the University of Cambridge. He is the co-author of the *Adelphi* book *Japan's Effectiveness as a Geo-economic Actor: Navigating Great-power Competition* with Yuka Koshino.

ACKNOWLEDGEMENTS

This *Adelphi* book is a compilation of decades-worth of strategic analysis published by the International Institute for Strategic Studies (IISS). The intention of the IISS Japan Chair Programme in producing this volume is to underscore the importance of studying past strategic thought to inform and refine present-day strategy-making, and to shed light on the evolution of Japanese strategic thinking against the background of interaction between Japan and the UK and Europe more broadly.

We owe a particular debt of gratitude to Dr Benjamin Rhode, Editor of the *Adelphi* series, for his guidance and editing throughout this project, and to Professor Hosoya Yuichi for his essay, which also helped shape the title of the book.

In undertaking this project, the Japan Chair Programme was fortunate enough to be able to interview former Research Associates seconded to the Institute by the Ministry of Foreign Affairs of Japan. The Programme would like to thank former Ambassadors Satoh Yukio, Fujisaki Ichiro and Sasae Kenichiro, and Professor Nishihara Masashi, for their valuable interviews, insights and stories, which have enriched the book. The Programme would also like to thank Sir John Chipman KCMG, IISS Director-General and Chief Executive (1 October 1993–1 October 2023) for his interview, as well as Christoph Bertram and the late Professor Robert O'Neill, both former Directors of the IISS, for their interviews and stories of experiences with the IISS.

We would like to thank the *Yomiuri Shimbun* for permission to publish its photographs, and Matsumoto Ken for his permission to publish the contribution of his late father, Matsumoto Shigeharu, founder of the International House of Japan, to this collection. We would also like to thank the Embassy of Japan in the UK, the Ministry of Defense of Japan and the Prime Minister's Office of Japan for their permission to use their photographs.

We are grateful to the Institute's stellar team of editors, designers and proofreaders who worked with us through hundreds of pages of republished material and were invaluable in helping to give shape to this book. We would also like to thank the Knowledge and Information Services team for their assistance in navigating the IISS archives, which were key to informing this project. Special thanks to Alice Aveson from the IISS Editorial Services team, James Parker from the IISS Design team and Nakano Shinsuke, former Research Assistant for the Japan Chair Programme, for their indispensable contributions.

Map: **East Asia**

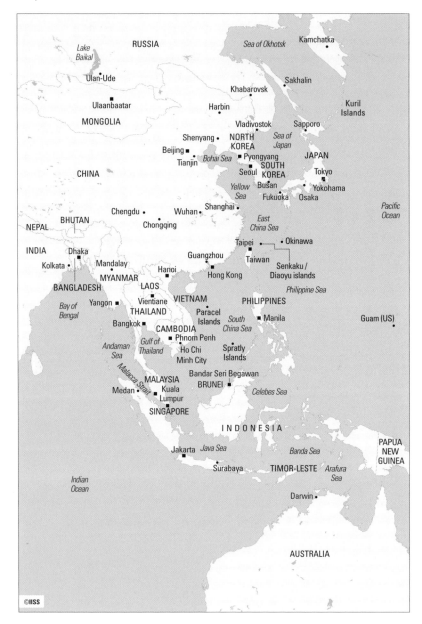

In the relatively short history of the International Institute for Strategic Studies (IISS), founded as the Institute for Strategic Studies (ISS) in 1958, the relationship with Japan has a distinguished pedigree.

The Institute was established as the Cold War was entering more dangerous territory. There was a need to think strategically about nuclear weapons and to develop ways to account for nuclear arsenals, the better to control them. A nuclear balance could not be maintained unless there were agreed ways to assess that balance.

British in origin, then transatlantic in disposition, the Institute determined early on that it had to become increasingly international in perspective and reach.

Engaging Japan, the only country to have suffered a nuclear attack, seemed a logical first step.

Brigadier Kenneth Hunt, who was Deputy Director of the IISS from 1967 until 1977, is remembered in the Institute for having made the first important outreach to Japan. I was told when I joined the Institute as a researcher in 1983 that before his first trip to Japan, he memorised a few sentences in Japanese, sensing that it would be polite to open a conversation with the Japanese, even if only briefly, in their own language. I recall that as one of my first lessons in effective diplomacy.

From that initiative grew a long and deep relationship with Japan, and 'Brigadier Ken' was always available to help Japanese thinkers who were beginning, with brave conviction, to enter the field of strategic studies. He wrote regularly for annual journals that their own institutes began to generate. On his 70th birthday in 1984, the Japanese government awarded him the Order of the Rising Sun in recognition of his work in helping a nascent strategic-studies community in Tokyo.

His efforts led to an agreement with the Japanese Ministry of Foreign Affairs to send one of its top rising young diplomats to the IISS each year. They ranged in personality from the conventional and cautious through to the eccentric and bold, yet all were brilliant in their own ways and flew to the top of the foreign ministry's hierarchy. They were kind fondly to remember their IISS association and help the younger generation of IISS staff.

The first to publish an *Adelphi Paper*, Satoh Yukio, became my guide to Japan from the late 1980s. He would help with appointments, but more importantly explain to me how to understand Japan's foreign policy as viewed from Tokyo.

While Japan's paramount strategic relationship was with Washington, these early connections to the IISS meant that many IISS alumni in the foreign ministry retained an instinct for seeking a 'second opinion', as it were, from non-Americans working at the IISS in London.

Japanese leaders have been associated with all of the Institute's landmark events. The IISS Annual Conference was for several decades the most important global conference in the strategic-studies world. The conference held in Kyoto in

1986 was acclaimed by many as the best ever. Prime Minister Nakasone Yasuhiro delivered the hugely prestigious Alastair Buchan Memorial Lecture, named after our first director. There have always been influential Japanese members of the Advisory Council, originally the Institute's governing body, and sometimes as many as three at a time.

Prime Ministers Abe Shinzo and Kishida Fumio both addressed the IISS Shangri-La Dialogue in Singapore.

When he travelled to other G7 countries in January 2023, Prime Minister Kishida did the IISS the signal honour of having only two appointments when in London, one with Prime Minister Rishi Sunak and one with me and the IISS Japan Chair, co-editor of this book and fluent Japanese speaker, Robert Ward. As if to complete the full circle of Japan's close relationship with the IISS, much of the conversation centred on how to prepare the elements of the G7 Hiroshima Summit in May that related to nuclear weapons, and the IISS was touched to have its strategic views again sought.

Our Institute has learned a great deal from our association with Japan's foreign-policy and strategic communities. Among Western-based think tanks, we were perhaps the first to conduct an 'Indo-Pacific tilt', long before that became strategically fashionable. We intend to build on this in the years to come, by recruiting to the Institute young analysts like the other co-editor of this book, Yuka Koshino, and by bringing more regularly our specialist expertise into the Japanese debate as the country moves further to develop its strategic personality.

This book records our happy past together. We hope that it foretells an ever-stronger relationship.

Sir John Chipman KCMG
Director-General and Chief Executive, IISS,
1 October 1993–1 October 2023

Introduction

Robert Ward

A volatile external environment

The essays collected in this volume trace the evolution of Japanese strategic thought from the beginning of the 1960s to the start of the third decade of the twenty-first century. By the start of this journey, Japan had already re-established itself after the post-Second World War hiatus as an important actor in the world economy and was emerging, in the words of one of the authors in this book, as an economic 'great power'.[1] Following the large-scale public protests against Liberal Democratic Party (LDP) Prime Minister Kishi Nobusuke's pushing through of revisions to the US–Japan Security Treaty in 1959–60 – the largest protests in Japan's modern history – and until the renewed turbulence of the 1980s, Japan's domestic political trajectory settled into what may now be seen as the 'core period' of the '1955 system' (*jisshitsu teki imi no 55 nen taisei*). The main characteristics of this system were the continuous dominance of the ruling LDP, despite prolonged periods of intra-party conflict; the pre-eminence of the Yoshida Doctrine, which prior-itised economic growth and saw Japan relying on the United States for security while it maintained only minimally armed military forces; and the deferral of socially divisive issues, such as formal constitutional reform, despite the LDP's formal commitment to revision.[2]

Japan was, however, far from strategically inert during this period. The 1960s–1980s were marked by major events that changed the international balance of power and had a significant impact on Japan's foreign-policy thinking. Three such examples stand out. Firstly, in October 1964, while Japan was hosting the summer Olympic Games, China became a nuclear power when it carried out its first nuclear test, conducting further tests in 1965–66 and detonating a thermonuclear bomb in 1967. Against a background of deteriorating Sino-Soviet relations and the ongoing Vietnam War, China's nuclearisation transformed its 'international bargaining power' and raised Japan's fears about its own security, not least the vulnerability of US bases in Japan to nuclear attack, even triggering debate about whether Japan should develop its own nuclear capability.[3] Secondly, in July 1971, the first of what remain known in Japan as the two 'Nixon Shocks' (*Nikuson Shokku*) of that year came with US President Richard Nixon's announcement that his national security advisor, Henry Kissinger, had visited Beijing to prepare for a presidential visit in 1972 to establish diplomatic relations.[4] Nixon intended US rapprochement with China to balance against the Soviet Union, but the lack of US consultation with Japan before the announcement – the Japanese government was only informed shortly beforehand – highlighted the precariousness of Japan's reliance on the US.[5] Finally, Mikhail Gorbachev's appointment as Soviet leader in 1985 proved to be a further external shock to Japan, heralding the beginning of the collapse of the Soviet Union and the end of the Cold War.

Against this background, one can discern increasing efforts by Japan's governments to take advantage of international geopolitical change to increase Japan's strategic agency. For example, Prime Minister Tanaka Kakuei's swift restoration of diplomatic relations with China in 1972, in order to stake out a more independent Japanese foreign policy; Prime Minister Fukuda Takeo's eponymous doctrine of 1977, which provided the first geo-economic blueprint for Japan's engagement with the Association of Southeast Asian Nations (ASEAN); and Prime Minister Ohira Masayoshi's Pacific Basin Cooperation Concept of 1979, a first for post-war Japan in terms of geographical range and strategic coverage, including political, diplomatic, economic and cultural issues.[6] But it was not until the administration of Prime Minister Nakasone Yasuhiro in 1982–87, the longest-lived Japanese government at that point since that of Prime Minister Sato Eisaku in the late 1960s, that the taboo on openly discussing military matters was lifted. Nakasone sought to tighten Japan's security relationship with the US by advocating, as he said in the 1984 IISS Alastair Buchan Memorial Lecture (see Chapter Thirteen), Japan's 'shift from a passive posture of responding to events, to an active posture of influencing events positively'. One example of this was the 1983 amendment of Japan's 1967 ban on arms and military-technology exports, and the approval of the transfer of Japanese military technology to the US.

The collapse of the Soviet Union in 1991 dovetailed with the bursting of Japan's economic bubble of the late 1980s and the end of the 1955 system, as a series of scandals involving the LDP and its failure to introduce promised political reform drained it of public support, leading to its fall from power in 1993. The impact of the disappearance of the stabilising domestic and external frameworks that had long guided Japanese strategic policy was evident in Japan's prevaricating response to the First Gulf War of 1990–91. Despite the direct threat to Japan's interests posed by Iraq's flagrant breach of international law in invading Kuwait and Japan's overwhelming reliance on the Gulf for oil imports, Japan was unready to assume global responsibilities commensurate with its economic power. But the trauma of the withering international response to Japanese failure also served to galvanise reforms in the late 1990s, which transformed Japanese decision-making and its strategic culture. These included Prime Minister Hashimoto Ryutaro's administrative reforms, implemented in 2001, which sharply increased the power of the prime minister, and Hashimoto's overseeing in 1997 of the first update to the Guidelines for US–Japan Defense Cooperation since they were first issued in 1978. These reforms provided a base on which the subsequent long-lived Japanese administrations of Prime Ministers Koizumi Junichiro (2001–06) and Abe Shinzo (second administration, 2012–20) could develop policy to realise their own political agendas of making Japan a more proactive global actor.

Consistent trends in Japanese strategic thought

Notwithstanding the considerable global flux of the past 60 or so years, the essays in this volume allow us to identify consistent ingredients in Japanese strategic thinking. One of the most important of these is the centrality of Japan's perennial need to triangulate its relations between the great powers in the region, and the ebbs and flows of its views of these bilateral relationships. The most important of these was and remains the security relationship with the US, a core interest of Japan since the signing of the US–Japan Security Treaty in 1951 – or, as Matsumoto Shigeharu notes in 'American–Japanese relations' (see Chapter Four), 'life insurance for which [Japan] must pay premiums'. Nevertheless, as the *Adelphi Papers* and articles in this book show, bilateral differences with the US frequently erupted. For example, the Vietnam War was unpopular with the Japanese public despite, for example Prime Minister Sato's political support and indirect assistance for the US during the conflict by allowing US bombers on missions to Vietnam to use US bases in Okinawa Prefecture. Conversely, another issue was Japan's concerns about the durability of the United States' commitment to the Asia-Pacific.[7] In the 1980s and early 1990s, Japan–US bilateral friction intensified, driven by US irritation at perceived Japanese 'free riding' on security and the widening bilateral trade imbalance in Japan's favour. It was not until the late 1990s and early 2000s that US–Japan relations began to stabilise, as Japan increasingly sought to demonstrate greater proactivity within the bilateral security alliance.

The pieces in this volume also illustrate Japan's long-standing ambivalent relationship with its other great-power interlocutor, China. Writing in 1967, in 'The Asian balance of power: a comparison with European precedents' (see Chapter Five), Royama Michio describes China as 'a Japanese obsession' and Asia as 'essentially an arc round the periphery of China'. Ogata Sadako's 1965 *Survival* piece 'The Japanese attitude towards China' (see Chapter Three) opens with the Johnson–Sato communiqué of 1965 in which Sato emphasises Japan's pragmatic policy towards China 'on the basis of the principle of separation of political matters from economic matters'. Known in Japan as *seikei bunri*, the intention of this policy was to allow Sino-Japanese engagement despite differences in ideology. She also notes that this communiqué was the first in which Japan and the US had disagreed over China policy. Ogata cites Japan's 'cultural affinity' and 'geographical proximity' with China as the reason why in Japan '[a] good neighbour policy has general appeal'. More recently, one can detect traces of this view in, for example, Abe's assertion in his de facto political manifesto from 2006, *Utsukushii Kuni E* (Towards a Beautiful Country), that Japan–China relations are 'unseverable and reciprocal'.[8]

While differing in their views about the scale of the challenge and coloured until the 1990s by the threat from the Soviet Union, our authors are also alive to the growing risks to Japan associated with China's rise. In the 1960s, Royama writes presciently of China's 'tacit national objective of achieving great-power status ... and eventually to defeat, Soviet leadership of the socialist world and American leadership of the "imperialist" or "bourgeois" world'. In 1987, in 'Prospects for security and co-operation between East Asia and the West' (see Chapter Seventeen), Okawara Yoshio warns that the 'Western industrialized nations should not take for granted the present Chinese posture towards the West', at a time of increasing Western warmth towards Beijing as China sought to modernise its creaking economy. The two Taiwan crises of the 1990s, rising concerns over China's needling on territorial disputes in the region – including in the South China Sea and around the Senkaku/Diaoyu Islands – and intensifying concerns over North Korea's weapons-of-mass-destruction programmes made integrating China more closely into the rules-based international system a more urgent priority for Japan. But as Bessho Koro suggests in 'Identities and security in East Asia' from 1999 (see Chapter Twenty-One), this was unlikely to be straightforward given China's history, in which 'in theory, there were no boundaries between the Empire and neighbouring nations' and 'thus, China is not part of Asia; Asia is China's periphery. Given this history, the belief in modern China as a world power comes naturally, while partnership with other Asian states does not.' Funabashi Yoichi echoes this point in his 2019 Alastair Buchan Lecture when he notes that China is 'rapidly becoming a revisionist power' rather than joining 'existing institutions under the current rules of the game' (see Chapter Twenty-Five).

Another recurring strand noted in this collection is that of Japan's own non-nuclear policy and its consistent commitment to nuclear non-proliferation. In his *Survival* article 'Japan's non-nuclear policy' from 1973 (see Chapter Eight), Kishida Junnosuke even goes as far as to advocate the denuclearisation of northeast Asia. The continued existence of the Three Non-Nuclear Principles, introduced by the Sato administration in 1967, in which Japan pledges not to possess, produce or introduce nuclear weapons to Japan, and the release at the 2023 Hiroshima Summit of the first G7 document to address nuclear disarmament underscore the deep roots of this stance in Japan. Thus, all the authors who write on the subject are agreed that Japan should not possess nuclear weapons, despite its latent capability to become a nuclear power as a result of its endeavours in civilian nuclear-power and space development. Given Japan's status as the only country to have suffered nuclear attack on the one hand and its desire to avoid antagonising its large, nuclear-armed neighbours – the Soviet Union, then Russia, and China – on the other, this is not surprising. But our authors fail, however, to resolve the contradiction between this resolute stand against nuclear weapons and the security provided by the United States' nuclear umbrella, which is seen as essential for the protection of Japan.

Strategic evolution

While some of the key preoccupations of Japanese strategic thought remain constant, the routes by which it seeks to achieve its aims have evolved, as this volume shows. One illustration of this is the proliferation of channels of interaction between Japan and the outside world, as Japan moves away from the Yoshida Doctrine and sheds the 'low posture' that Kosaka Masataka cites in his 1973 *Adelphi Paper*, 'Options for Japan's foreign policy' (see Chapter Nine). This is especially evident after the end of the Cold War. Although, as noted above, the US was and remains Japan's most important security partner, geopolitical flux after the collapse of the Soviet Union and Japan's desire to use its geo-economic power to maintain US post-Cold War interest in Asia and to engage China in regional issues led to more proactive Japanese foreign policy in the region. The Asia-Pacific Economic Cooperation (APEC) forum, launched on the initiative of Japan and Australia in 1989, is one example of this – Sasae Kenichiro writes in 1994 that APEC was established to 'confound Samuel Huntington's theory that there will be civilisational conflict in the unique Asia-Pacific geo-economic setting' (see Chapter Twenty). The ASEAN Regional Forum (ARF), which was launched in 1994 and for which Japan was an early agitator, is another example.[9] Although the ARF has failed to live up to early hopes that it would play an active role in managing the region's security problems, it remains an important dialogue channel, including, in addition to ASEAN members, major regional powers such as India and China as well as the US and Russia.

Starting in the 2010s, there has been a marked transformation of Japan's foreign-policy activism. This largely reflects Japan's response to China's rapid economic and military rise following its entry into the World Trade Organization (WTO) in 2001. Okamoto Yukio's *Survival* essay, 'Great-power relations in Asia: a Japanese perspective', from 2009, illustrates Japan's particular maritime concerns around the expansion of China's influence in the region when he writes that 'it is as though the East China Sea, the Taiwan Straits and the South China Sea have become China's internal waters' (see Chapter Twenty-Three). Here Okamoto prefigures the concern that Prime Minister Abe expressed in 2012 after his return to power that the South China Sea might become 'Lake Beijing'.[10] China's overtaking of Japan as the world's second-largest economy in 2010 and Japan's brief experience of Chinese economic coercion in the same year – when an escalation of the Senkaku/Diaoyu territorial dispute resulted in what was in effect a Chinese ban on exports of rare earths to Japan – were further triggers for the step change in Japanese external activism.

Japan's geo-economic influence in Asia developed rapidly under the second Abe administration in particular. This was expressed through an emphasis on Tokyo's support for and increasing desire to shape the rules-based order in the face of China's attempts to change the status quo. Abe's keynote address to the IISS Shangri-La Dialogue in 2014 (see Chapter Twenty-Four), in which he stated 'Asia for the rule of law. And the rule of law for all of us', was an important strategic marker for Japan in this regard. Abe's Free and Open Indo-Pacific (FOIP) concept of 2016 and his leading role in the rescuing of the Trans-Pacific Partnership – after US President Donald Trump withdrew the US from the bloc in 2017 – and its rebirth in 2018 as the Comprehensive and Progressive Agreement for Trans-Pacific Partnership (CPTPP) were two prominent examples of Abe's geo-economic strategy for the region. FOIP continues to function as an organising principle for Japanese statecraft in the region, and several 'like-minded countries' (dōshi koku) have since developed Indo-Pacific strategies of their own. The CPTPP, meanwhile, with its high standards for entry, has become an important vehicle for supporting the rules-based order in the region in the face of China's increasing economic gravitational pull. (China applied to join the CPTPP in 2021.) Japan's engagement of 'like-minded' partners from outside the Indo-Pacific in contributing to regional stability – for example, the Japan–UK Reciprocal Access Agreement, which was signed in early 2023, and the UK's accession in mid-2023 to the CPTPP – is a continuation of the FOIP policy.

The intensification of Japan's engagement with NATO since Russia's illegal invasion of Ukraine in 2022 underscores how Japan's geopolitical focus has become increasingly global. In his 2022 IISS Shangri-La Dialogue keynote address, Prime Minister Kishida Fumio links European and Asian security in his remark that 'Ukraine today may be East Asia tomorrow' (see Chapter Twenty-Six). In June 2022, Kishida gave physical expression to this point, becoming the first Japanese prime minister to attend a NATO summit (in Madrid), and in March 2023 he visited Kyiv, becoming the first Japanese prime minister since 1945 to visit a war zone. This *Adelphi* refers to Tokyo's previous tentative efforts to deepen Japan–Europe relations – the 'special relationship' between the Conference on Security and Cooperation in Europe in the early 1990s (from 1995 the Organization for Security and Cooperation in Europe) and Japan, for example. But overall, for many of the years this book covers, Japan–Europe relations were, as Takahashi Fumiaki writes in 1993 in 'What role for Europe in Asian affairs?' (see Chapter Nineteen), 'remote', with Japan concerned that Europe might 'further concentrate purely on European affairs' despite the importance of European engagement to the interests of the Asia-Pacific region. This and the comparison with Japan's tardy and limited contribution during the First Gulf War illustrate the strategic distance travelled by Japan since the 1990s.

This *Adelphi* also throws into sharp relief Japan's evolving thinking on military power since the 1960s. In the 1960s–1990s, our authors eschew Japan's building up of its military strength in favour of deploying its burgeoning economic power. Royama, for example, in 1967 cites the public resistance to 'countering force by force', and fresh and negative memories of the Japanese Imperial Army and Navy. Writing in 1972, Saeki Kiichi's *Adelphi Paper* 'Japan's security in a multipolar world' (see Chapter Seven) argues that Japan should 'organize economic resources and activity as a means of diplomatic influence' and to mobilise 'diplomatic influence by means of culture, science and technology'. This foreshadows Ohira's 'comprehensive security' thinking of the late 1970s, although he died in office before he could implement it, and even elements of the 'comprehensive national power' concept outlined in Japan's December 2022 National Security Strategy (NSS).[11] In 1981, Prime Minister Suzuki Zenko determined that, although Japan had the right of 'collective self-defence', to exercise it would exceed the use of force needed for individual self-defence and thus be unconstitutional.[12]

As we have already seen, there were inflection points from the mid-1980s to the 1990s under the Nakasone and Hashimoto administrations. The need for a strategic shift in the 1980s reflected Japanese concern at the Soviet military build-up in the Asia-Pacific, which included the deployment of SS-20 intermediate-range ballistic missiles in the region. These two administrations laid the groundwork for the security reforms of the 2000s. Those initiated under Koizumi's 2001–06 administration – for example, to allow the Maritime Self-Defense Forces (MSDF, Japan's de facto navy) to provide logistical support for the US-led coalition's campaign as part of the United States' 'war on terror' in Afghanistan – set new operational boundaries for the Self-Defense Forces (SDF, Japan's de facto armed forces) well beyond Japan. In another important landmark, legislation passed by the Diet (Japan's parliament) in 2015 by the second Abe administration expanded the scope of SDF activities by enabling 'collective self-defence' if Japan's survival was threatened. This legislation enabled implementation of the revised Guidelines for Japan–US Defense Cooperation, also in 2015. The December 2022 NSS in turn marked a decisive break with the Yoshida Doctrine along the lines that Kishida had suggested in his Shangri-La Dialogue speech, envisaging a 'fundamental reinforcement of Japan's defence capabilities' to boost its defence, deterrence and response credibility.[13]

A 'belief in world interdependence'

Linking the consistent and changing aspects of Japanese strategic thought is Japan's view of its connectedness to its external environment – or, as Kosaka writes in his 1973 *Adelphi Paper*, a 'belief in world interdependence'. During the early period covered in this book and despite its economic size, Japan was a reactive player, defining its strategies largely in response to the actions of others. For Kosaka, this low posture ultimately did not serve Japan's interests, and he argues that it was 'essential for Japan to contribute to the making of the global economic order, both by taking a more positive attitude in international economic relations and by improving her domestic structure'. Kosaka was thus an early advocate for Japan as a rule shaper.

In his 1965 book, *Kaiyō Kokka Nihon no Kōsō* (Japan's Vision as a Maritime Country), Kosaka situates Japan as a 'maritime power' but describes its often inward-looking foreign policy as that of an 'island nation' (*shima guni*), contrasting it unfavourably with the UK as a 'maritime nation' (*kaiyō kuni*) with an outward-looking foreign policy.[14] Japan's post-war strategic trajectory can therefore be read in part as a journey towards a more proactive role to, in Abe's phrase from his 2014 speech, 'make the world something more certain'. An important part of this is Japan's desire to be, as Funabashi said in his 2019 lecture, a 'rule shaper and proactive stabiliser in the Asia-Pacific and beyond'. But Japan has now moved beyond Kosaka's global economic order, as shown by its recent efforts to bolster its defence capabilities, secure greater agency within its security alliance with the US and preserve stability in the Indo-Pacific.

While the authors represented in this *Adelphi* volume were often prescient, like many others, they also failed to predict some key turning points. The collapse of the Soviet Union and the rapidity of the emergence of a less-than-benign China are two obvious examples. The speed of Japan's own strategic evolution over the past 15 years might also have taken some of the authors by surprise. The constraints of space have meant that we have had to omit many other excellent articles penned by Japanese authors for the Institute. The process of selecting the pieces has, however, been useful for illuminating current Japanese strategic thinking and for placing it in historical context, as well as highlighting the IISS's long history of association with Japan and its contribution to Japan's strategic culture. We hope that readers of this volume will find the writing in these chapters similarly enlightening.

NOTES

1 Michio Royama, 'The Asian
   balance of power: a comparison
   with European precedents', in *The
   Asian Balance of Power: A Japanese
   View, Adelphi Papers*, vol. 7, issue 42
   (London: IISS, 1967), pp. 1–16.

2 The LDP was formed in November
   1955 from the merger of two
   conservative political parties, the
   Japan Democratic Party and the
   Liberal Party. The merger came
   in response to the regrouping of
   the Japan Socialist Party, which
   had previously split, in October of
   that year. The LDP was in power
   continuously from 1955 until 1993.
   For a discussion of the 1955 system,
   see Sakaiya Shiro, *Sengo Nihon Seiji
   Shi* [Political History of Post-War
   Japan] (Tokyo: Chuko Shinsho,
   2023), p. 53.

3 Walter C. Clemens, Jr, 'Chinese
   Nuclear Tests: Trends and
   Portents', *China Quarterly*, vol. 32,
   October–December 1967, p. 129. See
   also Akiyama Nobumasa, '*Genshi
   Ryoku, Kaku Mondai*' [Nuclear
   Power, Nuclear Issues], in Tsutsui
   Kiyotada (ed.), *Showa Shi Kōgi (Ge)*
   [Lectures in Showa History, vol. 2]
   (Tokyo: Chikuma Shinsho, 2020),
   pp. 260–61.

4 The second 'Nixon Shock' came
   in August 1971, when Nixon
   suspended the convertibility to
   gold of the US dollar and imposed
   a 10% surcharge on imports into
   the US. The United States' ending
   of the global fixed exchange-
   rate system resulted in a sharp
   appreciation of the yen against
   the US dollar from the rate of
   ¥360:US$1 that had been fixed in
   1949 during the Allied occupation

   of Japan, destabilising the Japanese
   economy and threatening export
   competitiveness.

5 Murai Ryota, *Sato Eisaku, Sengo Nihon
   no Seiji Shidōsha* [Sato Eisaku, Political
   Leader of Post-War Japan] (Tokyo:
   Chuko Shinsho, 2019), p. 320.

6 See Seizaburo Sato, Ken'ichi
   Koyama and Shunpei Kumon,
   *Postwar Politician: The Life of
   Former Prime Minister Masayoshi
   Ohira* (New York: Kodansha
   International, 1990), pp. 523–24;
   and Fukunaga Fumio, *Ohira
   Masayoshi: Sengo Hoshu to wa
   Nani Ka* [Ohira Masayoshi:
   The Thoughts and Behavior of
   the 'Postwar Conservatives' –
   translation by the *Journal of Asian
   Studies*] (Tokyo: Chuko Shinsho,
   2013), pp. 236–37.

7 Glenn D. Hook et al., *Japan's
   International Relations: Politics,
   Economics and Security*, 2nd ed.
   (London: Routledge, 2005), p. 104.

8 Abe's exact phrase was '*Nihon to
   Chūgoku wa kitte mo kirenai "gokei
   kankei" ni aru no ron wo matanai*'.
   (There is no arguing that Japan–
   China relations are unseverable
   and reciprocal). See Abe Shinzo,
   Utsukushii Kuni E [Towards
   a Beautiful Country] (Tokyo:
   Bunshun Shinsho, 2006), p. 151.

9 Hook et al., *Japan's International
   Relations: Politics, Economy and
   Security*, 2nd ed., pp. 261–62.

10 Abe Shinzo, 'Asia's Democratic
   Security Diamond', Project
   Syndicate, 27 December 2012,
   https://www.project-syndicate.
   org/magazine/a-strategic-
   alliance-for-japan-and-india-by-
   shinzo-abe.

11   See Sato, Koyama and Kumon, *Postwar Politician: The Life of Former Prime Minister Masayoshi Ohira* for a brief discussion of this strategy. For a definition of 'comprehensive national power', see Government of Japan, Cabinet Secretariat, 'National Security Strategy of Japan', December 2022, p. 3, https://www.cas.go.jp/jp/siryou/221216anzenhoshou/nss-e.pdf.

12   Christopher W. Hughes, 'Japan's Strategic Trajectory and Collective Self-Defense: Essential Continuity or Radical Shift?', *Journal of Japanese Studies*, vol. 43, no. 1 (Winter 2017), p. 102.

13   'Japan's New National Security and Defence Strategies', IISS *Strategic Comments*, vol. 29, no. 1, January 2023, https://www.iiss.org/publications/strategic-comments/2023/japans-new-national-security-and-defence-strategies/.

14   Kosaka Masataka, *Kaiyō Kokka Nihon no Kōsō* [Japan's Vision as a Maritime Country] (Tokyo: Chūokōron-Shinsha, 2016). For a discussion of Kosaka's 'liberal realist' view, see Michael J. Green, *Line of Advantage: Japan's Grand Strategy in the Era of Abe Shinzō* (New York: Columbia University Press, 2022), pp. 38–9.

Japan's bridging role between Asia and the West: from the Cold War to the war in Ukraine

Hosoya Yuichi

'A bridge between the East and the West'

In his speech to the UN General Assembly on the occasion of Japan's admission to the UN on 18 December 1956, Shigemitsu Mamoru, then the country's deputy prime minister and foreign minister, concluded by stating that:

> The substance of Japan's political, economic and cultural life is the product of the fusion within the last century of the civilizations of the Orient and the Occident. In a way, Japan may well be regarded as a bridge between the East and the West. She is fully conscious of the great responsibilities of such a position.[1]

Since its accession to the UN, Japan has consolidated its national identity as a bridge between the East and the West in various ways. The United States has long recognised Japan's value as an ally with strong connections in Asia and Africa, with the establishment of the Asian Development Bank (ADB) in 1966, as a result of Japanese policy, being one of the most obvious examples of this.[2] The ADB was the first international institution that Japan created and led, and it enjoyed the support of Washington, which believed such an entity would support its strategic objectives in the region.

This identification of Japan's international role as a bridge was connected to the international politics of the mid-1950s. During this period, Tokyo perceived that such a bridge was both necessary and possible to mitigate the tension between the Western and Eastern blocs in the Cold War. Having restored its sovereignty with the ratification of the San Francisco Peace Treaty in April 1952, the Japanese government began to play a role in this effort.

The Japanese prime minister Hatoyama Ichiro (in office 1954–56) was aware of the need to diversify perceptions of Japan's international position beyond that of a loyal ally to the US within the Western alliance, recognising that Moscow would otherwise be unwilling to accept Japan's entry into the UN. Hatoyama visited Moscow in October 1956 to negotiate a peace treaty with the Soviet Union and successfully obtained an important understanding between the two former enemies. Moscow promised Hatoyama that it would support Japan's admission to the UN.[3]

Within Japanese domestic politics, both because of his own views and his perception of public opinion, Hatoyama was critical of the foreign-policy position of his predecessor, Yoshida Shigeru, considering it excessively focused on the US.[4] The so-called 'Yoshida Doctrine' was based on three pillars: Tokyo's military reliance on the US, minimal expenditure on its own armaments, and maintenance of a low profile internationally while prioritising economic growth. Sakamoto Kazuya, professor emeritus at Osaka University, has argued that 'there was also an inclination within the Hatoyama cabinet to keep a slight distance from the US and pursue a more autonomous diplomacy'.[5] In this way, Hatoyama's administration sought to make Japan a more autonomous power between the East and the West.

As part of his 1956 UN speech, Shigemitsu defined Japan as 'the fusion within the last century of the civilizations of the Orient and the Occident'. His description of Japan as a bridge should therefore also be understood from this civilizational point of view. Shigemitsu was a leading Asianist in his diplomatic thought, and had promoted this idea as foreign minister and then as minister of Greater East Asia in 1944–45.[6] Unlike Tojo Hideki (prime minister 1941–44) and his successors during the Second World War, as foreign minister Shigemitsu had argued that the 'Greater East Asia Co-Prosperity Sphere' could only succeed if other Asian peoples were treated equally and made efforts to promote their self-determination. However, in the context of the Second World War, Shigemitsu's diplomatic efforts were overshadowed by the view held by other Japanese leaders that Japan must dominate the region through military hegemony, mainly for the purpose of exploiting natural resources in the war. This reality naturally had a negative impact upon Japan's engagement in Asia for decades after the war.

Of course, Japanese occupation did not result in the independence of European colonies in Asia. Japan banned local political parties and, where local leaders were in charge, this was in name only and their remit was to carry out Japanese instructions. But the defeat of the colonial powers by an Asian state did give the independence movements a fillip. Shigemitsu's view, not shared by most of his colleagues, remained that Japanese victory over the colonial powers was a catalyst for the future independence of the subject peoples. Thus, as a defender of Asianist ideology, Shigemitsu endeavoured to promote the 'fusion of the Western and the Eastern civilisations, though his vision had anti-Western ideology before and during the war. Having updated his vision of Japan as a bridge, he was convinced that Japan, as a part of the Western Alliance during the Cold War years, needed to play a role in embracing the 'Orient'.

'Three basic principles': defining Japan's national identity

In September 1957, Kishi Nobusuke's cabinet released its first Diplomatic Bluebook – essentially the annual report on Japan's foreign policy – in which the 'Three Basic Principles' of Japanese foreign policy were defined.[7] These were: 'United Nations centrism', 'cooperation with free countries' and 'holding fast to being a member of Asia'.[8] To put it simply, 'the UN', 'the West' and 'Asia' were the three key pillars of Japan's post-war foreign policy. While desiring 'to occupy an honoured place in an international society', as stated in Shigemitsu's 1956 speech, Japan needed to belong to both the West and Asia.[9]

Harmonising these three principles was not always easy. The Japanese government tended to prioritise Japan's alliance relationship with the US over its position in Asia or the UN. However, in 1955, despite US reservations, Japan participated in the first Asian–African Conference in Bandung, Indonesia.[10] This was partly a result of Hatoyama's more autonomous foreign policy, prioritising Asia over the West. Underlining the importance of Japan's participation in the conference, Professor Miyagi Taizo (Faculty of Law, Chuo University in Tokyo) noted that 'the Bandung Conference was … the first international conference attended by Japan since the end of the war, and it was at Bandung that Japan came face-to-face with the newly born Asia for the first time'.[11]

The Japanese government exploited Japan's position as 'a member of Asia' as a diplomatic tool to strengthen Japan's international status. Prime minister Kishi Nobusuke was particularly skilful at this. A large part of Asia was under communist control in the late 1950s. Southeast Asia was the focus for Japan's Asian diplomacy, as a region in which Japan could expand its business opportunities. Kishi visited countries in Southeast Asia during his first trip abroad as prime minister, even before he visited the US. He believed that Japanese assumption of a leadership role in Southeast Asian development would put Japan and the US on more equal terms.[12] He toured these countries in part to promote his 'Asian Development Fund' plan.

Even though both the US and Southeast Asian governments were not eager at the time to collaborate with Japan on the basis of Kishi's vision for regional cooperation in Asia, Japan began to expand its diplomatic influence in Asia in the following decades through its official development assistance (ODA) and diplomatic engagements. Furthermore, the US government became aware of the merits of Japan's policy of strengthening its position as 'a member of Asia' while remaining part of the US alliance system.[13]

The creation of Japan's post-war national strategy

Together with the publication of the first Diplomatic Bluebook, in which the Three Basic Principles were defined, Kishi successfully formulated Japan's defence policy by publishing Japan's first Basic Policy on National Defense (*Kokubō no kihon keikaku*) in May 1957.[14] As Japan began to build up its own defence capabilities after the establishment of the Self-Defense Forces (SDF) in 1954, it needed to clarify its long-term national strategy for defending its people and territory. At this time, memories of North Korea's invasion of South Korea in June 1950 were still fresh. Communist groups were active in Japan as well, and 'indirect aggression' (i.e., subversion or revolution by communist forces) seemed plausible. Thus, the Basic Policy stated that:

> The objective of national defence is to prevent direct and indirect aggression, but once invaded, to repel

such aggression, and thereby, to safeguard the independence and peace of Japan based on democracy.

To achieve this objective, the following basic policies are defined:

1. Supporting the activities of the United Nations, promoting international collaboration, and thereby, making a commitment to the realization of world peace.
2. Stabilizing the livelihood of the people, fostering patriotism, and thereby, establishing the necessary basis for national security.
3. Building up rational defense capabilities by steps within the limit necessary for self-defense in accordance with national strength and situation.
4. Dealing with external aggression based on the security arrangements with the U.S. until the United Nations will be able to fulfill its function in stopping such aggression effectively in the future.[15]

Kitaoka Shinichi, a leading Japanese political scientist and professor emeritus at the University of Tokyo, pointed out in 2016 that the phrase 'indirect aggression' continued to be employed in Japan's Defense White Book.[16] According to Kitaoka, that was because the contents of the Basic Policy, 'attaching great importance to democracy, the United Nations, and international cooperation, as well as pointing out increasing patriotism and the gradual building up defence capabilities, as well as openly stating the reliance on the US-Japan defense system', still held true.[17]

Kishi was thus the prime minister who created the basis for Japan's post-war diplomacy and defence policy. These policies were necessary to create a more equal alliance relationship with the US. Kitaoka argued that 'Kishi sought to make the bilateral relationship more equal, requesting the review of the [US–Japan] security treaty and the return of the Ryuku and Ogasawara Islands'.[18] However, in reality, Japanese defence capabilities and security legislation were not adequate for such an equal partnership.

Kosaka Masataka: the rise of a strategic thinker in Japan

A new generation of Japanese strategic thinkers emerged in the 1960s. Before this, Japanese academia was overwhelmingly dominated by leftist intellectuals, many of whom energetically argued for the abolition of both the SDF and the US–Japan security alliance. In this environment it was not easy for Japanese academics to explore more realistic strategic thinking.

Kosaka Masataka, a professor of international politics at Kyoto University, was one of the first ardent defenders of the US–Japan alliance from a realist perspective. In September 1964, he contributed a groundbreaking article entitled '*Kaiyō Kokka Nihon no Kōsō*' (Japan's Vision as a Maritime Country) to *Chuo Koron*, a Japanese monthly magazine, in which he presented his original view on Japan's national identity in the international community.

According to Kosaka, 'we are not the East even though we are close to it, nor are we the West even though we are a distant part of it'.[19] Michael J. Green, a US Japan expert with many years of service in the US government, wrote that Kosaka 'predicted decades ago that Japan's torn identity between East and West would eventually become more acute because of the rise of Chinese power'.[20] Similarly, Ito Kenichi, a Japanese foreign-policy expert, commented that Kosaka argued:

> Japan belongs to neither the West nor the East and is consequently troubled by a loss of identity and he forecast that, despite the fact that Japan's defeat in

World War II, its subsequent dependence on the US, and its attempts to Americanize had led it to forget this concern for a time, the emergence of China as a major power would once again force Japan to confront the ambivalence of its stand between West and the East, indeed a perennial problem for Japan and the Japanese that today has once again been thrust before us.[21]

At the same time, in his biographical work on the political leadership of Yoshida Shigeru, Kosaka commended Yoshida for his accomplishments as prime minister in 1946–47 and 1948–54.[22] In particular, Kosaka valued the contribution the US–Japan alliance made to Japanese national defence. He regarded Yoshida's foreign-policy line as the foundation of post-war Japanese diplomacy.

Professor Alessio Patalano, a specialist in maritime strategy and doctrine and professor at King's College London, noted that Kosaka, who was later an adviser to prime minister Ohira Masayoshi (1978–80), 'was the first to adopt in the 1960s and 1970s the term "maritime nation" and "trading nation" to explain the distinctive features of Japan's successful industrial recovery'.[23] Kosaka argued that a maritime nation could promote a global view. Iriye Akira, a history professor at Harvard University, had written earlier that 'Kosaka's advocacy of a maritime strategy was significant in that he took a global view, seeing the oceans as Japan's frontier, and suggested that the nation was in a unique position to work out its own agendas.'[24]

Kosaka's global vision for Japanese foreign policy was further nurtured in 1973 during his time as a research associate at the International Institute for Strategic Studies (IISS) in London. Initially known as the Institute for Strategic Studies (ISS), the Institute was founded in London in 1958, less than two years after Japan's entry into the UN, and sought to navigate the turbulent strategic environment of the nuclear age. However, it originally had a fundamentally Atlanticist orientation, with its major strategic thinkers predominantly from Western Europe and North America. From 1968, however, members from Japan and Australia joined the Institute's Council.[25] Professor Hedley Bull of the Australian National University was elected as the first Australian member of the Council in 1968, and in 1977–86 Kosaka himself served as the Council member from Japan. The IISS was an important intellectual home for leading strategic thinkers and was becoming an increasingly global institution.

As a result of his research at the Institute, in 1973 Kosaka published an *Adelphi Paper* entitled *Options for Japan's Foreign Policy* (see Chapter Nine) in which he summed up post-war Japan's foreign policy as follows:

> When Prime Minister Shigeru Yoshida inaugurated his policy of 'economics above all' few were happy about it, though many thought that Japan had no other option. But it turned out a surprising success. Japan's security has been maintained at very low cost and her economy developed at a very rapid rate, while her status and influence have increased with the growth of her economic power.[26]

Kosaka's research at the IISS was a good opportunity to deepen his understanding of strategic studies, and his interactions with world-leading security experts may have influenced his involvement in formulating Japan's first National Defense Program Guidelines (NDPG) in 1976. The core strategic concept in the 1976 NDPG was that of the 'Basic Defense Capability' [*Kibanteki Bōeiryoku Kōsō*], and Kosaka played a key role within the 'Committee to Think about Japan's Defense'

[*Bōei wo Kangaeru Kai*] in formulating the concept of 'rejection power' [*Kyohiryoku*], which meant the power to deter aggression aimed at Japan.[27]

Nakasone and Thatcher

In the 1980s, the relationship between Japan and the United Kingdom, two island nations, was enhanced significantly, mainly as a result of the expansion of bilateral trade. Two prime ministers, Nakasone Yasuhiro and Margaret Thatcher, played a key role in this expansion, with a shared political ideology and understanding of global affairs.[28] Despite the hardening of trade frictions between Japan and the UK stemming from the UK's increasing trade deficit, Nakasone and Thatcher were aware of the importance of Western solidarity in order to counter the threat from the Soviet bloc.

Hugh Cortazzi, a British ambassador to Japan during the Thatcher years, noted that Nakasone was the Japanese prime minister with whom Thatcher developed the closest relationship.[29] When Thatcher first met Nakasone during the G7 Williamsburg Summit in May 1983, she had the impression that 'he was perhaps the most articulate and "western" of Japan's leaders in the period when I was Prime Minister, raising his country's international profile and fostering close links with the United States'.[30] Thatcher wrote in her memoirs that:

> Under the leadership of Prime Minister Nakasone, Japan began to take on a more active role in global issues. Hence, during his visit to the UK in June 1984, I felt that I was speaking with a leader who understood and sympathised with the values of the West and who was intent on moving in the right direction in terms of economic policy.[31]

Nakasone also had a good impression of Thatcher, describing her in his memoirs as having 'outstanding skill in perceiving the global situation'.[32] Nakasone was an exceptional Japanese political leader who deeply understood the geopolitics around Japan. The Reagan administration in the US wanted Japan to play a significant part in countering the Soviet threat.[33] Nakasone, who had been the director-general of Japan's Defense Agency, wanted exactly that. He stated in 1983 that:

> While the concept of the defence of Japan includes the defence of straits and sea lanes, I believe the most fundamental thing is to block an invasion by Soviet *Backfires* by covering the entire air-space over Japan with defence networks. *Backfire* is a powerful bomber, and once we face an emergency in which it demonstrates its abilities over the Japanese archipelago or the Pacific Ocean, we should be prepared for unavoidable and substantial damage to US–Japan defence cooperation. Therefore, in case of emergency, we must convert the archipelago to something like a big ship surrounded by high walls to block invasion by hostile foreign aircraft.[34]

Nakasone thoroughly understood the necessity of updating Japan's defence capabilities to realise this. In August 1983 he formed an advisory group tasked with drafting the new NDPG, of which Kosaka became the chair.[35] One of its greatest challenges was increasing Japan's defence spending in the face of strong public opposition.

Noting the intensified tension between the US and the Soviet Union, Kosaka warned that 1984 could be an *annus horribilis*. He wrote in January 1983 that the next year would become something like George Orwell's *1984* if the West did not act wisely. He argued that the Soviet Union was obsessed with its 'philosophy of force' and that the West would need to respond to it accordingly.[36] Based on this strategic assumption, Kosaka thought that Japan had to enhance its own defence capabilities.

Kosaka also published extensively abroad in English around this time and warned about the expansion of Soviet military activities in East Asia. In his article in a 1987 *Adelphi Paper* entitled *East Asia, the Pacific and the West: Strategic trends and implications: Part II* (see Chapter Fifteen) he wrote that 'there was good reason for pessimism' because:

> The failure of the United States in Vietnam did great damage to US capability and will. American prestige was tarnished and the trust of Asian countries in the United States as their guarantor was severely diminished. The Soviet Union, on the other hand, was vigorously building up its forces in the Far East. The days of American dominance in the Pacific seemed to be coming to an end.[37]

Taking a global perspective, both Nakasone and Kosaka perceived the connection between strategic trends in Europe and East Asia. This was one of the most significant intellectual and policy contributions that Japan's leading strategic thinkers have provided.

Conclusion

During the Cold War, Japan belonged to the Western alliance at the same time as being a member of Asia, as stated in its Diplomatic Bluebook. Tokyo often faced dilemmas about how to harmonise these principles. However, since foreign minister Shigemitsu described Japan's role as a bridge between the East and the West, both Japan's political leaders and its leading strategic thinkers have provided important possible answers to this difficult question.

Soon after Russia invaded Ukraine in February 2022, Japanese Prime Minister Kishida Fumio described Russia's actions as 'an attempt to unilaterally change the status quo by force', and 'an act that undermines the very foundation of the international order'.[38] By using the words 'international order', Kishida aimed to connect European strategic trends with those of East Asia. More directly, in the keynote address at the IISS Shangri-La Dialogue in June 2022 (see Chapter Twenty-Six), Kishida warned that 'Ukraine today may be East Asia tomorrow'.[39] In a January 2023 speech in Washington DC, he argued that 'Japan's participation in the measures against Russia transformed the fight against Russia's aggression against Ukraine from a transatlantic one to a global one'.[40]

Kishida's recent remarks therefore follow a long tradition of Japanese prime ministers seeking to connect the East with the West, to define Japan's perhaps unique ability to do so, and to delineate Japan's role in international affairs more broadly. Yet while these interventions represent a degree of continuity in Japanese foreign policy, they may also signal meaningful change: a more forceful and confident annunciation of Japan's hard security interests and of its role as an active partner in a global security order in which the European and Asian (and other) theatres are intimately connected.

NOTES

1   Government of Japan, Ministry of Foreign Affairs, 'Address of his Excellency Mamoru Shigemitsu, Deputy Prime Minister and Foreign Minister of Japan, Before the United Nations General Assembly on the Occasion of Japan's Admission to the United Nations on December 18, 1956', https://www.mofa.go.jp/policy/un/address5612.html.

2   Tanaka Akihiko, *Japan in Asia: Post-Cold-War Diplomacy*, translated by Jean Connell Hoff (Tokyo: Japan Publishing Industry Foundation for Culture, 2017), p. 86.

3   Hatano Sumio, *One Hundred Fifty Years of Japanese Foreign Relations: from 1868 to 2018*, translated by Carl Freire, Terry Gallagher and Tom Kain (Tokyo: Japan Publishing Industry Foundation for Culture, 2022), p. 398.

4   Sakamoto Kazuya, 'Conditions of an Independent State: Japanese Diplomacy in the 1950s', in Makoto Iokibe (ed.), *The Diplomatic History of Postwar Japan*, translated and annotated by Robert D. Eldridge (London: Routledge, 2011), p. 59.

5   *Ibid*.

6   Hatano Sumio, *The Pacific War and Japan's Diplomacy in Asia* (Tokyo: Japan Publishing Industry Foundation for Culture, 2021), pp. 321–22.

7   Sakamoto, 'Conditions of an Independent State: Japanese Diplomacy in the 1950s', p. 65.

8   Hosoya Yuichi, 'Japan's National Identity in Postwar Diplomacy: The Three Basic Principles', in Gilbert Rozman (ed.), *East Asian National Identities: Common Roots and Chinese Exceptionalism* (Stanford: Stanford University Press, 2012), pp. 172–75.

9   Government of Japan, Ministry of Foreign Affairs, 'Address of his Excellency Mamoru Shigemitsu, Deputy Prime Minister and Foreign Minister of Japan, Before the United Nations General Assembly on the Occasion of Japan's Admission to the United Nations on December 18, 1956'.

10 Hosoya, 'Japan's National Identity in Postwar Diplomacy', p. 172; and Miyagi Taizo, *Japan's Quest for Stability in Southeast Asia: Navigating the Turning Points in Postwar Asia*, translated by Hanabusa Midori (London: Routledge, 2018), pp. 1–29.

11 Miyagi, *Japan's Quest for Stability in Southeast Asia*, p. 3.

12 Sakamoto, 'Conditions of an Independent State: Japanese Diplomacy in the 1950s', p. 68.

13 *Ibid*.

14 Sado Akihiro, *The Self-Defense Forces and Postwar Politics in Japan*, translated by Noda Makito (Tokyo: Japan Publishing Industry Foundation for Culture, 2017), p. 49.

15 Government of Japan, Ministry of Defense, 'Overview and Fundamental Concepts of National Defense', https://www.mod.go.jp/en/d_act/d_policy/index.html#:~:text=The%20%22Basic%20Policy%20on%20National,and%20the%20Japan%2DU.S.%20security.

16 Kitaoka Shinichi, 'Kishi Nobusuke:

Frustrated Ambition', in Watanabe Akio (ed.), *The Prime Ministers of Postwar Japan, 1945–1995: Their Lives and Times*, translated by Robert D. Eldridge (Lanham: Lexington Books, 2016), pp. 108–9.

[17] *Ibid.*

[18] *Ibid.*, p. 109.

[19] Kosaka Masataka, *Kaiyō Kokka Nihon no Kōsō* [Japan's Vision as a Maritime Country] (Tokyo: Chūokōron Shinsha, 2008), p. 249.

[20] Michael J. Green, *Japan's Reluctant Realism: Foreign Policy Challenges in an Era of Uncertain Power* (New York: Palgrave, 2003), pp. 26–7.

[21] Ito Kenichi, *Japan's Identity: Neither the West nor the East* (Tokyo: The Japan Forum on International Relations, 1999), p. 1.

[22] Kosaka Masataka, *Saishō Yoshida Shigeru* [On Prime Minister Yoshida Shigeru] (Tokyo: Chūokōron Shinsha, 2006).

[23] Alessio Patalano, *Post-war Japan as a Sea Power: Imperial Legacy, Wartime Experience and the Making of a Navy* (London: Bloomsbury, 2015), p. 108.

[24] Iriye Akira, *Japan and the Wider World: From the Mid-Nineteenth Century to the Present* (London: Longman, 1997), p. 155.

[25] Michael Howard, 'IISS – the First Thirty Years: A General Overview' (*Adelphi Paper* 235, 1989), in *A Historical Sensibility: Sir Michael Howard and The International Institute for Strategic Studies, 1958–2019* (Abingdon: Routledge for the IISS, 2020), pp. 281–95.

[26] Kosaka Masataka, *Options for Japan's Foreign Policy*, Adelphi Papers, no. 97 (London: The International Institute for Strategic Studies, 1973), p. 1.

[27] Sado, *The Self-Defense Forces and Postwar Politics in Japan*, pp. 96–7.

[28] On the Japan–UK diplomatic relationship, see Hosoya Yuichi, 'Nishigawa dōmei kara Kokusai Komyuniti e – Taiei Gaikō to Jiyūshugi Shokoku to no Kyōchō' [From Western Alliance to the International Community: Diplomacy with the UK and Emphasis on Freemarket Countries], in Kokubun Ryosei (ed.), *Nihon no Gaikō* [Japan's Diplomacy], vol. 4 (Tokyo: Iwanami Shoten, 2013), pp. 219–44.

[29] Hugh Cortazzi, 'Margaret Thatcher, 1925–2013', in Antony Best and Hugh Cortazzi (eds), *British Foreign Secretaries and Japan 1850–1990: Aspects of the Evolution of British Foreign Policy* (Folkestone: Renaissance Books, 2018), p. 283.

[30] Margaret Thatcher, *The Downing Street Years* (London: HarperCollins, 2011), p. 412.

[31] *Ibid.*, pp. 683–84.

[32] Nakasone Yasuhiro, *Seiji to Jinsei: Nakasone Yasuhiro Kaikoroku* [My Memoir, Politics and Life] (Tokyo: Kodansha, 1992), p. 115.

[33] Sado, *The Self-Defense Forces and Postwar Politics in Japan*, p. 139.

[34] *Ibid.*, pp. 139–40.

[35] Hattori Ryuji, *Kosaka Masataka: Sengo Nihon to Genjitsu Shugi* [Kosaka Masataka: Postwar Japan and Realism] (Tokyo: Chūokōron Shinsha, 2018), pp. 246–48.

[36] Kosaka Masataka, *Gaikō Kankaku: Jidai no Owari to Nagai Hajimari* [The Sense of Diplomacy: The End and the Long Start of an Era] (Tokyo: Chikura-Shobo, 2017), pp. 168–69.

37 Kosaka Masataka, 'East Asia, the
    Pacific and the West: Strategic
    Trends and Implications: Part II', in
    *East Asia, the West and International
    Security: Prospects for Peace: Part
    I – Papers from the IISS 28th Annual
    Conference, Adelphi Papers*, vol. 27,
    no. 216 (London: IISS, 1987), p. 11.

38 Prime Minister's Office of Japan,
    'Press Conference by the Prime
    Minister Regarding Japan's
    Response to the Situation in
    Ukraine', 27 February 2022, https://
    japan.kantei.go.jp/101_kishida/
    statement/202202/_00014.html.

39 Prime Minister's Office of Japan,
    'Keynote Address by Prime
    Minister Kishida Fumio at the
    IISS Shangri-La Dialogue',
    10 June 2022, https://japan.
    kantei.go.jp/101_kishida/
    statement/202206/_00002.html.

40 Prime Minister's Office of Japan,
    'Japan's Decisions at History's
    Turning Point', Policy Speech
    by Prime Minister Kishida
    Fumio at the Johns Hopkins
    University School of Advanced
    International Studies (SAIS),
    13 January 2023, https://japan.
    kantei.go.jp/101_kishida/
    statement/202301/_00005.html.

CHAPTER TWO

The role of the IISS in bridging Japanese and Western strategic thinking

Yuka Koshino and Matthieu Lebreton

When ISS was founded nearly five and a half years ago, there was no other centre in Europe or the Commonwealth for the broad study of the role of force in international relations – which is what we have meant by strategic studies ... There is nothing comparable with the ISS annual conference as a meeting place of scholars and experts from all over the world, the Institute's publication fulfils a special international purpose as a meeting place of scholars and experts from all over, and though some of its services are most used by those within reach of London, they are at the disposal of serious scholars and students from all responsible countries.[1]

ISS Council Chairman Richard Goold-Adams, March 1964

The 1960s: nascent relations with Japan

Since its founding in 1958, the International Institute for Strategic Studies (IISS – the Institute for Strategic Studies; ISS until 1971) has been international in outlook, including in the composition of its staff and membership, and its governing body, the Council. The Institute's annual conferences, where its members could discuss current security affairs with a focus on nuclear policy, the Cold War international order and global security, were emblematic of this outlook. In its earliest years, however, interactions with Japan and other parts of Asia were limited, reflecting the Institute's predominant focus on European and United States strategic studies. Efforts to further internationalise its activities began in 1963 after the Council's fundamental review of the Institute's standing in the rapidly growing strategic community.[2] Japan was one of the target countries for deepening intellectual exchanges between IISS experts and local research institutes.[3]

Several initiatives deepened the Institute's relations with Japan. One was the publication of analysis by Japanese journalists, academics and diplomats in its flagship publications, including the journal *Survival* and the *Adelphi* series of papers and books. During the 1960s, *Survival* primarily reprinted articles that had first appeared elsewhere, but the inclusion of analysis by Japanese scholars and journalists was key in providing the Western strategic community with literature on international affairs and security in Asia. Debates on nuclear non-proliferation were also prominent during this time, reflecting the impact of China's nuclearisation in 1964 and the start in 1965 of negotiations on the Treaty on the Non-Proliferation of Nuclear Weapons (NPT). The NPT opened for signature in 1968 and Japan signed in February 1970.[4]

In-person interactions also began from around 1965. In April 1965, the ISS hosted Professor Momoi Makoto of the National Defense College of the Defense Agency of Japan as its first Japanese guest, to discuss 'Future Developments in Japanese Foreign Policy'.[5] In 1967, the Institute conducted a study of the 'Balance of Power in Asia' with ISS members – selected intellectuals and practitioners who were nominated by the ISS to play an active part in the Institute's activities – from Israel, Japan, the United Kingdom and the US.[6] In the same year, the ISS co-hosted the International Conference on Asian Security Problems with the *Yomiuri Shimbun* and the Japan Institute of International Affairs (JIIA) to discuss Asia's peace and stability; China's future and Asia; arms control and nuclear non-proliferation in Asia; and Japan's role in the prosperity of Asia. The four-day conference, which took place in Tokyo and Nikko, brought together 40 experts from ten countries (21 of whom were from Japan) to consider the major nuclear states' role in Asian security.[7] In 1968, Saeki Kiichi, then Executive Director of the Nomura Research Institute and former head of the

National Defense College (1961–64), and a participant in the ISS–*Yomiuri*–JIIA conference, was elected as the first Japanese member of the ISS Council. Saeki subsequently played an integral role in setting the direction of the Institute's research on Japanese and Asian affairs.[8]

These early exchanges confirmed that the Institute needed more voices from Japan on international affairs. During this time, the Institute's research programmes were largely composed of eight to ten research associates (RAs), all of whom were security experts and practitioners. During their one-year appointment, they would conduct research on their respective areas and were expected to publish *Adelphi* papers. The teams of RAs were international in composition, albeit mainly from the UK, Europe and Commonwealth countries. In an effort to increase input from Japan, at the end of the 1960s, Brigadier Kenneth Hunt, Deputy Director of the IISS in 1967–77, visited Tokyo to discuss with the Japanese Ministry of Foreign Affairs (MOFA) the possibility of developing a programme in which one of Japan's top mid-career diplomats would be seconded to the Institute each year to serve as an RA and write *Adelphi* papers on how Japan viewed pressing foreign-policy questions. In exchange, the Institute would train them to develop their analytical capabilities in security studies.[9]

The Japanese government was interested in deepening engagement with the Institute for its expertise. At that time in Japan, although a number of Western think tanks, particularly those in the US, enjoyed significant intellectual influence concerning strategic issues, the IISS was already regarded as the world's leading authority on issues of arms control, nuclear non-proliferation, the European balance of power and general security studies.[10] According to Christoph Bertram, Director of the IISS in 1974–82, '[MOFA] wanted a connection with a respected outfit on security policy'.[11] Sir John Chipman KCMG,

IISS Director-General and Chief Executive 1993–2023, also recalled that MOFA lacked particular internal expertise on these subjects.[12] In 1968, MOFA sent Noda Eijiro (who later served as ambassador to Vietnam in 1979–81, to Peru in 1981–83 and to India in 1987–90), to serve as the first Japanese RA to the ISS. In total, 29 Japanese diplomats were seconded to the Institute until the programme ended in 1999 (see Appendix, p. 76).

The 1970s: a hub for post-war Japanese strategic thinkers

By the end of the 1960s, the Institute's membership and its Council had become more international. In 1968, for example, the Council included members from Australia, Egypt, India, Israel and Japan.[13] Around this time, the number of security-focused research institutions also began to grow in the UK and continental Europe, but the Institute continued to stand out in terms of its international approach. Thus, as noted above, in 1971 the Council decided to rename the Institute as the International Institute for Strategic Studies to reflect its global reach.[14] As part of this process, and reflecting Japan's economic rise, the Institute's research programmes on Japan and Asia also expanded. In 1971, the IISS received its first funding from Keidanren, Japan's largest business association, and expanded its funding base to Asia. The 14th IISS Annual Conference – held in Quebec, Canada in 1972 – also focused on Asia for the first time, with the theme 'East Asia and the world system: China and Japan in the 1970s'.[15] In 1972, 1974 and 1978, the Institute held a number of conferences in Japan with partner institutions, including the JIIA, the *Yomiuri Shimbun* and the US-based Brookings Institution.[16] Bertram recalled that IISS Director François Duchêne's (1969–74) personal interest in Japan also contributed to the Institute's activities on Japan.[17] By 1975, Asian regional studies had become one of the four strands of the Institute's research.[18]

The beginning of the 1970s was marked by the end of the Vietnam War and the implementation of the Nixon Doctrine. The latter signalled a partial US military disengagement from Asia and a new multipolar world represented by US President Richard Nixon's surprise visit to China in 1972 to engage with the communist regime in Beijing in order to balance against the Soviet Union. These events raised questions concerning the Asian balance of power and, more specifically, Japan's role as an economic actor in the region and internationally. The end of the Vietnam War also highlighted the limits of US power, a particularly important development for Japan given its dependence on US security guarantees.[19]

Japanese perspectives became particularly valuable during this time. With the US retreat from Asia and widening rifts in the US–Japan relationship, Japan – with its 'pacifist' constitution and the world's second-largest economy – had to start thinking about how to proactively contribute to regional and global peace and security. Dr Robert O'Neill, IISS Director 1982–87 and an Institute member since the 1970s, recalled that 'more governments thought that the time was coming when Japan would have to be more self-reliant in terms of providing for its security'.[20] The contributions of Japanese IISS members, leading academics and strategists to *Survival* and the *Adelphi* series provided insights into Japan's budding foreign-policy responses to these major changes in its external environment. Their analysis reflected Tokyo's realisation that it needed to leverage its economic power and its persistent commitment to non-proliferation, and reduce its security reliance on the US.[21] Ambassador Satoh Yukio, a distinguished MOFA diplomat, long-time member of the IISS and an RA in 1979–80, recalled in our interview: 'I often used *Survival* as a means to let our policy be known to European and American thinkers.'[22]

Among the key thinkers from the Japanese academic community, Kosaka Masataka, a professor of international politics at

Kyoto University, played an instrumental role in bringing non-government Japanese perspectives to the IISS and the broader Western policy communities. Kosaka was one of post-war Japan's leading academics, focusing on international-relations history and European diplomatic history. He engaged in policy debates after making his name as a controversial thinker in his 1962 article, '*Genjitsu Shugisha no Heiwaron*' (A Realist's Theory of Peace). His 'realist' approach to security policies, including support for the US–Japan security alliance, was a bracing change of direction for a Japanese public used to the 'progressive' thinking in Japanese policy debates in the 1960s and 1970s, which, inter alia, called for Japan's unarmed neutrality.[23]

Kosaka's relationship with the IISS started in the 1970s when he attended the aforementioned IISS conference in Canada and submitted a paper entitled 'The Interests and Objectives of the Superpowers in Asia'.[24] He was formally affiliated with the IISS first as an RA in January–June 1973 and then as an IISS Council member in 1977–86. He contributed three *Adelphi* papers during this time, including his first, *Options for Japan's Foreign Policy*, in 1973 (see Chapter Nine).[25] According to Bertram, Saeki was 'rather discreet' but Kosaka was 'more outspoken' and 'liked to be controversial'. He further recalled

> Kosaka liked to engage in subjects far beyond Japan: international ones, conceptual ones, ethical ones. He was, of course, also among that group, a relatively small group of academics in Japan who actually felt that the country had to have a more serious position on its international role and the role of security in that international role. In many ways he was refreshing because of this position.[26]

During the 1970s, the IISS also played a major role in bringing its expertise in security studies to the policymaking community in Tokyo. Through invitations from the JIIA and other institutions as well as the Japanese defence minister, Hunt stayed in Japan for extended periods to cultivate relationships with pivotal practitioners from MOFA and contribute to the development of Japan's strategic community.[27] According to Satoh, Sakata Michita, Director-General of the Japanese Defence Agency in 1974–76, 'was listening to Ken [Hunt]'s views from time to time … Ken was very well known. I think the Japanese side took to him very much and his enthusiasm to bring Japan to the IISS'.[28]

The IISS also served as a model and source of inspiration for the Research Institute for Peace and Security (RIPS), a security-studies think tank with international perspective, established in 1978 by Inoki Masamichi. Inoki, another of post-war Japan's leading academics and Kosaka's academic adviser, was serving as the third dean of the National Defense Academy of Japan (NDA) when he first visited the IISS in London in 1976 to give a speech on Japanese security and defence policy. He was on a trip to give several lectures in the UK, France and Germany at the request of MOFA.[29] During most of Inoki's academic career, he focused on international-relations history and the history of contemporary Japan, rather than security studies. However, he later recalled in his memoir that his Europe trip was a turning point in his career, inspiring him to 'create a research institute and devote the rest of his life' to studying Japanese security and defence policies.[30] In 1977, Inoki resigned from the NDA and established RIPS.

Inoki's exposure to the IISS in 1976 and his acquaintance with Hunt and Bertram inspired the new think tank's early projects. In 1979, it began publishing an annual survey on Asian security issues, *Azia no Anzenhoshō (Asian Security)*, covering regions from Central Asia to the US.[31] The publication used the IISS's annual assessment of geopolitics, *Strategic Survey*, as a model but aimed to complement its Asia coverage. According to RIPS, Inoki, Kosaka and Saeki's relationship with the IISS was key to the success of the new publication. As a result of Hunt's personal relationship with Kosaka, Hunt assumed a major role in editing the English version, *Asian Security*, every year until 1992. He also served as an RA at RIPS every summer between 1979 and 1988 to support Inoki's work. In 1993, the *Strategic Survey* editor, Sydney Bearman, took on the role of editing the English edition of *Asian Security*, although the project was terminated after the Ford Foundation's support came to an end.[32] As of 2023, RIPS continues to publish the Japanese edition to educate 'students, journalists, SDF, and government officials'.[33] Hunt was later awarded the Order of the Rising Sun for his 'contributions to the development of strategic studies in Japan over many years'.[34]

In post-war Japan, only a handful of scholars were involved in security studies, but many of them had links with the IISS. Satoh recounted that security issues in Japan at the academic and government level were still 'a matter for heated debate' in the 1970s.[35] The public was still hesitant to engage in strategic debates or military affairs due to Japan's historical legacy. Kosaka and Inoki brought insights from their experiences abroad to share with Japanese policymakers. For instance, Kosaka was part of the expert group that advised Japan's first National Defense Program Guidelines (NDPG) under the Miki Takeo administration (1974–76). Inoki and Kosaka also led the Comprehensive Security Research Group, formed under the Ohira Masayoshi administration (1978–80). They engaged with the IISS to strengthen Japanese research institutes' capabilities on security so that Japanese policymakers could better navigate the turbulent multipolar geopolitical environment after the Vietnam War. The impact of the IISS's engagement with Japan was beginning to increase in scope and would come into full force during the following decade.

The 1980s: Nakasone Yasuhiro and the IISS's bridging role between the West and Asia

Building on these early relationships, IISS–Japan ties intensified in the 1980s. RAs from MOFA and authors for *Survival* and the *Adelphi* series regularly produced valuable and prescient material, articulating their perspectives on critical issues in Asia for the wider Western IISS member base. Moreover, from 1982, as IISS Director O'Neill expanded the Institute's activities and research programmes to analyse Asian security and its implications for Western policy. O'Neill recalled

> It was apparent to me that we had this imbalance, and, coming from the Pacific region, I felt that I ought to address this problem. In some ways there seemed to be greater dangers of wars occurring in East Asia and the Pacific than in the Atlantic area. Analysis of the security situation in Europe, complex and dangerous though it was, seemed to be a lot more soundly based than that of the security situation in East Asia. There was a mission for the IISS to undertake.[36]

Two key events further enhanced the Institute's relationship with Japan. The first was Prime Minister Nakasone Yasuhiro's delivery of the 1984 Alastair Buchan Memorial Lecture (see Chapter Thirteen), an annual high-level lecture series established as a tribute to the Institute's first director. O'Neill's visit to Japan in 1983 gave him the impression that Nakasone might accept the invitation to speak at the lecture in London, and Nakasone 'accepted readily' to speak as the first Japanese lecturer for this series.[37] Having served in the Japanese Imperial Navy during the Second World War and as Director-General of the Japanese Defense Agency in 1970–71, Nakasone possessed deep insights on Japanese security and defence policies and a keen interest in enhancing Japan's defence posture to meet the challenges posed by the Soviet Union in the early 1980s. According to O'Neill, Nakasone had 'a strong personal interest in strategic studies' and 'he looked positively on the IISS as a source of expertise ... But in particular, he liked the efforts we were making through developing the Japanese membership of the IISS'.[38] Nakasone also supported the MOFA secondees and listened to their advice when they returned to Tokyo.[39]

In his speech, Nakasone spoke about how Japan needed to take on greater international responsibility and shift from a passive to active diplomatic and security posture 'of influencing events positively'.[40] He called for cooperation between members of the 'Free World' on policies including nuclear disarmament, Western solidarity, responses to local conflicts in Middle East and the Korean Peninsula, revitalisation of the world economy and policy towards developing countries. He also emphasised the need for Western countries to form a nuanced understanding of the diversity among Asian countries and to adopt a flexible approach to Asian security matters.[41] O'Neill recalled that '[Nakasone] gave an excellent, vigorous address, and with his own strong and outgoing personality, he impressed many participants favourably'.[42]

The second event was the 28th IISS Annual Conference, 'East Asia, the West and International Security: Prospects for Peace', which was held in Kyoto in 1986 – this was the first such conference to be held in a non-NATO country. The conference, attended by several senior figures, including former US Secretary of State Henry Kissinger, was the result of work by many Japanese members of the IISS, but Satoh played an instrumental role in orchestrating it under O'Neill's leadership. Having attended these conferences several times himself, Satoh thought about bringing one to Asia, recalling that 'Bob O'Neill came in from Australia and had the same thinking right from the beginning'.[43] Satoh, who was serving in the Foreign Minister's Secretariat at the time, played a major role in organising the event, writing the welcome speech by Foreign Minister Kuranari Tadashi (see Chapter Fourteen) and securing funding from various groups, including the Sony Corporation.[44]

According to Satoh, the timing of the event was particularly important as the credibility of US extended deterrence in Asia was in question during the negotiation of the Intermediate-Range Nuclear Forces (INF) Treaty, when the US and the Soviet Union were negotiating the elimination of SS-20 missiles only from Europe. Thus, Kuranari's speech emphasised Japanese views on the nature of the Soviet SS-20 threat in Asia and the requirements for a credible US nuclear strategy and arms-control policy, which would seek either complete elimination of the SS-20 from both regions or 'the strategic balance that is well balanced globally'.[45]

The conference was only open to IISS members, but the strong IISS engagement in Japan had a notable impact. The attendance of Prime Minister Nakasone and Kissinger demonstrated to the global strategic community that Japan's approach to security was changing.[46] In the 1980s, many shared the view that Japan needed to contribute more to its own security and that of the rest of the world, and this served as a catalyst for widespread participation in the conference.[47] The conference's significance was magnified by its contrast with the general aversion during this time of the Japanese government and community to strategic and security studies, despite Nakasone's leadership. According to Professor Nishihara Masashi, who served on the IISS Council in 1987–94, 'the term strategy was not really popular then. … But the IISS climbed in while talking about strategy. So in that sense, it was different.'[48]

Japanese membership of the Institute increased following the Kyoto conference. Two Japanese members began serving on the IISS Council: Nishihara, and Okawara Yoshio (in 1989–98), a former Japanese ambassador to Australia and the US and adviser to Keidanren. With Saeki serving as one of the vice-presidents during this time, their participation 'strengthened Asian representation on the IISS Council'.[49] The Japanese members also established the Japan Committee of the IISS on 21 October 1988, although other than some significant fund-raising activities, this group remained inconspicuous.[50] The Committee lasted until the death of Okawara, its founder, a giant of Japanese diplomacy and former IISS vice-president, in 2018.[51]

The Alastair Buchan Memorial Lecture and the Kyoto conference, hosted amidst a Soviet military build-up in Asia, shed significant light on how such a threat perception forced a consolidation of US–Japan relations, a hardening of Japanese security policy and greater cooperation among Western states.[52] A major impression drawn from the IISS literature and events of the 1980s is their prescient emphasis on the inter-connectedness of Western and Asian security, and how Asian perspectives and international affairs can provide new frame-works for expanding the scope and effectiveness of strategic analysis.[53] These insights were a major motivating factor for the IISS to launch a review of its operations, research and financial base in 1988, the 30th anniversary of its founding, in order to expand its capacity in the 1990s in order to respond to the 'accelerating challenges of strategic change occurring in a scale unprecedented in IISS history'.[54]

The 1990s: the IISS and Japan's search for a new role

Several events in the 1990s persuaded the IISS to conduct a major reflection of its role in international strategic debate. These included the end of the Cold War in 1989, and the Gulf War of 1990–91.[55] The IISS Council recognised that the core issues of nuclear deterrence, force and armament reduction, and power relationships among nations are being fundamentally altered by the end of the Cold War. Problems caused by renascent nationalism, religious fundamentalism, ethnic unrest, refugee movements, as well as conflicts over natural resources and the environment are having an increasingly heavy impact on international security.[56]

In 1992, the IISS Council raised further concerns that 'fears about a new world disorder and chaos were growing'. It identified the threat from China's rise, stating that 'China [has] emerged as the potential post-Cold War equivalent of the USSR during the Cold War: a great power, potentially a very great economic and military power, determined to set its own rules rather than to accept those upheld by the West'.[57] Against this backdrop, the IISS launched a major appeal to double its capital base to expand in-house research capabilities.[58] Japanese members made significant pledges to this capital appeal.[59]

Japanese members also made several major contributions to the Institute's reflections on its role, including by supporting the 1992 Annual Conference in Seoul on 'Asia's International Role in the Post-Cold War Era'. This was only the second time in IISS history that the annual conference had been held in Asia. Satoh, who regarded the Seoul conference as a sequel of sorts to the Kyoto conference, again raised funds from Japanese businesses to enhance participation by members from Europe and new members from the former Soviet Union. During the conference, the IISS Council decided to organise the 1997 annual conference in Southeast Asia in order to maintain its Asian presence.[60]

At this time, Japan itself was also seeking to define its role in the rapidly changing global environment, and IISS RAs from

MOFA reflected the evolution of Japanese strategic thinking in their contributions. Sasae Kenichiro, an IISS RA who later served as Japan's ambassador to the US, explored the changing relationship between the US and Japan after the loss of a common threat, the Soviet Union, as well as Japan's role in the Asia-Pacific region (see Chapter Twenty).[61] Sasae recalled in our interview

> I think one of the issues I was addressing in my paper, and also Bessho addressed in his *Adelphi* paper, is how we have to face the history agenda and the relationship we have with neighbours when we address the relationship with [South Korea] and China and also other Asian countries … I thought and others thought as well that we needed to conclude the negative legacy of our history as early as possible. Otherwise, whenever we try to exercise security leadership, there could be concerns that they bring up past history … This is still not done yet. I'd say it has been 30 years since that time. I think we made progress step by step. I won't say we haven't made any progress, but the comfort of that process is that ASEAN and others don't express any serious concern, for example, for the recent Japanese efforts to expand its security role in the region. So, to some extent, I think our effort to support ASEAN development, both political and economic, is seeing fruit.[62]

The nature of the IISS relationship with Japan and Asia began to change after Sir John Chipman KCMG, the Director of Studies at the IISS, became Director in 1993. Chipman expanded the Institute's research capability and its impact on shaping policy debates, especially in Asia and the Middle East, in several ways. One was the appointment of senior fellows to drive the Institute's research activities on a longer-term basis than the RA's had done. Another was the development of Track Two diplomacy. The Institute began to play a major role in backchannel diplomacy in Southeast Asia from 1996, serving as the European secretariat of the Conference on Security Cooperation in Asia (CSCA) process related to the work of the ASEAN Regional Forum. The IISS also coordinated the work of the Council for Asia–Europe Cooperation (CAEC), which was connected to the Asia–Europe Meeting (ASEM) process. The 1996 Annual Conference, held in Singapore, confirmed that the time had come for strategic debate to deepen in this sub-region of Asia.[63]

The Institute's new senior fellow appointments and initiatives in Southeast Asia coincided with the termination of the RA programmes, including the secondment of MOFA diplomats, at the end of the 1990s. This reflected a number of factors, including, according to Chipman, changes to Japanese policymaking and personnel demands of MOFA driven by Japan's own global strategic evolution at the end of the 1990s.[64] Despite the end of the programme, interviews with previous MOFA secondees proved that the connections they made through their time at the Institute were long-lasting and often supported their diplomatic work after their return to MOFA. Fujisaki Ichiro, RA in 1987–88, recalled

> I got to know people. ... Lynn Davis was the director of studies. And I met her afterwards, when she became Under Secretary for Arms Control and International Security Affairs. Also, those people I still meet are Jim Steinberg ... John Chipman was the young regional director at the time, I think. And Kurt Campbell ... we found out that we were both alumni of the IISS. So, this really makes a huge, great network. 'Oh, you are someone'. It shows that. It is almost like I'd like to put in my *meishi* [business cards] that I was a Research Associate.[65]

IISS–Japan relations in the twenty-first century

Following the end of the MOFA secondment programme and changes to the IISS governance structure – in particular, establishing the IISS Trustees as a decision-making body and changing the role of the IISS Council into that of an advisory body, the IISS Advisory Council – the Institute's direct intellectual engagement with Japan continued through two new channels in the twenty-first century. The first was two major new dialogues launched by Sir John: the IISS Shangri-La Dialogue (SLD) in 2002 and the IISS Manama Dialogue in 2004 – premier security summits for the Asia-Pacific and the Gulf respectively. The former was important for Japan since it fundamentally transformed the IISS's engagement on strategic debates concerning Japan and Asia more broadly. The first SLD was held on 31 May–2 June 2002, and was at the time called the Asia Security Conference.

According to the IISS, 'with defence issues at the forefront of the discussions, this conference filled a major gap in the critical infrastructure of Asia's multilateral institutions'.[66] Chipman recalled that he was

> struck by the fact that in this region, presidents met, prime ministers met, finance ministers met, foreign ministers met, but there was no established forum for defence ministers to convene multilaterally … Having noticed this gap in the defence diplomatic marketplace, the IISS chose not to write a worthy academic article deploring the absence of a regional security institution … Instead, we decided to seek support to create it ourselves.[67]

The 1996 IISS Annual Conference in Singapore served as an inspiration to host the SLD in Singapore. The first SLD was attended by 14 defence ministers and 160 delegates, consisting of the expert community and journalists; by the 20th iteration in 2023, the SLD had expanded to include 34 full ministers, with 571 delegates from 54 countries and regions.[68] Moreover, 1,679 officials and security personnel also attended to support 121 bilateral meetings that took place on the sidelines of the dialogue.[69]

The SLD altered the Institute's relations with Japan and Asia in several ways. Firstly, it served as a platform for the IISS and the region to gain an understanding of regional security policies directly from senior defence policymakers. From its outset, the SLD was fundamentally different from the Institute's historical membership-based annual conferences. According to Satoh, the significance of the dialogue format lies in the fact that rather than simply inviting European and American members to Asia, 'it has given a venue for those countries' officials'. He observed that 'it was a very important and significant step that the IISS has taken'. [70] The annual nature of the forum underscored the IISS's permanent presence in Asia. Furthermore, the Institute set up its office in Singapore in 2000, and began to deepen its understanding of Southeast Asia. This was a shift from the Institute's previous predominant focus on Northeast Asia. In the same year as the first SLD, the annual conference was replaced by the Global Security Review, which was eventually disbanded in 2014.

Secondly, the SLD increased the IISS's profile with the Japanese government and broader public.[71] Since its inception, Japanese senior policymakers have attended the SLD with a view to gaining an international audience for their policies and thinking. Japanese defence ministers have attended the SLD every year since 2002 and held bilateral and trilateral defence ministers' meetings with their key counterparts. Two Japanese prime ministers have given keynote speeches at the SLD:

Abe Shinzo in 2014 and Kishida Fumio in 2022 (see Chapters Twenty-Four and Twenty-Six). The former called for the need for a rules-based maritime order amid growing regional concern about Chinese maritime assertiveness in the East and South China Seas. The latter condemned Russa's invasion of Ukraine – a violation of international law by a permanent member of the UN Security Council – as well as addressing the security links between Europe and Asia, and emphasising the need to further maintain and enhance the rules-based order.[72]

A long-time stakeholder in the Middle East, as one of the top importers of oil from the region, Japan has also been involved in the IISS Manama Dialogue.[73] Two recent highlights of Japanese participation were the attendance by Kono Taro both as foreign minister in 2017 and then as defence minister in 2019. In 2019, Kono gave his first speech at the Manama Dialogue as Japanese defence minister on Japan's 'Free and Open Indo-Pacific' (also known as FOIP) and Japan's active diplomatic and security role on the global stage.[74] Accordingly, Japan's engagement with the IISS expanded from East to Southeast Asia, and then to the Middle East as Japan's international security and geo-economic role expanded.

Also in 2019, Funabashi Yoichi, the founder of Japanese think tank the Asia Pacific Initiative (API) and IISS Advisory Council member became the second Japanese person to deliver the Alastair Buchan Memorial Lecture, in which he called for Japan to play a role as 'rule-shaper and proactive stabi-liser' to maintain international liberal order, together with the European countries.[75]

The second new channel facilitating direct intellectual engagement with Japan was the Japan Chair Programme, established in 2019 to 'provide first-class policy-relevant analysis on Japanese security issues for our global audience'.[76] The programme was enabled by funding from the Abe administration in March 2019 of some US$8 million to establish the Senior Fellow for Japanese

Security Studies position, or the Japan Chair, which serves as a 'major hub of Japan studies' for the 'global policy community'.[77] Robert Ward was appointed as the inaugural Japan Chair in December 2019, and Yuka Koshino was appointed as the first Research Fellow for Japanese Security and Defence Policy in January 2020.[78] Japanese government funding for think tanks had hitherto been focused on the US, so the IISS was the first such institution with a European headquarters to receive such an endowment. This marked 'an important new chapter in IISS engagement in the region'. Bill Emmott, Chair of the IISS Trustees, stated that the new programme was a 'very important and natural step … at a time of growing interest in the future of the Indo-Pacific and the role that Japan plays internationally'.[79]

Beyond 2023

The dynamic strategic environment in the post-1945 period – including the Cold War, the rise of China and the Indo-Pacific region, and reinvigorated transatlantic and Pacific strategic cooperation following Russia's invasion of Ukraine in 2022 – transformed both the IISS and Japan's role in international security affairs. The relationship between Japan and the IISS – originally fostered by several IISS directors, engaged IISS members and MOFA RAs – has expanded to encompass regular direct engagement with cabinet ministers, senior policy-makers and experts. The establishment of a permanent research programme has further enabled the Institute to continue publishing first-rate analysis on Japan's transformative security policies, and share with Tokyo more than 60 years of expertise on European and global international affairs to support such a transformation. The IISS will continue to find innovative and diverse ways to engage with the Japanese government, the private sector and the expert and opinion-forming community as Japan further develops its international strategic personality.

NOTES

1   Institute for Strategic Studies (ISS), 'Fifth Annual General Meeting', 24 March 1964, pp. 3–4, accessed in IISS Library Archives.

2   ISS, 'Fifth Annual General Meeting', accessed in IISS Library Archives.

3   ISS, 'Sixth Annual General Meeting Report: Chairman's Report', 28 April 1965, p. 2, accessed in IISS Library Archives.

4   See Ogata Sadako, 'The Japanese Attitude Towards China', *Survival: Global Politics and Strategy*, vol. 7, no. 9, 1965, originally published in *Asian Survey*, August 1965; Kishida Junnosuke, 'Chinese Nuclear Development', *Survival: Global Politics and Strategy*, vol. 9, no. 9, 1967, originally published in *Japan Quarterly*, 1967; and Imai Ryukichi, 'The Non-Proliferation Treaty and Japan', *Survival: Global Politics and Strategy*, vol. 11, no. 9, 1969, originally published in the *Bulletin of the Atomic Scientists*, May 1969.

5   ISS, 'Notice of Annual General Meeting: Chairman's Reports, Accounts', April 1966, p. 16, accessed in IISS Library Archives.

6   ISS, 'Notice of Annual General Meeting: Chairman's Reports, Accounts', April 1967, p. 4, accessed in IISS Library Archives.

7   See 'Ajia heiwa kokusai kaigi mikka me – anzenhoshō to kaku ni shūchū, taikoku no yakuwari o saguru' [Day Three of the International Conference on Asian Security Problems: Concentration on Security and Nuclear, Exploring Major Powers' Role], *Yomiuri Shimbun*, 10 April 1967. According to the *Yomiuri Shimbun*, the ten countries were Australia, Canada, France, Germany, India, Japan, South Korea, Sweden, the UK and the US. See also 'Ajia heiwa kokusai kaigi' [International Conference on Asian Security Problems], *Yomiuri Shimbun*, 30 March 1967, p. 1.

8   ISS, 'Notice of Annual General Meeting: Chairman's Reports, Accounts', June 1969, p. 14, accessed in IISS Library Archives.

9   Editors' interview with Dr Robert O'Neill, 23 November 2022.

10 Editors' interview with Professor Nishihara Masashi, 16 December 2022.

11 Editors' interview with Christoph Bertram, 20 December 2022.

12 Editors' interview with Sir John Chipman KCMG, 26 September 2022.

13 *Ibid.*

14 IISS, 'Notice of Annual General Meeting: Chairman's Report, Accounts', July 1971, p. 2, accessed in IISS Library Archives.

15 IISS, 'Notice of Annual General Meeting: Chairman's Report, Accounts', May 1973, p. 6, accessed in IISS Library Archives.

16 In March 1972, the IISS hosted a conference on 'Social and External Factors Influencing Japanese Foreign Policies during the 1970s', held near Mount Fuji. In March 1974, the IISS hosted a special working conference held with the JIIA and the Brookings Institution to discuss arms control. In October 1978, the IISS held a conference in Japan with the Brookings Institution and the *Yomiuri Shimbun*.

17 Editors' interview with Christoph Bertram, 20 December 2022.

18   IISS, 'Notice of Annual General
     Meeting: Chairman's Report,
     Accounts', June 1976, p. 5, accessed
     in IISS Library Archives.
19   Editors' interview with Dr Robert
     O'Neill, 23 November 2022.
20   Ibid.
21   See Saeki Kiichi, Japan's Security in
     a Multipolar World, Adelphi Papers,
     vol. 12, issue 92 (London: IISS, 1972);
     Admiral Uchida Kazutomi, Naval
     Competition and Security in East
     Asia, Adelphi Papers, vol. 16, issue
     124 (London: IISS, 1976); Kosaka
     Masataka, Options for Japan's Foreign
     Policy, Adelphi Papers, vol. 13, issue 97
     (London: IISS, 1973); Theo Sommer,
     Kosaka Masataka and Robert R.
     Bowie, 'Strategic Forum: American
     Policy After Vietnam', Survival: Global
     Politics and Strategy, vol. 15, no. 3,
     1973; Miyoshi Osamu, The Nixon
     Doctrine in Asia, in East Asia and the
     World System. Part I: The Superpowers
     and the Context: Papers from the IISS
     14th Annual Conference, Adelphi
     Papers, vol. 12, issue 91 (London:
     IISS, 1972); Muraoka Kunio, Japanese
     Security and the United States, Adelphi
     Papers, vol. 13, issue 95 (London:
     IISS, 1973); and Kishida Junnosuke,
     'Japan's non-nuclear policy', Survival:
     Global Politics and Strategy, vol. 15, no.
     1, 1973.
22   Editors' interview with Satoh Yukio,
     14 December 2022.
23   Nishihara Masashi, 'Heiwa
     Anzenhoshō Kenkyūjo no Ayumi:
     Sōritsu Yonjūsan Nen wo Furikaete'
     [The History of RIPS: Reflecting
     43 Years Since the Establishment],
     Research Institute for Peace and
     Security (RIPS), October 2021,
     p. 5, https://www.rips.or.jp/jp/
     wp-content/uploads/2021/11/

     bd7ca8c2c35528d30d7642b89f7789bf.
     pdf.
24   IISS, 'Notice of Annual General
     Meeting: Chairman's Report,
     Accounts', July 1971, p. 6, accessed in
     IISS Library Archives.
25   These include the following: Options
     for Japan's Foreign Policy; 'Crisis
     Control in Regional Conflicts', in The
     Diffusion of Power. Part II: Conflict and
     its Control: Papers from the IISS 18th
     Annual Conference, Adelphi Papers,
     vol. 17, issue 134 (London: IISS,
     1977); and 'East Asia, the Pacific
     and the West: Strategic Trends and
     Implications: Part II', in East Asia,
     the West and International Security:
     Prospects for Peace: Part I Papers from
     the IISS 28th Annual Conference,
     Adelphi Papers, vol. 27, issue 216
     (London: IISS, 1987).
26   Editors' interview with Christoph
     Bertram, 20 December 2022.
27   Editors' interview with Professor
     Nishihara Masashi, 16 December 2022.
28   Editors' interview with Satoh Yukio,
     14 December 2022.
29   Nishihara Masashi, 'Heiwa
     Anzenhoshō Kenkyūjo no Ayumi:
     Sōritsu Yonjūsan Nen o Furikaete'
     [The History of RIPS: Reflecting 43
     Years Since the Establishment], RIPS,
     October 2021, p. 1, https://www.rips.
     or.jp/jp/wp-content/uploads/2021/11/
     bd7ca8c2c35528d30d7642b89f7789bf.
     pdf.
30   Ibid., p. 1.
31   Ibid., p. 8.
32   Ibid., pp. 8–9.
33   RIPS, Azia no Anzenhoshō [Annual
     Report, Asian Security], https://
     www.rips.or.jp/en/publication/
     asian-security/.
34   IISS, 'Newsletter', July/August 1984,
     accessed in IISS Library Archives.

35 Editors' interview with Satoh Yukio, 14 December 2022.

36 Editors' interview with Dr Robert O'Neill, 23 November 2022.

37 *Ibid.*

38 *Ibid.*

39 *Ibid.*

40 Nakasone Yasuhiro, 'The 1984 Alastair Buchan Memorial Lecture', *Survival: Global Politics and Strategy*, vol. 26, no. 5, 1984, pp. 194–99.

41 *Ibid.*

42 Editors' interview with Dr Robert O'Neill, 23 November 2022.

43 Editors' interview with Satoh Yukio, 14 December 2022.

44 *Ibid.*

45 *Ibid.* For Kuranari's speech, see Kuranari Tadashi, 'Japanese Security Policy', *Survival: Global Politics and Strategy*, vol. 29, no. 1, 1987, pp. 84–6.

46 Editors' interview with Christoph Bertram, 20 December 2022.

47 Editors' interview with Dr Robert O'Neill, 23 November 2022.

48 Editors' interview with Professor Nishihara Masashi, 16 December 2022.

49 IISS, 'IISS Annual Report and Accounts: Notice of AGM', 10 July 1990, p. 4, accessed in IISS Library Archives.

50 IISS, 'Japan Committee of the IISS', 21 October 1988, accessed in IISS Library Archives; and personal communication from Professor Nishihara Masashi, August 2023.

51 Editors' interview with Professor Nishihara Masashi, 16 December 2022.

52 See Kuranari, 'Japanese Security Policy'; Satoh Yukio, 'The Changing Security Circumstances in the 1980s', in Satoh Yukio, *The Evolution of Japanese Security Policy, Adelphi Papers*, vol. 22, issue 178 (London: IISS, 1982); Tokinoya Atsushi, *The Japan–US alliance: A Japanese Perspective, Adelphi Papers*, vol. 26, issue 212 (London: IISS, 1986); and Kosaka, 'East Asia, the Pacific and the West: Strategic Trends and Implications: Part II'.

53 See Nakasone, 'The 1984 Alastair Buchan Memorial Lecture'; Henry Kissinger, 'East Asia, the Pacific and the West: Strategic Trends and Implications: Part I', in *East Asia, the West and International Security: Prospects for Peace: Part I Papers from the IISS 28th Annual Conference*; Sato Seizaburo, 'Convergence and Divergence in East Asian and Western Security Interests: Part I', in *East Asia, the West and International Security: Prospects for Peace: Part I Papers from the IISS 28th Annual Conference*; and Okawara Yoshio, 'Prospects for Security Co-operation Between East Asia and the West', in *East Asia, the West and International Security: Prospects for Peace: Part III Papers from the IISS 28th Annual Conference*.

54 IISS, 'Annual Report and Accounts: Notice of AGM', 13 July 1989, p. 4, accessed in IISS Library Archives.

55 IISS, 'Annual Report and Accounts: Notice of AGM', 16 July 1991, p. 4, accessed in IISS Library Archives.

56 *Ibid.*, p. 8.

57 IISS, 'Annual Report and Accounts: Notice of AGM', 20 July 1993, p. 4, accessed in IISS Library Archives.

58 IISS, 'Annual Report and Accounts: Notice of AGM', 16 July 1991, p. 4.

59 IISS, 'Annual Report and Accounts: Notice of AGM', 20 July 1993, p. 7.

60 *Ibid.*, p. 11.

61 Sasae Kenichiro, *Rethinking Japan–*

US relations, *Adelphi Papers*, vol. 34, issue 292 (London: Brassey's for the IISS, 1994).

62 Editors' interview with Ambassador Sasae Kenichiro, 16 December 2022.

63 IISS, '20th Asia Security Summit: The Shangri-La Dialogue: Seventh Plenary Session – Q&A', 4 June 2023, https://www.iiss. org/events/shangri-la-dialogue/ shangri-la-dialogue-2023/.

64 Editors' interview with Sir John Chipman KCMG, 26 September 2022.

65 Editors' interview with Ambassador Fujisaki Ichiro, 13 December 2022.

66 IISS, 'Annual Report and Accounts 2001/2002', 17 July 2003, p. 8, accessed in IISS Library Archives.

67 Sir John Chipman KCMG, '20th Asia Security Summit: The Shangri-La Dialogue: Opening Remarks', 2 June 2023, https://www.iiss. org/events/shangri-la-dialogue/ shangri-la-dialogue-2023/.

68 The SLD was not held in 2020 and 2021 because of the COVID-19 pandemic.

69 IISS, '20th Asia Security Summit: The Shangri-La Dialogue: Seventh Plenary Session – Q&A'.

70 Editors' interview with Satoh Yukio, 14 December 2022.

71 Editors' interview with Ambassador Sasae Kenichiro, 16 December 2022.

72 Kishida Fumio, 'The 19th Regional Security Summit – the Shangri-La Dialogue: Keynote Address', 10 June 2022, https://www.mofa.go.jp/ files/100356160.pdf.

73 IISS, 'A Decade of the IISS Manama Dialogue: Premier Regional Security Summit in the Gulf', 4 December 2014, https://issuu.com/iiss-publications/docs/a-decade-of-the-iiss-manama-dialogu/40.

74 Government of Japan, Ministry of Defense, 'Achieving the "Free and Open Indo-Pacific (FOIP)" Vision: Japan Ministry of Defense's Approach', https://www.mod.go.jp/ en/d_act/exc/india_pacific/india_ pacific-en.html.

75 Funabashi Yoichi, 'We Are All Small Countries Now': IISS 2019 Alastair Buchan Memorial Lecture, 13 November 2019, https://www. iiss.org/events/2019/11/iiss-annual-dinner-2019-yoichi-funabashi/.

76 IISS, 'The IISS Launches New Japan Chair Programme', 29 November 2019, https://www.iiss.org/ press/2019/the-iiss-launches-new-japan-chair-programme.

77 Government of Japan, Ministry of Foreign Affairs, 'Foreign Minister Kono Attends Dinner Reception to Mark the Launch of IISS Japan Chair', 5 June 2019, https:// www.mofa.go.jp/press/release/ press4e_002467.html.

78 The IISS Research Fellow for Japanese Security and Defence Policy was a two-year fixed-term position established by generous funding from Matsumoto Yasukane, Founder, Representative Director and Chairman of Raksul INC and Samata Anri, General Partner at ANRI through the Asia Pacific Initiative (API) in Japan.

79 IISS, 'The International Institute for Strategic Studies Announces New IISS Japan Chair', 5 March 2019, https://www.iiss.org/press/2019/ iiss-japan-chair/.

APPENDIX

IISS Research Associates from the Ministry of Foreign Affairs of Japan

Name	Date
Noda Eijiro	1968–69
Akiho Mitsutaka	1969–70
Hatano Yoshio	1970–71
Muraoka Kunio	1971–72
Matsuda Yoshifumi	1973–74
Kunihiro Michihiko	1974–75
Uchida Katsuhisa	1975–76
Matano Kagechika	1976–77
Endo Tetsuya	1977–78
Tajima Takashi	1978–79
Satoh Yukio	1979–80
Kawakami Takao	1981–82
Arafune Kiyohiko	1982–83
Tokinoya Atsushi	1983–84
Shigeta Hiroshi	1984–85
Noguchi Masaaki	1985–86
Asai Motofumi	1986–87

Name	Date
Fujisaki Ichiro	1987–88
Ando Hiroyasu	1988–89
Tanaka Hitoshi	1989–90
Yabunaka Mitoji	1990–91
Miyamoto Yuji	1991–92
Takahashi Fumiaki	1992–93
Sasae Kenichiro	1993–94
Ito Tetsuo	1994–95
Ishikawa Kaoru	1995–96
Harada Chikahito	1996–97
Bessho Koro	1997–98

TIMELINE OF EVENTS

1945–1960s

September 1945

Japan signs its surrender, officially ending the Second World War.

March 1946

Winston Churchill delivers his 'Iron Curtain' speech, ushering in the Cold War.

May 1946

Yoshida Shigeru becomes prime minister, serving most of the period until 1954.

October 1946

The Imperial Diet passes Japan's newly drafted constitution, defining the emperor as 'the symbol of the state'.

September 1948

The Republic of Korea (South Korea) is created in August and the Democratic People's Republic of Korea (North Korea) in September.

August 1949

The Soviet Union successfully conducts its first nuclear-weapons test.

October 1949

The People's Republic of China is established by Chairman Mao Zedong.

June 1950

North Korea invades South Korea, beginning the Korean War, which ends in 1953.

September 1951

The Treaty of Peace with Japan and the Security Treaty between Japan and the United States of America are signed. The US occupation of Japan ends; Japan regains sovereignty the following year.

April 1952

The Treaty of Peace Between the Republic of China and Japan is signed in Taipei, Taiwan.

August 1952

Japan joins the World Bank and the IMF.

October 1952

The UK successfully conducts its first nuclear-weapons test.

July 1954

The Japan Self-Defense Force (JSDF) is created, comprising three branches: the Japan Ground Self-Defense Force (JGSDF), the Japan Maritime Self-Defense Force (JMSDF) and the Japan Air Self-Defense Force (JASDF).

July 1954

The Geneva Accords establish North and South Vietnam along the 17th Parallel.

September 1954

The Southeast Asia Treaty Organisation (SEATO) is formed.

October 1954

Japan joins the Colombo Plan and begins providing technical cooperation.

January 1955

Japan's per-capita GDP returns to pre-war levels.

July 1955

Japan's Economic Planning Agency releases its first Economic White Paper.

September 1955

Japan joins the General Agreement on Tariffs and Trade (GATT).

 **DOMESTIC EVENTS**  **INTERNATIONAL ENGAGEMENT**  **KEY GLOBAL EVENTS**

November 1955

The Liberal Democratic Party (LDP) is formed.

October 1956

Japan and the USSR sign a Joint Declaration, restoring diplomatic relations.

December 1956

Japan joins the UN.

October 1957

The USSR launches *Sputnik*-1, the world's first artificial satellite.

January 1958

Japan becomes a non-permanent member of the UN Security Council (UNSC) for the first time.

February 1958

Japan disburses its first Official Development Assistance loan, with India as the recipient.

January 1960

The Treaty of Mutual Cooperation and Security between the US and Japan is signed, permitting US military bases on Japanese soil and committing the US to act in defence of Japan.

February 1960

France successfully conducts its first nuclear-weapons test.

January 1960

Major Anpo Protests during 1959–60, against the revision of the US–Japan Security Treaty, reach their zenith in June as protesters breach the Diet's compound. The treaty was revised in January 1960 to grant the US the right to establish military bases on Japanese soil in exchange for a defence commitment to Japan in a case of armed attack.

September 1960

The Organization of Petroleum Exporting Countries (OPEC) is created.

December 1960

Prime Minister Ikeda Hayato adopts the National Income Doubling Plan.

January 1962

The Komei Seiji Renmei (Clean Government League) is established. It is renamed Komeito in 1964, one of Japan's key political parties.

October 1962

The Cuban missile crisis occurs.

April 1964

Japan joins the Organisation for Economic Co-operation and Development (OECD). It also accedes to IMF Article VIII member status.

May 1964

The National Diet approves the Partial Nuclear Test Ban Treaty.

October 1964

China successfully conducts its first nuclear-weapons test.

October 1964

Japan hosts the 18th Olympic Games.

June 1965

The Treaty on Basic Relations between Japan and the Republic of Korea is signed, establishing bilateral diplomatic relations.

August 1965

Prime Minister Sato Eisaku becomes the first prime minister to visit Okinawa since 1945.

July 1966

The National Diet approves the establishment of the Asian Development Bank (ADB). The Bank opens in December 1966.

 **DOMESTIC EVENTS**    **INTERNATIONAL ENGAGEMENT**    **KEY GLOBAL EVENTS**

April 1967

Prime Minister Sato Eisaku establishes the 'Three Principles on Arms Exports and Their Related Policy Guidelines', stating that Japan will not export arms to communist countries, countries under embargo and countries involved or likely to be involved in international conflicts.

August 1967

The Association of Southeast Asian Nations (ASEAN) is created.

December 1967

Prime Minister Sato Eisaku declares Japan's 'Three Non-Nuclear Principles', which state that Japan will not possess, produce or allow nuclear weapons on its territory.

July 1968

The Treaty on the Non-Proliferation of Nuclear Weapons (NPT) opens for signing.

December 1968

Japan becomes the second-largest economic power in the world, surpassing West Germany.

July 1969

US President Richard Nixon announces the Nixon Doctrine, inter alia, reducing the number of US troops in Asia.

 **DOMESTIC EVENTS**   **INTERNATIONAL ENGAGEMENT**    **KEY GLOBAL EVENTS**

CHAPTER THREE

The Japanese attitude towards China

Sadako Ogata

Survival 7-9, 1965

Published in this volume with permission from University of California Press Journals. Originally published in Asian Survey, 1 August 1965.

An important debate on foreign policy is developing in Japan. The author of this article, who is Lecturer in International Relations at the International Christian University in Tokyo, examines that aspect of the debate which concerns relations with China.

In the United States-Japan Joint Communiqué of January 13, 1965, President Johnson and Prime Minister Sato stated the China policy of their respective countries as follows:

> The President emphasized the United States policy of firm support for the Republic of China and his grave concern that Communist China's militant policies and expansionist pressures against its neighbours endanger the peace of Asia. The Prime Minister stated that it is the fundamental policy of the Japanese government to maintain friendly ties based on the regular diplomatic relationship with the government of the Republic of China and at the same time to continue to promote private contact which is being maintained with the Chinese mainland in such matters as trade on the basis of the principle of separation of political matters from economic matters.

The most remarkable feature of this Communiqué was that Japan openly declared a policy of promoting trade with

Mainland China, which the United States had branded an aggressive power. It was the first occasion on which a Japanese Prime Minister expressed disagreement with the United States over China in a Joint Communiqué. At the time of Yoshida's visit to Washington in 1954, China trade was not even mentioned. The Kennedy-Ikeda conference in 1961 had merely committed the two nations to close consultation in dealing with China. What has pushed Sato to such a 'forward-looking' position on China? This change is all the more remarkable, since Sato has long been associated with the anti-Mainland China groups.

Changing relationship

One reason for the change might be found in the international position of the United States. Now that the United States is meeting greater opposition not only from neutrals but also from allies, Japan might feel freer to express disagreement over China than before. But another factor is the rising demand in Japan for closer relations with China, not only among left-wing intellectuals and politicians but also among conservative politicians and businessmen.

First of all, it is important to realize that not many Japanese regard Communist China as a 'cold war' enemy, nor do they accept the 'China-Communism-enemy' equation which is so widely held in the United States. This may be partly due to the fact that demilitarized Japan has become so accustomed to delegating her defence responsibilities to the United States that she has lost both the desire and the capacity for serious consideration of military matters. It may also be due to the absence of any strong apprehension of Communist invasion, and to a tendency not to treat militant Chinese revolutionary claims at face value, but rather to see them as a passing phase which will disappear when the Communist regime is more securely established and the standard of living has gone up. Opinion polls have indicated that more Japanese regard the United States bases in Japan as objects of nuclear attack that might involve Japan in war rather than as deterrents to Communist aggression against Japan.

To say that there is no intense fear of Communist invasion does not mean that the Japanese regard Communist China with friendly confidence. Broadly speaking the Japanese attitude toward China may be considered a mixture of fear, disdain, and a sense of kinship. For centuries, Japan had looked up to China as the greatest country in Asia until Chinese weakness was exposed to the world at the end of the nineteenth century. Yet Japan continued to hold her neighbour in awe and called her the 'sleeping lion' which might one day awake from her temporary slumber to shake the world. Though torn by internal and international wars, China's sheer size, man power and physical resources continued to impress the Japanese with its potential power. After fifteen years of Communist control, China today is seen as a unified and powerful nation, determined to surpass the advanced nations in industrial output, military strength and political influence. Moreover, it is armed with a revolutionary ideology and a monolithic political structure. The Japanese cannot but respond with fear to the emergence of Communist China.

Yet, if the Japanese are not exactly terrified by the appearance of a mighty neighbour, the reason may be that they have retained the sense of disdain toward China which was widely held in pre-war days. Many Japanese who were educated in the decades following the Sino-Japanese War, and who are over forty today, were accustomed to regard Japan as the leader in modernization in Asia, and China as a very poor second. *Chankoro*, or pigtailed fellow, was a typical expression of the disdainful way in which Japanese referred to Chinese. To these

Japanese, it is simply inconceivable that the same *chankoro* can now manage the most powerful nation in Asia and present a genuine threat to Japan.

Feeling of closeness

A sense of kinship is the third characteristic attitude of the Japanese toward China, and one that softens whatever sense of hostility may be caused by fear or disdain. Most Japanese refer to cultural affinity, racial similarity, and geographical proximity as providing the basis for a feeling of closeness toward China. The traditional phrase *dobun doshu*, i.e., common script and common race, is quoted frequently to reaffirm historical ties between the two nations. The simple fact of geographic proximity is invariably the starting point of any discussion advocating the resumption of Japanese relations with China. A good neighbour policy has general appeal. China is presented as Japan's most important neighbour with whom close relations should be established.

The sentiments of the millions of Japanese businessmen, technicians, civil servants, and former servicemen and their families to whom China is not a 'strange' land tends to strengthen the special feeling of kinship toward China. Whether or not these people went to China to exploit or fight the Chinese, they personally felt affection for the Chinese people and for the country. To many Japanese of the pre-war generation, the Chinese were not quite 'foreigners,' as were Americans or Europeans. Nor was China a completely alien land. Some advocates of Sino-Japanese solidarity today are motivated by their experiences in China before and during the war. Many others simply keep their experiences as personal memories quite unrelated to their present views on China. Yet the existence of a large number of China-experienced Japanese adds strength to the kinship feeling professed by the Japanese toward China. The attitude of the post-war generation toward China is considerably less marked by either feelings of disdain or kinship. To them China is a mysterious and frightening 'foreign' country. Fifteen years of estrangement from China have added distance between the peoples of China and Japan and may eventually result in material changes in the Japanese attitude toward China.

It is difficult to correlate the general attitude of the Japanese public with any specific policy argument regarding China. Nor can we draw from it enthusiasm for a rapprochement with the Mainland. Yet as long as the Japanese continue to possess a feeling of closeness toward China and as long as China holds the lure of a potential market, closer relations as such will not be opposed by the general public. In fact the polls have indicated a trend toward favouring recognition of Mainland China, and of promoting trade relations with it.

Moral obligation

The most common argument of the 'progressive' intellectuals who favour close ties with Communist China is that Japan mistreated China in the past and should now atone for its guilt. They claim that no individual Japanese is exempt from the 'China guilt,' because Japan carried out aggression and atrocities as an organized body. They consider Japan's rise to the status of a great power as having been attained through the sacrifice of China, and argue further that since Japan's military aggression launched China on the course of its 'national liberation' movement, Japan is morally obliged to approve China's present government. Many of these writers, publicists and scholars who have visited China in the past ten years returned feeling doubly guilty, as the Chinese expressed their willingness to forget the past. To some the sense of guilt is undoubtedly derived from the memory of their personal wartime experiences. Hotta Yoshie, a novelist and a known advocate of close relations with the Mainland, speaks of his repentant feeling when he witnessed the chaos in Shanghai in 1946. Ohara Soichiro, the president of Kurashiki Rayon Company – the first Japanese firm to export a vinylon plant to China – expressed his desire to compensate for the damages Japan inflicted upon China where he served as a soldier during the war. But to many others it seems probable that the 'China guilt' is little more than a plausible theme.

More important to 'progressive' intellectuals in determining their sympathy for China is their appreciation of the Chinese revolution as the model for Asian nationalist movements. They feel that China has won full independence from foreign rule and has achieved internal reform, and the fact that the Chinese revolution became a Communist revolution does not detract from their admiration. Many intellectuals who might be against a Communist regime in Japan, nevertheless accept the establishment of a Communist government in China, because this government has successfully transformed China into a powerful and unified nation.

Nationalist sentiment

Another important factor that brings the 'progressive' intellectuals close to Communist China is anti-American nationalism. Ever since the Nationalist Government moved to Taiwan, Communist China has pledged the 'liberation' of Taiwan and has regarded the United States as the main target of its nationalism. Today Communist China and the United States confront each other in a state of intense enmity in many parts of Asia. The Japanese intellectuals sympathize with China because of their own anti-American nationalism cultivated in the post-war years. In the years following the Japanese defeat, opposition to war, militarism, and nuclear armaments received support from most Japanese intellectuals.

The United States, as the predominant nuclear power and as the principal occupying force in Japan, became a natural target for this nationalist and pacifist sentiment. The progressive intellectuals as well as the Socialist and Communist parties capitalized on the nationalist and pacifist sentiment, and demanded the withdrawal of the United States military bases from Japan. They called for the abrogation of mutual security arrangements with the United States, and for the full independence of Japan from American control.

China was regarded as a 'fighting friend' against the 'common enemy of American imperialism' on the one hand, and a fellow 'peace force' against American militarism on the other. The former view was spelled out by the late Asanuma Inejiro of the Socialist Party and is said to have cost the party about one million votes. It represented the attitude of the militant left wing of the party as well as that of the intellectuals. According to this view, the Japanese opposition to American bases in Japan and Okinawa, and the Chinese determination to 'liberate' Taiwan, are one and the same struggle against American imperialism.

China's lapse

The Soviet nuclear explosion had already confused the leftist-oriented pacifists when the Chinese nuclear explosion took place on October 16, 1964, and placed the intellectuals and the political left in a painful dilemma. How should they explain the emergence of China as a nuclear power? Previously, they had regarded China as an object for atonement of Japan's past guilt and a fellow fighter for national independence and the cause of peace. But now, with the exception of the Communists, the left wing did not approve the Chinese nuclear explosion. The Japanese Communists, who had supported Peking in its opposition to the Test Ban Treaty, continued to argue that it was not fair to expect China to abstain when the United States encircled her with nuclear weapons. The Socialists, whose Fourth Mission was in China at the time of the explosion, announced that their Mission expressed regret and disapproval of the nuclear test in the presence of high Chinese officials, including Chou En-lai. The Mission had been placed in an extremely painful position, and showed understanding sympathy to China. Yet, the Socialists seemed to have felt that it was more important to reaffirm anti-nuclear, pacifist sentiments, and to assert independence from China. Pacifism and nationalism decided the Socialists' position.

Many intellectuals regretted the moral lapse of China, although some qualified their disapproval by pointing out that there were circumstances that made it inevitable for China to possess her own nuclear arms. Sakamoto Yoshikazu, a scholar and frequent commentator on China, stated that Chinese frustrations over Taiwan – to them a just demand for national unification branded as aggression by the United States – and their rejection from international society, had forced them to seek heroic means in order to strengthen their voice. More interesting was the reaction of the sinologist, Takeuchi Yoshimi, who agreed that the Chinese nuclear explosion was an unfortunate incident that should not have happened, yet emotionally he could not help applauding the Chinese for having achieved a phenomenal victory over the Anglo-Saxons and their supporters, including some Japanese. He considered the explosion comparable to Japan's victory in the Russo-Japanese War of 1904–05. Both were victories of nationalism and both had tremendously encouraging effects on the subjected peoples. With Takeuchi, it was nationalism and Asianism that determined his attitude toward China.

Promotion of trade

But it is the 'pro-China' conservatives, led by former Prime Minister Ishibashi Tanzan, the late Takasaki Tatsunosuke and veteran M. P. Matsumura Kenzo, who must be given more credit than all of the left wing for advancing trade with China. In 1959–60, when Japan faced the critical question of the revision of the US-Japan Security Treaty, all three visited Communist China with the hope of preventing any adverse effects that the revised treaty might have on Sino-Japanese relations. None of them were enthusiastic supporters of the Security Treaty. Since then they have revisited China and have been actively engaged in promoting relations with the Mainland. Matsumura and Takasaki collaborated in achieving the so-called LT, or the Liao Cheng-chih-Takasaki Trade Agreement, which is the private trade mechanism between Japan and China. These two men share a strong sense of guilt toward China, and a consciousness of Asian solidarity.

Takasaki, the founder of Toyo Can Producing Company, was the wartime president of the Manchuria Heavy Industries Company. After the war he joined the Liberal Democratic Party and attended the First Bandung Conference as the chief Japanese delegate. Matsumura, a member of the House of Representatives since pre-war days, has visited China many times and has many personal friends among the Chinese. Well versed in the arts and classics of China, and having had close contact in his Waseda days with revolutionary Chinese students and political refugees, Matsumura at eighty personifies the last of the traditional Pan Asianists who looked to China as a partner in the defence of Asia against Western domination. To him the feeling of 'common script and common race' is no empty phraseology. He considers Chinese Communism to be essentially an expression of nationalism. Underlying his appreciation for Chinese nationalism is his sympathy for the poor and exploited peoples of Asia who have recently gained their independence. Japan must assist them not only economically but also with understanding and trust. Japan and China, in particular, can and must trust each other in spite of differences in their political system. Hence, Matsumura has made it his life work not only to promote trade but to restore political relations with China.

Another important group within the Liberal Democratic Party is the Ajia Afurika Mondai Kenkyukai (Afro-Asian Problems Research Association) which was organized on January 28, 1965, as a rival to the pro-Taiwan Ajia Mondai Kenkyukai (Asian Problems Research Association) which was launched on December 16, 1964. The pro-Taiwan group, led by Kaya Okinori, comprises the mainstream of the Liberal Democratic Party and includes the majority of the Kishi, Sato, and Ishii factions. They are staunch anti-Communists, who are older in age and who organized themselves in order to prevent Prime Minister Sato from committing Japan to a pro-China course. The pro-China Ajia Afurika Mondai Kenkyukai consists of the younger House of Representative members, including the majority of the Miki and Kono factions. Matsumura serves as adviser to this group. Though they cannot claim numerical equality with the pro-Taiwan group, it is significant that they have drawn over eighty members cutting across established factional lines.

Asian nationalism

The spokesman for the pro-China Ajia Afurika Mondai Kenkyukai is Utsunomiya Tokuma, a junior member of the Ishibashi faction, who accompanied Ishibashi on his first trip to China, and since then has revisited China and South-East Asia. Like Matsumura, he sympathizes with the plight of the Asian people and supports their aspirations. He goes further than Matsumura, however, in attacking the crimes of colonialism in Asia, and in urging Japan to give positive assistance to contemporary Asian and African nationalist movements. He has a kind of guilt feeling that Japan betrayed Asia in the course of her modernization, and also a belief that the future lies with the Asian and African peoples.

Underlying the views of Matsumura, Utsunomiya, and other members of the Ajia Afurika Mondai Kenkyukai, is a tacit consensus that the time has come for Japan to free itself from American control. They feel that the United States has failed to appreciate Asian nationalism, that the situation in Asia calls for solutions by Asians, and that Japan can play a greater role in international society by obtaining a freer hand. They are nationalists, sharing the progressive intellectuals' and the left-wing politicians' desire for greater independence from the United States, but they do not share the latter's evaluation of America as an imperialist or militaristic power. To them, the United States is not bent on imperialistic aggression. When China's nuclear explosion became known, Matsumura was concerned that it would incite anti-nuclear feelings and turn Japanese public opinion away from China. He himself thought that the explosion made the resumption of Japanese relations with China all the more important, because a nuclear power should not be excluded from international society.

Attitude of businessmen

The attitude of business circles toward China has been based, understandably, on business interests. While there is general interest in the China market, many businessmen have been cautious because of their distrust of a Communist regime as trading partner and fear of adverse effects on trade with the United States and Taiwan. Nevertheless, the total trade volume has risen steadily in the last few years until it reached a peak of 311 million dollars in 1964. This is still only 2.13 per cent of total Japanese trade, as compared with 28.59 per cent with the United States. Chemical industries, potash and synthetic fibre, Japan's main export interests, are now badly in need of new markets. With the intensification of the Sino-Soviet dispute and the Chinese demands for advanced chemical, petroleum refining and electronic plants and techniques, however, Chinese trade with Western countries constituted 70 per cent of her total trade in 1963 as against 30 per cent with the Communist countries. England, France, West Germany, and Italy are showing marked interest in the China market. Japanese businessmen who have been actively promoting trade with the Mainland are apprehensive about the appearance of Western competitors. Okazaki Kaheita, chairman of the Nichu Sogo Boeki Renraku Kyogikai (General Council for Japan-China Trade) and president of the All Nippon Airways, who served in China for many years as a bank official, and Suzuki Kazuo, managing director of Nichu Boeki Sokushin Kai (Japan-China Trade Promotion Organization), share the beliefs of Matsumura and the pro-China conservative politicians that Japan and China are bound by special historic ties, that Japan should contribute to the peace and prosperity of Asia and that she should make decisions independently of the United States. They feel that they have already brought trade with Mainland China to the highest point possible under the limits of the present non-governmental agreement. Without the establishment of diplomatic relations, they argue, Japan cannot compete against the Western countries.

As we have seen, the China issue is closely bound with Japanese nationalism. Underlying all pro-China arguments, from the left-wing Socialists to traditional conservatives, is the desire to become more independent of the United States. Attempts at dealing with China have called forth nationalist assertions. China trade is frequently called *jishu boeki*, or independent trade, and pro-China diplomacy is referred to as *jishu gaiko*, or independent diplomacy. Sympathy with Asian 'national liberation' movements is largely sympathy with their nationalist aspirations even if they possess radical Communist overtones. It is precisely because of the nationalist element involved in the China issue that the Japanese government has been forced to take a 'forward-looking' position.

Government attitude

How has the demand for closer relations with China affected the Japanese government? Neither Ikeda nor Sato nor any of the leading members of the government seem to have any great desire to promote closer relations with Communist China. Communism is not an appealing ideology to an over-whelming majority of the Japanese. The Japanese economy has flourished in spite of negligible economic relations with China. The Japanese government has been fully committed to supporting the United States in military and diplomatic affairs. There is little desire to damage the close and highly beneficial ties with the United States. The problem of the government is one of walking along a narrow path that keeps its US relations intact, but forestalls demands for closer ties with China from developing into a major political issue or a mass movement.

The government has sought to achieve this objective by sepa-rating political and economic matters. Under this principle, trade with the Mainland has been allowed to expand by degrees. The government has tried to show a 'forward-looking' attitude domestically by pointing to the ardent China trade promoters within its own ranks. But obviously the economic importance of the China trade is still very limited. The motives of those Japanese expounding closer economic relations with China have been emotional and political, and they will not be satisfied regardless of how much trade may expand. The coming months will tell how far the demands of the pro-China group within the ruling Liberal Democratic Party will be met and at what speed. If they turn too readily toward abandoning Taiwan, neither the government nor the pro-Taiwan group of the Liberal Democratic Party will tolerate their intra-party opposition.

Here we must examine the question of Taiwan. The government has declared its intention 'to maintain friendly ties based on the regular diplomatic relationship with the government of the Republic of China'. If the government plans to promote economic relations with the Mainland, while maintaining diplomatic relations with Taiwan, this would be a step in the direction of the acceptance of 'Two Chinas'. The Socialist Party has been committed officially to a 'One China' doctrine, but even some of its members would support a 'One China, One Taiwan' settlement. It is probable that the Japanese people would readily accept either a 'Two China', or a 'One China, One Taiwan' settlement, although neither China will today accept this formula. Public opinion polls have shown that while a slight majority favour recognition of Communist China, only a very small percentage desire exclusive recognition of Peking.

The one concern shared by the government and all those who support close ties with China is that Japan should play an intermediary role between Communist China and the United States. Undoubtedly, improvement in Sino-American relations is the only way to decrease tension in Asia, and it is here that Japan wishes to play an active role. The government must now acknowledge the widely held desire for Japan to serve as the bridge between East and West, by taking more initiatives in Asian diplomatic relations.

CHAPTER FOUR

American–Japanese relations

Shigeharu Matsumoto

Survival 8-4, 1966

Published in this volume with kind permission from Matsumoto Ken (originally published in Japan Quarterly and Atlas, 1965).

Mr Shigeharu Matsumoto, a well-known commentator on foreign affairs, discusses the developing tensions of the American-Japanese relationship. The article was originally published in Japan Quarterly *in the form 'A Letter to an American Friend'.*

If things are left unsolved, I am afraid a serious crisis will result between the US and Japan within a few years. The present state of affairs in Japan constitutes a danger signal. It augurs that relations between the US and Japan will eventually turn from bad to worse. I can appreciate a growing impatience among Americans because you feel you cannot understand Japan and cannot make out what she is going to do. . . . I am not writing this merely because I wish to make any requests of the US. I am trying to tell you the peculiar circumstances in which we find ourselves.

Between the US and Japan there lie the problems of Communist China, of Vietnam and of South-East Asia in general. There is also the problem of Okinawa and the Security Treaty, which we expect will be an issue in 1970. All these problems involve basic Japanese attitudes. Unless Japanese leaders give serious thought to them and succeed in enlisting the support of the overwhelming majority of the people, the government will never be able to find an over-all solution. Japanese prime ministers and ministers of foreign affairs have repeatedly spoken of 'an independent foreign policy', but they have done nothing. Communist China and other Communist bloc nations severely criticize Japan. 'Japan is a colony of America', they say, 'the Japanese government is nothing but a robot controlled by Washington'. . . .

Yet Americans also feel uneasy over the state of things in Japan. Why is it, they ask, that Japan refrains from giving more positive cooperation to the US in Vietnam? How can responsible Japanese remain indifferent to the possible threat of Communist China? Why does Japan seek to expand trade relations with Communist China? Why doesn't it try to appreciate the strategic significance of Okinawa to the free world and act on problems pertaining to Okinawa in the light of such appreciation? Japan is in a position to decide on the continuance or the termination of the Security Treaty in 1970. Why isn't there any voice to bravely call for its continuance – since requests for its abolition or revision are already so very actively voiced?

My viewpoints on these questions, which I am going to relay to you, by no means represent those of the Japanese government. Kindly take them as the viewpoints of a critic on foreign affairs.

If I may speak frankly, I must say that, even in the days when US-Japan relations were, outwardly at least, in a 'honeymoon mood', many Japanese were uneasy. With 'muddy and bloody' battles now being fought in Vietnam, and with tension growing between the US and Communist China, public opinion in Japan is becoming, or rather, should I say, has become increasingly critical of US policies toward Vietnam. As US Ambassador to Japan Edwin O. Reischauer indicated in a recent interview, anti-American sentiment is growing from bad to worse. Although Japan's Liberal Democratic government is acting in concert with the American government – it is sending, as a formality, a small amount of medical supplies and drugs to the Saigon government – the overwhelming majority of the Japanese people eagerly urge peaceful settlement of the Vietnam crisis through efforts of the United Nations.

I am sure you are well acquainted with the criticisms of US policy voiced by the Socialists and other opposition parties. Particularly since the bombings of North Vietnam, the mass media are trying to cover the situation in detail to respond to the national sentiment of the Japanese for an early settlement. Needless to say, news sent from North Vietnam is covered by reporters who are neither Communists nor Communist sympathizers. Having had some experience in this field, I myself can see that their reports are based on a humanistic, objective viewpoint. These reports have tended to reinforce the sharp criticism of the US by the Japanese public.

As I see it, the core of US policy toward Vietnam is to check the advance of Communist China into the Indochinese Peninsula at South Vietnam and Thailand. Under present circumstances, where there seems little hope of political solution or diplomatic negotiation, I cannot help but conclude that Washington is determined to have US military forces stationed in these two countries for a long period of time, possibly several years. If I am mistaken, kindly point it out to me in your reply. . . . I would simply say that if the US had been interested in checking Peking's southward advance, it would have done better to assist Vietnam, so that it could develop as Yugoslavia has. I have written you this opinion of mine because I don't consider it 'locking the stable door after the horse has gone'. It is shared by many other reasonable Japanese. . .

Sacrifice hit

It is said that the US strives in Vietnam, in baseball terms, for a sacrifice hit, i.e., to show the world that the guerrillas there can never be successful militarily, and to check the efforts of Communist China and other Communist countries to Communize the whole world.

However, many Americans are well aware that guerrillas cannot exist without the support of the public. Aren't all guerrillas the same in this sense, whether they are Communist guerrillas, guerrillas fighting for the liberation of a people (as in Algeria), or Communist guerrillas masquerading as popular liberators? Even if the US wins a military victory in Vietnam, I see no evidence that this would amount to ultimate general victory.

Please excuse my quoting a rather outdated example, but at the time the Wang Ching-wei government came into existence in 1940, thanks to Japanese militarists, the Japanese Army, in order to better Sino-Japanese relations, suggested that along with the construction of a monument for the Japanese war dead in Nanking, a tombstone also be set up for the Chinese war dead. At the unveiling ceremony, the Japanese who were present got a shock. On the Chinese tombstone were engraved four Chinese characters written by Ching-wei. Their English translation is: 'Precious blue-blood for a thousand years'. It was as if they said they would not forget, for a thousand years to come, the blood shed by the Chinese in the war against Japan. What are the Vietnamese going to do about the blood shed daily in Vietnam?

Anti-war sentiment

Here I must mention the anti-war sentiment of the Japanese people. As you may remember, because of her victory in the Sino-Japanese war and in the Russo-Japanese war, Japan had been branded as a warlike nation. It was a viewpoint much accepted at one time in West European countries. But what of Japan today? Our anti-war sentiment is stronger than anyone else's. Those who visit Hiroshima or Nagasaki will appreciate why the resolution 'no more atomic bombs' is the strongest aspect of our national feelings. That is why even the conservative government party in Japan cannot help but voice opposition to nuclear experiments, regardless of which nation conducts them.

The anti-war sentiment can develop into an urge for peace. The primary principle followed by all Japanese cabinets since Kishi's is to act in concert with the United Nations in matters of foreign policy. However, the Japanese Communist Party regards Communist China as a peace-seeking nation. Under the pretext of safeguarding a peace-seeking nation from American imperialism, the Japanese Communists approve Communist China's nuclear experiments, which, however, the majority of the Japanese people oppose. In this connection, the overwhelming opinion is that Communist China be asked to join the UN disarmament conference. . . .

The anti-war sentiment was incorporated into our new Constitution promulgated during the Occupation days. The Constitution prohibits Japan from engaging in an act of war. The statement 'We don't like war', made while the cold war was raging between East and West, may be criticized as dangerously lacking in responsibility. Yet the Japanese nation, insofar as its anti-war sentiment represents its own wish for world peace, is proud of it.

There was 'a war to make the world safe for democracy' and also 'a war to end all wars'. But what was achieved? Aside from the fact that many developing nations have obtained independence, is it not true that Communist strength has drastically expanded? Is it not true that the two world wars proved to be among the most important factors in helping the Soviet Communist Party and the Chinese Communist Party come to power? Recognition of these historical facts has strengthened the anti-war sentiment of the Japanese people. In view of this, I do not believe any nation has the moral right to ask Japan to take up arms in violation of her own Constitution – just because the cold war has intensified.

The Japanese people were sent to war by a militarist government and bombed by the powerful US Air Force. They then underwent the dismal experience of an Occupation which lasted more than six years. After this the nation understandably desired a democratic government, as well as independence from the Occupation forces.

About that time (1949–51) the US was plunged into the Korean War on the heels of the counteraction against the Communist guerrillas in Greece. The Department of State wanted the early conclusion of a peace treaty with Japan, while the Pentagon took a negative attitude – it wanted to continue the military occupation of Japan, albeit on a limited scale. Dulles and Yoshida suggested a compromise – to sign simultaneously the San Francisco Peace Treaty and the US-Japan Security Treaty.

American umbrella

Due to the cold war between the US and the Soviet Union, only a very few nations blessed with special geographical and historical conditions managed to enjoy complete independence. Japan was obliged to stand under the atomic umbrella of the US. So were Great Britain, France and West Germany. As a result, they were obliged to behave with reserve toward the US or to co-operate with the US by providing her with military bases.

However, this situation could offer no solution to the various problems. . . . A father's feeling is noble in that he prays for the future happiness of his son. But the son, when he grows up, is apt to complain that 'Father doesn't understand me'. Perhaps it is natural that the father should want to keep his son under the protection of his atomic umbrella. But the son would wish to make an umbrella by himself, although it may prove useless. Or he would wish to leave his father's umbrella, without giving a thought to the umbrella of a wicked neighbour.

In view of this situation, the Japanese leaders feel that relations with the United States are based upon the US-Japan Security Treaty. So is Japan's foreign policy. It may offend you, but some people in financial circles who have a clear-cut view of the matter say, 'The Treaty is life insurance for which we must pay premiums'. A great many conservatives say: 'There will be no problem as far as 1970 is concerned. Nothing to it. We can manage to get the Treaty through'. A healthy democratic growth of Japan, however, demands political stability; I am one of those who cannot take an optimistic view of 1970 unless full preparations are made and a firm determination reached on the course to follow.

Open discussion

To face 1970 in a mood which satisfies the majority of the nation, it is absolutely necessary for the leaders and the people to engage in open discussions. As of now, opinion is divided: one view is to keep the Treaty, the other is to abolish it. However, with the remarkable technical progress made in nuclear weaponry, and certain drastic changes taking place in the international situation, a treaty revision in some form may be able to obtain the support of the Japanese majority. This may well develop into a political question, and, itself, become the subject of negotiation between the US and Japan.

Explaining the former Security Treaty to the nation, the then Prime Minister Yoshida said: 'The ratification of this treaty represents Japan's determination to share the fate of the US'. Both the Left and Right Socialist Parties (representing approximately one-third of the voters), not to mention the Communist Party, voiced strong opposition to ratification. Yet, for the sake of gaining independence from the Occupation forces and for the security of the nation, the overwhelming majority of people supported the Yoshida government. . .

Since 1957–58, to the surprise of the world, Japan's economic strength has grown rapidly. As the former Security Treaty was to Japan's disadvantage in many respects, Prime Minister Kishi wished to revise it so that Japan would be on a nearly equal footing with the US. He originally had in mind a new treaty which would replace the former Security Treaty. The US government was prepared to comply with Japan's request for revision, although it preferred to leave the Treaty as it had been. . . . Pushed into a passive position because of internal politics, Japan had to agree to joint US-Japan military operations should Japan's security be threatened (Article 5 of the Treaty) and a provision for US military bases (Article 6). Another result was an exchange of agreements concerning prior notice, in case of Treaty revision.

Sources of dissatisfaction

I am writing at tedious length on this subject to explain to you why there are a number of Japanese who are not satisfied with the new Security Treaty, although it is far more to Japan's advantage, in many respects, than the former one. I believe that some form of umbrella is necessary for Japan for the time being. I also believe it is rather hard for one who extends an umbrella to understand the feeling of one who is sheltered under his umbrella. Hence the Japanese people's frustration on these issues.

We must frankly express a certain dissatisfaction with the US. In the first place, to provide the US with military bases cannot help but give us the impression that we are still somewhat under Occupation. Please realize that this discrepancy will continue at least for five more years.

The second focus of dissatisfaction is the fact that it would not violate the Treaty for the US forces stationed in Japan to engage in military operations if they first moved to Okinawa

– because no stipulation is made in the Treaty as to US military operations originating in Okinawa. Many Japanese are displeased with the fact that if Okinawa is used as a stepping-stone in any military operations, prior consultation with Japan is not called for. The Japanese people are very much afraid of being involved in a war without their consent.

In the third place, the Japanese nation urges the earliest possible settlement of the Vietnam dispute. There are strong signs, however, that it will be prolonged. When reinforcement of US military forces there is completed, the war front will surely expand. Apparently the US is doing her best to solve the matter through negotiation. However, as you are well aware, even if the US achieves a military victory, a political solution will take longer than we expect. It will also require a large degree of concession on the part of the US.

Many demands

We are told that the US is determined not to resort to nuclear weapons in Vietnam and not to expand hostilities to involve Communist China. However, the Japanese people fear that if the dispute in Vietnam is prolonged, if it comes to involve Laos or if Hanoi-Haiphong is bombed, the result is not predictable. Should a war break out between the US and Communist China, there is ample danger that Japan would be divided in two – the pro-US camp and the pro-Communist China camp. Disturbances extending to the scale of civil war may take place.

I have taken the liberty of making many requests of the US. Actually the Japanese people are making stronger demands on their own government.

Their first demand is political stability. After the Security Treaty disturbances, Prime Minister Ikeda took a posture of 'tolerance and patience'. At the same time he reinstated trade relations with Communist China, a move which was not welcomed by the US. The Ikeda cabinet enjoyed popular support until its high-rate economic growth plan turned out to be an evident failure. This was because people, partly unconsciously perhaps, were pleased with political stability. It was also because they were pleased with the cabinet's posture, which was suggesting some spirit of independent diplomacy. The politics and foreign policy followed by the Ikeda cabinet stood for 'common sense'.

Last year, the Japanese economic delegation to the US explained that the trade between Japan and Communist China was being conducted in the same manner Western Europe conducted trade between its nations. As Japan's relationship with China is, geographically and historically, different from that of West European countries, it is natural that her relations with Communist China should be more intimate than those between West European countries and Communist China. Yet until last year, in speech and in action, the US had been taking a discouraging attitude towards Japan on the matter of plant export to China. Because of the intensification of the Vietnam crisis, the Sato cabinet, out of deference to the US, is temporarily suspending permissions for plant export. However, trade between Communist China and designated Japanese firms is steadily growing.

I wish Peking would develop a sense of proportion. It may be that Peking has its own reasons, but it is by no means to their advantage to make an issue of such a trifling matter as the problem of an Export-Import Bank. The fact that Communist China has been placed on a semi-war footing in response to the Vietnam crisis is a gloomy threat to peace in the Far East. Recent conclusion of another trade agreement may be an indication that Peking has not yet lost its composure. Or it could indicate that Peking is more eager to import Japanese goods and introduce Japanese techniques. I believe that the gradual increase of trade between Japan and Communist China helps to stabilize Japanese politics.

National defence

The second demand the majority of the Japanese make on their government concerns national defence. The problem has recently been taken up by the press; however, the government as well as the people should discuss it more actively. Have we ever seriously looked at the facts or the value of the American atomic umbrella? It is appalling that since the two treaties were signed in San Francisco, the office of Chief of Japan's Defence Agency, which is supposed to assume heavy responsibility for national defence, has been filled by twenty different people. Their average term is some eight months. No excuse can be made to US criticism of the conservative party on this point. As much as 8 to 10 per cent, of the total national budget amounting to 4 trillion yen [$10.8 million] goes for national defence. Why, then, has the morale of the Self-Defence Forces – Army, Navy and Air Force – not been raised as expected? Some say Article 9 of the Constitution [the anti-war clause] is at fault. However, I wonder if that is the real cause. We should surely live up to Article 9 which was born out of our bitter experience. On the other hand, although I am an amateur in this field, I believe that the Defence Force cannot safeguard Japan in a limited war – because the operation command is located elsewhere. I hear that even the joint military operations of the Saigon Army and the US forces have not been successful. It seems to me the only way we can turn our Defence Force into a real protection is to give it independence within a limited sphere of responsibility. Article 5 of the revised Security Treaty deals virtually solely with joint operations. Therefore, whether or not there is an act of genuine hostility, the defence of Japan is placed under the operational leadership of the United States. A thorough re-examination is required in order to make the necessary revision.

Plans for peace

I cannot agree to the nuclear armament of Japan. An effort to develop nuclear weapons may be inevitable under present circumstances, but I am sure the majority of the Japanese people oppose Japan's developing such weapons. It is more important for Japan to try to work out disarmament or armament control plans worthy of world attention.

Many plans can be worked out for the future defence of Japan. For example, the Self-Defence Forces could be given the task of safeguarding Japan in a limited situation, while still remaining under the US umbrella. For instance, couldn't Japan have a defence structure similar to Great Britain's, if it is too much to have one like France's? Aside from the work of a few specialists, serious study of this problem has just begun. . . . The Japanese people have long been displeased with the easy-going attitude of their political leaders, including those of the Socialist Party. It is easy to see how such dissatisfaction creates impatience among Americans. However, democracy is firmly rooted in the minds of the Japanese people. The majority would not want to turn Japan into a Communist country. True, our economic growth is not very strong at the moment, but it will soon recover and we will make further progress. Japan's scientific and technical standards are highly rated in the world. You cannot easily ignore Japan's population of 100 million and its skills.

The collapse of the former Japanese Empire created a vacuum as far as the stability of the Far East is concerned.

Communist China came into existence. Various South-East Asian countries became independent. The US, in spite of all her efforts, cannot expect to restore stability in the Far East all by herself. Fortunately, both US-Soviet relations and Japanese-Soviet relations are at a point where discussion is possible, and North-East Asia is now enjoying peace. The question is South-East Asia. The time has come when long-term assistance for the economic development of South-East Asia should be extended through the friendly co-operation of the US and Japan. It is important even among friends that they should respect each other's personality.

Please excuse my reiteration, but let me repeat once more what the Japanese people have in mind. They urge an early settlement of the Vietnam crisis. They ask that a future war between the US and Communist China be avoided and that no nuclear weapons be used in Asia under any circumstances. Before you get offended and say 'Is that any way for an ally to talk?', please give a second thought to the feelings of the Japanese people. As soon as the dispute in Vietnam has been settled, Japan will be willing to render positive assistance, both economic and technical. In the meantime, we will try to arrive at a sensible national consensus as far as the problems of national defence and foreign policy are concerned. I only hope that US policy toward Japan will not be such as to destroy Japan's political stability to the point where it cannot be restored. It would be very unfortunate if our conservative party were to turn into an ultra-rightist party. This would benefit neither Japan nor the US.

You know that I am regarded as an old liberal. I have worked all my life, although in a small way, for friendly relations between the US and Japan. I have written this letter to you, whom I hold in high regard, because I love Japan and because I love America.

CHAPTER FIVE

The Asian balance of power: a comparison with European precedents

Michio Royama

From Adelphi Paper 42, 1967

The transfer of concepts or techniques derived from the history of one area to the prospective future of another is necessarily a dangerous and delicate task. In this case it might seem an academic or even a mischievous one if the indigenous diplomatic traditions of Asia already provided workable answers to the security problems of that area. But though an attempt to make them do so may be read into the doctrine of non-alignment, the effort cannot claim much success. In the twelve years since the most ambitious enunciation of the doctrine, at Bandung in 1955, the 'area of peace' that non-alignment was supposed to provide in Asia has in fact been the scene of more military activity than any other part of the world, whereas the area organized on classic balance-of-power principles into two tight military coalitions, Europe, has witnessed only one minor military encounter lasting a few days, Hungary in 1956.[1] On the evidence of these years, one might say that the amoral traditions of the balance of power have done better (at least in respect of peace) for those who have lived by them than the moral aspirations of non-alignment.

One Western security-concept has admittedly been tried in Asia, to some extent in competition with non-alignment, the concept of containment, and it might be judged to have cost more, in terms of pain and death as well as money, and to have had no better success in terms of security or stability than non-alignment. But containment, a strategy which has been mistaken for a policy, is based on American assumptions which differ substantially from the European assumptions of the balance of power.

This essay will attempt to consider how far the traditional European concepts and experience can be applied to contemporary Asian security problems. It will be an Australian view in the sense that the author, as an Australian, must be conscious that her own country's efforts to provide for its future security should include some assessment of the prospects for such a balance. Perhaps there is a certain appropriateness to an Australian examination of this question, since Australians are the only group of Westerners who must remain fully and inescapably vulnerable to the diplomatic stresses arising in Asia, on whose periphery they live or die. The intellectual concepts involved are theirs by direct inheritance, and the possibility of applying them to this particular environment is more directly to their interest than that of any other group of Westerners.

The phrase 'an Asian balance of power' might be construed to mean either a balance of power intended to restrain any overweening ambitions in Asia, or a balance of power confined to Asian states (with Australians considered honorary Asians by virtue of proximity). I will consider both these interpretations, looking first at the question of what kind of balance could operate in the area, and second at the question of whether it would remain viable if non-Asian powers opted out of it. The notion of an Asian region will be held to cover the area from Pakistan east and north to Japan and Soviet Asia. There may be much to be said for regarding the Middle East as Western Asia, and for believing that it will ultimately share some of the interests and dangers of Southern Asia and Eastern Asia, but in the time-span which it is at present possible to contemplate, roughly to the late 1970s, the smaller definition of Asia seems the more useful.

Reflecting on the security history of this Asia, which is essentially an arc round the periphery of China, one must be strongly conscious [that to assess] Japan's short- and long-term political objectives, it is necessary to examine some basic factors which have conditioned post-war Japanese political thinking and behaviour.

Political climate and basic problems

Article 9 of the new Constitution of Japan, which was promulgated in 1947 when Japan was still under the Allied Occupation, is, needless to say, the symbol of post-war Japan: not only is it the earnest expression of a desire born out of the traumatic experience which ninety million people went through, including that of Hiroshima and Nagasaki, but it is also the product of five years of Occupation. During these years, when the Japanese people were living from hand to mouth and had not the time or the means to observe and assess what was happening in the outside world, many important changes in post-war international relations had already taken place, notably the development of the Cold War.

When Japan was gradually permitted to resume her normal relations with other nations in the period preceding the conclusion of the San Francisco Peace Treaty in 1951, the Cold War structure had already firmly established itself in Asia. It was, after all, the spread of the Cold War, i.e. the outbreak of the Korean War, which led the United States to accelerate the schedule for Japan's independence; Japan had practically no choice but to join the American camp if she wanted national independence at all. If one looks back over the sixteen years since the San Francisco Peace Treaty, the decision made by the Japanese Government under the leadership of Prime Minister Shigeru Yoshida was basically correct, including that of the conclusion of the Security Treaty between Japan and the United States, which set forth the basic structure for the maintenance of Japan's national security.

The decision's most obvious advantage was that it pushed Japan to a quick recovery from economic disruption, and made possible the unprecedented rate of economic growth which was triggered by the economic boom of the Korean War. Since then, in a ten-year span, Japan has attained a new power-status. If economic indices are the criteria of the status of power, Japan is certainly a great power in the world today. In 1966, she produced about 47.8 million tons of crude steel, or 10.3 per cent of the world total, being next only to the United States and the Soviet Union. In shipbuilding, she has maintained the world's top rank for the past ten years, producing 50 per cent (5.4 million tons) of the total world output (excluding the Soviet Union and Communist China). Even as a car manufacturer, she has already overtaken Great Britain, producing more than two million vehicles in 1966, and comes third after the United States and West Germany. In terms of GNP, which is now about $84 billion, she ranks fifth in the world, with a higher rate of growth than Germany or Britain, the third and fourth powers.

On the deficit side, however, the decision inevitably created the difficulties which have confronted Japanese political life ever since, and whose persistence has made them a part of the normal state of affairs. It brought into being the irreconcilable division of political opinion between the conservatives, represented by the Liberal Democratic Party (which has been continuously in power since 1946), and the progressives, or radicals, who have been represented mainly by the Japanese Socialist Party (JSP), which staunchly opposes the idea of the Security Treaty and the maintenance of an unconstitutional Self-Defence Force.

Of course, it would be wrong to try to draw conclusions about Japanese attitudes towards foreign and defence issues solely from election results, because the voters' behaviour is determined, more often than not, by factors other than foreign and defence policy issues.[2] However, if there was such a thing as the 'general will' of the people expressed in these election results, it would mean mainly two things: first, that the people have consistently endorsed the policies of the Liberal Democratic Government, policies which have allowed Japan's economy to grow rapidly to the point of affluence and have kept her parliamentary democratic politics on a moderately satisfactory level despite periodic tactical blunders; and, second, that while endorsing the general framework of close relations with the United States, including the security arrangement it provides, the people have given sufficient support to the progressives to enable them to prevent the conservatives from revising Article 9 of the Constitution, but not sufficient support to make possible the radical changes in the basic political, social, and economic structure that the Socialists and Communists certainly seek.

Despite the potential flaws in the structure of Japanese internal politics which the 1951 decision created, flaws capable of upsetting political stability (as was shown in the violent mass demonstration around the Diet Building in the summer of 1960), the decision has not been wholly disadvantageous politically. Since the creation of a 75,000-man Police Reserve Corps in August 1950, immediately after the outbreak of the Korean War, by the decision of General MacArthur, Supreme Commander of the Allied Powers, the Japanese Self-Defence Force has gradually grown, and has now become a fully fledged body of land, sea, and air forces of 250,000 men. This is still, however, a small number for the military forces of a nation which possesses such enormous economic power as present-day Japan. In the fiscal year 1966, Japan's defence expenditure constituted only 7.9 per cent of the total government expenditure, or 1.37 per cent of the gross national income. Despite the criticism frequently made by the opposition parties, and despite the pressures from the right-wing element within its own party, the Liberal Democratic Government has never been too keen on spending more money for national defence. In the face of the long-standing demand made by some defence-minded politicians and the Defence Agency personnel, the Government has still not made up its mind to raise the status of the Agency, which belongs to the Prime Minister's Office, to a full-fledged ministry. The anti-war sentiment of the general public, Article 9, and basic political weakness have always been used as its excuses to resist the American request to increase Japan's defence capability. In fact, the budget for the Third Defence Build-up Plan (1967–71) was finally approved at about £2,360 million, after hard negotiations for almost a year between the Defence Agency and the Ministry of Finance. Although this total is more than twice as much as the spending under the last Five-Year Plan, it does not reach 2 per cent of the national income, which has been the target set by the Defence Agency.

There is of course no universal criterion which establishes the proper ratio of defence spending to the national income needed to ensure the peace and security of a nation. In terms of economic capacity, Japan can afford to spend more only if she deliberately decides to do so, which could include the decision to go nuclear. But she simply cannot afford to make up her mind. The whole attitude of the Japanese people towards the problem of national defence is uniquely legalistic and sentimental, not strategic and realistic. What most concerns many Japanese is not the smallness of military expenditure, which normally means reduced national security, but the question of the unconstitutional nature of the Self-Defence Force. The Japanese mentality seems to be rather complex, and public opinion in recent years seems to have been fluid and changing; the Chinese development of nuclear capability naturally stirs up a sense of insecurity, but its effect does not appear to have been as great as many foreign observers might have expected. Generally speaking, the Japanese people are still largely pacific in their views, and resist the idea of countering force by force. While they reluctantly admit the *de facto* status of the Self-Defence Force, they do not want to revise the Constitution to legalize it, or to go back to the once abandoned idea that military force is an unquestionable symbol of power of a sovereign nation.

This attitude is partly derived from the people's own concept of the military, which was formed on their image of the Japanese Imperial Army and Navy. These were almost always used abroad as a means of aggression and seldom as a means to 'defend' their own country, while at home they were the military 'authorities' which interfered with domestic politics and suppressed civil liberty. Therefore, the Japanese people would conclude from their own experience that a foreign nation would allow them to live peacefully so long as Japan did not intervene in the domestic affairs of the foreigner. This conviction is further strengthened by the fact that Japan is an insular country, which in the world of today offers a reasonable basis for assuming that the possibility of direct aggression from abroad by a conventional means is small.

Although the general pattern of political opinion, which has persisted for more than fifteen years, is unlikely to change for many years to come, some new trends have, in fact, been recently observed in the Japanese political scene. One of the most apparent is a more pluralistic distribution of powers, which was brought about by the last general election, held in January 1967. It resulted from the gain of more seats by two parties: the Democratic Socialist Party (DSP), a moderate splinter from the Japanese Socialist Party, and the Kōmei Tō (KMP), which is the political front of the militant and well-organized new religious group, Sōka Gakkai. These parties are not yet very strong (30 and 25 seats, respectively), and though they have been regarded as belonging to the progressive camp, differences between them and the JSP concerning defence policy are considerable.

Another more subtle phenomenon is the cleft within the ruling Liberal Democratic Party, which takes two basically different political directions: one group has become more critical about the Government's traditional policy towards China, while the other, which belongs to the right wing of the party, has become more critical of the Government's passive attitude towards national security measures. These two groups are still minorities within the party and their influence is still small, especially in the case of the former group, but they cannot be disregarded when considered in conjunction with the over-all new multi-party trend.

So long as the basic division of opinion concerning foreign and defence policies continues, Japan's political stability, which, thanks largely to the expanding national economy, has so far been reasonably well maintained, is bound to remain apparent rather than real. All important issues in the fields of foreign and defence policies contain formidable potential energy, which is likely to explode if mishandled, as in the case of the revision of the Japanese-American Security Treaty in 1960, which cost Nobusuke Kishi his premiership. That was the lesson the late Prime Minister Ikeda learned when he succeeded Kishi, and that was why he maintained a so-called 'low posture' in the sphere of political action, while he made every effort to strengthen Japan's economic status in the world. The present Sato Government has been following the general line set by Ikeda, who resigned for health reasons in 1964. However, this policy of concentrating on economic activities in the past seven years, successful though it is, has unquestionably increased the dilemma which Japan as a great Asian power has to face.

The various images of Japan - as the wealthiest industrial power in Asia, as the power that in the past committed a grave act of aggression in Asia and arrogantly aspired for the leadership of the Greater Asia Co-Prosperity Sphere, and as the power that prospers under American military protection – are not adapted to form a cohesive whole. They produce suspicions in the minds of Asians, and anxiety in the minds of Japanese, while they create dissatisfaction in the minds of Americans. It is ironical that ever since 1963, when Japan was admitted into the Organization for Economic Co-operation and Development (OECD) as proof that she had achieved world status, and when she undertook to contribute one per cent of her national income for the economic aid of developing nations, this incohesiveness has been growing.

The Government's efforts to keep its promise to the OECD have imposed a considerable strain on the Japanese people because they are accustomed to thinking that all their energies have to be devoted to the national economy, since Japan is still far below the rank of a world power in terms of national income *per capita*.[3] However, this effort to give economic assistance abroad is at least less painful politically and better suited to the Japanese Government's line of thought because it is, after all, an inevitable extension of the policy to give priority to economic activities over political action, a field in which there is little scope for manoeuvre anyway.

At the beginning of 1967, encouraged by the apparent success of the initiatives it had taken in 1966,[4] the Japanese Government launched a new scheme for broader regional co-operation. The object is to create an Asian-Pacific Economic Sphere, which would be designed (1) to encourage an awareness of common destiny among Asian-Pacific nations; (2) to promote co-operation among the developed nations in the Pacific Basin; and thereby (3) to aim at solving North-South problems.[5] Since January 1967, the Japanese Foreign Office has been actively engaged in consultation with Australia and New Zealand, both of which have in recent years shown increasing interest in trade with Japan, and all three have agreed on the need to further solidarity and co-operation among Asian-Pacific nations.[6]

It is still too soon to assess the economic significance of these recent developments in the positive posture of Japanese economic foreign policy in Asia, but it is clear that this ostensibly 'economic' policy leads to political problems which Japan is not yet prepared to tackle. This is well illustrated by the very cautious attitude the Japanese Foreign Office has adopted towards the Asia and Pacific Council (ASPAC),[7] which was created as a result of the South-East Asia Foreign Ministers' Conference held in Seoul in June 1966. Japan's uneasiness about associating herself with this organization apparently grew after the Manila Conference of October 1966, comprising the seven nations fighting in Vietnam, for the members of ASPAC were almost the same as those of the Manila Conference. Although Japan did participate in the second ASPAC meeting, held in Bangkok in July 1967, Foreign Minister Miki declared at the meeting that the purpose of ASPAC 'is neither to create an exclusive group nor to advance an anti-Communist movement'.[8] Japan's basic objectives are to modify as much as possible the anti-Communist emphasis of ASPAC by inviting more neutralist nations to join, and to avoid political decisions or agreements which would restrict the freedom of participant nations. One of the most interesting aspects of this somewhat neutralist-inclined approach, which the Foreign Minister has been advancing since the beginning of 1967, was well expressed in the same address when he said that 'Japan will adopt a policy of peaceful co-existence *vis-à-vis* Communist China, since we believe that peaceful co-existence can transcend ideologies'.[9]

However, it is rather doubtful to what extent this posture can be consistent with traditional policy towards Communist China. The view that this series of Japanese efforts in regional co-operation is an instrument of Japanese-American economic aggression in Asia or an adaptation of the Greater Asia Co-Prosperity Sphere has been expressed not only by China and the Soviet Union but also by some of the Asian nations.[10] In fact, at the opening ceremony of the second meeting of the South-East Asian Ministerial Conference for Development, which was held in Manila in April 1967, President Marcos of the Philippines gave a clear warning that 'Asia would refuse economic control by any country'.[11]

If Japan must succeed in convincing her fellow Asian nations that she is not party to an American conspiracy, she must also reconcile her interests with American policy in this sphere. How far can she assert her own independent view? To what extent can she co-operate with the United States, Taiwan, South Korea, Thailand, or, for that matter, Australia and New Zealand, while at the same time trying to pose as *non*-anti-Communist? These are 'political' problems, which seem to have been raised as a result of Japan's pursuit of an ostensibly 'economic' policy.

China: a Japanese obsession

The problem of China, which was created and has been developed by forces beyond Japan's control, has been a political obsession of the Japanese.[12] Had Japan not signed the peace treaty with Taiwan in 1951, things could have been much easier. However, unless she had been willing to forgo independence in 1951, it is doubtful whether she could have resisted Mr Dulles's pressure to recognize Chiang Kai-shek's regime: for the recognition of Taiwan was the *sine qua non* for the ratification of the Japanese Peace Treaty by the United States Senate. Not that Japan disliked the Chiang regime – on the contrary, a majority of Japanese were grateful for the tolerance shown by the Generalissimo, his waiver of war reparations, etc. – but the decision has restricted Japan's freedom to deal with Communist China, whose existence cannot be ignored, towards whose 700 million people the Japanese people feel the guilt of aggression, and with whom they feel they have special historical and cultural relations.

The only way which the Japanese Government has devised to deal with this problem has been the development of non-political relations with Communist China, i.e. the so-called principle of 'the separation of economic from political affairs'. Through this clumsy and uneasy approach, Japan has been able, while trying not to offend Taiwan by treating the problem of seating Communist China at the United Nations as an 'important matter', to increase the volume of trade with Communist China to a sizeable level of $620 million in 1966.

So far, Japan's trade with Communist China has been carried out under two separate arrangements. One is called 'friendship trade', meaning trade conducted by traders who are regarded by Peking as friendly towards the Communist regime, which was the only form of trade permitted to resume in 1962 after all trade relations had been temporarily suspended in 1958. The other arrangement is called 'L-T trade' which was established in 1963, when an agreement was reached between the late Tatsunosuke Takasaki, an elder Liberal Democratic politician, and Liao Ch'eng-chih, chairman of the Chinese Afro-Asian Solidarity Committee and the China-Japan Friendship Association, both of whom acted in a private capacity. However, although in 1966 actual trade reached $240 million, the amount agreed under 'L-T trade' for 1967 remained $180 million. This disappointing result is attributed to the fact that China regards the present Sato Government as very unfriendly towards China.

Whereas Japan would welcome expansion of 'L-T trade', the 'friendship trade' arrangement presents a rather unwelcome problem to her national interests. For ideological reasons, or more often with the self-interested object of obtaining a better deal, and sometimes under pressure from their Chinese part-ners, the traders involved tend to identify themselves with the political cause of Communist China. Furthermore, since the ideological rift between Maoist China and 'revisionist' Soviet Russia began, almost every one of the left-wing organiza-tions in Japan – the Japanese Communist Party, the Japanese Socialist Party, and their affiliated organizations – has been affected by severe factional strife, and the friendship traders are not exempt from repercussions. So far as Japan's relations with Communist China are concerned, it has become apparent that application of the traditional policy of 'the separation of economic from political affairs' is limited, and it is also obvious that the 'friendly trade' approach does not serve the long-term national interests of Japan if she wants to be truly independent. But how should she respond to this problem?

'1970' as a political issue

The significance of the impact of developments in China and of the Vietnam War on Japan becomes clearer when it is viewed in conjunction with Japan's domestic political issue, 'the year 1970', which arises directly from discussion of the termination or revision of the present Japan-US Security Treaty.[13] The discussion has become more animated as 1970 approaches, and especially since the intensification of the American bombing of North Vietnam. The main battle has been fought between, on the one hand, the Government and the Liberal Democratic Party, which want to keep the treaty, and, on the other, the Japanese Socialist Party, which wants to seize the opportunity for developing a big campaign designed to get rid of the treaty altogether. It is in a sense a fight to settle once and for all the whole question of national security in the context of the increasing menace of Chinese nuclear armament and the escalation of the Vietnam War.

The official position of the Government concerning the issue of 1970 has been that it would not take any action on the question of Article 10, so that the treaty could automatically continue. At the same time, political parties have been developing a variety of policies towards the problem of over-all national security arrangements.

There are basically three positions, each of which is further divided into two:

1. *Maintaining the present arrangement provided for by the Security Treaty –*
   a. continuation of the treaty for a specific term (another ten years) by revising Article 10 after its expiration (the plan advanced by the right-wing group of the Liberal Democratic Party);[14]
   b. automatic extension – non-action (the policy the Foreign Office seems to follow).[15]

2. *Conditional acceptance of a collective security arrangement –*
   a. fundamental revision of the treaty to provide a new security arrangement under which American forces would only be available in times of emergency and American

bases would be withdrawn (the policy of the Democratic Socialist Party);[16]

b. gradual dissolution of the present arrangement (within ten to twenty years) to correspond with the progress of disarmament measures and international security arrangements undertaken by the UN (the policy of the Kōmei Tō Party, which is fundamentally religious-pacifist but recognizes the necessity for a pragmatic approach).[17]

3. *Abrogation of the treaty* –
   a. abrogation of the security treaty by diplomatic means: maintenance of national security through neutralism and unilateral disarmament, to be guaranteed by a network of non-aggression treaties covering US, China, USSR, Korea, and Japan, and the creation of a demilitarized zone (the policy of the Japanese Socialist Party);[18]
   b. neutralization of Japan by a united people's democratic front (the policy of the Japanese Communist Party).[19]

Of these various proposals and policies, the only practical approach seems to be the present official policy of the Government, namely an automatic extension of the treaty. In view of the general political-psychological climate in Japan, it would certainly be unwise to stir up a political row by taking any positive action on this issue. It would also be very tactless to revive the criticism that the one-sidedness of the American obligation under the present treaty aroused in the United States Senate during the deliberation of the treaty in 1960, while the present Administration seems to be quite satisfied with it. In this respect, the American presidential election of 1968 may become crucial to Japanese domestic politics in 1970, for, if a more 'hawklike' President were elected, the United States might reappraise her obligation.

Although the discussion of national security issues in Japan has become livelier and technically more sophisticated than it was ten years ago, the central problem remains unchanged. It is still the conflict between two irreconcilable views on the interpretation of causes of international tensions, and on the validity of the balance-of-power policy. Therefore, the problem of nuclear deterrence, which is the vital core of the present defence arrangement, and which is essentially the problem of the balance of power, tends to be discussed in all-or-nothing terms, while only a very limited number of specialists participate in technical discussions which would help clarify problems peculiar to Japan's strategic situation. Under these circumstances, the recently begun discussion of the problem of nuclear proliferation tends to become either an abstract imitation of debates which have been conducted in other countries – Germany, India, Sweden, the United States – or else a mere expression of nationalism which has little to do with the reality of defence policy or the industrial development of nuclear energy.

The Japanese Government now seems to accept the fundamental desirability of a treaty to prevent further nuclear proliferation, though it is still pleading for certain principles to be recognized in a non-proliferation treaty. They are (1) the obligation of nuclear powers to strive for general and complete disarmament in order to make equitable the obligations which a treaty would impose on non-nuclear powers; (2) the need for measures to ensure the security of non-nuclear powers sufficiently; (3) non-discrimination between nuclear and non-nuclear powers in the peaceful use and development of nuclear energy; and (4) the necessity for provisions for revision or redeliberation of the treaty to meet the changing political and technological environment (e.g., every five years).[20]

The basic weakness of this attitude towards a non-proliferation treaty is that, although it seems very reasonable and natural for a near-nuclear power, it is not consistently supported by attitudes and policies in related fields. Neither the Japanese Government nor the people in general has expressed any desire to become a great power competing with other powers in every field of the nation's activities. The Government has never appeared to consider the military application of nuclear energy, even in the face of the Chinese nuclear threat, nor has it doubted the desirability of IAEA inspection, which it has already accepted. In so far as it has an objective, it would seem to be to keep open the option of expressing Japanese nationalism. As such, it could not be useful even as a diplomatic lever, since the present Government seems to have neither the intention nor the capacity to use it.

The Vietnam War

From the American point of view, Japan is most valuable in terms of her strategic location, for American interests and commitments extend beyond Japan towards South Korea, Taiwan, the Philippines, South Vietnam, and Thailand. Almost indispensable in strategic terms are the Ryukyu Islands (which are under direct American control and therefore not under the jurisdiction of the Security Treaty, Japan holding only 'residual sovereignty'), for they are only 440 miles from mainland China and almost the same distance from Tokyo, Seoul, Manila, and Hong Kong. They really constitute 'the keystone of the Pacific' for the American strategic set-up.

The strategic value of Japan in the American effort to contain China and, to a certain degree, to keep vigil over North Korea and Russia is not that of a nuclear base. *Polaris* submarines are much more effective weapons than the *Mace* B missiles which are now deployed in Okinawa, and the *Minuteman* missiles on the American continent are more stable deterrents against Russia and China as well.

Some experts in both Japan and the United States have been arguing, and many Japanese who wish to see the early recovery of Japan's full sovereignty over the Ryukyus have been hoping, that the progress of military technology has diminished the Ryukyus' strategic value. Many of them believed that the apparent success of the operation 'Quick Release', which was carried out in the Pacific in January 1964 (comparable to 'Big Lift' in the NATO theatre), was additional proof of their argument that overseas bases were becoming unnecessary. However, this kind of argument has been proved wrong in the context of over-all American strategy. Lt-General Albert Watson, the former United States High Commissioner of the Ryukyu Islands, left no doubt as to the strategic value of the islands when he spoke in September 1965. He declared: 'Despite all the talk about "push button" warfare, the United States continues to require a close-up support base in the Western Pacific'.[21] It is obvious that the strategic value of the Ryukyu Islands has increased, rather than decreased, since the United States war effort in Vietnam was intensified. This fact creates rather difficult problems for Japan and the United States, and also reveals a fundamental question which has much relevance to the consideration of the balance of power in Asia.

One of the curious outcomes of the relative stabilization of mutual nuclear deterrence between the United States and the Soviet Union is that, while it has greatly decreased the possibility of all-out nuclear war between the two super-powers, it has also decreased the ability of the super-powers to influence the behaviour of other powers. Collateral to this, the advance in weapon technology seems to have extended the spectrum of modes of violence at both ends, raising the relative level of tolerance for political violence at one end, and raising the so-called 'fire-break' line at the other. The kind of uncivilized behaviour exhibited by the Chinese Red Guards in recent months, the scale and intensity of their harassing activities against foreign diplomats in Peking, could very easily have become a *casus belli* seventy years ago. Conversely, the type of war which is being fought in Vietnam between the mightiest power in history and a small underdeveloped country could not have become the subject of universal concern if nuclear weapons had not existed and if the conventional war-making capability of the United States were not so high.

The paradox of the Vietnam War is precisely that it continues with increasing intensity, not *despite*, but *because of*, the development of 'push button' warfare technology. However strongly Kosygin may be aggravated by the war, and however resolutely Mao Tse-tung may want to eliminate the influence of imperialist America from Asia, they simply cannot 'punish' the United States by employing the means which the most advanced modern technology provides.

To the Japanese people, who are still technically in a state of war with Communist China, the situation in Vietnam is most disturbing. It has done much harm to Japanese-American relations. Although the Japanese Government has officially supported the American cause in Vietnam, apprehension and feelings of ambivalence have become increasingly noticeable even among Government officials and conservative politicians, not to mention the opposition parties and intellectuals.

The potential conflict between the national interests of Japan and the United States with regard to the latter's military policy was clearly evidenced recently by the view expressed by the Japanese Foreign Office that 'the danger of indirect aggression in Asia cannot possibly be removed, even if the war in Vietnam ends, unless developed nations, such as the United States and Japan, co-operate in improving the economic well-being of the peoples of South-East Asia'.[22] The emphasis of this opinion is on the problems which would come after the ending of the

Vietnam War, but it also implies that the problem of South-East Asia cannot be solved by a military approach. Foreign Minister Miki in fact said on one occasion that 'an early settlement of the Vietnam War is necessary, but it will not be possible to settle this war by military means'.[23] The crux of the matter was very well presented when Mr Miki said further that 'if a world war were to break out in Asia, it would be the result of a combination of three elements: namely, nuclear armament of Communist China and the resultant nuclear proliferation, aggravation of Sino-American relations, and escalation and dissemination of regional conflicts'.[24]

Japan is really concerned about the implications of the Vietnam War, and the United States does not seem to understand this too well. Mr McNamara was probably a little too optimistic when he testified before the House Appropriations Committee this year that 'Japan's fear of direct involvement in the war as a result of escalation has not disappeared, but this fear of Japan's has decreased to some extent as she becomes well informed of US objectives and the actual progress'.[25]

It is quite obvious that the Vietnam War has become an American nightmare, and many responsible Americans, including President Johnson and Secretary McNamara, have been trying to find a solution to this seemingly insoluble question. The Japanese Government has been trying, within the bounds set by the constitution and public opinion, to co-operate with the United States as a faithful ally; but it will be impossible for the Government to maintain its support indefinitely without endangering its own position. Mr McNamara is probably wrong to interpret Japanese apprehension as a function of the information available, since some of the more important problems of the Vietnam War, theoretical as well as practical, seem to revolve round the following points:

1. A protracted war of attrition, such as the one going on in Vietnam, seems to present a set of problems which are not given adequate consideration by limited-war strategists:

   a. Because of the dimension and complexity of the tactical problems – e.g., the relative length of the chain of command; the time taken to put into effect a high-level decision; the tendency for human error, fear, or animosity to result in the imprecise execution of a decision; difficulty in gathering information – the impact of a decision on the opponent becomes ambiguous, or misleading, and the chances of misinterpretation and miscalculation by the opponent become greater. Thus in practice a military action cannot be relied upon to convey the intention of the decision-makers who instigate it, although in limited-war theory this function is very important.

   b. Rational thought and behaviour, which are also important elements in academic discussion of limited-war strategy, nuclear or conventional, are inevitably liable to become blurred by the intrusion of irrational elements. The very nature of a protracted war of attrition, and the ideological origin of the Vietnam War, cause political decision-making to be much influenced by ideological, emotional, and moral arguments, as well as such factors as the presidential election, which are all foreign to purely theoretical strategic discussions.

Because of these characteristics, Mr McNamara's strategy of controlled 'punishment' has succeeded neither in persuading the enemies nor in satisfying the allies of the United States, except the few whose very existence is totally dependent on American military presence or aid.

2. The combination of strategic theory and political philosophy, which was especially noticeable in the Kennedy-McNamara period, does not seem to exist at present. Kennedy's recognition of the necessity for a change in the American attitude towards Soviet Communism played an important role in the Soviet-American *détente* when it was supported by McNamara's strategic thinking, which was quite well suited to the type of 'game' played between the two super-powers during the Cuban Crisis.

3. The state of socio-politico-economic development of most South-East Asian countries often renders unapplicable ideas and concepts of Euro-American origin, such as 'modern sovereign nation', 'government', 'liberty', etc. These countries are still essentially in the pre-nation-state stage, and political-military conflict is an unavoidable phase in the process of national consolidation, whether Communism is involved or not.

However, the initial approach of the United States to Vietnam was unfortunately wrong owing to the attitude of mind which she had acquired from her experience in the Cold War, the Chinese Civil War, and the Korean War.

American presence and intervention in South-East Asia have now made it very difficult to assess the real significance of the danger of Communism in the region, because they have introduced a positive feedback into the system, which comprises the actions and reactions of the United States and her Communist opponents. In fact, a who-started-first attitude exists on both sides, although it is generally absent from the more thoughtful game theorists, whose ideas were also believed to be applicable to Vietnam War strategy.

An assessment of Chinese objectives

Most Western analysts of Chinese affairs agree that China has two main objectives: first, the declared ideological objective of achieving world Communism; and, second, the tacit national objective of achieving great-power status, great enough initially to challenge, and eventually to defeat, Soviet leadership of the socialist world and American leadership of the 'imperialist' or 'bourgeois' world.

The two objectives are hard to separate. This has become especially true since the Sino-Soviet conflict began, because the second objective has become essential to accomplishing the first, but the distinction has always been blurred because the motivation of Mao Tse-tung's political commitment was to unite a sick, weak China and expel foreign imperialists. The first objective may change in the long run, and the means of attaining it could certainly change, though so far the only precedent is that of Soviet Russia. In the 1970s, it will be possible to assess the course of China more accurately, as the relative success or failure of Maoism will have become clearer. However, the second objective, China's desire to achieve great-power status, would remain relatively unchanged, for such a desire is more natural and appropriate to China.

In this connection Japan's problem is that she has to face a great nation with a firm political objective and considerable nuclear capability. How should Japan react to this situation? A combination of nuclear capability and rampant Red Guards is hardly a reassuring spectacle.[26] Is it a threat to Japan? If it is, what is its substance? This question deserves some analysis.

First, the prospect of direct Chinese aggression, conventional or nuclear, for the purpose of territorial gain or control, seems remote. If China desired to utilize Japan's industrial potential, she could probably attain this end more effectively by political and psychological means than by military force. One of the reasons why the Japanese people has been free from fear of Communist China is that there is no major issue between the two countries which can be utilized by Communist China as a pretext for launching an attack on Japan. Another reason is that China lacks a large-scale conventional capability for an overseas campaign, at least for the time being.

Second, the likelihood of indirect aggression or assistance to a Communist insurrection within Japan is also small. Japan's social, political, and economic foundations are entirely different from those of South-East Asian countries. However, so long as potential political instability exists, this possibility cannot be ruled out, although the Japanese Communist Party does not seem to be in agreement with its Chinese comrades on the subject of revolutionary strategy.[27]

Third, there is of course at least a theoretical possibility of Chinese nuclear blackmail when China has reached the stage at which she has a crude form of nuclear deterrence. For instance, China might hold Japan hostage to deter an American nuclear attack on China, if and when Sino-American relations deteriorated to a point where a direct confrontation of the two powers became imminent, possibly as a result of unexpected escalation of the war in Vietnam.

During this first period, which will continue for about another ten years, China's greatest fear will be that of an American nuclear attack on herself, and therefore China seems less likely to move inadvertently towards blackmailing neighbouring countries, including Japan.

If this analysis is sound, no substantial nuclear threat need be expected from China for the foreseeable future. However, it is foolish to dismiss the possibility altogether, simply because it is very small. Nobody can be sure that Chinese leaders will never act inadvertently; China might launch a suicidal nuclear attack on neighbouring countries out of fear, if the situation in

Vietnam went beyond the control of either the United States or North Vietnam. However, since, in the case of China, the effectiveness of nuclear blackmailing depends on complicated triangular psychological interplay between a blackmailer and his potential victim, the blackmailer and the protector of the potential victim, and the protector and the protected, there can be no easy set answer. The most valid question to be raised from the Japanese standpoint is, would the blackmailer actually use the weapon if his potential victim had disregarded the blackmail? If it is assumed that he would, then the purpose of his blackmail would be lost because the reason for blackmail could not be the same as the reason for a nuclear attack, which could not be executed without inviting a reprisal. Therefore, if the credibility of the American nuclear umbrella over Japan is reasonably high, and Japanese national morale is strong enough to withstand nuclear blackmail, it would not work. There is reason to believe that China might not consider it advantageous to employ blackmail tactics against Japan, for Japanese reactions to such a situation are not too predictable. If such blackmail produced an unexpected reaction in Japan strong enough to persuade her to revert to a policy aimed at establishing a 'militarily strong, anti-Chinese Japan' – not an improbable reaction – the effect of blackmail would be adverse, unless China's intention was to procure such an effect, which would be inconceivable.

At any rate, China will have an excellent opportunity to try Japanese morale when she reaches a stage at which she has to conduct a series of ICBM tests. She will naturally choose the Pacific Ocean as a testing ground, because the Chinese land mass is not large enough for such a test. This will be a severe trial for the political and psychological stability of Japan, because it is more than likely that the test will coincide with a political row about 'the year 1970'.

Basic requirements for Japan's defence

A strategic problem peculiar to Japan is that there are two potential threats to the country's security. The Soviet Union, having reached a stage of relatively effective mutual deterrence in relation to the United States, is becoming more and more a *status quo* power, and the conflict between her and Communist China is intensifying. This, in turn, has tended to create a sort of common interest between the United States and the Soviet Union which serves to accelerate the *détente* between them while also causing the posture of China *vis-à-vis* the two super-powers to harden.

At present the strategic relationship between the United States and China, unlike that between the United States and the Soviet Union, is quite asymmetric, since China is just beginning to put into operation a limited quantity of vulnerable nuclear striking forces, In these circumstances, a weapon system, such as *Polaris*, which is supposed to work as a stabilizing factor between the two superpowers, does not necessarily work in the same way *vis-à-vis* China, to whom it is nothing but a deadly and efficient weapon system aiming at her targets from a hidden place deep in the ocean. The Chinese reaction is rather to strengthen the urgent effort to counterbalance. It is quite natural for China to feel that way, particularly since Mr McNamara has not denied that the United States might use nuclear weapons first against her.

From the Japanese point of view, this situation presents a danger and a dilemma. As Chinese nuclear capability develops, demands within the United States for the deployment of ABM defence will increase, and there may result a renewed arms race between the two superpowers. Should the delicate balance of terror be disturbed by this, the Russian threat towards Japan, which, though potentially far bigger than that of China, has remained theoretical, will become real. There could then be no feasible defence plan for Japan. This is another reason why an early settlement of the war in Vietnam is desirable.

In considering Japan's defence plans for the 1970s, one must realize how vulnerable Japan would be under nuclear attack. Japan is heavily populated and the majority of her population is concentrated in large cities like Tokyo, Osaka, Nagoya, Kita-Kyushu, etc. A few hydrogen bombs dropped on these cities would be sufficient to cause Japan to cease functioning as a modern industrialized society. A distinction between counter-force attack and counter-city attack does not make any great difference, and an attack from China, if it were to come, would have to be a counter-city attack anyway.

Is it therefore inevitable that Japan should consider seriously the possibility of becoming the sixth nuclear power, in order to deter the Chinese threat? At present a very small number of Japanese people think that it is, and many foreign observers seem to agree. However, I believe that there is no sense in taking such a grave step, which would risk Japan's domestic stability, unless there is clear assurance that Japan could not otherwise survive, and that Japan's nuclear armament would positively deter any nuclear threat.

Some Japanese experts, stressing the purely defensive character of ABMs, argue that Japan should deploy ABM defence, presumably under some agreement with the United States, in order to attain security without provoking either Japanese national sentiment or a sharp reaction from China. I do not see any wisdom in this suggestion, chiefly because no ABM system can be perfect in operation, however much money may be spent on its development. Japan's geographical and demographical characteristics render a damage-limiting sort of strategy unacceptable. How could an ABM system safeguard the life of the people if there were no intensive civil defence programme? To judge from the state of mind of the Japanese people, the situation in which an intensive civil defence programme would cause least panic would be one in which the deployment of a nuclear offensive weapon system were permissible. In that case, offensive weapons would be preferable, because they would be more effective as a deterrent. An ABM deployment seems to be useful only when it accompanies ICBMs. In short, ABMs are not necessarily effective defensive weapons, particularly in the case of Japan.

What becomes clear from the above analysis is that, so far as Japan's defence against a nuclear threat is concerned, there is no worthwhile alternative to continued reliance on the American nuclear umbrella if Japan's political stability is to be maintained. Obviously, at this point the question of 'credibility' comes into play. However, the so-called American nuclear umbrella – a notion which is normally associated with an image of a 'defensive shield', and which is therefore a misleading one – can be assumed to function reasonably well, unless the Chinese were convinced that the United States would *never* retaliate under *any* circumstances for fear of a counter-reprisal on American cities. 'Uncertainty', which causes doubt about the credibility of nuclear protection, is at the same time the very basis of the function of nuclear deterrence.

Broader strategic problems

When China has managed to build a reasonably invulnerable system of nuclear deterrence, with a quantity of ICBMs which are capable of retaliating to an attack from either the United States or the Soviet Union, a certain degree of stability is likely to be established. However, this situation will probably not arrive before the mid-1970s: witness Mr McNamara's statement on 23 January 1967 that 'it appears unlikely that the Chinese Communists could deploy a significant number of operational intercontinental ballistic missiles before the mid-1970s'.[28] However, according to a noted science correspondent, Mr J. Kishida, the Chinese effort and ability in the development of solid-fuel rockets cannot be underestimated, and the operational deployment of these weapons might be realized earlier than Mr McNamara anticipated.[29]

During the next few years there will probably be a rather rapid development of a Chinese nuclear deterrent, which will certainly create strategic instability among the three super-powers (or two super-powers and one semi-super-power). This unstable situation could be compared to American-Soviet strategic relations during the period between 1954 and 1962, from the successful testing of the Russian ICBM to the Cuba crisis, during which time the strategic balance between the two super-powers was changing, and nuclear strategy itself was also changing. It was the period of Cold War under bipolarity, and it is worth noting that, particularly in the earlier part of it, the United States was exposed to the temptation of nuclear pre-emption, which derived from an asymmetry of strategic postures. There also existed, at least in theory, an inclination towards a first strike on the part of the more vulnerable side, Soviet Russia. Although China has the advantage of pursuing her development of nuclear weapons in the wake of four predecessors, and can draw on numerous studies of nuclear strategic problems which must make her realize the importance of making her nuclear deterrent invulnerable, the danger of instability during the development period is still unavoidable. It is probably correct to assume that the problems arising from a triangular nuclear-power situation will be more complex and formidable than the two-power situation that we have so far experienced.

An examination of the Sino-American strategic relationship reveals two important differences between it and the Soviet-American relationship. First, the United States has no diplomatic relations with Communist China, whereas Soviet-American diplomatic relations were maintained even during the height of Cold War tension. Second, in the Vietnam War there is an inherent danger of escalation which might eventually lead to direct confrontation between the United States and China. If President Johnson was in earnest when he said in his letter to President Ho Chi Minh, 'It may be that our thoughts and yours, our attitudes and yours, have been distorted or misinterpreted as they passed through these various channels. Certainly that is always a danger in indirect communication',[30] he must recognize a much greater danger of lack of direct communication with Communist China. If the lessons of the process of stabilizing American-Soviet mutual deterrence can, and should, be applied to the Sino-American case, it would be wise for the United States to try to clarify, before a three-power situation has emerged, the causes which might drag the United States into a situation which she does not want. The same logic applies to China. Communist China must realize that she cannot afford to be dragged into confrontation with the United States, or Soviet Russia, once she has reached the status of a super-power.

Conclusion: Japan's objectives redefined

One of the basic difficulties in trying to analyze power patterns in Asia today, in an effort to form some idea of what policies are likely to be in the 1970s, is that nobody knows exactly what the vast majority of peoples in this part of the world are thinking about themselves today, their life, their country, and their future. 'Asia' is a vague concept, and it may be no more than a historical and geographical concept. And yet 'Asia' is there, embracing more than half the world's total population, a majority of them undernourished and sometimes starving, demanding a remedy.

It has already been proved that hasty intervention in Asian affairs by outside powers tends to aggravate rather than improve the situation. However, it is also clear that there is no 'Asian' solution to the problem, because it is structurally interwoven in the central power-balance of the world, and also because Asian nations alone are too weak to tackle the problem. Japan in particular, who must inevitably take into account her domestic political climate and her realistic capacity for political action, puts special emphasis on the importance of stability in this central power-balance of the world.

Ever since Japan regained her national independence, her relations with the United States have been the keystone of her foreign relations. It is highly desirable to maintain the basic aspects of the relationship in the future. On the other hand, it is also obvious that friendly relations with the Soviet Union are essential, not only for Japan's basic national security but also for greater economic prospects which such relations provide.

In order to maintain, or even promote, stable and friendly relations between the United States and the Soviet Union, if Japan wishes to remain relatively weak in a military sense and yet strong in terms of national wealth, she must be prepared to accept even super-power condominium, an idea that some European powers may abhor. An important fact which is becoming more apparent is that the nuclear weapons of the super-powers are not an effective means of coercing other nations. The threat to use them might deter, but would hardly persuade. Therefore, the real greatness of the superpowers is due to the greatness of their whole capability, which cannot be contested. As long as Japan's principal interests remain economic, this situation will be advantageous to her.

By the same logic, it could be argued that a *détente* between Communist China and Soviet Russia would not necessarily be an unwelcome phenomenon, provided that it did not result in a renewal of the rigid confrontation of two hostile power-blocs. For it seems very likely that if such a *détente* occurred, it would have been brought about by the revision of attitudes on the part of China, rather than by a reversion on the part of the Russians to Stalinist ideology and policies. If this assumption is correct, then this situation would also enable the United States to improve her relations with China – the situation which Japan wishes to see realized.

In recent years the relationships between the three super-powers have been strained because of the Vietnam War. What can Japan do in this situation without losing what she has gained in the past?

Unfortunately, the scope of immediate action open to Japan seems to be extremely limited. Japan does not possess the sort of political leverage which can be efficiently applied to the United States, not to mention North Vietnam or China. The only approach left for her, then, is to redefine and take initial steps towards a bold, long-term objective which could contribute to the general stabilization and development of Asia – and this is naturally a problem for more than the 1970s.

There is no reason why Japan should reject, or disfavour, the idea of closer co-operation among the bigger powers in Asia – Japan, India, Australia, and perhaps Indonesia – if it could save the situation. However, there seem to be more obstacles than incentives for such an attempt, if it is designed to create a cohesive counterbalancing system or a military alliance against the immediate Chinese threat. It is bound to fail, for the situation in Asia is so different from that in Europe, and there is no real common basis or bond that would make such a scheme a natural one.

If there is an ideal regional co-operation which Japan could dream of, it should be the one that includes both China and Korea, which are more natural partners in terms of geographical propinquity and special historical relations. However, the political reality conditioning present-day China and dividing the two Koreas is such that the ideal pattern of cooperation in the Far East cannot emerge before other basic problems in Asia have been solved. Unfortunately, the Korean problem is not so much the cause as an expression of trouble in Asia, which essentially revolves around China.

The point has already been made that there is no military solution to the problem of South-East Asia, and in this respect the direction of the steps taken by the Japanese Government in the recent past is basically correct. Japan should increase her economic and technical aid to developing nations in South-East Asia, and should recognize that it is a positive political decision which must be given priority. She must determine to perform this difficult task of assisting the development of fellow Asian nations with every means available to her. In this context, assistance to other nations is not charity, but a long-term investment designed to develop a stable environment in which Japan may live in security. Of course, it is not an easy task. There must be a clear realization that a viable scheme for assistance requires thorough preparation and, in particular, that a scheme must be designed to answer not only economic but political, sociological, and cultural needs. (It is clear from American experience that the power of money alone does not work.)

In order to make such a decision really practicable, however, Japan must make a fundamental political decision: to recognize Communist China, or at least to instigate diplomatic action leading to recognition. Admittedly, this would be difficult, and probably there would be no immediate results; Taiwan would feel insulted, and others would be offended. But it must be remembered that there will be no long-term stabilization in Asia if short-term interests are allowed to prevail. Japan must be single-minded in defending her real interest, which is the same as that of South-East Asia or of Asia as a whole. The United States can be persuaded, if Japan takes up this problem seriously and resolutely, because it will serve her long-term interest also. If Japan adopted a tactful approach, agreement could be reached on a division of diplomatic labour whereby Japan would try to establish an official channel of political communication with Communist China, while the United States tried to persuade Taiwan. An initiative must be made to interrupt the present vicious circle of Sino-American relations.

Japan's advance towards recognition might not be successful at the first attempt, but the important thing is to make the attempt. This would not be appeasement, but an act aimed at averting two threats: Chinese nuclear power, especially its blackmail potential, and Japanese political instability. If Communist China responded to a Japanese move favourably, it would improve Japan's security. Even if she did not, Japan's political stability would have increased, because the Japanese Government would have shown itself able to take such an action.

The deterrent effect will be higher if action is taken soon, and by the Liberal Democratic Government. A decision to afford recognition would be regarded as an act of appeasement if it were taken after Chinese capability had become much greater, and its whole significance would be lost if it were taken by a socialist government.

Until the Japanese Government decides to adopt such a policy, the situation in Asia cannot be expected to change, and Japan's role in Asia will not develop in the direction of the general welfare and security of Asia. If such action were successfully taken, however, it is not inconceivable that Japan could play an important role as a leader in Asia, having the 'industrial and intellectual capability' to tackle the problem of insecurity arising from underdevelopment, but lacking the 'military power' which would enable her to become a menace to others. There is no reason why the two super-powers should consider this situation detrimental to their long-term interests, or why Communist China should reject it.

NOTES

1 Even this was not quite a military encounter in the conventional sense, but rather a military suppression of a city-based insurgency.

2 In terms of the distribution of total votes cast and seats held in the House of Representatives, in January 1967 the relative strength of the two opposing forces was 66.1 per cent (325 seats) for the conservatives, as against 24.5 per cent (115) for the progressives. The conservative Liberal Democratic Party, in power all through the period, while being able to retain a comfortable majority, has been steadily receding from the position of a two-thirds majority which is needed for taking decisions on such important issues as the revision of the Constitution. On the other hand, the support for the Japanese Socialist Party, which is the single largest opposition representing the socialist, neutralist, and pacifist segment of the population, has been almost constant: 27.56 per cent (145 seats) in 1960, 29.03 per cent (145 seats) in 1963, and 28 per cent (141 seats) in 1967.

3 National income *per capita* in 1966 was about $870.

4 Namely, the Ministerial Conference for the Development of South-East Asia (April); the meeting of the creditor nations of Indonesia (September); the inauguration of the Asian Development Bank, to which Japan subscribed $200 million (November); and the South-East Asian Conference for Agricultural Development (December).

5 Address delivered by Foreign Minister T. Miki in Tokyo on 22 May to a meeting of businessmen (*Asahi Shimbun*, 23 May 1967).

6 Japanese-Australian Joint Communiqué, 17 January 1967, and Japanese-Australian Joint Communiqué, 20 January 1967.

7 Australia, Japan, Laos, Malaysia, New Zealand, the Philippines, South Korea, South Vietnam, and Thailand.

8 *Asahi Shimbun*, 5 July 1967 (evening edn.).

9 *Ibid.*

10 This view is also shared by the Japanese Socialist Party.

11 *Asahi Shimbun*, 26 April 1967. At this conference Indonesia participated as a full member, while Cambodia remained an observer, as in the first conference.

12 The whole problem of Japan's relations with Communist China is excellently dealt with by Shigeharu Matsumoto, 'Japan and China: Domestic and Foreign

Influences on Japan's Policy', in A. M. Halpern, ed., *Policies Toward China: Views from Six Continents* (New York, Toronto, London: McGraw-Hill, 1965).

[13] Article 10 of the Treaty of Mutual Co-operation and Security between Japan and the United States reads: 'After the Treaty has been in force for ten years, either Party may give notice to the other Party of its intention to terminate the Treaty, in which case the Treaty shall terminate one year after such notice has been given'.

[14] Interim Report of the LDP National Security Studies Council, 22 June 1966.

[15] Private Proposal drafted by Z. Kosaka, Vice-Chairman, LDP Foreign Affairs Studies Council, 26 July 1967.

[16] DSP, 'Our Basic Policy for National Security and Defence', 19 May 1966.

[17] 'KMP's Attitude Towards Japan's National Security: Our Plan (Interim)', 14 July 1966.

[18] JSP, 'Our Basic Policy Concerning National Security and Defence', 14 May 1966.

[19] 'Neutralization and International Guarantee', *Akahata* ('Red Flag'), 1 September 1966.

[20] Ministry of Foreign Affairs, 'On the Attitudes of Japan Towards a Nuclear Non-Proliferation Treaty', which was used as the basis of consultations with leaders of the three opposition parties which took place on 15 April 1967. All three parties, JSP, DSP, and KMP, seem to accept the view that the conclusion of a treaty is desirable, in consistence with their traditional attitudes of opposition to the nuclear weapons of all nations. JCP, however, is utterly against it, as it was to the test-ban treaty of 1963.

[21] An address given at the Foreign Correspondents Club in Tokyo, 29 September 1965. He pointed out that 'the conflict now going on in Asia employs both conventional and primitive weapons. The problem still is to have men and weapons in a forward position, from which they can move quickly to prevent threatened aggression or to stem actual invasion of free nations'. He also listed various requirements which the Ryukyu Islands satisfied: '(1) freedom to move troops and equipment without delay; (2) freedom to stockpile equipment which may be necessary to deter aggression and to help stem actual invasion; (3) freedom to dispatch troops, equipment, aircraft, and ships to any area which the United States has pledged to assist in preserving its national integrity; and (4) freedom to provide logistical support to United States forces, wherever they may be required to operate in pursuance of our treaty'.

[22] It is reported that this line of argument was developed by the Japanese Foreign Office representative at the 6th Japan-US Informal Consultative Meeting, which was held in May 1967, when the Asian-Pacific Economic Sphere scheme was discussed. *Asahi Shimbun*, 25 May 1967.

[23] Foreign Minister's address before a meeting of the Naigai Josei Chōsa Kai (the Council for

National and International Affairs) in Tokyo on 13 April, reported by *Asahi Shimbun*, 14 April 1967.

24 *Ibid.*

25 AP (Washington); *Asahi Shimbun*, 4 March 1967.

26 The failure of the Japanese Socialist Party in the January 1967 general election has been partly attributed to the success of Liberal Democratic Party propaganda which criticized the pro-Maoist tendency of the JSP.

27 As a matter of fact, it was reported that Secretary-General Miyamoto of the JCP, during his stay in Peking in the spring of 1966, had a collision with the Chinese Communist Party on this subject. He is understood to have insisted that a Sino-American war could be avoided, and that revolution by force did not fit Japanese conditions, while the Chinese demanded that the JCP revise its platform and adapt more militant tactics because the war was inevitable. *Asahi Shimbun*, 23 February 1967.

28 On 17 September, in San Francisco, Mr McNamara repeated this judgment, though phrasing it in a slightly different manner.

29 Junnosuke Kishida, 'Chinese Nuclear Development', *Japan Quarterly*, Vol. XIV (April–June 1967), No. 2.

30 Early February 1967, reprinted in *Survival*, June 1967.

CHAPTER SIX

The non-proliferation treaty and Japan

Ryukichi Imai

Survival 11-9, 1969

There is some considerable Japanese interest in the implications for Japan of the Non-Proliferation Treaty (NPT), and indeed in arms control in general. The following article, by a consultant to the Japanese Foreign Ministry on nuclear energy, is a particularly thorough examination of some aspects of the Treaty from a Japanese viewpoint.

Japan is the one country in the world that is legally committed to the non-use of military power as a means of resolving international disputes. Article IX of the Japanese constitution states this principle, and Japanese dedication to it remains high after 16 years under the constitution.

Because of the experiences of Hiroshima and Nagasaki, the Japanese public is very sensitive to anything pertaining to nuclear power. For example, public reaction to even the peaceful use of radiation is such that selection of a site for nuclear facilities is a difficult problem. 'Nuclear allergy' is the phrase coined by the conservatives to describe the prevailing psychology. Public discussion of the political or military implications of nuclear weapons has been taboo for a long time. To discuss it is in itself regarded as an admission of evil force. In fact, the most prevalent criticism of NPT has been that it does not go far enough: states possessing nuclear weapons in effect force others to accept the *status quo* but fail to specify measures for complete disarmament. In this case, the argument does not represent a bargaining position *vis-à-vis* nuclear powers, but is a genuine expression of high ideals.

The foregoing helps to explain Japanese criticism of the US nuclear presence in Okinawa, for example. Anyone who proposes a realistic assessment of the high ideal is a 'realist', and in this case 'realist' is a dirty word. However, increasing numbers of 'realists' are beginning to be concerned about the direction in which the prevailing idealism might lead Japan. An obvious concern is that while we are closing our eyes to the great importance of nuclear weaponry in international politics, we lose opportunities to promote the ideal of disarmament itself. Instead of participating in international nuclear arms-control efforts, such as the Eighteen-Nation Disarmament Committee in Geneva, or presenting Japan's own version of NPT to the world, all we accomplished was to propose minor modifications in the wording of the draft treaty at the UN General Assembly.

The other concern is more domestic. Through the recent period of economic development, a resurgence of something like a great-power complex is noticeable in Japan. Japan has acquired the technical and industrial capability to manufacture at least a few plutonium bombs. Although this course of action is highly unlikely because of political realities and Japan's social and industrial structure, there is no denying the theoretical possibility that a 'great-power' complex might one day lead the nation into a weapons-oriented psychology. Combined with Japanese interest in space, our nuclear development may be inviting the suspicion of others and encouraging what is today a very small militaristic minority within the country. After all, we have had some experience with our own military–industrial complex leading the country into Asian wars.

Pax Russo–Americana

The essence of the Treaty for Non-Proliferation of Nuclear Weapons is in Articles I and II, in which each nuclear weapon state undertakes 'not to transfer nuclear weapons or other nuclear explosive devices or control over them to non-nuclear states, not to assist, encourage or induce non-nuclear-weapon states to manufacture or otherwise acquire them'.

Non-nuclear states are obligated 'not to receive the transfer of . . . not to manufacture or otherwise acquire . . . and not to seek or receive any assistance in the manufacture of nuclear weapons or other nuclear explosive devices'. This is a unilateral arms-control obligation on the part of the non-nuclear-weapon states. Nuclear states accept only a general obligation, according to Article VI: 'Each of the Parties to this Treaty undertakes to pursue negotiations in good faith on effective measures relating to cessation of the nuclear arms race at an early date and to nuclear disarmament, and on a treaty on general and complete disarmament under strict and effective international control.'

These fundamental characteristics of the treaty have been clear from the outset. After the Partial Test Ban Treaty of 1963, the Eighteen-Nation Disarmament Committee took up non-proliferation, and by August 1965, the United States presented a draft. Agreement by the great powers was soon reached and in the spring of 1967 there was already a joint US–USSR draft. Discussion at the 22nd General Assembly prior to the signature represented their concerted effort to accommodate the wishes of other countries in return for accepting what is basically a *status quo* treaty.

Looking back over the history of negotiations on nuclear disarmament since the UN Atomic Energy Committee Conference of 1946, one is amazed at the extent of mutual understanding the United States and the Soviet Union could achieve with the appearance of NPT. What was once divided between Geneva (disarmament and arms-control discussion) and Vienna (International Atomic Energy Agency, peaceful atomic and international safeguards) has been joined together again. Instead of constant disagreement and denunciation which have characterized the era of the cold war, the picture we see today is one of basic understanding between the two countries, the United States and the Soviet Union together trying to persuade the rest of the world to accept the product of their understanding.

Of course, it is rather an over-simplification to say that the growth of nuclear deterrent forces has solved all the problems between the two countries. Like the August incident in Central Europe, there can still be unpleasantness which, with a bit of human error, can lead the world into a grave situation. Nevertheless, if the cold war represented an era in which the bipolar world operated to consolidate spheres of interest around the two great powers, we are definitely out of it today.

America and Russia have now seen the merit of limiting other powers in the building of nuclear weapon capabilities that would disturb the delicate balance between the two. It is also logical that the two will work towards agreement to restrict mutual efforts which might change this balance. An increase in offensive or defensive forces in an attempt to obtain a first-strike capability will be a basically futile exercise. Talk of a new *entente* on anti-ballistic missiles is an expression of this logic.

This is the coming of the era of Pax Russo–Americana, and the expression is by no means an accusation of either nation. It is an objective description of the world of NPT. With regard to the treaty, many Americans have asked, 'Is it not better for Japan to have assurance that none of her neighbours will have nuclear weapons?' Set in that framework, the answer is obviously 'Yes'. It is indeed the major characteristic of a Pax

Romana that a great power can say to smaller powers, 'By observing my order, ye shall indeed live in peace'. As far as Japan is concerned, there is no merit in trying to challenge the existing and growing Pax Russo–Americana at this time; nor does any country, for that matter, possess the capability to challenge it seriously. At the same time, it becomes clear that there is no logical relationship between NPT, which is a reflection of the Pax (and arms-control measures within that framework), and the possibility of complete nuclear disarmament which is a denial of the very basis of the Pax.

The problem of security

During the UN-sponsored Conference of Non-Nuclear Weapon States (Geneva, September 1968) many of the general debates referred to the problem of national security 'in view of the recent event in Central Europe'. Of these, one delivered by the West German Foreign Minister was by far the most eloquent. A cynical comment heard at the time was: 'That was the best he could do – to make an eloquent speech. There is nothing he could have done now to improve German security.'

Guarantee of national security in return for renunciation of rights to nuclear weapons has been one of the central issues of NPT. In practical terms this involves both a pledge by the great powers not to use nuclear weapons and a pledge to come to the immediate assistance of a nation incurring a direct nuclear attack or threat of nuclear attack. The latter is the major content of the so-called nuclear umbrella. There are a number of problems. The first concerns the qualifications for receiving such a guarantee. Is it all parties to NPT, or does it include countries outside of the treaty who pledge against the manufacture of nuclear weapons and voluntarily submit their peaceful nuclear facilities to IAEA safeguards? Does the inspection system *have* to be under the IAEA? What about 'international safeguards as provided for in the NPT' if they are different from the IAEA system itself? There is a certain possibility that Euratom safeguards might fall under this category according to Article III of the treaty.

More important still is the so-called Kosygin formula that 'the nuclear-weapon states would undertake not to use nuclear weapons against the non-nuclear-weapon states party to the NPT which have no nuclear weapons on their territories'. This is obviously meant to exclude West Germany from Soviet guarantee. President Johnson sent a message to the Disarmament Committee in 1966 that said, 'The nations that do not seek the nuclear path can be sure that they will have our strong support against threats of nuclear blackmail.'

This leads immediately to the second problem. The strength of the nuclear umbrella lies in its credibility, and credibility is a product of objective assessment of nuclear deterrent forces, relative strength of spheres of interests, and a psychological pattern of action-reaction by the two great powers. Statements by the United States or the Soviet Union or by other countries may theoretically extend the nuclear umbrella, but in themselves cannot render the necessary credibility to make it useful. Mr Johnson's statement about 'strong support' may in reality not have added anything to existing US obligations under the UN Charter, as the State Department is reported to have explained to the Congress. Of course, to say so openly does not seem to be in good taste.

Negotiations at the September Geneva Conference about the wording of security resolutions were therefore nothing more than reconfirmation of various countries' positions in the bipolar world, and did not serve any useful purpose in changing the reality. It did not take very long before the Conference realized the futility of such negotiations. Probably not much more could have been usefully added on this subject to the Joint Declaration at the 22nd General Assembly by the United States, the Soviet Union and Great Britain.

Whether or not a country joins NPT would not seem to affect that country's security, for NPT is essentially a *status quo* treaty. What interests us more is what NPT cannot do, and that is the third problem. There is no doubt that the proposed arrangements will reduce the probability of a small-scale and/or accidental nuclear exchange. It will not stop China from becoming a major nuclear power one of these days. Since China is not a party to the treaty, and since its development of nuclear warheads and delivery systems is obviously self-sufficient, the NPT can expect to have no real influence on China's course of action. During the process of global readjustment of relative influence due to the emergence of the third power-centre, we will have to face the sort of security problems which NPT has, by definition, failed to provide for. Being China's immediate neighbour, Japan will feel this impact very strongly.

Science and technology

During NPT negotiations, there were several attempts to define 'nuclear explosive devices'. These efforts were not successful. Definitions were either too narrow and might exclude some form of future weapons, or too broad and might include facilities which may be used for peaceful nuclear development in the future. One of the ideas that came up was to make specific exceptions and say that nuclear explosive devices for the purposes of this treaty do not include nuclear excursion facilities to evaluate the safety of the fast breeder reactors or facilities for fusion application studies. The obvious shortcoming of this approach is that we do not know all the facilities that may be involved in peaceful nuclear development in the next 25 years. What we fail to accept today may turn out to be important tomorrow. Indeed, it is a well known fact in the history of science and technology that mankind has never predicted with any accuracy its own progress 25 years in advance. By placing restrictions on weapons activities, countries may be deprived of essential privileges to carry out research and development for their scientific and technical future. In this era of 'big science', when scientific and technical capabilities can well determine national well-being, restrictions on future possibilities could become a serious handicap.

Still another factor to be considered is the theme of 'spin-off from weapons-oriented R&D'. If one looks at the cost-effectiveness of spin-off and discusses short-term benefits arising out of military R&D expenditures, spin-off may be a grossly exaggerated concept. There is, however, a longer range point of view. Military R&D is unfortunately the best and often the only means for national investment in research-and-development activities which profit-seeking private capital cannot undertake. This is very clear in a country like Japan, which lacks a military outlet for uneconomical expenditures and therefore suffers from insufficient national investment in R&D activities. In the area of power reactor development, gas-graphite reactors are an outcome of plutonium production facilities; light water reactors are offsprings of submarine propulsion studies; the high temperature gas reactor is related to the nuclear rocket; and the molten salt reactor is an outcome of airplane reactors. Activities such as the *Plowshare* project either for very large-scale civil engineering works such as canal digging or for trans-uranium elements production, could not have started except as an application for surplus nuclear warheads.

One outstanding example of this phenomenon is uranium enrichment. All five of the countries which now possess enrichment plants have spent billions of dollars to develop the technology and construct facilities solely for the purpose of manufacturing the bomb. Today, enriched uranium is the major source of power reactor fuel, demand for which is expected to exceed 35,000 tons separative work by 1980 (free world estimate). Whether or not private capital can finance such a large-scale and uncertain investment is the current issue in the United States, as the plants may be now transferred from the government into private hands. According to the US Atomic Energy Commission, a facility for 17,500 tons separative work per year built with today's technology will require a capital investment of one billion dollars. The electric power requirement for such a facility will be around 5,000 megawatts, and unless it can obtain electricity at 4 mills per kilowatt hour (cheaper than the cheapest nuclear power generation) and can always operate with a 100 per cent load factor, the facility may not be able to compete with the current AEC charges for uranium enrichment.

It is fair to say that a nuclear industry of a much smaller scale than that of the United States will find it extremely difficult to support such a facility, unless other than commercial investment is available. The Japanese demand for enriched uranium will be about 4,000 tons separative work per year by 1980, too small to seek domestic economic enrichment. Europe, on the other hand, may support its own facility by 1980. Uranium enrichment technology and naval reactor technology are classified under the Atomic Energy Act of 1954, thus making it more inaccessible to non-nuclear-weapon states.

These arguments by no means lead to the conclusion that NPT itself needs immediate modification. In fact, according to Article IV, 'All Parties to the Treaty have the right to participate in the fullest possible exchange of scientific and technological information for the peaceful uses of nuclear energy.' As was proposed by Japan and Western European countries during the Conference of the Non-Nuclear-Weapon States, this provision of access to information needs to be interpreted in view of what non-nuclear-weapon states have renounced. This does not mean that in the absence of NPT these countries would immediately go ahead with weapons activities, thus reaping abundant spin-offs from them. The important point is that they would have renounced such a possibility.

Although rights of classifying or declassifying essentially belong to the country possessing the information, it is very much in the spirit of NPT that nuclear weapon states should declassify as much technical information as possible and treat it on a purely commercial basis. This is particularly so with regard to uranium enrichment technology in view of its commercial value as nuclear fuel. International safeguards in Article III essentially remove the reason for keeping such information classified. NPT in a sense puts into writing the advantages of the nuclear weapon states. It is important that there is some form of guarantee that these advantages will not be employed for industrial or trade gains by the nuclear weapon states.

International safeguards

Safeguards are a technical means to achieve political ends, namely to provide an effective tool for executing NPT. Safeguards are aimed at discovering early indications of military diversion of special fissionable material, and thus also serve the purpose of making diversion difficult. There are a number of practical difficulties involved, and it is essential that nuclear weapon states accept the application of safeguards to all their peaceful nuclear facilities. This is because that is the only way to appreciate the practical difficulties of safeguards, and without such appreciation by nuclear weapon states, who also have the greatest influence in determining actual safeguard procedures, it is impossible to devise a system that is both effective and practical. Past experience with IAEA safeguards teaches this lesson. For years, Japan has tried to call the attention of the international nuclear community to these difficulties. Given Euratom's position with regard to Article III, Japan is likely to become the only advanced nuclear country in which an international safeguard system is fully applied.

Let us look at some of the practical difficulties. There is no 100 per cent effective safeguard technology. A simple example is plutonium build-up in power reactors. Computer calculations of isotope compositions in power reactor fuel elements from actual plant operation records are based on three sources: computer codes that simulate in-core physics, readings of in-core nucleonic instrumentations with appropriate calibration for neutron effects, and neutron cross-sections of different isotopes against a wide spectrum of neutron energy. For one thing, the technology is far from perfect and calculational accuracy is reported to be around 5 per cent. For another, a good deal of the normalization process in the calculations is proprietary information of reactor manufacturers. Similar uncertainties exist in chemical determination of plutonium content at the dissolver tank, where irradiated fuel elements are chemically treated. At the present rate of power reactor construction, we will soon reach 'a bomb a week' rate of diversion possibilities, even with the best of safeguard technology available.

Nuclear industry is developing into a very complex entity – with uranium enrichment, various shapes and types of fuel elements to be fabricated, with different reactor concepts, different methods of fuel reprocessing, and plutonium being recirculated back as fuel material. For many years to come, as the industry matures, the actual flow of fissionable material will be far from whatever mathematical model one may adopt for the purpose of analysis. Even within the accepted range of uncertainties mentioned above, safeguards will be a considerable disturbance to the industry and will require many qualified inspectors, many exotic instruments, and a large budget.

If safeguards are regarded as a problem in technology with a given aim (that is, without the possibility of a feedback mechanism to change the aim itself), the only feasible way to get efficiency is to hire an army of inspectors and station them at all conceivable strategic points 24 hours a day, so that nuclear facility operators have no chance to do anything irregular. To believe this to be possible even on a minor scale is an absurdity, because industry, be it nuclear or non-nuclear, simply does not operate in such a fashion. It is often joked about that one will have to hire one inspector per operator. Disclosure of commercial secrets through inspectors has become a serious issue, because the current system presupposes an inspector's right of access at all times to all places.

These difficulties will remain insoluble if the great powers continue to regard safeguards as an independent and separate technology. We will have a complicated, over-computerized system that costs $100 million a year, and is unpleasant and unsatisfactory, being far beyond the present capabilities of the IAEA to administer. There will be constant complaints of 'inequalities' because for one thing, the present NPT exempts military but non-weapon uses of nuclear power from inspection; for another, Euratom has openly demanded special treatment under Article III.

Early recognition and acceptance of the intrinsic limitations of safeguards seems to be the essential step. One does not always have to count plutonium atoms in order to detect military diversion. One should look at safeguards technology as a technical complement to the formulation of political judgments. After all, if suspicion of diversion is discovered, the international community has nothing but political means either to prevent it or to exercise sanction.

The problem of safeguards could be resolved by acceptance of a regional or national system of materials accountability (which is required by industrial-goods management in the handling of so many dollars per gram of fissionable materials), then giving the IAEA the right of verification to exercise according to more non-technical considerations on a case-by-case basis. This is in fact what Euratom is asking for. This is the only system which the US will eventually find acceptable both in terms of simplicity and of cost.

Proliferation of technology

Article IV declares that 'Parties to the Treaty in a position to do so shall also co-operate in contributing alone or together with other states or international organizations to the further development of the applications of nuclear energy for peaceful purposes, especially in the territories of non-nuclear-weapon states Party to the Treaty'. Very often, developing countries have taken this as a *quid pro quo* for accepting Russo-American domination of the post-NPT world. This was also apparent at the Conference of Non-Nuclear-Weapon States. The developing countries made a very strong point of this subject. A considerable number of resolutions were adopted calling for strengthening IAEA technical assistance (concern against expansion and domination of the Division of Safeguards among the IAEA activities); study of new international arrangements to finance assistance; freer access to scientific and technical institutions of advanced countries.

One of the important factors that made NPT necessary is the rapid spread of nuclear technology throughout the world during the past fifteen years. Both the United States and the Soviet Union have done a great deal to assist it by offering facilities (such as research reactors), by making educational and training facilities available, or by distributing scientific and technical documents. Increase in technical assistance, which seems to be an inevitable trend regardless of NPT, will further accelerate international proliferation of general nuclear technology, and in turn, of potential nuclear weapon capabilities. The most direct expression of this contradiction is Article V, in which each party 'undertakes to co-operate to insure that potential benefits from any peaceful applications of nuclear explosions will be made available through appropriate international procedures to non-nuclear-weapon states Party to this Treaty on a non-discriminatory basis and that charges to such Parties for the explosive device will be as low as possible and exclude any charge for research and development'. Needless to say, here we are talking about the hydrogen bomb itself!

Nuclear power represents the new technology and scientific progress and promises to meet the huge energy need of the twenty-first century (an estimated multi-billion-dollar industrial activity in the US alone). It is expected to influence widely scientific research and development, and one cannot just go back to the pre-nuclear age nor confine nuclear benefits to a limited number of countries. Efforts of the past 15 years to promote wider acceptance of this new technology cannot be branded folly or amateur idealism just because they increase the weapon potential. This is an intrinsic contradiction of nuclear power, and one should look for means to reconcile its military and peaceful outlets. That mechanism is effective safeguards.

Technical and economic assistance to developing countries must undergo extensive review and re-evaluation. In this sense, nuclear power is no different from other areas of technology except that it requires a wider basis of technical, industrial and economic build-up in order to be truly effective. This is partly because nuclear power is still very much a developing technology.

Article V contains a point of particular interest to Japan. The basic premise of that Article is that nuclear weapon states agree to offer products of peaceful nuclear application, but under no condition to reveal the technology itself. It is doubtful whether scientists and engineers of advanced nations can be content with such arrangement for long. For instance, it is doubtful that safety authorities will agree to leave the essential information undisclosed and still issue permits to carry on the work itself. Japan is interested in the technology itself because of its many possibilities for the future. Whether technical assistance of this kind should be left to the discretion of assisting countries alone is a rather important question.

Japan's reservations

To point out the problems of NPT does not mean that it is better not to have an NPT. As mentioned at the outset, as far as Japan is concerned, the relative advantage of accepting the treaty outweighs the disadvantage. However, Japan would do well to point out three reservations before ratifying the non-proliferation treaty. One limitation concerns the effectiveness of NPT. If, for example, China should gain strength as a major nuclear power, while non-aligned, developed countries acquired a nuclear weapon capability as a consequence of increased technical assistance, the international picture would be very different. There is no mechanism within the treaty to deny this possibility. Even though we should accept the treaty, Japan must face now the possibility of the basic structural support of NPT losing strength and the treaty losing efficacy even before the end of its 25-year life.

Another limitation concerns nuclear science and technical information, to which freer access should be arranged by some sort of international mechanism to assure that the extent of access to such information shall not be decided by the discretion of nuclear weapon states alone, and that such information will not be used by nuclear weapon states for their political or industrial advantage.

The third point concerns international safeguards. The concept of safeguards today seems to be developing around a somewhat unbalanced philosophy between technical and political judgments, and this is causing unnecessary complications. Formulation of safeguards should be a collaboration between political and technical minds. It should not be left to scientists alone.

1970s

February 1970

Japan launches its first satellite, *Ohsumi*, becoming the world's fourth space power.

March 1970

The NPT enters into force, signed by Japan and 61 other nations.

March 1970

The Red Army Faction of the Japan Communist League hijacks Japan Airlines Flight 351 and flies to Pyongyang, North Korea, known as the 'Yodogo Hijacking Incident'.

June 1970

The Treaty of Mutual Cooperation and Security between the United States and Japan (the US–Japan Security Treaty) is automatically renewed, triggering another round of Anpo Protests.

October 1970

Japan publishes its first Defense White Paper; the second would be released in 1976.

April 1971

The US–Japan Economic Consultative Committee is created.

June 1971

The US and Japan sign the Okinawa Reversion Agreement, returning Okinawa to Japanese sovereignty in May 1972.

July 1971

The Nixon Shocks: US President Richard Nixon announces that National Security Advisor Henry Kissinger paid a visit to China, paving the way for his own visit to China in February 1972.

July 1971

An OECD report shows that Japan is the world's second-largest aid contributor to developing countries.

August 1971

The Nixon Shocks: US President Richard Nixon ends convertibility of the US$ to gold.

October 1971

The Republic of China (Taiwan) is expelled from the UN and replaced by the People's Republic of China.

December 1971

The Smithsonian Agreement is announced and sets the exchange rate at ¥308 per US$1.

April 1972

Japan approves the deployment of the JSDF to Okinawa.

May 1972

The first Strategic Arms Limitation Talks (SALT) treaty is signed by the US and USSR, wherein the two parties agree to limit their ballistic-missile arsenals.

September 1972

Prime Minister Tanaka Kakuei visits Beijing to normalise relations with China.

January 1973

The Japanese embassy in Beijing officially opens.

April 1973

The Japanese government votes to open domestic industries to foreign ownership after lifting restrictions on foreign investment.

September 1973

Japan and North Vietnam officially establish diplomatic relations.

 **DOMESTIC EVENTS**    **INTERNATIONAL ENGAGEMENT**    **KEY GLOBAL EVENTS**

October 1973

The members of the Organization of Arab Petroleum Exporting Countries (OAPEC) proclaim an oil embargo, greatly affecting Japanese energy security ('The First Oil Shock').

November 1973

Japan announces a new Middle East policy in an attempt to preserve Japan's energy security, breaking away from the US.

January 1974

Japan and China sign a trade agreement.

May 1974

India detonates its first nuclear bomb.

August 1974

The Japan International Cooperation Agency (JICA) is established.

August 1974

President Richard Nixon resigns from office following two years of the Watergate Scandal.

November 1974

US President Gerald Ford visits Japan, being the first US incumbent president to do so.

April 1975

The fall of Saigon to North Vietnamese forces marks the end of the Vietnam War.

November 1975

The first G6 summit is held in France, attended by France, Italy, Japan, the UK, the US and West Germany.

June 1976

The Japanese government ratifies the NPT.

July 1976

Former prime minister Tanaka Kakuei is arrested and charged with accepting bribes from Lockheed Martin.

October 1976

The Japanese government develops the first National Defense Program Guidelines (NDPG), recommending the building of a 'Basic Defense Force' to prevent a power vacuum from emerging in East Asia.

November 1976

The Miki Takeo administration makes a cabinet decision to limit defence spending to 1% of GDP.

March 1977

The first Japan–ASEAN forum is held in Jakarta, Indonesia.

August 1977

Prime Minister Fukuda Takeo delivers a speech in Manila, Philippines, introducing the 'Fukuda Doctrine', which reiterates Japan's commitment to never again become a military power, increase mutual confidence and trust, and to develop equal partnerships in Southeast Asia.

September 1977

Kume Yukata is abducted in Japan by North Korean agents. North Korean abductions of Japanese citizens continues until 1983.

May 1978

Narita Airport opens in Tokyo.

August 1978

The Treaty of Peace and Friendship between Japan and the People's Republic of China is signed.

September 1978

The Camp David Accords are signed by Egypt and Israel, leading to a peace treaty between the two nations.

 **DOMESTIC EVENTS**    **INTERNATIONAL ENGAGEMENT**    **KEY GLOBAL EVENTS**

November 1978

The first Guidelines for US–Japan Defense Cooperation are approved by the 17th Japan–US Security Consultative Committee.

January 1979

Vietnamese forces seize the Cambodian capital Phnom Penh, ending Pol Pot's Khmer Rouge regime.

February 1979

The Iranian Revolution topples the Shah and subsequently leads to the establishment of the Islamic Republic.

February 1979

Chinese Vice-Premier Deng Xiaoping visits Japan for the second time, the first being in October 1978.

June 1979

Japan hosts the 1979 G7 Summit in Tokyo.

June 1979

The second SALT treaty is signed by the US and USSR, where in the two parties agree to reduced strategic forces.

July 1979

Sony begins sales of the Walkman. The portable audio player would have a global impact and sell over 385m units by 2009.

December 1979

The USSR invades Afghanistan, signalling the end of the Cold War detente.

 **DOMESTIC EVENTS**  **INTERNATIONAL ENGAGEMENT** **KEY GLOBAL EVENTS**

CHAPTER SEVEN

Japan's security in a multipolar world

Kiichi Saeki

From Adelphi Paper 92, 1972

I. The US response to a multipolar world

The world in the 1970s is said to be a multipolar world. More accurately, it should probably be called a world of political and economic multipolarity with military bipolarity. A simplified characterization of the world in the 1970s as a US–Soviet–Chinese tripolar structure or a pentagonal structure with the addition of Japan and Western Europe could very well lead to dangerous misunderstandings of reality.

It would appear that the American leadership now attaches prime importance to adapting their policies to the new international environment which is increasingly multipolar in politics and economics alike. The so-called Nixon Doctrine is designed to readjust the external role of the United States to this changed context. It is quite natural to consider it unrealistic for the United States to continue playing the same international role as in the past twenty-five years, since the burdens of that role have exhausted her and led to a relative decline in her national strength. Again, President Nixon's desire to strike a bearable balance between

American commitments abroad and national strength and the national interest is a very rational one.

One cannot say, however, that the consequent readjustment of American foreign policy has been entirely successful. Confusion and contradictions can be perceived in it. Perhaps this is partly due to the distortion of President Nixon's purpose by tactics and rhetoric geared to the Presidential election campaign. More fundamentally, however, the cause is probably to be found in the fact that the image of a future multipolar world that he is aiming for, itself contains elements of ambiguity and confusion. At times he seems to place the main emphasis on maintaining the bipolar military structure and to use the concept of a multipolar political structure as a cloak for stabilizing that structure, and as a tactical aid in the United States' negotiations with the Soviet Union. At other times he seems to stress the concept of a pentagonal world as a rationale for alleviating the American burden in relations with allies, and for promoting the dialogue and negotiations with countries hitherto hostile to the United States. President Nixon has also stressed the necessity for strength, partnership and negotiations as means of adapting to a multipolar world; and here he seems to be running the risk of sacrificing partnership with long-standing allies for the sake of furthering negotiations with long-standing enemies. Sometimes, too, he seems to overemphasize the degree of balance in the power relations in a five-polar political structure.

In a speech delivered at Kansas City in July 1971, President Nixon stated that the United States was entering a period of declining vitality, just as the Greeks and Rome had once done, and predicted that within five to ten years, five great powers – the United States, Western Europe, the Soviet Union, China and Japan – would control the world. Again, in a special interview which appeared in *Time* magazine, he expressed the opinion that if the United States, Europe, the Soviet Union, China and Japan could maintain a balance of power among themselves, it would be a better and more stable world.[1]

If this opinion was a carefully considered one, what it means, as George Ball has pointed out, is a complete renunciation of the central strategy that the United States has followed since World War II.[2] It also suggests that the long-range strategy of the United States contains within it the possibility of Europe and Japan being treated eventually not as allies, but from the standpoint of American power politics on the same terms as the Soviet Union and China.

In Japan, the term 'Nixon shock' refers to the announcement in July 1971 of President Nixon's plans to visit China; the announcement in August of a series of new economic policies including the imposition of a surcharge on American imports and the suspension of dollar convertibility to gold; and the subsequent textile negotiations ultimatum that went so far as to threaten Japan with the application of the Trading with the Enemy Act. This is supposed to have been a shock to Japan because there was no prior consultation with Premier Sato on the President's trip to China, or because the style of American diplomacy rubbed the Japanese up the wrong way. It seems to me, however, that there is a more basic reason for the 'Nixon shock'. It was probably due to the fact that while the United States' announcement of Presidential plans to visit China dramatically symbolized the end of the bipolar structure which had dominated the post-war world and the cold war, and the announcement of the New Economic Policy the collapse of the postwar international economic order known as the Bretton Woods system, neither announcement did much more than suggest considerable impending change and confusion in the future direction of American policy because of failure to set forth a clear vision or image of a new politico-economic order to replace the old.

II. The Japanese response to a multipolar world

In these ambiguous circumstances, how should Japan cope with a world which is becoming multipolar? It is of fundamental importance that Japan should indicate her own vision as to how to cope with political multipolarity. One cannot be sure either that President Nixon's apparent vision of a multipolar political structure with a balance of power among the various poles is a carefully considered one, or that the specific content of the Nixon doctrine is necessarily clear. In addition, both the Soviet Union and China seem to have their own respective images of the world which differ from that held by the United States. The fundamental aim of the Soviet Union will probably be to expand her external influence as much as possible while establishing a system of peaceful coexistence as well as the Soviet–American structure of military bipolarity. China seems neither willing nor able to rise to become a global power on a par with the United States and the Soviet Union. Her basic attitude is inward looking, and her efforts will be concentrated on consolidating her national strength and improving her domestic institutions for some years to come. Instead of challenging the Soviet Union or expanding her influence in competition with the United States and the Soviet Union, China seems intent upon establishing an international position shielded from the influence of the super-powers, while constituting herself as the protector of the Third World. Although European economic integration will probably make further advances, it is doubtful to what extent an economically integrated Europe will be able to push forward political integration and be able to exercise global influence. Also, one cannot be very optimistic about the extent to which the newly-emerged countries of Asia will be able to gain strength and self-confidence and increase their regional solidarity, and the North–South Problem will present as many difficulties as ever. In the final analysis, Japan will have to clarify her aims in coping with a multipolar world by studying the options open to her. The basic point here is the gap that is presently appearing, or that might possibly appear, between President Nixon's basic vision for coping with a multipolar world and the direction in which Japan is heading.

President Nixon appears to place Japan at one of the five poles of the balance of power which should guarantee peace in a world marked by a relative decline in the United States' strength. He appears to think that it is unrealistic to expect a country, such as Japan, which is entirely dependent on another country for its security, to become a first-rate power, and has said that there will clearly be a change in the US–Japan defence relationship as Japan regains her national strength and pride. He has warned that measures to maintain friendly relations will have to be adjusted to the changing world situation. He has also pointed out that the question is not so much whether Japan and the United States intend to maintain their mutually beneficial partnership, as how to inject into it the measure of reciprocity which is indispensable to its continuance.

In short, in President Nixon's image of the world, there seems to be an implicit expectation that Japan will be able to take up a position as one of the poles in the pentagonal political structure by becoming strong enough to maintain a partnership of equality and reciprocity with the United States. Naturally, the balance-of-power President Nixon is talking about does not mean simply a military balance of power. Nor is he saying that Japan might arm herself with nuclear weapons or that it is necessary for her to aim at becoming a military power in order not to be entirely dependent on another country for her security, and to introduce equality and reciprocity into her relationship with the United States. Nevertheless, so long as President Nixon anticipates a pentagonal political structure with a balance among the five, and expects Japan to build herself up as one of the poles of such a balance, the logical conclusion is that the United States expects Japan to take the road towards becoming a military power.

If President Nixon's vision of a pentagonal political structure is indeed a carefully considered, deep-rooted one, and it gradually takes a clearer shape Japan, which up to now has maintained a close, co-operative relationship with the United States, will find herself forced to choose one of the following four courses: (1) to build up military capacity to become a great power able to play a role as one of the five poles of the pentagonal world structure; (2) to mobilize her resources in other than military fields to produce the strength necessary to sustain a great-power diplomacy; (3) to drop out of the role of a great power; or (4) to try to adjust the discrepancies between Japan's own long-range vision and that of President Nixon.

III. The first alternative: nuclear armament and major military power

Bearing in mind the nature of the world in the 1970s and the conditions governing Japan's role in it, an attempt to become a major military power continues to seem inappropriate: it would not only be undesirable for Japan, it could be dangerous.

Certainly, Japan should possess the defensive conventional armaments directly necessary to the protection of her own territory. Even here, there seems little need for their quantitative expansion beyond the present level, in the absence of any emergency or tension giving serious cause to fear a threat to Japan herself or the use of military pressure to force her to make political concessions.

In considering the size and nature of the self-defence forces which Japan should have for the 1970s, the three main aspects which should receive careful study are: (1) securing safe trade routes for Japan; (2) preventing conflicts over peninsulas and islands in close proximity to Japan and, in the event of such conflicts arising, not becoming entangled in them; and (3) deterring strategic threats or pressure from the Continent against the political, economic, and military centres of Japan.

This first question basically lends itself to more effective solution through economic and diplomatic efforts, than through any military response. Any threat to marine transportation in peacetime should be identified as a challenge to the imperative rule of international law mandating freedom of navigation on the high seas and resolved diplomatically through international co-operation. Economic and diplomatic efforts are more effective means of alleviating animosity on the part of those who would threaten Japan's sea-lanes.

The question of how to safeguard maritime transport routes in case of a total war is a less important one than how to handle the third question. There is very little possibility of total war; and it is unlikely that any which should erupt would be protracted. Any limited war or conflict which might arise will be subject to considerable limitations of size, duration and theatre, and so stockpiling and alteration of trade-routes are more effective means of coping with such an emergency. In any event, protecting trade-routes is no reason for expanding significantly the size of Japan's peace-time naval forces, although present strength levels are perhaps unsatisfactory.

With reference to the second question, one might reason that the possibility of international armed conflict involving Taiwan, and the chances for Japanese or American involvement in such a conflict are virtually nil in view of the establishment of Sino–Japanese diplomatic relations on the heels of the Sino–American *rapprochement*. In the Korean Peninsula, efforts are being made in accordance with last July's joint communiqué by the Republic of Korea and the People's Democratic Republic of Korea towards relaxation of tension and the establishment of conditions for peaceful coexistence, paving the way for better mutual understanding and expanded exchanges between North and South, and leading to the peaceful unification of this divided country by the Korean people themselves. As long as the United States, China, the Soviet Union and Japan, all of which have interests in the Korean Peninsula, are basically in a position from which they can support the Korean joint communiqué, one may assume that the trend is towards an easing of tensions in the Peninsula. It would be difficult to argue that there is a greater need for stronger Japanese defence forces in order to prevent conflict in the Korean Peninsula from spilling over to Japan.

Although political instability may continue to plague Indo-China even after the Vietnam War and the political situation in the Philippines, which is now under martial law, remains unstable, there is no need for Japan to increase her defence forces beyond their present level in order to prevent disputes from occurring in these areas, or to keep Japan from becoming involved in such conflicts. Such an approach would not be effective nor is it desired by the countries of South-East Asia.

While the third question is by no means a pressing issue, it is one that no independent country can neglect. This question also relates to the issue of Japanese nuclear armament. However, it should be recognized that, basically, Japan can cope with the situation posed by this question only by relying upon the US–Japan Security Treaty.

It is of the utmost importance that Japan should draw a clear line between nuclear and non-nuclear armament. If Japan goes ahead with nuclear armament, it will become very difficult to control her level of military strength and set a clear limit to her armaments. So long as a policy of no nuclear armament is maintained, there is an automatic check on the scale of conventional armament as well. Large-scale use of conventional weaponry or of non-nuclear strategic offensive capacity would heighten the risk of nuclear intervention by either the enemy country or another power, and neither the use nor the maintenance of such conventional armaments would make sense to a country without the nuclear deterrent power to minimize the attendant risks.

In any case, Japan should not attempt to acquire nuclear weapons. First of all, Japanese nuclear armament is not as easy a matter as some foreigners may think. Any effort to revise the Japanese Constitution in the ways necessary to legitimize the first steps to nuclear armament would stir up serious domestic social and political tensions. Technically, it would be almost impossible to find a place within Japanese territory to conduct nuclear tests. It would take at least ten years after making a political decision to reach the minimum meaningful level of nuclear armament, that is, one with some deterrent effect against a nuclear threat from China. And all this would be risked for the most doubtful gains. It is inconceivable that nuclear armament could more effectively guarantee Japan's security. The opposite is likely – that it would endanger both Japanese security and world peace. While Japan would have to pay a high price for nuclear armament, it would get no proportionate dividend in national security and would run great risks.

One reason for the scanty return from nuclear weapons is that Japan is small in area and densely populated: approximately 32 per cent of Japan's total population is concentrated in the three separate 50-kilometre radial areas around Tokyo, Nagoya and Osaka. They are also where important political, economic, and military functions are concentrated. Of all major countries, Japan is peculiarly vulnerable to nuclear attacks. Thus, if Japan wanted an effective nuclear deterrent against China, she would have to strive for sufficient superiority in nuclear armament to compensate for her disadvantages in geographic and demographic conditions. At the very least, she would have to far surpass any rival so as to remove the fragility of her own nuclear defence. If Japan were to seek an advantage in nuclear armament over China, or concentrate greater efforts on nuclear armament than China, this might appear to Chinese eyes as Japanese military provocation. To foster China's hostility and an endless nuclear arms race with her would increase the threat to Japan rather than bolster her security.

Again, a decision by Japan to arm with nuclear weapons would perhaps invite a deterioration in relations with the United States, and it would most certainly not improve them. Since Japan's nuclear armament would be rooted in lack of confidence in the American nuclear deterrent, there is a danger that it would induce suspicion and resentment of Japan in the United States. As Japanese nuclear armament grew, this could, in some circumstances, drive US–Japan relations towards hostility. At the least, there is the risk that Japan's nuclear armament, far from supplementing the deterrent of the American nuclear umbrella, would replace it with a more fragile and less effective one.

If one adheres strictly to the logic that national security must be guaranteed by a national nuclear deterrent, to achieve a balance of power or offset a decline in the credibility of the American nuclear umbrella, Japan must be ready to deter any nuclear threat from the Soviet Union and United States as well as from China. But there is no chance at all that Japan could, in the 1970s, develop the nuclear second-strike capability to maintain a balance of deterrence or military power with the Soviet Union and the United States, and scant possibility of this even in the 1980s. During all that time, Japan's efforts at nuclear armament would inject a dangerous degree of tension and confrontation into relations with both super-powers and constitute a challenge to the world peacekeeping mechanism, the core of which is the US–Soviet bipolar military structure.

It should be recognized that the American nuclear umbrella under the US–Japan Security Treaty, although not without credibility problems, can provide better security for Japan than an independent Japanese nuclear arsenal. It is highly undesirable that Japan should strive for nuclear armaments to secure a balance of power. As President Nixon wrote in his 'Building for Peace' report to the Congress: 'Nuclear fighting power is the element of security our friends either cannot provide or could provide only with great and disruptive efforts. Hence, we bear special obligations towards non-nuclear countries'.[3] Although one would like to think the United States will always be prepared to reaffirm this position, the fact that there seems to be some wavering on the part of American intellectuals on this point gives cause for concern. Professor Brzezinski of Columbia University, for instance, has expressed the opinion that although nuclear proliferation was against the American national interest when the United States enjoyed nuclear superiority, it could be to her advantage in a situation of American–Soviet nuclear parity (and even more so should the United States be in a position of inferiority) since it could, in particular, complicate the strategic-political planning of the country in a position of nuclear superiority.[4]

IV. The second alternative: exploitation of other than military resources for great power influence

Granted, then, that there should be a curb on any great increase in Japan's military strength, it will be necessary to find effective ways to mobilize other factors of influence to sustain her vision and policy goals. The first priority in the 1970s will be to organize economic resources and activity as a means of diplomatic influence. The trend is towards ever stronger economic interdependence between nations, and many countries still seem to attach high priority to the pursuit of economic values.

It should, therefore, be easy to transform economic capability and activity into political influence. In this field, Japan, the third-ranking economic power in the world, is blessed by the capacity to compete with any country, either as an equal or with the advantage.

Of course, Japan will not be able to make an adequate response to the multipolar world of the 1970s by economic diplomacy alone centering on aid and co-operation. Nevertheless, her highest priority will be not to build up military strength but to discover good ways to channel economic strength into political and diplomatic strength. Although one cannot claim that Japan has succeeded in this so far, there seems to be plenty of room for her to change her thinking and make an effort. From this point of view, Japan's economic assistance to South-East Asia and economic co-operation in the development of Siberia are highly significant test cases. With foreign exchange holdings in excess of $17 billion and with long-term prospects for a continued favourable balance of payments amounting to more than 1 per cent of GNP, Japan has sufficient accumulation of resources and power to enable her to venture a number of ambitious experiments in this area.

It will also be necessary for Japan to find ways of mobilizing diplomatic influence by means of culture, science and technology. Basically, through comprehensive efforts in these spheres, she should muster all her energies to help create an international environment in which there is less dependence on military power.

V. The third alternative: renunciation of a great power role

It remains doubtful that Japan will be able to become a great power and one of the poles of the pentagonal world envisaged by President Nixon either through a military build-up, or by exploiting her non-military sources of power. Nevertheless, it would also be unrealistic for her to attempt to follow an existence unrelated to this multipolar political structure by deliberately renouncing any potential role as a great power. Japan cannot help but continue to have economic influence over other countries, as the third economic giant in the world, the second in the non-Communist world and the first of all the major economies in terms of growth, with the potential to become absolutely and relatively an even greater economic power than she is today. Given these facts, Japan cannot be irresponsible about her own influence. Nor can she be freed from the international role and responsibility of an economic power by dropping out as one of the poles of the multipolar political structure. Neutrality is only possible for countries which play a small role in shaping their environment; this is not, and cannot be, the case for a country of the size Japan has now become.

VI. The fourth alternative: readjustment of US–Japanese relations

What becomes necessary, then, is to adjust the contradictions between the Japanese vision and the American vision of a multipolar world. The non-military future that most Japanese think desirable for Japan is possible only if there can be adjustment to the multipolar world envisaged by President Nixon. The precondition for Japan to walk the path of non-nuclear economic power is the continuation of the kind of relations between Japan and the United States, including the US–Japan Security Treaty, that would permit her to flourish. It is to be hoped that President Nixon's vision of a pentagonal political structure is flexible, or can be made flexible, enough to embrace this kind of US–Japan relationship.

In a press interview in Tokyo on 12 June, 1972, Dr Henry Kissinger, Special Assistant to President Nixon, indirectly suggested that the concept of a politically quintopolar system with balanced power relationships is not yet firm in Mr Nixon's mind. He stated that although the world is essentially bipolar in military terms it is economically multipolar, while politically it is somewhere in between. He also noted that the US–Japan Security Treaty is necessary for the time being and that it should be maintained for the foreseeable future. He further indicated that he did not expect Japan to acquire nuclear arms.

One can no longer say, however, that the continuation of such a relationship is self-evident. This applies particularly to the US–Japan Security Treaty. President Nixon, while affirming that the United States has no intention of entering into any agreements to promote communication with long-standing enemies which might sacrifice relations with long-standing allies, has not forgotten to warn of the need to adjust the means of expression of friendly relations as the world changes, and to anticipate changes in the US–Japan defence relationship as Japan regains her national strength and pride. There is a problem on the Japanese side as well. The political and social conditions for understanding and the acceptance by Japan of the equality and reciprocity wanted by the United States seem to have been weakened by increasing distrust of the United States, following the so-called 'Nixon shock'. There seems a growing possibility of considerable discrepancy between American and Japanese views as to what constitutes the equality and reciprocity to be introduced into the US–Japan partnership.

In any case, the adjustment of relations with allies and enemies in a world of political multipolarity is both complicated and fluid, and adjustment of US–Japan relations has become a problem too important and too complicated to be viewed with any complacency on either side. At the same time, the common interests of Japan and the United States in economics, security and diplomacy, seem to be so broad and so entrenched as to warrant the assertion that there is no possibility at all that Japan might break with the United States, provided her choices are governed by reason. If, in spite of this fact, US–Japan relations seem fragile and feeble, this is because Japan is showing a tendency to want to keep her position of relative inferiority in the partnership with the United States, even in a future marked by a measure of instability, while the United States appears to be no longer willing to put up with such a relationship and is pressing Japan hard for equality and reciprocity.

A more basic problem which may be pointed out here is that, despite the strength of the United States and the weakness of Japan in their absolute sense, the relative decline in America's international influence and the relative increase in Japanese economic might has made it all the more difficult to introduce into their relationship those elements of equality and reciprocity which are essential for the maintenance of an effective partnership between the two countries. The problem is that the measures with which to judge equality and reciprocity in the relations between the two nations have grown confused, and the possibility of considerable discrepancy between American and Japanese conceptions of what is equal and what is reciprocal is increasing.

The US–Japan relationship cannot be defined in terms of a balanced, quintopolar political structure. The United States and Japan must perceive correctly the changes in the power relationship between them as well as the absolute gap between their magnitudes of power, and must strive for a common identification and understanding of the characteristics of equality and reciprocity which must be introduced into the relationship in order to maintain an effective US–Japan partnership. This means that equality and reciprocity in the overall US–Japan relationship must be sought. It would not be conducive to effective solution to perceive the US–Japan relationship broken down into its separate economic, political, cultural, security and other aspects, and then to seek equality and reciprocity in those fields in isolation.

One of the questions which is of increasing importance from the point of view of introducing equality and reciprocity in the America–Japanese relationship, yet which will likely defy easy solution, is that of the US military bases in Japan. For the time being, however, the main priority is on solving economic problems. In a way, the fact that the relative economic strength of the United States has declined while Japan's economic might has shown a relative increase has confused the images of equality and reciprocity in the co-operative economic relations between the two nations, thus making it difficult to adjust these economic relations. This also means that, while the United States has come to feel that Japan's repayments in the economic arena are not commensurate with what she receives from America within the total context of the US–Japan relationship, including the security commitments, the Japanese public sees the situation as the exact opposite; all of which make it necessary to adjust US–Japan economic relations in conjunction with security arrangements.

Economic issues will continue to be important to US–Japan relations in the future. The adjustment of US–Japan economic relations will be made all the more complicated if, the Vietnam War over and the United States relieved of her military burdens in Taiwan and Korea, the United States should succeed in a total revitalization of its economic power against the backdrop of *rapprochement* in its relations with the Soviet Union and China. The questions of economy and security are very closely related in US–Japan relations, and Japan will find it all the more necessary to promote greater co-operation in economic areas in order to promote greater co-operation in the defence field. However, it may be increasingly difficult in Japan for the

Japanese Government to obtain the support of all the people in such endeavours.

The US–Japan relationship must be developed in such a manner as to permit adaptation to the trend of political multipolarization. In this sense, it is desirable that issues between the two countries, whether they concern defence or economic matters, should be handled within a wider, multilateral framework rather than on a purely bilateral basis of Japan and the United States.

In economic terms Japan's relationship with the United States must be closer than with any other country. Yet to maintain this relationship effectively, Japan must be prepared to develop a co-operative tripolar relationship linking the United States, Europe and Japan in such areas as currency, trade, investment and economic assistance. Japan must also pay greater attention to developing varied relationships of co-operation with the emerging nations of East Asia and the rest of the world, China, and the Soviet Union all of which are important to Japan as markets for Japanese products and sources of raw materials. Particularly in her approaches to the Soviet Union as a future supplier of energy resources, Japan must act with utmost prudence in consideration of adjustments in the US–Japan relationship of competition and co-operation and Japanese relations with a China in conflict with the Soviet Union.

It is desirable that security problems be handled in a wider framework.

It would be better for US–Japan relations, in the fields of security or economics, to be handled in a multilateral framework rather than on a purely bilateral basis. To continue the US–Japan Security Treaty is desirable, but it is neither desirable nor possible any more in a multipolar world for Japan to depend decisively on the United States for any length of time.

To lessen Japan's dependence on the United States while maintaining the US–Japan Security Treaty it would be necessary not to revise that Treaty, but to try to fit it in with overlapping, multilateral security agreements.

Professor Shinkichi Eto of Tokyo University has proposed the idea that the US–Japan security system be reinsured by means of a Japanese non-aggression pact with China and economic and cultural co-operation abroad. It may even become necessary to study the possibility and effectiveness of reinsurance by means of a Soviet-Japan non-aggression pact, despite the unpleasant memories which such a pact would arouse. Since the Soviet Union will probably be more bent on deterring the Chinese nuclear threat than the United States when a stage of considerable advancement in Chinese nuclear armament has been achieved and she feels more directly threatened, one cannot deny the possibility that, from Japan's point of view, the Soviet nuclear umbrella might more actively, and in another sense, deter the Chinese nuclear threat, than the American nuclear umbrella.

VII. Relations with China and the Soviet Union

It is probably more realistic to understand a politically multipolar world in terms of a system more complicated and more fluid than a pentagonal architecture of mutually balancing powers. Just as the United States, as the curtain rises on an age of political multipolarity, is engaging in active negotiations and dialogue with both the Soviet Union and China, so Japan must discard the idea that she ought to stand against the Soviet Union and China so as to maintain relations of alliance with the United States. One might even say that the most effective way to maintain friendly relations with the United States is to improve relations with the Soviet Union and China. Perhaps a situation in which the

United States lives in a state of peaceful co-existence, characterized by simultaneous negotiation and rivalry with both the Soviet Union and China, while tension between the Soviet Union and China continues short of war, may provide an international environment very much to the advantage of Japanese diplomacy, for such an environment could be expected to heighten the relative attractiveness of Japan to all three countries.

Although it is true that Japan's historical experience of the Soviet Union has bred distrust and caution, and her experience of China a strong interest mixed with familiarity and vigilance, Japan should in future attempt a *rapprochement* with both, keeping her distance from each as equal as possible, and not be bound by traditional concepts.

With the visit of Prime Minister Tanaka to China, the basic course for the normalization of Sino–Japanese relations has been set. This may be characterized as the basic path to the normalization of diplomatic relations in such a way as will meet the test of time and lay the groundwork for long-term friendly relations between China and Japan. Specific steps to this end should, however, be implemented at a steady, unhurried pace. The basic path runs in the direction of 'one China, not now' and recognition of the People's Republic of China as the sole, lawful government of China. It is a policy of maintaining existing economic relations with Taiwan as much as possible, despite the severance of formal diplomatic ties, and one in which neither Japan nor China seeks hegemony in Asia.

Japan's giant neighbour, the Soviet Union, has the potential to deal her a fatal blow and is the greatest rival of the United States, but is also, in view of her proximity, a promising future customer for Japanese industrial products and a major potential source of raw materials and energy.

There are also several compelling reasons why the Soviet Union might want to improve relations with Japan, not the least being the *rapprochement* between the United States and China. Japan should work for *rapprochement* with the Soviet Union on the basis of sound calculations of interest and, without diluting her claim to her lost northern territories, Habomai, Shikotan, Etorofu and Kunashiri, temper her inherited distrust from the past with an accurate objective appraisal of current possibilities.

Still, there is a limit to the unfolding of multilateral diplomacy to cope with an age of political multipolarity. There is probably no possibility, whatever, in the foreseeable future that Japan might get close enough to the Soviet Union and China to make Soviet–Japanese and Sino–Japanese relations equidistant with American–Japanese relations, or profit by such a degree of *rapprochement*. It will take a long time to overcome completely the political, social and institutional barriers which lie between Japan, the Soviet Union and China respectively. In the foreseeable future, Japan's Security Treaty with the United States will continue to have greater significance than any possible security arrangements with other countries.

NOTES

[1] 'We must remember the only time in the history of the world that we have had any extended periods of peace is when there has been balance of power. It is when one nation becomes infinitely more powerful in relation to its potential competitor that the danger of war arises. So I believe in a world in which the United States is powerful. I think it will be a safer world and a better world if we have a strong, healthy United States, Europe, Soviet Union, China, Japan, each balancing the other, not playing one against the other, an even balance.' *Time*, 3 January 1972.

[2] See *Adelphi Paper* No. 91, p. 40.

[3] *US Foreign Policy for the 1970s: Building for Peace. A Report to the Congress* (Washington, D.C.: US Government Printing Office, 1971).

[4] See Zbigniew Brzezinski, *The Fragile Blossom: Crisis and Change in Japan* (New York: Harper and Row, 1972).

CHAPTER EIGHT

Japan's non-nuclear policy

Junnosuke Kishida

From Survival 15-1, 1973

As long as a completely unexpected change does not take place in the world's military situation, Japan will not choose to become a nuclear power in the foreseeable future.

Herman Kahn of the American Hudson Institute keeps repeating at every opportunity that Japan will decide, some time in the mid-1970s, to become a nuclear power. There is no likelihood whatsoever of his prophecy being fulfilled. Professor Zbigniew Brzezinski of Columbia University wrote his book, *The Fragile Blossom – Crisis and Change in Japan,*[1] on the basis of a six-month study tour in Japan. He states that the possibility of Japan deciding to become a nuclear power cannot be entirely ruled out and that, if so, the United States should co-operate in order not to turn Japan into an enemy. This too seems very unlikely.

President Richard Nixon in a speech made in July 1971, in Kansas City, pointed out that the future world would probably revolve around five poles – the United States, the Soviet Union, China, the European Community and Japan. Subsequently, argument arose in various quarters in Japan as to whether the basic structure of the world would remain bipolar, revolving around the United States and the Soviet Union; or tripolar, revolving around the United States, the Soviet Union and China; or whether it would become pentagonal, as predicted by President Nixon. The general conclusion reached seems to be as follows:

(1) Militarily, the world would be bipolar, with the United States and the Soviet Union forming each of the two poles; while the Asian region would basically become tripolar in structure revolving around the United States, the Soviet Union and China.

(2) Japan and the European Community would be added to these bipolar and tripolar structures. In these circumstances, the expression, 'pentagonal structure', would serve only to invite misunderstandings.

This conclusion is based on several facts. The European Community has the built-in restriction of not being one nation, while it is the general consensus that Japan cannot become a great military power and that Japan should take precautions to avoid moving in the direction of establishing herself as a pole, since this would not be in Japan's national interest.

The basis for Japan's non-nuclear policy

In particular, nuclear armament is becoming increasingly distasteful to Japan. In the first place, compared with the past, the military value of nuclear weapons has become increasingly doubtful.

It is true that the nuclear balance between the United States and the Soviet Union has brought about a situation of stabilized mutual deterrence between the two countries. This is proof of the military efficacy of nuclear weapons as a deterrent. There is no doubt that the deterrent effect of nuclear weapons has played a role in the relaxation of tensions between the United States and the Soviet Union. The conclusion of the treaty and agreements on the Strategic Arms Limitation between the United States and the Soviet Union was made possible by the deterrent effect of nuclear arms. At the same time, however, the nuclear deterrent has served to create a state in which the nuclear super-powers will resort to nuclear weapons only when their own national security is about to be dealt a direct and fatal blow. In other words, the nuclear deterrent has created a state of no-war between the nuclear super-powers.

Many countries have come to feel that the nuclear deterrent exists only between the nuclear powers and does not have much relevance to the security of non-nuclear states. In fact, some specialists go to the extreme of saying that the only thing which nuclear arms are now deterring are rash actions of the nuclear powers themselves.

The political value of nuclear arms also continues to decline. It has been sustained by the belief that only countries with advanced technologies and vast economic power could possess nuclear weapons. However, China's achievement of nuclear power status has destroyed this myth. China proved that as long as a country is determined to have nuclear arms, it can, regardless of any lag in technology or lack of economic power, acquire them without great difficulty. From the moment China proved this fact, nuclear status ceased to be a symbol of political power and the political value of nuclear arms began to decline.

In addition, the acquisition of nuclear arms by the second-class nuclear powers, judged solely on past performance, has proved to be a hindrance to the economic development of each of these countries. Nuclear arms have not helped to elevate the political positions of these countries.

The third reason why nuclear armament is distasteful to Japan lies in the progress made in the peaceful uses of atomic energy. If the prospects of utilizing nuclear technology for peaceful and economic purposes were non-existent, it would not be at all surprising for nations to feel it indispensable to produce nuclear arms as the quickest way of developing a nuclear technology. However, today the generation of electric power by atomic energy has become economically competitive with the conventional fossil-fuel power plants. Nuclear technology, for military and for peaceful purposes, has much in common. The peaceful development of nuclear energy leads directly to an increase in the potentialities of a nation to become a military nuclear power. The potentialities of Japan for becoming a nuclear power have greatly increased, as a result of her efforts in the field of the peaceful uses of atomic energy and space development. The position that Japan has already achieved in international politics is not only due to her being the third greatest economic power in the world, but also due to the fact that Japan is being given credit for her potential ability to become a great military power within a short space of time, should she so choose. Because Japan's ability to become a military power has been generally accepted, the need for Japan to fulfill her potentialities has been further reduced. She has reaped the political advantages without incurring the economic and political costs of going nuclear.

Particular attention must also be given to a new phenomenon: a change in the concept of national security. As a result of economic development, all advanced countries stand more to lose than to gain through international disputes. Most countries have now come to realize that even if a situation of considerable conflict should develop there would be no other way of settling such conflicts, except through peaceful means.

At the same time, the multipolar world of today is going through a period in which problems are multiplying and becoming multidimensional. The threat to a nation's security does not only arise from a specific military action by a specific nation, but can also arise internally. Increases in crime, the spread of narcotics and environmental pollution can also create threats to the security of societies. Threats from sources other than purely military ones are drastically increasing for all civilized nations. The security policies of a nation must check the tendency to fall into the trap of resorting to military measures to cope with threats to its existence, and must take into account the diversification of security threats. What is needed is a new approach to the allocation of resources in the planning and the building of peace and security.

Japan is a country which, from the standpoint of geography and resources, must restrain any orientation towards becoming a strong military power. In terms of the size of her territory, she is extremely small. This makes her highly vulnerable to nuclear attack. Even if Japan were to develop into a military nuclear power and were to acquire the same quantity of nuclear arms as the super-powers, the deterrent effect would in no way be comparable to theirs because of their vast land masses. Furthermore, a small country has to rely on others for the greater part of its resources. In short, Japan must adopt a policy of mutual reliance with all other countries at all times and in all situations, and must studiously avoid becoming a militarily strong nuclear power and thereby arousing distrust among other states.

The deep-rooted fear among Asian nations of the militarization of Japan must be taken into constant consideration. It is in the common interest of all Asian countries, including Japan, for Japan not to become a strong military power.

The efficacy of militaristic policies in Asia is lower than in other regions of the world. There are many developing countries in Asia. It is inevitable for every country to be oriented toward a change in the *status quo*. If Japan's security policies are to embrace the changes and the flexibility sought after by Asian countries, emphasis necessarily will have to be placed on non-military expedients, with their greater flexibility and adaptability, rather than on military measures.

The changing nuclear umbrella

For these reasons, Japan will continue her non-nuclear policy in the future. In order to stabilize her non-nuclear policy on a still firmer foundation, Japan must make every effort to establish the conditions necessary for this, both internationally and domestically.

Domestically, Japan must build up public opinion against any trend toward nuclear armament and must adopt policies that will prevent the militarization of Japan's industries. More importantly, Japan must seek some way of escaping from her feeling of reliance on the nuclear umbrella of the nuclear super-powers.

It has been said that in the nuclear age every country must rely for its security on the nuclear deterrent, that, in other words, the nuclear umbrella of the nuclear super-powers is indispensable for the security of non-nuclear nations. Japan has concluded a security treaty with the United States and, as a result, is now relying upon the nuclear deterrent of the United States. The Nixon Doctrine reconfirms this situation.

If we maintain this premise, it means that as long as Japan remains a non-nuclear power, she will have to look to the American nuclear umbrella for protection. However, this implants in the Japanese consciousness a feeling of being a protégé of the United States. At times, this generates impatience in the 'great economic power' that Japan has now become.

Naturally, as Japan becomes economically stronger, the more the demand for greater independence will also grow.

But the nuclear umbrella plays the role of crystallizing the present world order, created after World War II as a result of the development of nuclear arms. This world order is a four-tier pyramid; with the two nuclear super-powers, the United States and the Soviet Union, at its apex; the second-class nuclear powers in the layer immediately below; the nations with nuclear potentialities in the third tier; and the developing countries in the bottom stratum. In the case of the countries allied to the nuclear super-powers, the greater the demand for independence the greater the feeling of unbearable resentment against the political implications of the nuclear umbrella, as exemplified in the present structure of world order.

The effort to overcome this unnecessary feeling must be made both by the nuclear powers and the countries allied to the nuclear powers. In the case of the advanced countries, treaties of alliance with nuclear powers are no longer determined by their original military purpose, but have become mutual assurances of lasting friendship. It is in the interests of both the nuclear protector and the protégé to remove as far as possible the factors that could hinder the continuance of alliances of friendship between the countries concerned. In this sense, even if a nuclear power may feel it is providing a nuclear umbrella to an allied country, it should not act in a manner which could indicate to its allies that they have the responsibility for paying for the protection provided by the nuclear umbrella, or to accuse their allies of getting a 'free ride' on the grounds that the allies are not completely co-operative toward the nuclear powers.

Today, the existence of what might be called a 'world-wide nuclear umbrella' looms much larger than at any time in the past. As a result of the stabilization of the military bipolar structure and the establishment of mutual deterrence between the United States and the Soviet Union, both are becoming more strongly oriented toward the maintenance of the *status quo.* If this analysis is correct, both countries will try to work out the measures needed to prevent any changes in any part of the world contrary to their interests. This, in practice, functions as a world-wide nuclear umbrella.

The umbrella spreads over all countries, regardless of whether they are allied specifically with either of the two nuclear super-powers. Of course, since this is not based on any treaty, there are limits to its theoretical credibility, but the more stabilized the military bipolar structure, the more credible the umbrella becomes. Today, the weight of this world-wide nuclear umbrella is much greater than the particular one of any nuclear power. And since the super-powers have established the umbrella of their own volition, they cannot force any country to pay for the protection it affords. Both arguments together provide a foundation for solid non-nuclear policies.

No first use of nuclear weapons

Japan, as a non-nuclear power, can prevent the stratification of nations on the basis of nuclear armaments and escape from the position of a protégé of a nuclear power. Such a process, however, would actually result in Japan removing herself from the security of nuclear protection. Thus, in adopting such a policy, Japan should take parallel steps to work out measures that would enable her simultaneously to withdraw herself to safety from the threat of nuclear arms.

The first task which must be tackled is the conclusion of an agreement binding nuclear powers not to be the first to use nuclear weapons. This would reduce the weight of nuclear arms in today's world order. It would not only be most desirable for non-nuclear powers, but would also have the result of putting brakes on the nuclear arms race between the nuclear powers themselves. Judging from the fact that the United States and the Soviet Union have concluded their Strategic

Arms Limitation Agreements, there is no reason to believe that a treaty banning the first-use of nuclear weapons would run counter to the nuclear policies of the nuclear powers.

Would China be an obstacle to such an agreement? At every opportunity, China keeps 'solemnly' declaring that she will not be the first to use nuclear arms under any circumstances. She also says that a pledge not to use nuclear weapons is indispensable as the first step towards nuclear disarmament. China's advocacy does not necessarily stem only from good intentions on nuclear disarmament. If by such a pledge the nuclear super-powers could be prevented from using their nuclear arms, then, China, even with her limited nuclear capability, would be able to achieve a political position equal to those of the nuclear super-powers. For China, who has no present plans or ability to acquire the same panoply of nuclear weapons as the super-powers, a pledge not to use nuclear arms first is the best way of exploiting her own nuclear weapons to their greatest political advantage. Besides, each nuclear country must recognize the fact that the proposal not to use nuclear weapons first is an appeal which has considerable attraction for many countries.

China has not, as yet, indicated her willingness to participate in discussions on nuclear disarmament. However, she would not be able to boycott any discussion aimed at a treaty barring the first-use of nuclear weapons. From the standpoint of bringing China into disarmament discussions, negotiations on this subject might offer significant advantages.

Of course, China is not the only nation that has proposed non-use of nuclear weapons. The Soviet Union submitted a draft resolution on the non-use of nuclear weapons to a subcommittee of the United Nations Disarmament Committee in June 1954. Since then she has made similar proposals on a number of occasions. These moves have been interpreted as an effort, on the part of the Soviet Union, to overcome her inferiority in nuclear armaments *vis-à-vis* the United States. But in 1972, after achieving parity with the United States, the Soviet Union has repeated her proposal and asked that the subject of the non-use of arms, centred on a permanent ban on the use of all nuclear weapons, be included in the agenda of the United Nations General Assembly. Both Great Britain and France agreed in 1955 to the conditional non-use of nuclear arms, the one reservation being the right to use nuclear arms for defence against aggression.

Till now, of all the nuclear powers, the United States has been most clearly opposed to a commitment not to use nuclear arms first. The reason given is the desire to maintain the deterrent effect of nuclear weapons. However, even in the case of the United States, a number of symptoms of change have recently come to the fore. One of these symptoms is America's ratification, in May 1971, of Protocol II to the Treaty on the Denuclearization of Central and South America. The United States agreed not to use nuclear arms and not to resort to nuclear threat in these areas. Further, President Nixon committed the United States in 1969 not to be the first to use chemical weapons. This can be interpreted as an admission on the part of the United States of the fact that no first-use of chemical weapons would not have any great effect on her deterrent strategy.

In an article in *Foreign Affairs,* Professor Richard Ullman of Princeton University contends that a ban on the first-use of nuclear arms would not be of disadvantage to the United States and that the deterrent effect of nuclear weapons would not be impaired:

> China will step up its 'peace offensive' in the United Nations and the United States' attitude to the non-use of nuclear weapons must take this into full consideration. Today, when the United States has adopted a second-strike strategy, the conclusion of an agreement on the no

first-use of nuclear arms would have no impact whatever on the deterrent effect of this strategy on a nuclear power from launching a nuclear attack on the United States. Even in the case of Europe, where there is the biggest danger of an attack using conventional weapons, the demarcation of an absolute boundary between nuclear and conventional weapons, would enable a clearer decision to be taken on counter measures and would increase the effectiveness of the NATO forces.[2]

The attitude of most nuclear-weapon states and the debate in the United States suggest that there are today considerable possibilities for drafting a treaty on the no first-use of nuclear weapons. To prevent the conclusion of a treaty banning the first-use of nuclear weapons only serving to stimulate a conventional arms race, the agreement could stipulate that it would not apply in the case of defence against aggression by large conventional military forces.

Negotiations on such an agreement would be undertaken principally between nuclear powers. However, this does not include the various non-nuclear powers from taking the initiative in proposing such a treaty.

The denuclearization of North-East Asia

Another way in which nations can weaken the link with a nuclear umbrella without weakening their security, and reduce the nuclear threat against themselves is the establishment of denuclearized zones. In the case of Japan, the denuclearization of North-East Asia would be the first goal.

To date non-nuclear zones have been established by the Antarctic Treaty signed in 1959, by the Treaty on the Denuclearization of Central and South America concluded in 1967 and by the resolution passed by the General Assembly of the United Nations in 1961 on the Denuclearization of Africa. In other words, nuclear demilitarization has been achieved only in areas which do not have any nuclear weapons at present, and which are of little military importance to the nuclear powers.

In the case of the Central and South American Denuclearization Treaty, Protocol II which stipulates the non-use of nuclear arms or nuclear threats, requires ratification by all the nuclear powers before it becomes effective. At the present time, only the United States and Britain have ratified the protocol, while the other three nuclear powers have not even signed the agreement. The conditions enabling Central and South America to escape nuclear attack as a denuclearized zone have, therefore, not as yet been fulfilled.

The establishment of nuclear-free zones is therefore not simple, but as a result of China's return to the United Nations, the time has come seriously to consider declaring North-East Asia a nuclear-free zone. China herself proposed the establishment of a non-nuclear zone in the 1971 General Assembly of the United Nations. Japan succeeded in normalizing her relations with China at the end of September 1972 and, in the joint statement issued on that occasion, agreed to the establishment of peaceful relations with China on the basis of five principles of peace, and mutually confirmed her resolve not to resort to military means in the settlement of disputes. This could provide the basis for a study of the problem of regional arms-control by the countries concerned.

In order to make agreement on a non-nuclear zone more feasible, it would be best to limit the area to the territory, the territorial waters and the territorial skies of the non-nuclear countries in North-East Asia. It might even be smaller, to include only Japan, the Republic of Korea and North Korea. The smaller the area of a non-nuclear zone the less effective the denuclearization treaty. However, the greater possibilities of achieving agreement on such a small zone are of great importance. A small zone can become the starting point for a greatly expanded zone in the future.

What would be the political effects? First, a nuclear-free zone would give international credence to Japan's policy of keeping at a distance from nuclear weapons, as stipulated in Japan's three non-nuclear principles, *viz.*, not to possess, produce or acquire nuclear arms. It would contribute to the stabilization of Japan's security policies. Also, the suspicion of various countries that Japan might want to become a nuclear-weapons power would be allayed, while the basis for criticism against the militarization of Japan would disappear. If stipulations such as those contained in Protocol II to the Central and South American Denuclearization Treaty were to be incorporated into the non-nuclear zone agreement, it would have the effect of heightening the security of a non-nuclear Japan.

Second, the agreement would help to stabilize further the Korean Peninsula as a buffer-zone between the United States, the Soviet Union and China and would help to lull tensions in this area. The inclusion of both countries of the Korean Peninsula in this non-nuclear zone takes the possible development of the recently started dialogue between North Korea and the Republic of Korea into account. Following the normalization of relations between Japan and China, a normalization of relations between Japan and North Korea should also make progress. The possibility of establishing a nuclear-free zone embracing the three countries of North and South Korea and Japan is much greater today than it was a year ago.

The establishment of a nuclear-free zone in Asia should start with comparatively limited areas, where the possibilities of realization are great. It should be extended gradually in scope as the political situation allows. Other possible areas include the region covered by the Association of South-East Asian

Nations (ASEAN). The ASEAN declaration adopted in 1971 proposes joint action aimed at the neutralization of South-East Asia; one of the targets of this action would be the establishment of an ASEAN nuclear-free zone. Again, the scope of the non-nuclear zone would be limited to the territory, the territorial seas and the territorial skies of the ASEAN nations. None of these nations has nuclear arms, and if there should be American nuclear weapons in the area, they can easily be removed. The Indo-China Peninsula, after the end of the Vietnam War, might also qualify as a possible nuclear-free zone.

Hand in hand with disarmament measures designed for the entire world, such as the complete nuclear test ban now being discussed by the Geneva Disarmament Committee, disarmament must be expedited in each region. The normalization of relations between Japan and China has increased the possibility of achieving actual regional disarmament in East Asia.

NOTES

[1] *The Fragile Blossom – Crisis and Change in Japan* (New York: Harper & Row 1972).

[2] Richard H. Ullman, 'No First Use of Nuclear Weapons', in *Foreign Affairs*, July 1972, pp. 669–84.

CHAPTER NINE

Options for Japan's foreign policy

Masataka Kosaka

From Adelphi Paper 97, 1973

Introduction

In Japan there have been contradictory feelings about her foreign policy. On the one hand there seems no need for any major change, since it suits Japan splendidly; on the other, there is persistent concern that she is vulnerable because she depends upon resources over which she has very little control. With this latter concern goes a sense of frustration, arising from the feeling that Japan's destiny has been decided too much by others and too little by herself. The main criticism of foreign policy among the Japanese themselves has thus taken the form of pleas for a more independent line – pleas repeated so often that they have become almost a cliché – yet whenever there is a specific discussion of policy, and rational calculation dominates, it always results in confirmation of the existing line.

This ambivalence is natural in view of the unique nature of Japan's post-war foreign policy, which can be described as one of 'low posture' or of 'economics above all', and in the light of its remarkable success. The basic characteristics of the policy are: dependence on the United States for direct and indirect security interests (the American military forces are vital not only for the defence of Japan herself but also for the defence of Korea, which is also important for Japan's security); utmost caution in the conduct of external affairs, so as to avoid offending anyone (which really amounts to taking no diplomatic initiatives – hence the term 'low posture'); and concentration of Japan's main energies on economic development, which is seen most clearly in the surprisingly low expenditure on armaments (hence the label 'economics above all').

The above policy was not so much a result of choice as of necessity. For in 1951 Japan was poor and powerless and was occupied, nominally by the Allied Powers but in practice by American forces. When Prime Minister Shigeru Yoshida inaugurated his policy of 'economics above all' few were happy about it, though many thought that Japan had no other option. But it turned out a surprising success. Japan's security has been maintained at very low cost and her economy developed at a very rapid rate, while her status and influence have increased with the growth of her economic power.

Though 'virtue' has played some part in Japan's success story, fortune has clearly played a much larger role. Since Japan has become militarily a small power, she has found that she can do without military strength, thanks to American protection and perhaps also to the changed nature of world politics, in which military force now has only marginal utility – or at least has lost its 'positive' function of making other people obey. Having lost what few sources of raw materials she had had, Japan has found that she can get them through trade, and since the end of World War II raw materials have been abundant (until recently, that is) because of the many technological developments there have been. Trade has been free because the Bretton Woods system was basically a sound one and because old blocs were destroyed as a result of decolonization, to be replaced by global interdependence made possible by the extraordinary advances in transportation. Japan did not contribute to any of the above changes, but she benefited from them. So she was lucky – and may indeed have been too lucky, since she gained more than those countries which helped to create the new situation. Moreover, she was lucky in another sense also, in that the United States destroyed her military establishments and carried out large-scale social reforms which made the Japanese social structure better suited to the needs of modern industrial society. It is no wonder, then, that there is in Japan no real sense of having achieved anything, but only the fact of achievement. From this stems the sense of frustration.

Significantly, however, the basic situation has remained unchanged despite the growth of Japan's economic power – and may even have become more pronounced because of it. Japan depends almost entirely upon the outside world. She depends upon the United States for her security, while for her economic well-being she depends upon a certain minimum of stability in the countries from which she obtains raw materials, and upon the healthy functioning of the free-trade economy. Hence the concern for greater independence. And yet the basic soundness of her post-war foreign policy still persists, because it is not only the expression of her weakness but also a remarkably wise (though unconscious) adaptation to the new realities of world politics in general and to the basic international position of Japan in particular.

Japan is a relatively small island country close to the Asian mainland. She has few natural resources, but is highly industrialized. She is Westernized as a result of the success of industrialization, but the roots of her civilization are in Asia and she still retains Asian characteristics in her culture. It is not difficult to deduce her basic interests from the above facts. Japan is a maritime nation in that her security is threatened if hostile powers gain control of the surrounding seas, and in that she must live by trade, for which she is suitably located. So long as the American Navy controls the Western Pacific, therefore, the only sensible security policy is a close security relationship with the United States. Moreover, so long as such a relationship gives Japan very reasonable protection, a security policy based upon strong armaments of her own is apparently of doubtful value (her own nuclear weapons would be difficult to acquire, too costly in economic, political and social terms, and of dubious utility for her security).[1]

It is doubtful whether a country can develop strong military forces without nuclear weapons, since the active use of conventional forces is effectively deterred by the nuclear weapons of other countries. Thus, a militarily powerful Japan is indeed an unreal option. The role of global trading power is, on the other hand, a natural one for her. Therefore, as long as Japan's future policy is discussed in terms of a clear-cut choice between the continuation of the present course and a major change, the discussion will not be very meaningful, for the rational option is bound to be the former. It is no wonder, then, that responsible Japanese opinion still favours continuing as before, despite the so-called 'Nixon Shock' and the subsequent soul-searching.

But it would be intellectually idle to be satisfied simply with elaborating upon the basic soundness of the post-war foreign policy. For one thing, Japan may not be able to carry out a rational policy. There is an air of unreality in the Japanese Government's reiteration of policies which are basically the extension of past and present ones. The government says Japan will not go nuclear; she will maintain security ties with the United States but try to be friendly with every country; she will increase her imports and try not to disturb the international economy; and she will play an active role in giving aid to developing countries. Nobody doubts the desirability of such policies, but the statement is unrealistic in two senses.

Firstly, it is by no means easy to act in this way. The Japanese Government may not be able to continue the Japan–US Security Treaty in view of the strong domestic opposition to it, while a liberalization of imports such as some countries are demanding is a difficult task for any government. Secondly, a world in which the above policy is relevant is a world without trouble for Japan, and to base a policy on it is thus to wish away all problems. Who can be sure that military force will not again acquire greater political significance?

The world situation will certainly not change drastically – and to draw up theoretical scenarios in which Japan has to abandon her present policy is therefore too speculative – but it can change gradually, and has indeed already changed to a certain extent, requiring important modifications of Japan's foreign policy, although not a major change. The world political situation is entering a new stage, as many have pointed out; the days of bipolarity are over and a so-called multipolar world is emerging. The United States has now ceased to be all-powerful and has been disengaging from Asia, so the 'American hegemony' in the Far East is past.

The change is not one which demands a major alteration of Japanese policy, since it has not seemed to alter the basic power arrangements in Asia. It is a change from the 'cold war' to the 'era of negotiation', and tension in the region is therefore less acute, but the basis of the *détente* in Asia, as in Europe, is the recognition of the *status quo* by the important actors in the area. The recent adjustments of Sino–American and Sino–Japanese relations were made on this basis: though Japan has more or less recognized the sovereignty of the People's Republic of China over Taiwan, the actual relations between Taiwan and Japan have not drastically changed and, more importantly, China is not now opposed to the Japan–US Security Treaty. The developments in the Korean Peninsula also reflect movement towards *détente* on the basis of the *status quo*: the two governments of Korea recognized each other's existence for the first time by pledging not to resort to arms. It appears that the existing security system has become the basic framework of international relations of the *détente* era.

With the relaxation of tension, however, the characteristics of international politics have changed in subtle but important ways. One can see changes both in inter-state relationships and in the nature of international politics. The cold war coalitions are losing their former cohesion, and friend–enemy relations are no longer clear, while the focal point of international politics seems to be shifting from the military to the non-military aspects – especially trade relations and technological exchanges. Theoretically, this must make for a better world for Japan, which is weak militarily and influential in non-military fields. But the new situation is also a more difficult one for Japan because she adapted herself too well to the former world of cold war and American hegemony, when a 'low posture' policy suited her magnificently. The United States was dependable, and bold diplomatic initiatives were either impossible or undesirable, because the dividing line between the two opposing blocs was sharply drawn. An assertive economic policy was possible, however, partly because people focused their attention on security matters and were indifferent to other problems, partly because any economic development was considered to help to strengthen the 'Free World'. None of the above statements are valid today. Protection by the United States is no longer automatic, Japan can and must take diplomatic initiatives, and economic problems have come to the top of the diplomatic agenda. It does not follow that the Japan–US security relations are obsolete or undesirable, or that the economic orientation of the Japanese foreign policy should be changed, but care must now be taken over maintaining the security relationships, and concentrating energy on economic activities can no longer be considered as a 'low posture'.

The growth of Japanese economic power, due to continuous, rapid development, has itself changed the situation. It has increased both the vulnerability and the influence of Japan. Twenty years ago, strangely enough, she was less vulnerable economically than she is now. Though she needed markets and sources of raw materials – and in economic terms it was no easy task, for she had to try hard to produce attractive goods to sell abroad, so as to overcome her balance of payments problem – Japan was safe from political interference because of the smallness of her needs. In other words, Japan could live anonymously twenty, or even ten, years ago; but now her exports, because of their volume, create problems in other countries. And if raw materials should become less easy to obtain Japan would suffer more because she now needs them in larger quantities.

Japan's influence has increased with the growth of her economy, and she is now making some impact on the world economy. But unconscious, undirected impact can only cause chaos, and impact without will, which cannot properly be called influence, is a disadvantageous rather than an advantageous factor. Japan has become vulnerable, but is not using her potential influence to overcome her vulnerability, and, making her impact on the world in a quite chaotic way, has become a 'problem child' in the eyes of some. Herein lies the necessity for modifying the past policy of 'low posture'.

The combination of the rise of non-military problems to the top of the diplomatic agenda and the rise of Japan as an important economic power has suddenly brought her to the forefront of world politics, to the surprise and annoyance of both the Japanese and others. Adjustments are obviously necessary, but they may not be easy. If Japan cannot make them, this may gradually change the world situation in the wrong direction from her point of view: a process which could ultimately lead to a situation in which a major change in Japanese foreign policy does become necessary.

In this paper, therefore, I want to consider the difficulties and problems Japan may face, failure to solve which may have a cumulative effect, leading to a gradual change in the environment of her foreign policy and finally to a major change of the policy itself. In this way I will try to avoid both speculative forecasting of the future (disregarding the probability problems of scenarios) and being a lazy advocate of continuation of the *status quo* in the hope that nothing serious will happen. I shall start by examining the difficulties and problems involved in continuing the present policy, and shall then extend this analysis to examine the difficulties and problems involved in variations of this policy.

The problems of Japanese–American relations are discussed first, as this relationship has been the core of Japan's foreign policy and will remain so for some time at least, since close relations with the United States are still (rightly) preferred by the Japanese policy-makers. The problems of economic intercourse will be discussed next, not only because these constitute a major factor affecting Japanese–American relations but also because one of the main features of Japan's foreign policy has been to try to become a global economic power. I shall then turn my attention to the domestic factors constraining her foreign policy.

As the discussion is likely to throw some doubts on the simple continuation of the present policy, I shall then examine two variations of it: a policy stressing the Pacific–Asia area and one stressing improved relations with the two Communist powers. The former has been advocated by a few Japanese for some time, while the possibility of the latter was opened up by the recent *détente* and multi-polarization of the international relations of Asia. These are not speculative scenarios, therefore, but real possibilities, though they may not in the event become actual alternatives. In conclusion, I will try to draw policy implications and will discuss some concrete measures.

VI Findings and policy suggestions

I have tried to find out the problems and difficulties Japan will face in her foreign relations. My aim in so doing is not to show that Japan's diplomatic future is bright or bleak, nor to argue for drastic changes in her policy by pointing out the problems involved in the continuation of the present policy. I have examined the problems and difficulties because I believe that a realistic policy can be built only upon cool recognition of the problems and difficulties. In view of the above examination, then, what policy should Japan follow?

The first option she can take is to stick to her present policy in spite of the difficulties involved. This is not so unreasonable as some might think, for close relations between the United States and Japan are clearly in Japan's interests. Also, pursuing one policy but disregarding the other options has the merit of clarity: one can be determined and devoted to the cause. This has been the attitude of the Japanese policymakers until recently, and rightly so. Moreover, such a commitment can give considerable bargaining power, as has been proved by the past performance of Japan's foreign policy; the negotiation of the reversion of Okinawa is a recent example.

As we have seen, however, there are dangers in such a course. To begin with, it poses a large psychological burden on the parties concerned, particularly when Japan tries to assert herself. Binding one's hands gives considerable bargaining power and might achieve quite a lot, but it does not give the satisfaction of a feeling of achievement; the strange psychological situation after the decision on the reversion of Okinawa proved that. Such a psychological price can no longer be dismissed lightly, on account of a more assertive mood in Japan and the less generous and more xenophobic attitude of the United States to international affairs. In fact, sticking adamantly to the policy of close co-operation with the United States was a policy best suited to a 'weak' Japan, which is now no longer the case.

Moreover, disregarding other options carries its own uncertainty, for changes can create wide repercussions. Examination of the future development of Japanese politics has shown that one cannot rule out the possibility of the termination of the Japan–US Security Treaty, but no one can foresee what will happen then, and this in itself could be a cause of instability in Asia. It may appear as a potential danger at present, but it might in time become actual.

The second option is that of global economic power. This is only a small step from the first option, and Japanese policy has actually developed in this direction. There might therefore be some who doubt the point of dealing with this as a different option; yet there are several meaningful differences. It is true that such a policy would be still based on the Japanese–American security relationship, but the security aspects are de-emphasized in the second option and the perspective broadened. Accordingly, the balance sheet of Japanese–American relations would be drawn up in a different form.

Again, much can be said for this. It would suit Japan's geographical conditions, which provide her with considerable security and easy access to most parts of the world, and it would also suit Japan's efficient industries. Moreover, such a policy might suit contemporary world politics, where military forces do not play a large role. Many Japanese, including myself, prefer this policy, but it is not without its difficulties, for one cannot lightly dismiss the rising tide of nationalistic economic policy or protectionism in several parts of the world. Such a tendency appears to be the result of two factors. One is the change in the structure of the international economy: the increased interdependence of national economies has sometimes produced unfavourable reactions, and rapid growth in the economies of most industrial countries, together with the gap between rich and poor nations, might once more bring the supply of raw materials into question. A second factor is the rapid increase of Japan's exports, which has brought some hostile reaction. Japan can consider herself unlucky that the former system of free trade began to change at the very moment when she was able to act in accordance with it, and she might justifiably criticize the attitudes of others as a selfish reaction to Japan's success, but this will not solve her problems.

She might, however, be able to cope with the problems by de-emphasizing the export factor, switching her energies to domestic requirements and maintaining the high efficiency of her economy. As no protectionism can be absolute, especially today, Japan can hope to enjoy a considerable volume of trade so long as her economy can maintain its high efficiency, and, with a healthy economy at home, her need to export will not be so great. Strangely, such an attitude resembles that of Richard Cobden, the Victorian English statesman; Cobden failed in the nineteenth century, but Japan in the twentieth century might succeed, especially if her economy remains efficient.

She can also hope that present reaction to her economic expansion will diminish with the passing of time; after all, West Germany experienced the same treatment and has now been accepted by other countries, even with 11 per cent of world trade in her hands. But this figure is in fact misleading: out of that 11 per cent of world trade, trade with the countries of the European Community (i.e., trade with politically guaranteed markets) occupies some two-thirds. When Japan has 11 per cent of world trade (in 1980), therefore, her impact on the world economy will be far greater than that of West Germany, and it is unlikely that such sizeable economic activity can be achieved without any political impact.

There is a third option, in which Japan plays a political role, mainly through a loose co-operative organization in the Asia–Pacific region. But playing a political role demands the will on the part of the people to do so. Whether, and how, such will can be fostered is the problem for Japan. My assessment has shown not only the necessity for this, but also the possibilities; but only if Japan can free herself from narrow economic considerations will those possibilities attain any reality. But this precondition cannot easily be met by Japan, due to domestic constraints; also, she cannot play a political role by disregarding the three super-powers.

Thus, we turn to Japan's relations with the two Communist powers. Clearly it is the most important 'frontier' for Japanese foreign policy, but it may not present any alternative to the present policy – because the relative smallness of the two nations' economic power and the difference in their political and economic systems inevitably limit the scope for co-operation in quality and quantity, and because the Sino–Soviet conflict inhibits very close relations with either of them. However, Japan can no longer keep the two powers at arm's length, as she has so far done. This is not only impossible but would also be against Japan's interests, for better and closer relations with the two Communist powers are necessary for her active participation in Asian politics. Also, Japan's relations with the United States will be maintained without great cost only by an improvement in relations with the Soviet Union and China. The most difficult problem involved in this is, of course, the danger that Japan might become involved in Sino–Soviet conflict.

There are two ways of improving Japan's relations with the Soviet Union and China. The first is to do so on a bilateral basis, using the utmost caution to avoid the danger of antagonizing either of them. Japan might be able to go to considerable lengths to achieve this, but there is a certain element of opportunism in it, and therefore dangers. There is not only the possibility that one of them might be antagonized, but also that the United States might become anxious if Japan should achieve a certain success. It could then be argued, cynically, that Japanese policy was a variation of balancing the three against each other, and as Japan increased in power and independence, such an accusation could become valid. If this process resulted in a cynical balance-of-power game, Japan would find herself in a disadvantageous position, and in the end might well feel the need for strong military forces as a necessary instrument of bargaining. She should not take this risk by embarking upon a policy of balancing the three (it should be noted that Japan can increase her freedom of action safely only by successfully de-emphasizing the role of military force). Sooner or later, therefore, Japan must try to involve the three major powers in a political programme to create a framework for the stability and security in which she can hope to manage her relations with them. I want to conclude by discussing possible frameworks for such stability in more detail.

The value of such a framework for Japan is that, by creating some kind of co-operation in the security field, she can act both economically and politically with less risk of being involved in the Sino–Soviet conflict and with a smaller dependence on the United States.

But constructing such a system will not be easy, indeed it will be more difficult than in Europe. For such a system becomes possible when there is a clear need for co-operation, when the parties concerned have some confidence in it, and when there are some prospects of benefiting from it; moreover, the need for co-operation and the advantages to be gained must be balanced sensitively. Such would appear to be the case in Europe now, but in Asia the bitterness of the Sino–Soviet conflict makes it difficult to have confidence in such co-operation. Whenever one listens to Chinese criticism of the Soviet proposal of a 'collective system of security in Asia', one cannot help feeling pessimistic about security co-operation.

In my opinion, however, the lack of clear needs and the wide divergence of advantages to be gained are more important inhibiting factors. To begin with, the United States appears to feel no strong need to create a system of co-operation for security in Asia, for her Asian policy has changed: she now puts more emphasis on self-help by the Asian countries and, for herself, seems to have decided to start some sort of co-operation with China, though not with the Soviet Union. Having started, and tried to maintain, some semblance of co-operation with the Soviet Union as regards the central balance and the European system, she then chose to co-operate with China in Asia and has been keeping the Soviet Union out in the cold. China is a more important power for the stability and security in Asia, and, given China's considerable influence there, the United States must co-operate with her, and can afford to neglect the Soviet Union, which is in a relatively weak position in the area. Also, keeping the Soviet Union in the cold helps to keep the American global position superior to the Soviet Union's. Thus, the necessity for co-operation between them is small, and the prospective advantage from co-operation is smaller than that to be gained from non co-operation. Moreover, since there is at present little likelihood of security co-operation among the three major powers, the United States must choose between China and Russia, and her choice is bound to be China.

As for China, she feels no strong need for co-operation among the three. For one thing, her concern with the Soviet Union overshadows all others, and in addition her security interests are fairly limited, due to her geopolitical condition and to the fact that she is the weakest of the three powers. Basically China wants to be left alone, and does not want to expand her security interests greatly; thus her security policy had been one of trying to drive away outside influence from neighbouring areas. She had been opposed to the network of bilateral treaties which the United States created, but she now seems to be not unhappy with the American presence in Asia and is content with the American policy of keeping the Soviet Union in the cold.

Only the Soviet Union is therefore interested in a new and wider framework for security, because she hopes by this means to emerge from the cold and acquire a role and political influence. Her insistence that the Brezhnev system for security in Asia must supersede all others, even those originating in Asia, is proof of this basic objective. When Kosygin met Tun Razak on 26 September 1972, he did not support the plan for the neutralization of South-East Asia which the latter had advocated;[2] the Soviet Union had been repeating the allegations that the ASEAN was potentially a military bloc manipulated by the West, and dismissed the Kuala Lumpur Declaration, advocating the neutralization plan, as 'only a piece of paper'. Though her attitude to the plan has softened recently, the Soviet Union still does not favour it, for neutralization will strengthen ASEAN, which is an organization the Soviet Union cannot hope to influence or control. She is certainly interested in the stability of the area, since turmoil there can only give China better opportunities, but she is much more interested in a form of stability in which she can play a role. The 1969 Soviet proposal for Asian collective security was taken by some as an anti-Chinese pact and one cannot deny that the proposal had such an aim, but, as *Le Monde* pointed out at the time, it was not as important as had been thought. The Soviet Union's basic objective has been to use the proposal to secure an entry into Asian politics – something to which China is strongly opposed.[3]

But the possibility of co-operation is not always slight, nor the lack of need clear cut. In an area such as South-East Asia tension is not high and co-operation is not impossible. As has been pointed out, no major outside powers consider the area as vital, so that they might therefore be able to co-operate in pledging non-intervention. On the other hand, and for the very same reason, the incentive to act may be weak.

Needs are a more important factor, and there are both general and particular ones. The former stems from the dangers of a policy of trying to keep the Soviet Union in the cold in Asia. The Soviet Union has only the vaguest idea of her 'collective security system'; and it is not difficult to find weak elements in her proposals. Firstly, one cannot hope to create a single collective security system in Asia, because there is no such thing as a single Asia; it must be divided into at least three regions: South, South-East and North-East Asia. Secondly, some of her proposals are either meaningless or made with a specific country in mind: for example, the principle of inviolability of borders can be considered either as too general to be useful or else as directed at China and perhaps Japan. Again, the principle of 'extensive development of economic and other co-operation on the basis of complete equality and mutual advantage' can be used in several different ways.[4]

Thirdly, the Soviet Union can and will advance her own particular interests under the banner of a 'collective security system' in Asia. She appears to regard her treaty with India as the prototype for others, and, if this really is the case, some might argue that it is not a 'collective security system' she seeks but a Soviet-style web of bilateral security pacts.[5] It is undeniable that the Soviet–Indian Treaty has an element of alliance in it, and so it might be said that the Soviet Union has been advancing her influence while at the same time trying to destroy the old arrangements by advocating a 'collective security system'. It might therefore be better to invite the Soviet Union into Asia and jointly define her role there than to keep her out in the cold, leaving her to spell out her plan by her actions.

The need for such co-operation can be demonstrated more specifically, in that co-operation between the three, and probably four, major powers in the area (i.e., the three plus Japan) is necessary to further progress towards *détente* in Asia. The United States clearly seems to feel that this further progress should be made in such fields as arms control, especially in nuclear weapons, and a recent policy paper prepared by the Brookings Institution for the US Arms Control and Disarmament Agency can be considered as a good example of such thinking.[6] It argues for arms control measures in the transitional period when the United States will have a significant counter-force capability *vis-à-vis* China, so that, since the United States has decided to rely on deterrence rather than damage denial capability, a more or less stable balance will emerge in future. But for some time to come, the United States, which plans her nuclear force in relation to the Soviet Union, inevitably also has a counter-force capability in relation to China; the paper therefore suggests reducing Chinese fear of American nuclear attack by measures including efforts to explain American strategy, a bilateral No-First-Use Agreement, and avoidance of 'moving towards greater reliance on tactical nuclear weapons for deterrence and defence'. Instead it suggests reducing reliance on nuclear weapons by maintaining in conjunction with allied forces, as strong a conventional force capability as might be needed to deal with conflicts in North-East Asia, but reducing this force 'as diminishing tensions warrant'. Regional arms-control measures are both desirable and essential for such a policy, and a Korean arms-control plan is also advocated in the report.

As for the first two measures, discussions will be limited to bilateral talks between the United States and China, because there seems to be no possibility of contacts between China and the Soviet Union or between the three. Bilateral Sino–American talks can have only a limited meaning, but the hope would be that they would develop into wider arrangements. It is clearly impossible, however, to have meaningful discussions about regional arms-control measures, or about Korea, without the participation of the Soviet Union and possibly Japan, and since security co-operation is actually a requirement in Korea, this might provide the chance to begin the political process of enlarging the framework.

There is a good chance that such a system of co-operation might be achieved. The United States has adopted a policy of low profile and, while maintaining sufficient conventional forces in Asia, she is trying to ease the tension so that she can reduce her troops stationed there. China has been on the path to co-existence with the United States, and does not want conflict in the Korean Peninsula. As for the Soviet Union, Morton Abramowitz writes: 'The Soviets have repeatedly expressed their desire to achieve greater stability or defuse the situation in Korea, although they must be circumspect here to protect their position in Pyongyang *vis-à-vis* the Chinese. There is ample opportunity for the United States to take the Russians up on these interests and a similar rationale as for talks with China on the Korean question.'[7] Such a system of co-operation is highly desirable for Japan, because the situation in Korea to a certain extent affects the security of Japan. It may not be so important as many Japanese thought some decades ago and some still think today – and clearly it does not warrant direct Japanese intervention – but Japan cannot remain indifferent to the situation either. The possibility has already been noted that China and Japan might clash in Korea and that Japan might suffer from a difference of opinion with the United States over that country. Therefore, if the situation in Korea can be stabilized politically the concern of the Japanese will be eased.

Security co-operation is both possible and necessary in view of developments there. In 1972 the two governments of Korea took a major step towards *détente* and co-existence. While it is beyond doubt that the diplomatic process leading to *détente* in Korea must begin with the actions of the two Korean governments, after the process is started and shows signs of progress it will become necessary for the outside powers to back the two Korean governments' efforts and make the result certain and fixed. The necessity for such an action can be best understood from an examination of the present stage of *détente*. After the joint declaration of 4 July 1972, the two Korean governments started diplomatic initiatives towards the countries of the 'opposite' bloc, with the establishment of formal diplomatic relations in mind. But the result has unfortunately been poor; though North Korea opened diplomatic relations with Sweden in 1973, South Korea has not achieved any success. This shows that there are certain limits to diplomatic efforts on a bilateral basis and that the ice cannot be broken piecemeal. Clearly international backing is necessary, and perhaps now is the time to give it.

What are the necessary measures and what kind of regional arms-control measures can be envisaged? First, there are two political measures. One is the establishment of formal diplomatic relations with the 'opposite' bloc. The second is that the two governments are given some status in the United Nations, possibly as more-or-less full members. As the world will shortly have to tackle the problems of the two German governments in the United Nations, this formula could be a fruitful one.

Second, there are several arms-control measures. The basic one is the renunciation of the use of force by the two Korean governments and the international guarantee of such a renunciation. As both governments made such a renunciation in their declaration of 4 July 1972 the process has already been started; the next step will be a change in the deployment of their forces, and eventually their mutual reduction (actually the disbanding of North Korean special troops is believed to have been done).

Both countries are badly in need of such reduction, being crippled by huge military budgets.

There are three difficult points worth consideration. Firstly, there is the co-ordination of development within Korea and between Korea and outside powers. Undoubtedly the former is of basic importance, but at the same time many of the measures discussed above have to be taken through joint efforts. For many can be used as bargaining assets in many different ways. Thus, it would be against the interests of South Korea for such countries as the United States and Japan to set up diplomatic relations with North Korea unless South Korea can also widen her diplomatic relations. Also, the handling of the Korean question in the UN will have a very different impact on the two Koreas, depending upon the way in which it is handled. Therefore something like a North Asian Security Conference seems necessary after the basic groundwork has been done.

Secondly, there is the problem of the area to which arms-control measures are applied. Can one limit them to Korea? Clearly the military balance among the Soviet, Chinese and American forces is the basic condition for arms control in Korea. Also, the two Koreas might raise objections to the fact that only their forces had been limited; therefore, Japan might have to formally limit her forces (which seems not to be difficult in view of the present low level of her forces), coupled with the lease of some bases to the United States. Moreover, limitations on the movement of the forces within a certain area might be explored to advantage.

Thirdly, there is the problem of guarantees. Here we must reject the two extremes, one of which is to make a treaty without any guarantee, while the other is to try to set up very complete, and therefore intricate, machinery. The former is not trustworthy, while the latter is both impossible and

undesirable. Perhaps international supervision of the demilitarized zone will be both possible and sufficient. Happily, the
Korean Peninsula is not Vietnam, where the boundaries are too
long and cannot be watched, and where the opposing forces do
not form any distinct fronts.

Still, one may well be sceptical about the possibility of the
co-operation of the four powers in the security field. If one thinks
about the difficulties involved in the co-ordination mentioned
above, one realizes that much groundwork has to be done and
that *détente* in the Korean Peninsula will be a very long process.
Moreover, any important advance may be impossible, except
in the medium- or long-term, in view of the harshness of the
Sino–Soviet conflict. In other parts of Asia, co-operation in
security measures will be more difficult because the situation
is far from clear.

It is, however, extremely important for Japan to act in the
international relations of North-East Asia with her eye on such
a medium- or long-term objective, even if she has to deal with
the two Communist powers on a bilateral basis for a while. She
should not try to exploit the fluid triangular relations according to the mechanistic concept of the balance of power, for,
though she might gain by it in the short run, in the long run
she would suffer.

It may not be impossible for Japan to contribute to the
making of a new framework if she clearly shows such an intention and takes initiatives. For example, when Japan negotiates
with China over the problem of the Senkaku Islands or the
demarcation of the seabed she can do so with her eye on the
long-term goal of creating a wider co-operative system. The
seabed can become a very serious issue if the countries involved
pursue their narrow national interests, and it is therefore not
only desirable but necessary to try to create a wider framework
in which nations can settle issues amicably and co-operate in

development. The South China Sea, in addition to the Korean Peninsula, may provide the opportunity.

Another possible field for the Japanese initiatives is the renunciation of a nuclear option in return for some *quid pro quo* on the part of the three powers. Such a *quid pro quo* might be, for example, moves towards a regional security system in the Korean Peninsula, a guarantee by the United States against nuclear attack or blackmail, or the pledge by the three powers, jointly or separately not to use nuclear weapons against a non-nuclear power. Depending upon its timing, such an agreement could have considerable impact on the international relations of the area. Again it is no easy task, but it is worth while for Japan to explore the possibility, since she more than anybody else needs a stable and peaceful framework in North-East Asia.

Last but not the least, it should be pointed out that such a policy is the logical extension of Japan's basic philosophy of international relations, i.e., belief in world interdependence. The rejection of the idea of the mechanical balance of power is merely a logical conclusion of this basic view. It is therefore essential for Japan to contribute to the making of the global economic order, both by taking a more positive attitude in international economic relations and by improving her domestic structure. It will clarify her basic posture and increase the confidence of others in Japan, and hence improve her capability to act in the difficult context of the quadrilateral relations in Asia.

NOTES

[1] In addition to several technological difficulties – e.g. miniaturization of warheads, development of long-range sea-borne missiles and the construction of deep-diving submarines – Japan's extreme vulnerability, due to the small size of her territory and the concentration of population, makes it almost impossible for her to create a state of mutual deterrence. Targeting also poses serious difficulties. Strong domestic opposition and unfavourable international reaction to Japan's acquisition of nuclear weapons seems almost certain, and in view of this it is better for Japan to remain a threshold power than actually to become a nuclear power. On Japanese capability for nuclear armament, see *Strategic Survey 1972* (London: IISS, 1973), pp. 40–42. For a representative Japanese view, see Kiichi Saeki, 'Japan's Security in a Multipolar World', in *East Asia and the World System: The Regional*

Powers, Adelphi Paper No. 92 (London: IISS, 1972), pp. 23–28.

[2] *Asian Analysis*, November 1972.

[3] *Le Monde*, 10 July 1969.

[4] At the 15th Congress of Soviet Trade Unions Brezhnev advocated a system of collective security based on such principles as the renunciation of the use of force between states, respect for sovereignty and the inviolability of frontiers, and extensive development of economic and other co-operation on the basis of complete equality and mutual advantage (*Soviet News*, 4 July 1972).

[5] *Asian Analysis*, May 1972.

[6] *The Implications of Chinese Nuclear Force for US Strategic and Arms Control Policies* (Washington: Brookings Institution, January 1973).

[7] Morton Abramowitz, *Moving the Glacier: The Two Koreas and the Powers*, Adelphi Paper No. 80 (London: IISS, 1971), p. 24.

CHAPTER TEN

The energy problem and alliance systems: Japan

Makoto Momoi

From Adelphi Paper 115, 1975

The energy problem, long anticipated but emerging graphically with the October war, showed Japan herself and the world how vulnerable Japan's economic basis was and will be, and how strikingly Japan lacked politico-economic bargaining power in dealing with the oil crisis. As a corollary, it introduced a subtle, if not fundamental, change in a hitherto militarily-oriented concept of national security based on Japan's alliance with the United States. Indeed, it has become fashionable when discussing national security in terms of economic and military security to place a heavier emphasis on the former, as is indicated by an alleged statement of a policy-maker: 'With or without a nuclear deterrent, there is no national security without oil.'

Japan's reaction to the crisis, however, was at first complacent, then pessimistic, and finally fatalistic. When the war broke out, few Japanese realized that their country was about to face an oil embargo which she had successfully escaped during the 1967 six-day war by remaining politically neutral. When the embargo was imposed, there were cries of 'Japanese Economy Without

Maps',[1] or 'Capitalism Gasps For Breath'.[2] On 22 November, thirty-five days after the embargo was announced, Japan abandoned her neutralism for a pro-Arab stance, even at the risk of antagonizing the pro-Israeli United States. Civilian oil consumption was curtailed and some military exercises halted.

A number of official and private studies have since been undertaken to reassess Japan's position and future course of action. The government has yet to adopt a particular policy, but several proposals and recommendations (most of them for intramural study only) reveal Japan's extremely limited range of options, both in ensuring stable energy supplies and in reassessing the alliance system. This Paper is a brief attempt, first, to review how Japan reacted to the oil crisis, what she has learned from it and how she now plans to deal with energy problems in general. Secondly, it tries to reassess how the realities of the energy problems affected Japan's concept of the Japan–United States alliance and what future course of action she might contemplate against the background of the changing nature of the alliance.

Alliance for Japan

For such an attempt, one needs to know something of the uniqueness of the Japan–United States alliance. First, it is the only alliance the United States has under the treaty of *mutual co-operation* and security. Second, the treaty has a unique sentence in the second paragraph of Article II: 'They [the parties] will seek to eliminate conflict in their international economic policies and will encourage *economic collaboration* between them' (italics added).

No similar phrase can be found in any of the 'mutual defence' or 'security' treaties the United States has with forty-one other nations. The words 'mutual co-operation' and 'economic collaboration' have been regarded by Japan as being just as important as other aspects of the security arrangement. Her spokesmen, in every official statement, have confirmed a desire to 'firmly maintain' the security treaty – a symbol not only of common defence but of economic collaboration.

In the defence field Japan is not obliged to 'act to meet the common danger' except in the case of an 'armed attack against either Party in the territories under the administration of Japan.' In the economic field she undeniably took advantage of an easy access to the American market. The access was so easy that Japan became dependent on American sources for 29.5 per cent of her total imports and 28.3 per cent of exports in 1973 (as against the figures for 1972 of 29.8 per cent and 34.8 per cent respectively).

Such a unilateral defence arrangement, combined with such an economic dependence on the United States, inevitably prompted former Secretary of Defense Melvin Laird, in his 1973 Final Report to Congress, to call for 'mutuality in both trade and security', after indirectly carpeting Japan in these terms: 'Our allies, particularly those which have developed strong and thriving economies through easy access to American markets, while enjoying the luxury of a nuclear shield financed solely by the American taxpayer, must be brought to the realization that they, too, have responsibilities and burdens to bear for their own and free world security and prosperity.'[3]

Former President Nixon also warned Japan in his 1973 foreign policy report that 'without conscious effort of political will, our economic disputes could tear the fabric of our alliance'.[4] For most Japanese these warnings were a far from pleasant reminder that the alliance system had already begun to show signs of deterioration, for three main reasons. The first of these was that, when faced with American criticism of 'free-riding', the Japanese were, as a diplomat put it, 'apt to consider the security pact imposes obligations only on Japan' because 'Japanese obligations are visible to everyone in terms of the presence of bases [in Japan]'.[5] The second was that the warnings followed a series of economic–diplomatic 'noises': American criticism of Japanese dumping of television sets (December 1970), American pressure on the 'undervalued yen' (May 1971), American overtures to Peking 'over Japan's head' (July 1971), the forced devaluation of the yen (December 1971) and textile disputes over two and a half years that ended in January 1972 with Japanese concessions. The third reason was that Japan began to notice a change in the nature of nuclear deterrence following the May 1972 agreement between the two super-powers on the avoidance of nuclear war and the Nixon–Brezhnev pledge of 22 June 1973 on the prevention of continental war and on refraining from 'the threat or use of force against ... the allies ... and other countries'. By implication the pledge weakened the contractual nature of the nuclear umbrella, if it did not furl the umbrella completely.

Nevertheless, the super-powers' agreement was welcomed as a political framework within which Japan hoped to continue her economic activities without fear of catastrophic disruption resulting from a super-power global confrontation. She knew, of course, that nuclear *détente* does not necessarily spell peace in relations either between super-powers and others or among the rest of the world. Nor would it automatically lead to non-nuclear and politico–economic stability.

The October war proved beyond doubt Japan's basic politico–economic vulnerability when she found that political neutrality was seen by the Arabs as an unfriendly posture and that the United States was concerned not so much with 'economic collaboration' as with a global strategic balance. Japan's options were extremely limited: she could either follow the leader (the United States) which, with relatively independent oil resources, reportedly wanted Japan to remain non-committal to the Arabs and tolerate the embargo for a few months without any assurance from the major oil companies of an emergency supply; or else Japan, which then had 59 days' oil stockpiled, including that aboard tankers en route, had to defy American pressure and reach a political accommodation with the Arabs, at the risk of further deterioration in the alliance. She chose the latter – that is to say, a subtle process of de-Americanization.

Post-mortem and policy review

Now that the crisis is over, at least quantitatively, a series of intensive post-mortems has been undertaken against the background of a drastically changed producer–consumer relationship. In addition, Japan must face another set of already existing vulnerabilities, most of them invariables she can do little about.

(a) Japan cannot be completely independent of the United States in political, economic and military terms: her pro-Arab posture can therefore never approach that of France or Britain.

(b) Japan has little to offer the Arabs, who are limited both in products they have to export (except for oil) and, because of demographic conditions, in the market they can offer for Japanese goods (parliamentary resolutions ban Japan from arms sales, and technological–legislative limitations keep her from joining the United States, France and Britain in a 'nuclear reactor sales war').

(c) Japan still relies on the major oil companies for the bulk of her oil imports (or about half of the demand expected towards the end of the 1970s) and for downstream operations, since her national oil companies are limited in size and operational experience.

(d) Japan, a relative newcomer to the Middle East scene, is ill-prepared to deal with a possible crisis, arising for instance between Iran and Iraq, or from a split between a Saudi–Egyptian group and an Iraqi–Syrian–Libyan faction.[6]

(e) Japan's economy would suffer a fatal blow from another prolonged interruption of energy flow, since in 1969 about 60 per cent of imported energy (or about 80 per cent of the total imported and domestic energy supply) was used by industry.

Japanese options: some proposals

Against this background the Comprehensive Energy Study Committee (CESC), an advisory organ to the Ministry of International Trade and Industry, published its 39-page interim energy report on 25 July 1974.[7] It stresses three major policy goals: a secure, stable supply of energy; gradual reduction of Japan's dependence on overseas energy, in particular oil; and conservation, stockpiling and exploration of new energy resources.

First, the committee recommends that priority be given to stable supply: stability should come first because of its possible critical impact on the socio-economic situation in the event of another oil crisis. Second, it sets a goal of an annual average increase in energy supply of 5.7–7.6 per cent until FY 1980, and then, until FY 1985 of 5.7–7.8 per cent. Such rates will be far less than the average over the past ten years of 11.9 per cent. This could partially offset higher prices. Third, the CESC calls for an intensive effort to conserve and stockpile energy and explore new energy sources on a crash basis in collaboration with other oil-consuming countries, in particular the United States.

On the other hand the report reveals two interesting features:

(1) It does not mention government-to-government collaboration among consuming nations in ensuring oil supplies, but it does stress that the international oil companies, 'though their role might relatively diminish', may still play a big role in the international oil market with their long experience, technological know-how and vast capital reserves. To this extent Japan prefers to live in harmony with the major oil companies, if not necessarily with their mother governments.

(2) In the field of research and development, however, Japan evidently wants to 'positively cooperate with US government agencies which have high technological potentials',[8] and for this purpose signed an Agreement on Co-operation in the Field of Energy and Research and Development in Washington on 15 July 1974. Under this, the two governments will undertake co-operative projects related to energy resources, conversion and transmission, and conservation. In most of these projects Japan depends on the United States and only in some, such as solar energy application ('Project Sunshine'), are the two interdependent. In that sense, the agreement is evidence that the emotionalism which emerged during the crisis has partially disappeared.

Future plans and difficulties

A series of 'Nixon shocks' and trade disputes in the early 1970s provoked Japanese suspicion that the United States might fail to recall the unique aspect of the alliance system with Japan: common defence and economic collaboration. The initial American reaction to Japan's vulnerability during the oil crisis simply deepened the Japanese suspicion that the spirit of economic collaboration had virtually been struck out of the American text of the treaty. After an objective survey of the factors behind her vulnerability, however, Japan found no options other than seeking collaboration with the United States. This is also true of Japan's future plans, as well as her efforts to overcome related difficulties.

Development of continental shelves is promising indeed, and vast oil and natural gas deposits might exist in Japan's continental shelves and their peripheral seabeds. But their development entails vast financial outlay, complicated international legal issues and technological problems. Without direct or indirect American participation, development might take too long and cost too much.

In order to deal with drastic changes in international situations in future, Japan may have to diversify her sources of oil by extensive development of oil deposits in untapped regions overseas (including China, Chinese offshore areas and the Soviet Union) if technically feasible and politically agreeable.

While relying on the international oil companies for about 50 per cent of demand, Japan will increasingly engage in bilateral deals: direct deals by private companies and government-to-government transactions with oil-producing countries. Both will eventually require stronger government control and management.

Japan hopes to bring her total oil stockpiles up from an expected 68.9 days at the end of August 1974 to the European-American level of 90 days by 1979.[9] The government is also ready to join actively in an international joint stockpiling programme and an emergency burden-sharing system.

As for technological R&D, Japan is interested in every item listed in the recently concluded United States–Japan energy R&D agreement; she is also to launch a national movement for energy conservation by organizing a Resources–Energy Conservation

Headquarters, and will draft a long-range plan to change her industrial structure to a less energy-intensive industry.

The plans sound promising, but face a number of inherent problems. First, extensive, long-range R&D programmes require national consensus on huge financial outlay, for in the post-war years Japan has relied mainly on importing technological know-how, in particular from the United States. The oil crisis has brought a subtle change in this easy-going attitude, but public opinion is not yet ripe for taxpayers to swallow a huge outlay. Secondly, the cost will multiply when Japan embarks on her planned series of overseas-development investment projects in the Middle East, South-east Asia and the Far East. For instance, a single Siberian natural gas project at Yakut may cost up to $3,400 million if undertaken without American participation.

Thirdly, there is resources nationalism: a phenomenon not limited to the Third World but also existing in industrial export markets. For both commercial and financial reasons demand for Japanese goods is declining and import regulations are getting severer. Some people fear the world might sooner or later be divided into a few economic blocs, but if Japan were forced to organize one in Asia, the argument goes, she would be in a disadvantageous position *vis-à-vis* other advanced nations, because South-east Asia today accounts for less than a quarter of her trade (only 24.2 per cent of exports and 20.7 per cent of imports). Japan desperately needs industrialized markets, particularly the American market.

Fourthly, Japan theoretically could and should diversify sources of resources supply and potential markets, and should include China and the Soviet Union, which are in fact making approaches to her. The prospects, however, are not necessarily optimistic, mainly because of Sino–Soviet disputes (which require extremely discreet and, above all, balanced approaches by Japan), politico–economic instabilities inherent in socialist systems, the huge financial outlay involved, and Japan's lack of some specialized technology (e.g., pipeline-laying in frozen soil and offshore, or deep-sea oil exploration). Japan has therefore hoped for Japan–United States joint participation, though, in the absence of a favourable American reaction, the Soviet Union is 'likely to ask for Japan's participation at least in the Yakut plan ... without waiting for the US to take part', as a financial leader observed on his return from a Soviet tour.[10] The government has yet to give the green light, but Japanese business circles are 'not so seriously concerned about the diplomatic impact of Japan's participation in the natural gas project', since 'pipelines cannot carry tanks or troops'.

The fifth difficulty is Japan's lack of bargaining power, which proved near fatal during the oil crisis. Only a limited range of Japanese goods has achieved a sizeable share of the market in only a few countries while other sources of supply are readily available. Since Japan will have virtually no bargaining power when she faces another crisis, no counter-embargo will be credible, and another quick political accommodation might again become imperative. However, some official circles argue that Japan's only bargaining power might lie in technology, which would be extremely effective in international collaboration, if not for retaliatory use in a crisis. But Japan has yet to understand fully such political implications of technology.

Finally, there is a psychological difficulty: nuclear allergy. The CESC report argues that one way to deal with another crisis is for Japan to accelerate nuclear power generation from the present 0.7 per cent of total energy supply to 10.3–11.4 per cent in FY 1985. 'Once placed in a reactor,' the report explains, 'nuclear fuel will last longer than a year ... with some stockpiling it is possible to tide over a short interruption of energy supply.'[11] On the other hand, the report points out the extreme difficulty of siting nuclear power plants, because of a lack of geographical locations themselves and strong resistance from local communities.

All this reveals how badly Japan needs collaboration with the United States. Japan cannot simply afford to let the alliance deteriorate any farther than it did during the oil crisis. On the other hand, the oil crisis has reinforced the shift in emphasis on the Japanese side from the defence to the economic aspects of the alliance.

Alliance reassessed

From the day the treaty was revised under the existing title of 'mutual co-operation', Japan had placed equal weight on common defence and 'economic collaboration', but the emphasis gradually shifted to the latter. When economic and trade disputes increased she tended to make politico–economic accommodations under the spirit of economic collaboration – without which, in her view, there could be no common defence. The United States, on the other hand, seemed to have somewhat ignored the spirit, being too concerned about a global strategic balance under the Nixon administration to pay too much attention to the shift of emphasis in the treaty relationship with Japan. The argument for 'mutuality' of trade and security evidently reflected American emphasis on the latter in the form of criticism of Japan's 'free-riding'.

According to Webster's Dictionary, to collaborate is not just to co-operate but to 'co-operate voluntarily as a nation with another or other nations in international political or economic adjustment'. 'Voluntarily' and 'adjustment', the two key words, were evidently missing during the oil crisis. Japan had nothing to adjust voluntarily in a military sense (no staging base was used nor any arms supplies asked for), but she desperately wanted an adjustment in the economic/political field, where the

United States failed to adjust voluntarily or to collaborate with Japan. She thus had no choice but to reach a political accommodation with the Arabs. It was therefore a pleasant surprise when President Ford, in his first address to Congress, pledged to the Allies in the Atlantic community and Japan 'continuity in the loyal collaboration on our many mutual endeavours'. Now the question is how it can and will be implemented.

The first priority is to modify or reverse the process of de-Americanization that Japan adopted, along with her pro-Arab stance, during the oil crisis. Post-crisis experience has already revealed this stance has a limit. It should and will be maintained, but not at the price of further deterioration in the alliance with the United States – particularly now that the latter is making successful overtures to the Arabs. The de-Americanization can and should be halted for economic, political and technological reasons; but what about the military aspect?

During the crisis, Japan remained a concerned observer of its military aspects, and learned a crucial strategic lesson, too: that a new strategic weapon – oil – proved far more powerful as a political instrument than any arms, coercing even third parties, including Japan, to give up a position of neutrality. Thus on 17 October, only eleven days after the war broke out, the concerned observer suddenly found herself involved in the conflict as a major politico–economic target. Interestingly enough, no cry for a military response was heard in Japan: only solutions in economic and political terms were sought. This experience led to a reassessment of the strategic vulnerability of Japan which had been predicted in August 1969 following the six-day war of 1967. Editors of an almanac[12] warned against two basic strategic vulnerabilities: virtual dependence on a single source of oil supply (the Middle East), and the need to transport the oil by sea over a long distance. They were particularly pessimistic about the problem of sea transportation.

This is a many-sided problem, involving distance (about 6,800 nautical miles), narrow straits (e.g., Malacca and the entrance to the Persian Gulf), unstable strategic arenas (the Indian Ocean and the Taiwan Strait), increasing Soviet naval expansion and a declining or over-stretched American naval presence along the sea-lanes used by Japanese tankers.

All this indicates that even today Japan's oil transportation is vulnerable to all sorts of disruption or harassment. In fact, some people deduce that Japan could be politically coerced by a threat of oil embargo, physically punished by sealing off the Persian Gulf only, and economically harassed by disrupting passage through the Malacca Strait (forcing tankers to make a voyage three days longer and increasing freight costs by about 10 per cent). Furthermore, the long distance entails risks of encountering sea guerrillas, other acts of non-territorial harassment, and legal restrictions evidenced in the recent Law of the Sea conference.

To all these possibilities, however, Japan can think of no military response. In fact none other than a defence minister publicly ruled out the validity of what has been called 'destroyer diplomacy'. 'The use of military means to protect overseas interests is not only anachronistic but useless', he said.[13]

Moreover, military means are of limited effectiveness in countering the sealing of the Persian Gulf or harassment in the vast Indian Ocean. They are completely useless against legal restrictions imposed on the basis of international agreements. All this means that Japan must look for options other than military response.

First, Japan should refrain from diplomatic action which might undermine the basis of the super-power *détente*, lest the deterioration of American–Soviet relations should lead to the collapse of the political framework within which Japan can ensure economic and military security.

To this end, Japan must be prepared to pay a price: offering economic and development assistance (if necessary, going beyond commercial considerations) to the Soviet Union and accepting a politico-economic accommodation with the United States.

Secondly, intensive diplomatic efforts should be made to cultivate friendly relations with resources suppliers and the coastal nations of the Indian and Pacific Oceans, so as to minimize the chance of violation of Japanese overseas assets, and to obtain assistance in any emergency involving ships and other means of transport.

Thirdly, in the military field, Japan may have to build up a capability sufficient to take care of herself in a local, conventional armed conflict not only so as to defend herself but also so as to relieve the United States of her security burdens in the Far East, enabling her to divert her naval-air capabilities to areas where Japan cannot make any military contribution.

Fourthly, in order to meet the overall energy problems, Japan must make all necessary investment in R&D and other projects designed to reduce her dependence on overseas resources. The financial outlay might reach an unprecedented amount which would be acceptable only if the public is convinced of its reasonableness as a security cost and as a means to obtain a powerful bargaining instrument.

Finally, but not least important, Japan should try to extend international collaboration in the field of economic security to the Atlantic community. During the oil crisis, Japan shared with Europe the problem of relations with the United States, the possibility of partnership as oil consumers and a common concern about the Soviet Union. A closer European–Japanese relationship would in the first place be an attractive psychological counterweight to the bilateral relationship with the United States – which is basically an alliance of protector and protected. Secondly, the relationship can be expanded to a functional, and later institutionalized, trilateral link for pooling industrial and technological resources in order to solve energy and other problems.

Already the problems the world faces today – energy, pollution, population and food, among others – are so global in scope and so urgent in nature that their solutions require multinational collaboration.

NOTES

1 *Weekly Economist* (Japanese), 11 December 1973.

2 *Monthly Economist* (Japanese), January 1974.

3 Melvin Laird, *Final Report to the Congress of the Secretary of Defense*, 8 January 1973, p. 24.

4 *United States Foreign Policy for the 1970s* (Tokyo: USIS Special Report, 3 May 1973), p. 103.

5 Takashi Yasukawa, Ambassador to Washington, in an interview with *Sankei Shimbun*, 16 June 1973, p. 2.

6 Editorial, *Nihon Keizai Shimbun*, 20 August 1974.

7 Sogo Energy Chosa-kai (Comprehensive Energy Study Committee), *Chukan Torimatone* (Interim Report) (Comprehensive Subcommittee, 25 July 1974).

8 Reference to the text of the 15 July agreement on Co-operation in the Field of Energy Research and Development.

9 Two obstacles to this are a shortage of locations and the cost: 20 million sq. metres of land and about $5,000 million will be needed to stockpile an extra 30 days' reserves.

10 'Siberian Development – Japan's Sole Participation Hoped', *The Asahi Evening News*, 14 August 1974.

11 CESC *Interim Report, op. cit.*, p. 14.

12 *Anzen-Hysho* (National Security), 1969 ed., pp. 240–84. Published annually by Asagumo Shimbun (a Japanese *Stars and Stripes*).

13 Naomi Nishimura, 'My Philosophy of Self-Defense – on the Strategy of Limited Response', speech at the Tokyo Foreign Correspondents' Club, 11 October 1971.

CHAPTER ELEVEN

Naval competition and security in East Asia

Admiral Kazutomi Uchida

From Adelphi Paper 124, 1976

It is difficult to write on the subject of sea power without acknowledging the debt that we owe to such men as Alfred Thayer Mahan,[1] who was the first to theorize about sea power, and Halford Mackinder,[2] who reminded people of the importance of sea power by formulating his theory of power on land.

Recent events in Indochina have lent credence to Mackinder's theory, that power from the heartland, flowing toward the oceans, has overcome sea power. If Mackinder's land power is to be construed as consisting merely of Communism and military power, he has been proved right; if, on the other hand, it is to be understood as the value of the integrated culture of mankind, there is no relationship whatsoever between his theory and the situation in Indochina. The sea powers of the world today have cultures which are far more free and humane than those of the land powers, and these cultures have permeated, and are still permeating, the continents.

The concept of sea power has changed since Mahan's days. At that time the sea was the symbol of freedom, and the object command of the sea, but nowadays the peoples of the world are endeavouring to divide among themselves the wealth of the oceans. Nobody can predict whether this course will promote the future welfare and happiness of mankind.

War, with all its tragedy, has been a means by which nation states have been founded and consolidated. If war is also used to create a new order on the sea, mankind may well be said not to have grown any wiser over the centuries. A new age needs new rules; though we must treasure inherited theories and principles, we should also use them to help us to arrive at bold new ideas, going beyond inherited ones where necessary.

In our discussion of sea power, it is necessary to introduce the element of *dialogue based on mutual trust*, in addition to the considerations of *force* or of *weapons* which older generations included as a matter of course. We need to reflect on the fact that the majority of past international conflicts occurred as the result of misunderstandings about others.

The sea and East Asia

Let us look briefly at the importance the sea has for East Asia. World seaborne trade in 1973 is estimated to have amounted to some three billion tons, and of this Japan transported through the seas of East Asia six hundred and fifty million tons, or about 22 per cent. Some 33 per cent of Japanese imports was oil from the Middle East; of her exports 28 per cent was manufactured goods for the United States, while 24 per cent went to Southeast Asian countries. By value, Japan's trade in 1973 amounted to some $75 billion. The figures for other East Asian countries for that year were (approximately):

- South Korea $7.5bn
- Taiwan $8.2 bn
- Philippines $3.5 bn
- Indonesia $5.6 bn

The volume of China's trade is estimated to have been about $12.5 billion. Merchant shipping in the possession of the East Asian countries in 1974 is shown in Lloyd's Register to have been:

- Japan   38,700,000 tons
- South Korea   1,230,000 tons
- Taiwan   1,410,000 tons
- Philippines   770,000 tons
- Indonesia   760,000 tons

China is estimated to have possessed 1,560,000 tons, and Soviet ships in the Far East to aggregate some 2,000,000 tons.

Though East Asia is a focal area of important sea lanes, not many Japanese are aware of the fact. On the contrary, people write scenarios involving a future war of only short duration (about three months), in which the effect of warfare against shipping will be slow to make itself felt. As a consequence they argue that such warfare will not be undertaken in the future, or they assert that anti-submarine warfare is so difficult technically and so expensive that Japan cannot easily afford it. Perhaps it might be a good idea to paint a 'Dove of Peace' on every Japanese merchant ship, hoping that potential aggressors would not destroy the naive dreams of such people. But the scenario writers might contend that, since the dove could be mistaken for a hawk from the periscope of a hostile submarine, this would only cause the ship to be attacked.

Causes of international conflict

There are a number of potential causes of international conflict in East Asian waters.

Title to islands

(a) The Senkaku Islands, between Okinawa and Taiwan, became the territory of Japan as a part of the Okinawas in 1895, but in 1971 both Taiwan and China laid claim to them. The results of surveys conducted in 1958 by Japan, South Korea and Taiwan, with the co-operation of the Economic Commission for Asia and the Far East, revealed the possibility that the continental shelf of the East China Sea contains rich oil deposits. The problem of title to the Senkaku Islands, together with that of the exclusive economic zone involved, has now become impossible to ignore.

(b) In the South China Sea title to the Paracel Islands has been claimed by both China and Vietnam; at present they are occupied by the former. Title to the Spratly Islands has been claimed by Taiwan, the Philippines and Vietnam, and the three countries are now occupying their respective portions of the islands. As important sea routes pass through waters surrounding these islands, any military conflict that involves them might cause serious hindrance to maritime trade. Conflict might also arise between the countries concerned over seabed oil deposits.

(c) Take shima in the Sea of Japan was placed outside Japan's administrative jurisdiction under the occupation policy of General MacArthur and is now occupied by South Korea. Japan, however, does not acknowledge that her title has been lost, and this, along with the associated exclusive economic zone, will become a problem between Japan and South Korea in the future.

(d) Taiwan is geographically an island but possesses every condition necessary for an integrated state. We cannot deny this fact, even though she holds no seat in the United Nations and is not recognized by certain states. But James Schlesinger, US Secretary of Defense, said in a press conference on 1 May 1975 that as long as the United States has a treaty obligation, Taiwan would be defended. This treaty continues in effect, as does the American legal obligation.

Law of the sea

As far as the law of the sea is concerned, we have only the Informal Single Negotiating Text, prepared by the chairmen of the three Committees of the Geneva Conference on the Law of the Sea, as a guide. It is difficult at the moment to predict the eventual outcome with any certainty, but it is probable that the 12-mile territorial sea, 200-mile exclusive economic zone and the archipelago doctrine, and so on, will finally be agreed to by the majority of the participating nations. If so, the following problems are likely to arise in the future:

(a) The Straits of Malacca, Lombok, Ombai-Wetar, Tsugaru, Soya, etc., will be international straits, through which the Informal Single Negotiating Text now advocates uninterrupted transit passage. If, however, states with international straits within their territorial waters impose troublesome conditions beyond those related to safety and pollution, there may be many hindrances to maritime traffic passing through these straits.

The width of the Tsushima Straits is 25 miles. If the extent of the territorial sea should become 12 miles, there would remain a free-water zone one mile wide along the median line, but it would demand great skill on the part of a submerged submariner to pass through such narrow free waters.

(b) As long as the right of innocent passage through archipelago waters, as claimed under the archipelago theory of Indonesia and the Philippines, is recognized, and free passage through the sea lanes or routes normally used is allowed, few problems are likely to arise. But if it is not, sea traffic through these waters may be subject to difficulties and hindrance.

(c) In the Sea of Japan, the Yellow Sea, the East China Sea, the South China Sea, etc., the exclusive economic zones will be delimited by the respective coastal states. In this case, if China forcibly puts forward her cherished thesis of natural prolongation of continental territory, most of the sea bed of the East China Sea will belong to her, and this would deal body blows to the other states concerned with regard to sea-bed oil resources. Since the average depth of the East China Sea is only some 188 metres, resources can be exhausted by means of advanced technology, and so China's claim to its sea bed is of particular importance.

Japan has decided to carry out the Japan–South Korean joint development undertaking in the area to the west of Kyushu, which is to become the exclusive economic zone of Japan. A problem to be resolved later is how the division of the continental shelf and exclusive economic zones at the median line should be dealt with.

The oil deposits in the sea beds of the South China Sea and the Bay of Siam look very promising, and may also create a number of problems for future settlement.

(d) There are various questions concerning fishing rights within the exclusive economic zones, but so far negotiations and compromises have been reached between various coastal states and others concerned. Negotiations are now under way between Japan and China concerning the Yellow Sea and the East China Sea.

(e) In 1973 the Soviet Union made public a map of manganese nodules in the Pacific Ocean. The South Pacific Ocean is also regarded as a promising area for these, so that various problems related to the delimitation of exclusive economic zones may arise between the states concerned. Under such circumstances, unless mutual understandings as to the law of the sea are reached after discreet discussions, the law thus enacted will give rise to many international disputes.

If the tasks of protecting interests arising out of the provisions of the new law, or of keeping watch over infringements, are entrusted to the navies of the states concerned, there may be no navy in the world able to carry out such duties satisfactorily. It is for this reason that a new rule of dialogue based on mutual trust must be introduced.

Security organization

The organizations which play important roles in the security of East Asia are the United States' Bilateral Treaties of Mutual Defense with Japan, South Korea, Taiwan, and the Philippines, together with the South-East Asia Treaty Organization (SEATO)[3] and Australia–New Zealand–United States (ANZUS) pacts. These organizations are not so grandiose as NATO. As the East Asian countries differ from one another in their problems and their environment, there may be more advantages in bilateral treaties with the United States than in membership of a multilateral defence organization. There will be fewer frictions, and a more speedy response to emergencies.

As against this, the North Korea–Soviet Treaty of Friendship, Co-operation and Mutual Assistance is in force in the Communist countries, and there is also the Sino–Soviet Treaty of Friendship, Alliance and Mutual Assistance. Though the latter treaty is effective until 1980, relations between the two countries are such that it is doubtful if it has any practical application.

The Soviet Union is now proposing that a collective security treaty should be concluded between Asian countries, including Japan. One of its objects is alleged to be the containment of China, and most Asian countries are unlikely to welcome it, not only because they realize it may bring new confrontations among themselves but particularly because some of them are showing more inclination to approach China in the wake of the collapse of South Vietnam in 1975.

On 11 May 1973 Lee Kuan-Yew, Prime Minister of Singapore, suggested while on a visit to Japan that a task force, consisting of naval units of the United States, Australia, New Zealand, Western European countries and Japan, should be formed with a view to defending the peace and security of the sea areas of South-east Asia. In my view this suggestion is more realistic than the Soviet proposal for a collective security organization in Asia, but it seems to me that Japan, in the light of her Constitution, cannot at this stage agree to this 'Lee Theory'. Japan cannot, however, isolate herself from other countries, since she is dependent upon foreign supplies for resources of every kind, not least for large amounts of food and oil.

The military situation

It is quite incomprehensible why, in order to liberate themselves, the peoples of Indochina should have been subjected to military aggression in a period of international détente. If there is force in the slogans that peace is a war without bloodshed, and that political compromise is only the preparation for establishing a new front, then there will always be a threat to those who regard freedom as essential. The threat can be made explicit or otherwise; it can be manipulated according to the situation and strategic objective at a particular time or in a particular place. Even when no threat is visible, it does not mean that it is not there.

Looking at East Asia with this in mind, it would seem that threats of three kinds exist: (1) the basic and long-term threat of the expansion of the Soviet Navy and the growing extent of its movements; (2) the urgent threat of confrontation between South and North Korea, which needs attention now; and (3), less urgent but always needing attention, the threat of confrontation in the Taiwan Straits.

The Soviet Navy

As far as the Soviet Navy is concerned, we feel very uneasy, because its strength in the Far East is very considerable:

- Total tonnage   1,100,000 tons
- Aircraft   2,300
- Submarines   about 110, including some 36 nuclear and about 48 missile-firing
- Guided-missile ships   about 60

This strength is still increasing. The repair facilities in the Far East are being modernized, and at Komsomolsk construction of cruisers, and perhaps of nuclear submarines, may be possible. Construction of the second Siberian Railway is thought to have started, so that the logistic capacity of the fleet will increase. The Soviet supply of weapons to North Vietnam has been remarkable. The Soviet Union is reported to have asked for the use of Cam Ranh Bay in return, and she may get it sooner or later, in spite of counter-moves by China.

The movements of the Soviet Union's naval vessels in support of her merchant ships have increased year by year. In the *Okean* exercise in April 1975 four task groups were operational in the Pacific Ocean, and the number of aircraft approaching Japanese air space amounted to 126. The Japanese Air Self-Defence Force carried out more than 30 scrambles. Oceanic survey by Soviet intelligence and survey ships is very extensive, indeed unparalleled, as is clearly shown by the large number of ships involved: about 47. There is only the US Seventh Fleet to rely upon as a main counter-weight to this Soviet sea power.

An anti-submarine capability must be the first charge on the resources of any nation precipitately faced with the possibility of starvation and exhaustion by hostile blockade. A force structure based upon the overall striking force of the United States and the regional defence forces of various indigenous nations must be the basic military concept in East Asia.

Korea

The threat of conflict in Korea is described above as urgent because of the danger of the North invading the South through a miscalculation of the current military balance and the application of the US–South Korean Mutual Defence Pact. The threat is either of occupation of South Korea by mass attack or of the instigation of internal disturbances in South Korea by secret-service units or fanatic groups, or both. The recently discovered tunnels into South Korea, and others now being excavated, and the activities of North Korean submarines and missile-boats, show that there is danger. Tension has become particularly high around the coasts and islands in the vicinity of the demilitarized zone, and if these islands are attacked by bombardment or bombing, we would be seeing the signal for commencement of all-out invasion of the South. There would be fears that it might lead to another world war.

North Korean guerrillas have been infiltrating into South Korea by land or sea, in the belief that, since the South was on the verge of revolution, they would be welcomed as heroes. This is a very dangerous miscalculation. The South Korean Navy, of some 75,000 tons, is a crack force which has been built up to full strength and prepared against possible invasion from the North. Without naval success, even a full-scale land invasion could hardly succeed, because once North Korea had been defeated on her sea flank there would be a danger of being attacked in the rear by combined US and South Korean amphibious forces. An invasion carried out by North Korea alone would have no probability of success, and other Communist countries should not encourage her in this ambition.

Taiwan

Taiwan faces the same problem as Japan, in that she is very vulnerable to blockade by hostile submarines, which need only be few in number. It is, however, inconceivable that Taiwan would be subjected to such a blockade at present. China is in a very strained situation on her northern border and would hardly want to risk being involved in three-way operations against the United States, the Soviet Union and Taiwan – even though she possesses some 50 submarines and over 600 fast motor boats of various kinds. The Taiwan Navy, which is getting submarines from the United States and has begun ASW training, is a well-balanced force of some 140,000 tons and must pose a considerable regional deterrent.

In contrast to the problem of the Taiwan Straits, the seas to the south can be said to be in a relatively stable environment. The 130,000-ton Indonesian Navy, the 105,000-ton Australian Navy and the naval bases at Subic Bay in the Philippines and Singapore are playing their respective roles in ensuring the security of these southern sea areas.

Maritime competition

The above is a bird's-eye view of threats and naval competition in East Asia. We should, however, remember that the continental countries do not, in the last analysis, depend on sea power – nor, therefore, do they need it as much as the maritime countries, for whom it is essential for progress and survival. Mere physical equivalence in sea power would leave the Free Nations fatally handicapped; the maritime countries' sea power must be superior if they are to compete with that of the land-oriented countries. Greater co-operative efforts are therefore needed.

The role of Japan

Since the collapse of Vietnam the attitude of Japan, in particular, has become a focus of attention in the world. The United States President and Secretaries of State and Defense have emphasized the importance of Japan and have repeatedly pointed out that the security of South Korea is necessary for the security of Japan. The Japanese economic assistance and technical co-operation offered to the various Asian countries has been favourably commented on, but where the security of East Asia is concerned she has been criticized for not having fulfilled her responsibilities as a large trading country towards ensuring the safety of the sea lanes. There are some misunderstandings in such criticisms.

The present interpretation of her Constitution prohibits Japan from sending her troops overseas, but, making full use of her geographical environment, she has strengthened the naval defences of the important straits within her jurisdiction. She has enhanced her anti-submarine hunter-killer capability, thereby endeavouring to deter hostile submarines from being deployed in the outer seas and oceans and also contributing to the safe movements of the US Seventh Fleet in East Asian waters. But, with only a small force of some 160,000 tons and 1,000 aircraft, her control of the air space over and sea space on her surrounding waters is clearly insufficient. An effort is therefore being made to build up these forces as a matter of high priority.

It is evident that the security of Japan should be firmly established within the framework of the overall security of Asia, including that of South Korea. Although Japan will not send her troops overseas, even for the sake of that security, she should support the freedom of movement of any American forces which may be necessary for the security of Asia.

In spite of having the capability for nuclear development, the Japanese government has adopted non-nuclear-weapon principles (which most nations seem to welcome) which prohibit the manufacture, possession and bringing into Japan of nuclear weapons. The definition of 'bringing into Japan' is construed by the Japanese government to include transit of nuclear weapons through her territorial waters, giving rise to criticisms that this is inconsistent with her reliance on the US nuclear umbrella for her protection. I believe that these principles are the expression of the Japanese government's earnest desire to avoid any use of nuclear weapons. This, just as much as the American–Soviet numerical balance in nuclear weapons, is an important psychological factor in deterring any use of nuclear weapons.

Japan welcomes foreign military students of her security affairs. Exports of weapons to countries involved in military conflicts are prohibited in Japan, but the export of technology for peaceful purposes will be willingly undertaken. This is the type of co-operation that Japan can best offer and one that can leave a legacy of good in the long term.

I have some personal proposals for a fuller role for Japan in security affairs – based, however, on the premise that the US Navy should never withdraw nor decrease the strength of the Seventh Fleet against the wishes of the Asian nations. It is desirable that Japan, with the co-operation of the US Navy, should carry out joint studies for the control of shipping, the conduct of rescue operations and the gathering of intelligence necessary in case of emergencies. To provide early warning of dangers, it is hoped that a joint plan might be made to launch reconnaissance satellites into orbit. I also hope that some joint research and development organizations and funds can be established with the United States acting as promoter and sponsor, perhaps with the headquarters in Hawaii and with branches established in the relevant country. Nuclear weapons have shown how an overwhelmingly superior weapon can become a factor in obtaining political and military advantage, and it will be important to pool ideas and efforts on other important weapon technologies – the laser, for example. Developing nations may have excellent ideas but few funds and facilities for research and development; developed nations should be prepared to share these with them.

The national defence policies of Switzerland and Sweden are excellent examples for Japan in her choice of role. Japan is, however, far more dependent on the sea than these two nations and so she should put more effort into consolidating her regional sea power.

Epilogue

I began by saying that in a new age new rules should be introduced. A proper dialogue is certainly one of these, but discussion can only be sustained if it is underpinned by power. Mackinder said that land power backed by sea power becomes formidable, and we now see each of these elements still flourishing. I would like to emphasize therefore that, in order to counter the threat, we should form an organic framework of the global and regional sea powers. It is urgent for our free nations to aggregate their power and co-operate with one another, improving mutual understanding and friendship through effective consultation, through dialogue.

NOTES

[1] See A. T. Mahan, *The Influence of Seapower upon History 1660–1783* (1890) (London: Methuen, 1965).

[2] Halford J. Mackinder, *Democratic Ideals and Reality* (London: Constable, 1919).

[3] At the SEATO meeting in September 1975 it was decided to phase out the standing treaty organization but to leave the treaty itself in force.

TIMELINE OF EVENTS

1980s

April 1980

The 30-year Treaty of Alliance between the USSR and China expires, in effect leaving them in a no-treaty state.

September 1980

The Iran–Iraq War begins.

September 1980

Japan, in a joint initiative with Australia, establishes the Pacific Economic Cooperation Council (PECC).

January 1981

Ronald Reagan is inaugurated as the 40th US president.

May 1981

The government of Prime Minister Suzuki Zenko rules that collective self-defence is banned under its constitution, so Japan cannot contribute to the defence of allies abroad.

March 1982

US President Ronald Reagan submits a budget proposal to Congress, requesting a 13% defence-spending increase.

April 1982

The Falklands War begins between the UK and Argentina.

November 1982

Nakasone Yasuhiro is elected prime minister.

December 1982

The UN Convention on the Law of the Sea (UNCLOS) opens for signing and enters into force in 1994.

October 1983

Japan and China demand that the USSR reduce its number of SS-20 *Sabre* missiles deployed in Asia.

November 1983

Ronald Reagan makes his first official visit to Japan as president.

December 1983

Prime Minister Nakasone Yasuhiro forms the first coalition government since the LDP's creation in 1955, following the dissolution of the Diet in November 1983 (a result of former prime minister Tanaka's conviction).

June 1984

Prime Minister Nakasone Yasuhiro delivers the 1984 IISS Alastair Buchan Memorial Lecture in London.

September 1984

South Korean President Chun Doo-hwan visits Japan, the first South Korean president to do so since the 1965 normalisation of bilateral ties.

October 1984

Indian Prime Minister Indira Gandhi is assassinated by her bodyguards.

November 1984

Despite doubts over the LDP's political stability, Nakasone is re-elected leader of the LDP.

March 1985

Mikhail Gorbachev becomes leader of the Soviet Union.

September 1985

The Plaza Accord is signed, weakening the US dollar against the yen and helping to fuel Japan's asset-price bubble.

 **DOMESTIC EVENTS**    **INTERNATIONAL ENGAGEMENT**    **KEY GLOBAL EVENTS**

April 1986

The Chernobyl nuclear reactor in the USSR explodes.

May 1986

Japan hosts the 1986 G7 Summit in Tokyo.

August 1986

Japan agrees to limit its semiconductor exports, at the behest of the US and during a period of intense US–Japan trade friction.

September 1986

The IISS Annual Conference is held in Kyoto, Japan, opened by Foreign Minister Kuranari Tadashi and attended by Dr Henry Kissinger, Professor Kosaka Masataka and former ambassador of Japan to the US, Okawara Yoshio.

September 1986

Doi Takako is elected head of the Japan Socialist Party and becomes the first woman in Japan to head a political party.

March 1987

The *Washington Times* breaks the Toshiba–Kongsberg scandal, wherein Toshiba and Kongsberg, a Norwegian company, were found to be exporting machinery to the Soviet Union that could greatly enhance its submarine systems.

April 1987

Japanese National Railways is privatised and divided into six regional railway companies.

June 1987

The 'June Democratic Struggle' protests take place in South Korea, eventually forcing the government to hold free elections.

May 1988

Prime Minister Takeshita Noboru announces Japan's 'International Cooperation Initiative' while in Europe, comprising three pillars: the strengthening of cooperation to achieve peace, the strengthening of international cultural exchange and the expansion of Japan's Official Development Assistance (ODA).

June 1988

The *Asahi Shimbun* breaks the 'Recruit Scandal', a corruption and insider-trading scandal that leads to the resignation of several politicians, including then-finance minister Miyazawa Kiichi.

June 1988

The Intermediate-Range Nuclear Forces (INF) Treaty enters into force. The Euro-Atlantic signatory countries destroy a category of nuclear-capable ground-launched ballistic and cruise missiles.

September 1988

The European, Canadian, Japanese and US space agencies sign the Space Station Cooperation Agreement, setting the groundwork for what would become the International Space Station.

November 1988

Japan becomes a signatory of the Convention on the Physical Protection of Nuclear Material, which entered into force in February 1987.

December 1988

Japan's first national consumption tax bill is forced through the Diet by Prime Minister Takeshita Noboru.

January 1989

Emperor Hirohito dies, ending the Showa era and ushering in the Heisei era under Emperor Akihito.

January 1989

George H.W. Bush is inaugurated as the 41st US president.

April 1989

Prime Minister Takeshita Noboru resigns amid the ongoing Recruit Scandal.

 **DOMESTIC EVENTS**  **INTERNATIONAL ENGAGEMENT**  **KEY GLOBAL EVENTS**

May 1989

The Bank of Japan implements the first of a series of interest-rate rises, heralding the end of the late 1980s economic bubble.

November 1989

The Japanese Trade Union Confederation (also known as RENGO), Japan's largest national confederation of trade unions, is founded.

November 1989

The Berlin Wall falls.

June 1989

Chinese People's Liberation Army forces kill and wound large numbers of student protesters in the Tiananmen Square massacre.

November 1989

The first Asia-Pacific Economic Cooperation (APEC) meeting is held in Australia, attended by Japan and 17 other nations.

December 1989

By the end of the decade, Japan has surpassed the US as the world's largest provider of ODA.

 **DOMESTIC EVENTS**    **INTERNATIONAL ENGAGEMENT**    **KEY GLOBAL EVENTS**

CHAPTER TWELVE

The changing security circumstances in the 1980s

Yukio Satoh

From Adelphi Paper 178, 1982

Soviet challenges

The most serious aspect of the deteriorating security situation in the 1970s was the continued Soviet military build-up, both nuclear and conventional. The attempts of the Soviet Union to use every possible opportunity to expand her influence over strategically important areas in the Third World, directly or by use of surrogates, contributed to a sense of unease in Japan. Such attempts appeared to be aimed at obtaining military ascendancy over the United States and her allies and at establishing Soviet political influence world-wide.

In conjunction with the American involvement in the Vietnam War and the sluggishness of efforts to strengthen US military capability in the aftermath of that war, the relative waning of American military superiority over the Soviet Union became a subject of increasing speculation in the course of the 1970s, as the strategic nuclear balance between the two super-powers shifted to one of perceived parity. The qualitative superiority of NATO forces, which used to be assumed to offset the quantitative superiority held by the Soviet bloc in a conventional force balance in Europe, began to decline. Improved Soviet air and naval projection capability began to limit the global influence of US forces and increased the Soviet ability to project power to distant areas. Soviet expansion of influence to strategically important countries in the Third World, such as Ethiopia, South Yemen, Vietnam and Afghanistan, strengthened the Soviet strategic position, particularly in the area surrounding the oil-rich Gulf States.

Furthermore, under the influence of these changes, the political momentum for detente in East–West relations declined in the United States towards the end of the 1970s. Most importantly, differences of perception emerged between Washington and West European capitals concerning detente and the need for East–West political dialogue and economic relations. It is reasonable to presume that Moscow saw opportunities to divide the Atlantic Alliance over the issue of detente.

The Asian and Pacific region was not excluded from Soviet attempts to put pressure on allies of the United States. The Soviet Union deployed a new generation of offensive weapons to the region, including a *Kiev*-class aircraft carrier, an *Ivan Rogov*-class amphibious assault ship, *Backfire* bombers and SS-20 missiles. She acquired access to air and naval facilities in Vietnam and increased her continuous naval presence in the Indian Ocean using new facilities acquired from Ethiopia and South Yemen. These developments, together with an increased military presence along the Sino–Soviet border since the late 1960s, added to the Soviet ability to project power in the Western Pacific and into the Indian Ocean. What was particularly alarming in Japanese eyes was the development of Soviet military bases and the stationing of up to a division of ground combat forces on the islands of Etorofu, Kunashiri and Shikotan off the northern coast of Japan, in defiance of the outstanding Japanese territorial claims to the islands, and in the absence of any military threat from Japan.

These Soviet attitudes may have derived from anxiety that the USSR was becoming encircled by what she perceived as an emerging United States–China–Japan alliance against her. However, irrespective of Soviet intentions, the growth of Soviet military power in the Far East and in the Indian Ocean, together with a shift of the global strategic balance to something like parity, clearly made American intervention in the region more costly than before. Yet, contrary to Soviet hopes, the military build-up has increased Japanese interest in defence, and has caused a reappraisal in ASEAN of the need for American military support. While it is quite reasonable to presume that the growth of her deployed military power – and her increased naval presence in the Pacific and Indian Oceans in particular – was partly designed to enhance the Soviet Union's political position in the Asian and Pacific region, she has so far failed to translate her military power into political leverage.

The military presence of the United States in the Far East underwent many changes in the course of the 1970s. Politically, these changes had a direct impact on the Asian scene. The intention to minimize US military involvement in Asia became apparent with the enunciation of the Nixon Doctrine, the withdrawal of forces from South-east Asia, and the announcement by the Carter Administration that it would withdraw ground combat forces from South Korea. All these aroused misgivings among US allies in Asia about the credibility of the American commitment. Although a number of steps were subsequently taken by the United States to reassure her allies that her commitment remained, and a general shift of American public opinion in support of stronger military capability alleviated much of the anxiety on the part of America's allies in Asia, the public reaffirmation of a 'swing strategy' and the deployment of naval vessels of the US Seventh Fleet to the Indian Ocean to protect Western interests in the Gulf demonstrated, in the eyes of the Japanese and other Asians, the scarcity of US forces in the Western Pacific. The much discussed deficiencies in the combat readiness of the American forces added to their anxiety.

It is broadly assumed that the Soviet Union will continue to expand her military power at least through the 1980s. Neither the increasingly difficult economic situation which the Soviet Union will have to face nor the change in her leadership which is expected to take place during the decade seems likely to affect Soviet policy in this respect.

Moreover, it seems probable that the Soviet Union will place an even higher military priority on the Far East in the 1980s. She would be prompted to do so both in order to cope with what she views as the emergence of a United States–China–Japan alliance against her and to confirm her position as a super-power in the international politics of the region. Her attempts to appease the anxiety of the West European public (for the sake of dividing Western Europe from the United States) might result in moving some of her military resources deployed in Europe to the east of the Urals. The need to defend strategically important naval bases in the Far East will grow, since a stronger naval presence in the Western Pacific and the Indian Ocean will become increasingly important in any Soviet strategy directed towards Asia and the Gulf. Accordingly, it is expected that Soviet military capability in the Far East, particularly naval and air, will continue to increase, both to enhance Soviet ability to project power and for purposes of defence. The economic development of Eastern Siberia, and the eventual completion (possibly late in the 1980s) of the BAM (Baikal–Amur) trunk line – the second Siberian railway to connect Tayshet to the northwest of Irkutsk and Sovetskaya-Gavan on the strait of Tatar at the northern end of the Sea of Japan – would greatly help the logistic support of Soviet forces in the Far East. Furthermore, the negotiations between the United States and the Soviet Union on the reduction of intermediate-range nuclear missiles might lead to an increase in SS-20 and other intermediate-range missiles in Asia, should the negotiations be focused only on reducing weapons capable of reaching Western Europe.

Politically, too, it is likely that the Soviet Union will attempt to influence Japan away from the United States and China. President Brezhnev's unusual emphasis at Alma Ata in August 1980 on the prospect of expanding economic ties with Japan, and his speech at Tashkent in March 1982 emphasizing Moscow's readiness to improve relations with Japan, for example, seemed to be aimed at driving a wedge between Japan and the United States and China. (The Tashkent speech seems also to have been designed to upset relations between the United States and China, taking advantage of Sino–US wrangles about American arms sales to Taiwan.) There were not many attractions for Japan in such a shift of allegiance, however, because of continued Soviet denial of Japanese territorial claims over the Northern Territories.

The American response

Given the heavy spending on naval power detailed in the Reagan Administration's defence budget, American military capability in the Western Pacific and the Indian Ocean also seems set to grow in the course of the 1980s. However, it will be some time before increased expenditure can be reflected in force numbers. Moreover, it is quite likely that American efforts to improve the military balance with the Soviet Union will be directed in the first instance to the modernization of nuclear forces, and, in the field of conventional capability, to more vulnerable areas (such as the Gulf and the Indian Ocean) which will require more immediate attention. The concept of a Rapid Deployment Force (RDF) to move American forces in the Western Pacific to Europe or the Gulf in the event of an emergency in those areas will make it probable (at least theoretically) that her military capability immediately available in the Far East would be limited in the event of a concurrence of crises. Furthermore, the forward-basing of American forces in the Western Pacific will not be without problems. The presence of US forces in South Korea and the Philippines will become increasingly costly under the pressure of inflation. In the case of the Philippines, the United States had to agree to pay $500 million from 1980 through 1984 in order to obtain the right to use military bases (Subic Bay and Clark Field) under the Agreement of 1979, which will be subject to review before 1984. The political stability of both South Korea and the Philippines cannot necessarily be depended on in the future.

China

China attracted much attention from Western strategists as they saw the increasing global challenge from the Soviet Union in the late 1970s. From the Western viewpoint, China's movement towards closer economic and political, and possibly military, co-operation with the United States, Japan and Western Europe appeared to provide an opportunity for improving the global military balance against the Soviet Union. Indeed the existence of China, hostile to the Soviet Union, aids the West in the context of the East–West military balance, because it to some extent diverts Soviet strategic attention and resources away from the West.

However, the implication of the 'China factor' for the East–West military balance in this region is more complex. First, suspicion, deepened by the normalization of US–China and Japan–China relations, seems to have inclined the Soviet Union to strengthen her military capability in the Far East as well as to undertake diplomatic countermeasures such as a Treaty of Friendship with Vietnam. Second, a rapid increase in Chinese military power, should it occur, would have disturbing implications for the security of the South-east Asian countries. Third, it is very questionable whether China would be disposed to cooperate externally with the West beyond pursuing her own interest of strengthening her position with respect to the Soviet Union. And, fourth, US–China political relations might become strained over issues relating to Taiwan, and particularly American arms sales to Taiwan.

During the next five to ten years China will continue to be pre-occupied with the domestic problems deriving from post-Mao power struggles for leadership and from the modernization process in the country. Moreover, the modernization of Chinese conventional forces (which are at present no match in qualitative terms for Soviet military capability) will take a long time. In fact the modernization of China's military capabilities was given the lowest priority among the four targets of modernization – agriculture, industry, science and defence. Given the speed of the Soviet military build-up, it is more likely that the gap between Soviet and Chinese military power will widen in the coming years. But the most important factor is that China's political direction remains unpredictable. It is too early to judge whether what the Western analysts consider as the pragmatic approach in foreign policy of Deputy Chairman Deng Xiaoping and his group will prevail. Their position could become vulnerable if the social and economic changes which they have been advocating run into serious problems. The effects of the eventual replacement of leaders by the next generation are also important but difficult to gauge. However, it seems likely that China will take a more neutral position between the super-powers in order to increase her room for diplomatic manoeuvre.

All in all, it is more plausible to assume, at least for planning purposes, that China could add only a little more than she does now to the East–West military balance in the 1980s, particularly in the area of conventional forces. Her nuclear capability will be modernized gradually in line with the advancement of her science and technology, but there is little reason to assume that Chinese nuclear capability will affect the East–West strategic balance during the 1980s any more than it does now. While it is important for Western nations to make efforts to keep China close to the West, it might be rather imprudent for them to play the so-called 'China card' against the Soviet Union, particularly in the context of the East–West strategic balance in Europe.

The regional balance of power

None of this implies, however, that Soviet military capability in the Asian and Pacific regions will come to exceed that of the US in the 1980s. The basic weakness of Soviet forces in this region persists. This weakness is a result of the difficulty of sustaining logistic supplies through tenuous lines of communication along the Sino–Soviet border; the vulnerability of Soviet naval vessels to blockade in the straits around Japan; the severe natural conditions of Siberia and the Soviet Far East, which limit the manoeuvrability of forces during the long winter; and the lack of reliable allies in the region. All these elements will remain basically unchanged during this decade.

Yet American military operations in the Western Pacific will be increasingly limited by Soviet air and naval forces in the event of a military confrontation. In the context of Japanese planning, it ought to be taken into consideration that, in the event of a Soviet armed attack on Japan, the American forces necessary to support Japan would meet considerable interference.

This does not mean, however, that a Soviet attack on Japan is imminent. The question of whether the Soviet Union will attempt a direct armed attack needs to be considered in a much wider context than that of the narrow military balance around Japan. Although it is impossible to read the Soviet mind, it seems most unlikely that the Soviet Union will dare to take such a risk so long as the Japan–US Alliance appears solid, and the Japanese defence posture seems likely to promote resistance to any Soviet military attempt to invade Japan. To attack Japan under such circumstances would be too costly, militarily and politically.

On the other hand, Japanese lifelines (such as the routes for oil supply) extend world-wide, so that any increase in Soviet influence in other areas – South-east Asia, the Indian Ocean and the Gulf, for example – would have serious implications for Japanese security. In this context, Japan can no longer be indifferent to the East–West global military balance, and American efforts to deter Soviet control of these regions will be a matter of vital interest. This will be increasingly relevant as the global implications of Soviet military capability become apparent in the 1980s.

The security of oil supply

Securing a steady oil supply presents another serious challenge to the security of Western industrialized democracies, and of Japan in particular. Japan imports over 99 per cent of her oil to produce three quarters of the energy required to sustain her economy. The fact that over 70 per cent of the oil she imports comes from Gulf states makes peace and stability in the Gulf region, and the security of the sea-lanes connecting the Gulf and Japan, a matter of vital importance to her security.

In the interests of minimizing the strategic vulnerability caused by her heavy dependence on oil – and Gulf oil in particular – Japan, in common with other countries, has been taking such measures as (a) placing oil in reserve storage (sufficient to run the economy for over 90 days); *(b)* diversifying the sources of oil supply (Indonesia, China, off-shore Sakhalin, Mexico and Alaska have been explored); *(c)* intensifying measures for energy conservation; and *(d)* encouraging the use of alternative energy resources (such as coal and nuclear energy) as well as the development of new energy ones (for example, solar and terrestrial heat and energy from nuclear fusion). Yet it is widely assumed that a heavy dependence on oil will continue throughout the 1980s and thereafter (in 1990, some 58% of total energy demand will be for oil). The Gulf states are expected to continue to be Japan's largest source of oil for the whole of this period.

This dependence will, therefore, continue to cause Japan constant anxiety about security in the 1980s and possibly afterwards. There are, however, a number of questions relating to oil supply which the Western industrialized nations have not yet solved.

First, the geographical proximity of the Gulf to the Soviet Union makes the region vulnerable to Soviet military interference. The disappearance of a militarily strong pro-Western regime in Iran (which the United States once tried to make a regional stabilizing power) and the Soviet military invasion of Afghanistan have adversely affected the United States' (and therefore the Western) strategic position in the region. The reluctance on the part of many local Arab states to allow the United States access to military bases (except for limited facilities in Somalia, Oman and, further away, in Egypt) makes it even more difficult for the United States and her allies to counter-balance the Soviet geographical advantage.

Second, relations between Gulf states are likely to remain unsettled for a variety of reasons, such as religious and ethnic antagonism and rivalry as well as the differences in political systems. The Iran–Iraq war was a typical example of purely indigenous instability. The Arab–Israeli dispute, too, remains a constant cause for concern. Regional conflicts could easily disrupt the outflow of oil, as happened in the case of the Iran–Iraq war. Moreover, regional differences might be exploited by the Soviet Union to increase her influence.

Third, many regimes in the oil-rich Gulf states do not appear domestically stable in the face of Islamic fundamentalism and looming financial difficulties. Social and economic changes, brought about by economic and social modernization, might affect the present political structure (as in the case of Iran). In this context, the future stability of many Gulf states under traditional rulers cannot be counted on; nor are other regimes in the region any more stable.

Fourth, the Arab states might use oil as a lever to achieve their political aims, as they did in 1973 (public denial notwithstanding), although such a possibility may have become somewhat less likely for a number of reasons – such as the preparedness (if still insufficient) of the industrialized nations for such an eventuality; the internal splits in the Organization of Petroleum Exporting Countries (OPEC); the restraining pressure from non-oil-producing developing countries, who would suffer most from the deterioration of the world economy which such measures would cause; and the increased need of some oil-producing countries to maximize sales of oil in order to carry out their own economic and military projects.

Of course the Soviet Union is not necessarily in a position to be able to exploit these vulnerabilities. The Gulf States are basically on their guard against possible Communist infiltration, which would constitute a threat to the present regimes. The Soviet invasion of Afghanistan added to their political and psychological concern about possible Soviet interference, but the Soviet Union could well be tempted to manipulate Gulf politics in order to strengthen her position *vis-à-vis* the

West. The assumption that the Soviet Union herself might run into difficulties over oil – at least to export to Eastern Europe – would add to her motivation to seek more assured access to Gulf oil.

All in all, there is no panacea to cure the constant sense of insecurity of the Western industrialized democracies deriving from their critical dependence on Gulf oil. How political, economic and military resources could be organized to protect the common interests in the Gulf region will therefore remain a major preoccupation of the Western industrialized democracies.

Such co-operation will have to cover a broad range of issues including, among other things, military preparedness to secure a steady oil supply against local disturbances and to deter possible Soviet military interference, political efforts to stabilize the region, economic and technical assistance to meet the requirements of Gulf states as well as efforts to minimize Western dependence on Gulf oil. Yet to organize such co-operation among the Western industrialized nations will be far from easy, as was demonstrated in the case of economic sanctions against Iran over the issue of the American hostages. There will be differences in perceptions of Arab politics, in the evaluation of the efficacy of military measures, and in political and economic interests involved in the region. Above all, there will be competition for oil. All these differences and rivalries among the Western nations will add to the difficulties of organizing concerted efforts among them.

Moreover, no organizational mechanism for co-ordinating such efforts is readily available. Neither NATO arrangements nor the Japan–United States Security Arrangements can be a basis for such co-operation because their functions are geographically limited by their respective Treaties. Summit meetings tend to be too confined to economic issues and can hardly deal with detailed matters. It is highly desirable that some sort of mechanism be created to manage the co-ordination of all the policies of the Western industrialized democracies towards the Gulf.

Irrespective of the difficulties involved in organizing Western efforts, it is quite likely that the United States and some West European countries will move towards the adoption of certain programmes for concerted action to protect their common interests in the Gulf. They might ask Japan to contribute, in one way or another, to such programmes, because she would clearly benefit from them. The need for a rapid increase in Japanese self-defence capability will be emphasized in this context, because it could release some of America's resources to be deployed for the purpose of protecting Western interests in the Gulf. Japanese economic and technical co-operation with strategically important countries in and around the Gulf – such as Oman, Turkey, Egypt, Somalia, Kenya and Pakistan – will be pursued. Demands for financial contributions from Japan either to offset or to share a certain portion of the costs for a concerted Western military effort to secure the flow of Gulf oil (as well as to deter Soviet military intervention in this region) might be forthcoming. Furthermore, although the United States and Western Europe are aware of the constitutional restraints on Japanese military contributions in this area, they might well eventually come to consider it appropriate for Japan to contribute to purely defensive operations (such as minesweeping). Should her co-operation be sought, for example, in the area of mine clearance for the purpose of securing the safe passage of Japanese vessels through the Gulf, it would be extremely difficult for her to refuse, particularly as the mine-sweeping capability of the Japanese Maritime Self-Defence Forces (MSDF) is regarded internationally as 'one of the world's most modern'.[1]

Tensions in the Asian and Pacific regions

Military tension in the Korean Peninsula, in South-east Asia and along the Sino–Soviet border will continue to have an impact on Japanese security.

The Korean Peninsula

It is very likely that any large-scale military conflict in the Peninsula would involve Japan, at least indirectly. The United States' military support of South Korea in the event of an armed conflict in the Peninsula would depend upon the use of bases in Japan, while the close geographical location of, and the affiliations between, Japan and Korea (over 680,000 Koreans are resident in Japan, for example) make it probable that a large number of refugees would arrive in Japan in the event of a military conflict. Japan also has considerable economic interests in South Korea. It would be extremely difficult, therefore, for her to keep herself detached from any large-scale military conflict in the Korean Peninsula.

Since 1953 the US, China and the USSR have combined to avoid any outbreak of armed conflict in the Korean Peninsula (which would inevitably involve them), although there have been frequent military incidents along the demilitarized zone (DMZ) and political turbulence in the South, including the assassination of President Park. North Korea can hardly contemplate a large-scale military offensive without the support of the Soviet Union, upon whom she relies for the supply of modern military equipment and oil. Both the Soviet Union and China have been reluctant to become involved in a direct military conflict with the United States, whose forces are stationed in South Korea. Nor has the United States wanted to be involved in any military conflict on the Korean Peninsula, an involvement which would inevitably involve Soviet or Chinese intervention.

It is in the interests of all that a political settlement be worked out through talks between the parties involved that would ensure a more stable peace in the Korean Peninsula and replace the Armistice Agreement (which has been in effect since 1953). However, the possibility that things can be made to move in such a direction still appears somewhat remote. Great power self-restraint, and equilibrium in the military balance between North and South (including the US forces) must be maintained. The presence of American forces in South Korea will be indispensable for both purposes, particularly in the light of the increase in the military capability of North Korea. President Carter's decision to postpone the withdrawal of the Second Division and the assurance of President Reagan to President Chun that America would maintain the present levels of military forces in South Korea were therefore welcomed in Japan.

The modernization of South Korean forces within the framework of American–South Korean security arrangements, and the political stability and the economic development of South Korea are equally important for preserving peace in the area.

Japan has long been expected by South Korea and the United States 'to provide all support short of military forces to the broad deterrence equation',[2] and has been responding to such expectations through economic and technical co-operation. With respect to military co-operation, both the United States and South Korea are well aware of the constitutional restraints which make it impossible for Japan to make a direct military contribution to the security of South Korea. Her contribution has been confined to the provision of the bases to allow American forces to carry out their commitment to the defence of South Korea (although the use by US forces of facilities and areas in Japan as bases for military combat operations is subject to prior consultation with Japan).[3] The increase in Japanese defence capability is also expected to make an indirect contribution.

However, relations between Japan and South Korea remain difficult. They have been much hampered in recent years by the Korean authorities' handling of the leading dissident Kim Dae-Jung, who was widely believed in Japan to have been taken away forcibly from Japan by agents of South Korea. The commutation of the death sentence on Kim Dae-Jung into one of life imprisonment seems to have improved political relations between the two countries to some extent, but his treatment by the South Korean Government may still remain a potential source of political tension. On the other hand, the South Koreans tend to see the Japanese as unappreciative of the sacrifice which they have been making for the sake of peace in the entire Far East, including Japan. Reflecting such sentiment, the South Korean Government has recently made explicit demands that Japan demonstrate her support for the South Korean efforts to deter the North in the form of increased economic assistance.

A more self-confident and assertive younger generation in both Japan and South Korea will add a new dimension to the bilateral relationship. It could even provide an opportunity for the two nations to bury the historical memory of the Japanese annexations of Korea. However, it is just as possible that the rivalry between the two nations could increase.

All in all, relations between Japan and South Korea will continue to require careful handling, and intensive efforts need to be made by both sides to create a new relationship. Should political relations become strained, it would threaten Japan's immediate security and might well affect Japan–US security relations.

South-east Asia

The stability of South-east Asia is also important to the security of Japan. Japan is deeply involved economically and politically with the countries of ASEAN. Japanese trade with ASEAN countries, which includes the import of oil from Indonesia (14.3 per cent of crude oil imports in 1980) reached $34.2 billion (12.7 per cent of Japanese trade) in 1980. Furthermore, the sea-lanes connecting Japan and the Gulf states pass through this area, including the vital Malacca Strait.

Neither the withdrawal of US forces from Indochina nor the unification of Vietnam by Hanoi has brought lasting peace to Indochina. In December 1978 Vietnam sent her troops into Kampuchea to establish a puppet regime in Phnom Penh. In February 1979 China launched an attack along the Sino-Vietnamese border for the alleged purpose of 'punishing' Vietnam. The Chinese troops were later withdrawn, but the Vietnamese troops remain in Kampuchea, posing a threat to Thailand. The Soviet Union, which concluded a Treaty of Friendship and Co-operation with Vietnam in November 1978, supported the Vietnamese military campaign in Kampuchea and took the opportunity of the Chinese attack to obtain regular access to Vietnamese military facilities, particularly to the strategically important naval facilities at Danang and Cam Ranh Bay. Meanwhile, the exodus of refugees from Vietnam and Kampuchea became a destabilizing factor in South-east Asia.

The countries of ASEAN have united politically behind Thailand. They became diplomatically active in pursuit of the withdrawal of the Vietnamese troops from Kampuchea and the self-determination of the Kampuchean people. They also became increasingly interested in their mutual security. Yet the members of ASEAN are inclined to place more emphasis on the political stability of the region and on the development of their own economies than on collective military arrangements to counterbalance Vietnamese interests, let alone Soviet interests.

The Japanese economic and political commitment to ASEAN deepened with Prime Minister Fukuda's visit to all five countries in 1977. Diplomatically, too, Japan has backed ASEAN, particularly in attempting to alleviate the destabilizing effect of the Indo-Chinese refugees, in seeking the withdrawal of Vietnamese troops from Kampuchea and in promoting a political settlement for that country. She increased her economic assistance to Thailand in the wake of the Vietnamese invasion of Kampuchea and at the same time suspended her economic assistance to Vietnam. These Japanese initiatives were welcomed by the ASEAN countries, not least because they were deeply concerned at the decline of American interest in South-east Asia in the aftermath of the Vietnam War and because Japan was expected to be able to provide much of what the ASEAN countries needed, especially financial and technical assistance and political support. Prime Minister Zenko Suzuki also visited the five countries in 1981 making these his first official visits to foreign countries on coming into office.

Looking to the future, Vietnam will almost certainly continue to be a destabilizing influence in the region. Vietnamese efforts to control Kampuchea and the rest of Indochina will continue to threaten neighbouring countries, and the antagonism between China and Vietnam could again result in armed conflict. China would almost certainly support Thailand against Vietnamese aggression. Yet Vietnam will not be able to continue her campaign in Kampuchea, let alone a larger military campaign beyond Kampuchea, without the support of the Soviet Union, and the Soviet Union might be unable to refrain from attacking China should the latter once again attack Vietnam.

Political and economic difficulties in ASEAN could also lead to internal turbulence and subversion. More important, the coherence of ASEAN, which was prompted by the challenges from Vietnam, remains yet to be consolidated; differences of interests and perceptions among the ASEAN countries, deriving from their different historical, cultural and racial backgrounds as well as from differences in economic structure and development, might come to the surface as they pursue national objectives.

The roles to be played by the United States and Japan in this region seem set to increase in the 1980s. The United States is likely to demonstrate her interest in the security and independence of the ASEAN countries by providing military assistance as well as economic assistance and political support. Moreover, the presence of American military forces in the Western Pacific will serve to defuse the sense of insecurity felt by the ASEAN countries as they are increasingly pressurized by the increasing Soviet military capability in the region. Japan's efforts to increase her ability to defend herself will contribute in the long run by making it possible for the United States to spread her limited resources more widely, but there will be considerable reluctance on the part of the ASEAN countries to countenance a rapid increase in Japanese military capability. The bitter memory of the Japanese occupation during World War II remains.

Politically and economically, Japan will be expected both by the ASEAN countries and the United States to further increase her contribution. Economic and technical co-operation and political support to the ASEAN countries will define the Japanese role in this region. Diplomatically, Japan will also be expected to persuade the United States to turn her attention more to South-east Asia and to persuade China to refrain from assisting Communist elements in the ASEAN countries.

The Sino-Soviet border

It is likely that Sino-Soviet political confrontation will continue for at least the next five to ten years, despite the recent Soviet calls for dialogue with China. Although it is possible that a Chinese attack on Vietnam might provoke a Soviet counter-offensive against China, it is reasonable to assume that the Soviet Union would avoid a large-scale military move against China. While *rapprochement* between the USSR and China, should it occur, would have a drastic effect on the global East–West military balance, any large-scale military confrontation between the two Communist rivals would also destabilize security patterns in Asia. However, while it seems unlikely that either of these possibilities will occur, the implications of Sino-Soviet *political* confrontation for Japanese security will remain more or less a subject for speculation.

Western political pressure

Pressure from the United States, and possibly from Western Europe, for larger Japanese contributions to the common security interest will be another important feature of the external circumstances which Japan will face in the 1980s. Japan has long been a passive partner in her Alliance with the United States, particularly in the area of security. Although during the 1970s the United States wanted her to take on a greater share of the responsibilities and burdens for the political stability of Asia as well as for her own security, the US refrained from pushing Japan too hard. This was partly due to the fact that Japan began in the latter part of the 1970s – and without pressure – to take a number of diplomatic initiatives aimed at maintaining international stability, particularly in South-east Asia. She began also to step up her efforts to provide for her own security. Perhaps another reason why the United States did not exert any pressure was to avoid any recurrence of the political flurry caused in the American–Japanese Alliance by the 'Nixon shocks' at the beginning of the 1970s. There was also a prevailing view among American experts on Japan that too much pressure would be counter-productive.

However, the US has increasingly felt that Japanese defence modernization is still too little and too slow. Preoccupied with a more imminent, global challenge from the Soviet Union since the late 1970s, she has begun to express greater interest in Japanese efforts for self-defence, particularly in the wake of the Soviet invasion of Afghanistan. Through a series of high-level talks, which began with the visit of Defense Secretary Harold Brown to Tokyo in January 1980 and culminated in the talks between Prime Minister Ohira and President Carter in May 1980, the United States is reported to have pressed Japan to expedite the modernization of the SDF planned under the *National Defence Programme Outline*. More specifically, the US requested Japan to complete the implementation of the Japanese Defence Agency's Medium-Term Defence Build-up Plan (FY 1980–84) a year earlier than originally scheduled. The Reagan Administration, with its particular emphasis on the need to improve the East–West military balance, became more than ever insistent in demanding a rapid increase in Japanese defence efforts (and in defence spending to this end). Since Prime Minister Suzuki stated at the National Press Club in Washington in May 1981 that Japan could, within the limits of her Constitution, defend her own territory, the seas and skies around Japan, and her sea-lanes to a distance of 1,000 miles, the US Government has been pressing the Japanese Government to attain such a defence capability as promptly as possible. The United States stresses that 'to satisfy those critical defence missions will require increases in defence spending substantially greater than the current annual growth rate'.[4] US Defense Secretary Caspar Weinberger reportedly presented a view to the Japanese Government in March 1982 that Japanese defence spending would have to be increased by 12 per cent annually in order to attain the capability to defend sea-lanes to a distance of 1,000 miles.[5]

The United States' motivation for requesting greater Japanese efforts in the area of security is no longer simply to dispel Congressional criticism that Japan is getting a 'free ride' on security. Indeed such criticism intensified in Congress as a result of a worsening of the trade imbalance with Japan. Underlying it is a perception widespread in the United States that Japan is spending too little on defence for her economic capacity, while the US is making painful efforts to produce a huge military budget which helps defend Japan (and West European allies). Yet there is now a strong conviction in the United States of the need for all-out efforts by herself and her allies to increase their military capability in order to counterbalance a rapid Soviet military build-up in global terms. This, too, seems to underlie US pressure for larger Japanese (and NATO) defence efforts, along with the feeling that Japan should shoulder a larger share of the burden of her own defence, so as to release American military resources for the defence of Western interests in the Gulf and the Indian Ocean. There also seems to be a US desire to demonstrate politically the solidarity of the Western Alliance by organizing concerted military efforts to meet the Soviet challenge.

In the future, American demands for larger Japanese defence efforts (and therefore for more defence spending) will grow more strident. Japanese defence policy will become more than ever a subject of alliance politics between Tokyo and Washington. It is alleged that the Reagan Administration has so far been emphasizing its intention to avoid exerting public pressure on Japan over the issue; yet there is growing frustration in Congress and among US defence and foreign policy experts over what they perceive as the sluggishness of Japanese defence efforts, and it may be difficult to contain demands for a rapid improvement. The American public, favourably disposed towards the strengthening of military power against the Soviet Union, will no doubt support such demands.

Western Europe will no longer remain a silent bystander in this process. For example, those countries which wish to see greater American military efforts to protect Western interests in the Gulf region without jeopardizing the security of Western Europe will seek a Japanese contribution to the cause of protecting the common interests in the Gulf. As in the US, rapidly mounting West European frustration over Japanese behaviour in trade will foster criticism of what is perceived as the Japanese 'free ride' on security. It is also conceivable that a growing tendency to count Japan as a member of the Western Alliance in a broader context will make West European countries more candid about Japanese security policy. Although the impact of West European views on Japanese security policy will be somewhat limited, pressure from Western Europe will no doubt add to the need for Japan to consider the possible implications of her security policy for her political position among the Western industrialized nations.

Nuclear arms control

Arms control and arms reduction, particularly in the nuclear field, are another important dimension of international affairs with significant implications for future Japanese security.

Backed by public abhorrence of nuclear weapons deriving from the experience of nuclear holocaust, Japan has been appealing internationally for the reduction of nuclear weapons and their ultimate abolition. Despite a capability to produce them, she has not done so, and, in the context of the Japan–US Security Arrangements, she has consistently refused to contemplate the introduction of American nuclear weapons into her territory, even though she has been (and is) dependent upon American nuclear deterrence for her safety. The United States, well aware of this strong feeling has allegedly respected the Japanese position. In the context of security, Japan, trusting

American extended nuclear deterrence, has appeared to sense little threat of nuclear attack on the country. Indeed, many Japanese consider that the prospect of a nuclear confrontation between the two superpowers is remote, and that the possibility of Japan being attacked with nuclear weapons is even more unlikely so long as American nuclear weapons are not stored there. Whether or not the United States would risk a nuclear war for the sake of Japan remains a matter for concern, but the Japanese have been less persistent than the West Europeans in questioning the credibility of American nuclear deterrence - possibly because they are reluctant to be involved in American nuclear strategy.

Nevertheless, Japan is bound to become more sensitive to the state of the nuclear balance between the two super-powers. The drift in the US–Soviet strategic military balance, from American ascendancy to perceived parity, has already tended to place in doubt the reliability of American nuclear deterrence. It has increased, at least theoretically, the possibility that the Soviet Union might be tempted (should she see an opportunity) to make nuclear threats against Japan, on the grounds that waning nuclear superiority would cause the United States to hesitate before risking a nuclear confrontation with her. As long as the US–Soviet nuclear balance remains one of perceived parity, however, the Japanese seem likely to be able to convince themselves of the credibility of American nuclear deterrence, but any signs of further deterioration would seriously undercut that credibility and have important implications for Japanese security policy.

In this context, the Soviet–US negotiations on strategic nuclear arms will become a subject of much more acute interest to Japan than before. The negotiations on reducing intermediate-range nuclear weapons will seem even more important, for these will have a more visible bearing upon the regional

East–West nuclear balance in Asia. The particular features of SS-20 missiles which mean that they could be used against Japan without posing a direct threat to the United States will add to Japanese concern, just as they have been alarming Western Europe. So long as the reduction of intermediate-range missiles is addressed in a global context, with due consideration of the implications for Asia, it could serve the security interests of Japan. But should the United States and her NATO allies concede Soviet demands that the reduction in Soviet weapons should be confined to those capable of reaching Western Europe, this would be harmful to Japanese security interests. Such arrangements might allow the Soviet Union to increase the number of such weapons in Asia, and China gives her a pretext to do so. Politically such an outcome, carrying with it the implication that the Atlantic Alliance is seeking to pursue its security interests at the expense of the Japanese interests (or Asian interests more generally), would force Japan to question how far her security interests coincide with those of the other Western industrialized nations.

It appears that Japan has not so far been particularly sensitive to the deployment of SS-20 missiles to Asia. This is largely due to the fact that, with so many Soviet nuclear systems already in Asia, the addition of SS-20 missiles does not appear, at least to the Japanese public, to make a fundamental difference. However, as the Japanese come to know more of the particulars of these missiles, and their implications for Japanese security, they will become as seriously interested in their reduction as are the West Europeans.

Other developments

There are also a number of other external developments which would significantly affect the future direction of Japanese security policy. The North-South relationship, East–West trade and, more broadly, the world economy are also issues which, among others, would affect Japan's security perceptions, but their impact on her security policy would be less direct than those described above.

Clearly domestic conditions, both political and economic, will also have a significant bearing upon the direction of Japanese security policy, but domestic conditions (like security policy itself) will not remain unaffected by external circumstances. More significantly, the direction Japanese security policy takes is likely to affect the evolution of Japanese politics in the coming decade. This will be discussed in Chapter IV.

NOTES

[1] Japan's Contribution to Military Stability in North East Asia (a report prepared by the US Arms Control and Disarmament Agency for a Sub-committee on East Asian and Pacific Affairs of the US Senate Foreign Relations Committee, June 1980), p. 34.

[2] Richard L. Sneider (former US Ambassador to the Republic of Korea), 'Prospects for Korean Security', Part II.6 *of Asian Security in the 1980s: Problems and Policies*

for a Time of Transition, (Santa Monica, Calif: Rand Corporation, November 1979).

[3] Exchange of Notes between Japanese Prime Minister Nobusuke Kishi and US Secretary of State Christian A. Herter, 19 January 1960.

[4] Remarks by US Secretary of Defense Caspar W. Weinberger before Japan National Press Club in Tokyo, 26 March 1982.

[5] *Asahi Shimbun,* 2 April 1982.

CHAPTER THIRTEEN

The 1984 Alastair Buchan Memorial Lecture

Prime Minister H.E. Yasuhiro Nakasone

Survival 26-5, 1984

The Alastair Buchan Memorial Lectures were established as a tribute to the Institute's first Director. The 1984 lecture was delivered on 11 June 1984 by H.E. Yasuhiro Nakasone, the Prime Minister of Japan.

Asked to predict on a political scene, one of Japan's most enduring politicians once said, 'In politics, one inch ahead, it is pitch dark', meaning that one cannot predict what the future holds.

Today, the future of our world is also unknown and unknowable. Anything could happen.

In such times as ours, one can write an infinite number of scenarios for the future. Each possible scenario must be closely studied, and most of these scenarios need to be put in separate files, for possible later use.

When something happens, then we must decide which file to open, and which scenario to act upon. The course we choose has profound consequences for our peoples. So it is all the more important that our scenarios be carefully thought out and constantly updated.

The decision on which scenario to adopt can be discussed among friends, because friends have common concerns and can act together. Today, friends often gather to talk about many scenarios, and to reach consensus as to which scenarios are more likely and viable. At the Williamsburg and London Summits, we discussed economic, political and peace-keeping issues, and examined common choices among the possible scenarios.

Today I should like to review one scenario – to explain the choices that Japan has made and will make, and to suggest a policy orientation for the Free World.

The path Japan has taken

Out of the ashes and ruins of World War II, and with deep remorse for the past, the Japanese people dedicated themselves to international peace, and resolved never again to go to war. They set, as their goal, to make Japan a 'nation of peace and prosperity'.

Left with the ruins of war and lacking its own natural resources, Japan needed peace if we were to rebuild our economy and feed our hundred million people. Japan also needed to achieve domestic stability by forming the broadest possible popular consensus. For these reasons, our objective of 'peace and prosperity' was chosen carefully and wisely.

Japan has been especially careful in its handling of security questions. The Japanese people sincerely believed that their nation should never again fall prey to militarism or become a military power. And this belief was consistent with the wishes of Japan's neighbours.

When East–West tensions grew, and brought conflict to East Asia, Japan opted for self-defence arrangements under its newly adopted 'Peace Constitution'. Japan signed a security treaty with the United States, and created its own self-defence forces. Consistent with our Constitution, these Japanese self-defence forces were not to possess such military capability as to threaten our neighbours, and their purposes and nature were limited solely to self-defence.

In the years since, Japan has sought to ensure its own security and to contribute to the maintenance of peace and stability in the Far East, through strengthening its ties of mutual trust and co-operation with the United States, and by gradually building a moderate defence capability.

In this way, Japan's course was firmly set in the direction of 'peace and prosperity'. Blessed with a hard-working people and favourable circumstances, Japan has achieved spectacular gains in its economy and industrial technology. In these decades, the nations of Europe, and the nations of the Asia–Pacific region, have also made great economic progress.

During this period, there were many changes in the international situation, including the Vietnam War, the shaking of the Bretton–Woods system, two oil crises, and normalization of Sino-American relations. Also, the once-predominant economic and military strength of the United States saw a relative decline.

As the world underwent such major structural changes, it became clear that Japan could not simply keep on responding passively to changing circumstances. Japan's position demanded that we work actively for world peace and prosperity.

In the cause of maintaining world peace, Japan was called upon to play a more active role in its own defence. With its enormous economic strength, Japan was also called upon to provide more economic co-operation to the developing countries, so as to promote world peace and prosperity.

Despite Japan's best efforts, when I assumed the office of Prime Minister in 1982, the situation was serious. A vast gap still existed between the Japanese reality and what the rest of the world expected of Japan.

One of the first things I did in office was to address the people on Japan's need to move towards an 'international nation' –

a nation that bears international responsibilities in keeping with its international position. I stressed the need to open our trade and capital markets; the need to speak out with a greater political voice for international peace and conventional and nuclear arms control; and the need to strengthen our economic co-operation with the developing countries. In essence, I advocated that we shift from a passive posture of responding to events, to an active posture of influencing events positively.

In the year and a half since then, Japan has enacted four separate packages of market-opening initiatives. At the Williamsburg Summit last year, I strongly supported the need for co-ordinated international political action. Whatever difficulties this may cause at home, I am determined to pursue the course I have taken.

Japan's choice

In the present situation, what policies does Japan choose?

First, Japan chooses as national policy to maintain our peaceful and stable society on the basis of political and economic co-operation and solidarity among the countries of North America, Western Europe and Japan – countries that share common values of freedom and democracy.

Our three regions – North America, Western Europe and Japan – account for half of the world's economic production. Together, we form the backbone of the Free World. Together, we have great responsibilities to maintain our solidarity, in order to secure world peace and security, and to uphold our common values.

The seven-nation Summit Meeting of industrialized democracies is an important forum for our trilateral co-operation. To commemorate our tenth Summit Meeting, it is entirely appropriate that we have adopted the London Declaration on common democratic values, and have reaffirmed our solidarity.

Japan is determined to continue to contribute positively to our trilateral solidarity.

Second, Japan chooses to look to its future as a nation of the Asia–Pacific region. With a long and distinctive cultural and social heritage, Asia is now finally on the threshold of a new economic prosperity. Japan is resolved, with the global perspective of an Asian nation, to strengthen our friendly relations with neighbouring countries in the region.

President Theodore Roosevelt was one of the first to talk about a 'New Pacific Era'. At the start of the twentieth century, he spoke of the shift of the point of importance from the Mediterranean to the Atlantic and once more from the Atlantic to the Pacific.

Today, we see the Pacific region gaining world attention as a centre of economic growth. The countries of the region are overcoming various difficulties, and are achieving solid economic development – not just the United States, Canada and Japan, but also in North-east Asia, the ASEAN nations, Australia, New Zealand and Latin America.

I know that some people in Europe have mixed feelings about the dynamic economic development under way in the Asia–Pacific region, and the increasing attention which the United States is giving to this region. But we should not think in terms of the Atlantic versus the Pacific, or Europe versus Asia. It is not a question of one against the other.

The Asia–Pacific region includes the United States and Japan – two nations that share with Western Europe the values of democracy, freedom and the market economy. Dynamic development of this region will benefit the entire Free World. And Asia–Pacific economic development is impossible without co-operation and interdependence with Western Europe.

Building on its long experience of internationalism, its efforts to forge homogeneous and strong regional bonds, so well exemplified in the development of the European Community, Europe is assured an influential and leading role in world affairs, certainly for as far as we can see into the future. My dream is that of a strong Europe and a developing Asia–Pacific linked together in mutual prosperity, and working together for the common good of all peoples.

Third, Japan attaches great importance to Japan–China relations.

China has set itself the goal of raising its per-capita income from $250 in 1980 to $1,000 by the end of the century. To achieve this ambitious goal, the Chinese people have embarked upon a bold industrial and social reorganization – the so-called four modernizations. China seeks to lay the foundations for its development as a great modern nation by easing social controls and raising individual living standards. If China is to succeed, peace in the region and realistic and independent Chinese policies must be maintained.

People often talk about the so-called 'China card'. But in the light of independent and realistic policy of today's China, could there really be a China card?

I believe that Japanese efforts to promote our friendly relations with China can help to improve the climate for world peace and stability.

Fourth is Japan's relationship with the Soviet Union. These relations are strained, not only because the basic issue of Japan's Northern Territories remains unresolved, but also because of the deterioration in East–West relations since the Soviet intervention in Afghanistan.

Yet, like Europe, Japan and the Soviet Union are neighbours, and neither can move away from the other. Thus, we believe the more strained our relations become, the more important it is that we patiently maintain and strengthen our dialogue with the Soviet Union.

Fifth are the policy choices Japan has made in its relations with the developing countries.

A hundred years ago, Japan was itself a developing country. Only recently did Japan join the ranks of the advanced industrialized countries, becoming the only Asian member of the OECD, and the only Asian country to take part in the seven-nation Summit Meetings. Our conscience reminds us not to forget the past, and to co-operate economically, technologically and culturally with the developing countries.

Many developing countries are members of the non-aligned movement, but they are not all the same. Their non-alignment or neutrality is an expression of their national pride, anticolonialism, independence, aversion to external interference in their affairs, of a piece with their desire for economic development.

I have long said 'there can be no prosperity for the North without prosperity for the South'. For the South's development, we must promote the smooth flow of capital and technology, and the mutual exchange of resources. Special attention must be paid to technology transfer, and the building of managerial, academic and other skilled human resources. In all these fields, Japan intends to step up its efforts.

The choice for the free world

Next, I wish to turn to the policy choices I see for the Free World, as we seek to ensure world peace and prosperity.

Nuclear disarmament and East–West relations

The gravest problem facing the world today is how to prevent nuclear war and preserve world peace. We must never allow World War III to occur. This is not a choice, but an imperative.

World peace today is tenuously maintained by a balance of deterrence between the nuclear super-arsenals of the United States and the Soviet Union. We must find a way out soon from such day-to-day peace under this sword of Damocles, towards a secure and lasting peace for mankind. The first step is to agree on effective, realistic and verifiable nuclear arms control.

The Free World needs a common strategy – with both short- and long-term perspectives and flexibility – to respond to the Soviet challenge. We should be neither subservient nor inflexible. We should broaden our perspective – beyond the military, to include the political, economic, cultural, and other human aspects of our relationship – in our patient and determined quest for peaceful co-existence.

Western solidarity

Such a response is impossible without Western solidarity – the second of our policy choices.

In the Free World, we will always have discussion, debate and friction. The interaction of ideas is vital for our progress and development. In East–West relations, however, we must unite behind our common decisions, and co-operate in implementing them. We must consult closely with each other, constantly exchanging information and opinions.

The development of *Pershing* II and cruise missiles begun at the end of last year was one vital step the West took jointly in facing the Soviet Union.

The prevailing speculation is that the Soviet Union will not return to the INF and START negotiations until after the American Presidential election. However, as I said at the outset, the future is unknown and unknowable. We should be prepared for whatever may happen. Maintaining the strength of our unity, we should collectively and actively call on the other side for peace and negotiations.

Responding to local tensions

Our third choice concerns the important question of how to respond to such local conflicts and tensions as the Iran–Iraq conflict, the Lebanese problem and the situation on the Korean Peninsula. These conflicts and tensions do not only mean suffering and sacrifice for the immediate region. The problems created for safe passage in the Gulf by the Iran–Iraq conflict, and the impact this has had on the Western countries show how local conflicts have global significance. With East–West tension now on the rise, local conflicts and tensions can easily escalate into East–West confrontation.

The conflict between Iran and Iraq has already caused terrible loss of life and property, and is posing a major threat to world peace. It is imperative that international efforts be made now to prevent any further escalation of the conflict.

The situation on the Korean Peninsula remains serious. Terrorist attacks, such as happened last year in Rangoon, are inhuman and impermissible, and carry the risk of heightening tensions.

Promoting a meaningful dialogue between North and South Korea is most important for improving the situation. I hope that all countries concerned will, while respecting the views of both North and South Korea, work together to ease tensions, facilitate dialogue between them, and thus create a climate conducive to the Peninsula's long-term stability.

Efforts to revitalize the world economy
Given our countries' economic strengths and growing inter-dependence, the world economy is another area in which our joint responses are needed. This is our fourth choice.

Our post-war world economy owes much to the very open and outward-looking policies developed within the IMF and GATT frameworks. In this climate, the engines of the free-market economies were able to run at full throttle, achieving for us an unprecedented level of material wealth. Economically, our free-market countries today stand head and shoulders above the socialist states.

However, serious economic problems have arisen in recent years, including slower growth, fiscal deficits, high interest rates, growing unemployment, and inflation. Under pressure to respond to these problems, we now face the danger that we may look only at our own domestic difficulties, and adopt closed or inward-looking policies. The developing countries, too, now find their development programmes seriously hampered by the burden of mounting international debts. All these issues demand our attention. Any one of them could bring down the post-war economic order, if not handled properly.

We must breathe new life into the free-market economic system for the twenty-first century. To do this, it is essential to maintain and expand the system of free economic exchange among nations. The free-trade system can only be sustained by the untiring efforts of all countries.

The London Summit affirmed the need to prepare for a new round of trade talks, taking up where the Kennedy and Tokyo Rounds left off. This is of great significance. We must make constant efforts to counter the trend for protectionism. The proposed new round is just like pushing a car uphill. If we idle even for a moment, the car will roll back down and free trade may revert to protectionism. The time has come not to limit ourselves to trade, but to promote industrial co-operation and structural adjustment, and to build up transnational ties of all kinds among enterprises.

We also need to promote co-operation in science and technology, to bring a new wave of innovation to our market economies. The world is on the verge of a new era of technological break-through. We are entering the age of the 'information society' – with technologies that will open up new frontiers for human civilization in the twenty-first century.

Policy towards the developing countries

No less important is the fifth choice of policy for the Free World, that of strengthening our dialogue and co-operation with the developing countries.

For the sake of all mankind, the industrialized countries should help the developing countries improve their living standards, achieve social and economic stability, and build up their infrastructures. We must act to preserve world peace and prosperity, by seeking co-operative and friendly relations with as many countries as possible.

We should remember that some countries regard the Summit Meetings as a forum where rich nations get together to ensure their continued dominance. We must dispel such misunderstanding. But it is true that the interests of the industrialized and developing countries do sometimes conflict.

The developing countries' debt problem, for instance, has confronted the industrialized countries with a dilemma. If the industrialized countries raise interest rates to hold down domestic inflation, this will drive the debt-burdened countries deeper into debt. If we help the developing countries export more to pay off their debt, we run the risk of damaging industries in the importing countries.

Europe has a long history of involvement with the developing countries, especially in the Middle East and Africa. Japan hopes to learn from Europe's experience, and to work with Europe for the stability of these regions. I think there is a great need for such co-operation between Europe and Japan.

I said earlier that 'there can be no prosperity for the North without prosperity for the South'. We must never forget that we all live on one planet, that we need each other, and that we share a common destiny.

Better summit meetings

Finally, I should like to comment on the Summit Meetings of the industrialized democracies. These Summits have focused primarily on economic issues. Recent world developments have made it increasingly important to preserve the peace and ensure our common security, as the basis for our economic prosperity. It is only natural that our Summit Meetings should be able to respond flexibly to important trends and changing circumstances.

As I have said, we should be ready for whatever may come. In our age of infinite scenarios, it is vital that the Summit nations meet regularly to reaffirm and defend their shared values. Our discussions have great political significance and influence. And I believe our joint resolve to defend our common values speaks more strongly than any ordinary treaty.

I believe the Summits should continue as a forum where a small number of world leaders speak frankly with one another. It is also important that cabinet ministers or experts be able to meet for discussions, whenever an important international issue arises. The Summit countries have shown they can take concerted action on such problems as the oil crisis, hijackings and international terrorism.

Conclusion

I have tried here to sketch Japan's policy choices and those for the Free World. Before I conclude, I should like to give you my impressions of the differences between Europe and Asia, the kind of differences existing between engineering and medicine, as they affect our strategic outlooks.

In my travels to the Republic of Korea, the ASEAN countries, China, Pakistan and India, I have felt anew how each country differs in geopolitical terms and in national personality. There is great diversity among the culturally distinct and geographically separated countries of Asia.

Some countries are aligned with the United States. Others adhere to non-alignment. Still others are independent-minded socialist states. Some are under transitional military rule; others are full-fledged parliamentary democracies.

There is a rich mosaic of religions: Buddhism, Islam, Hinduism, Christianity, Confucianism and many more. Even within a single country, there may be three or four main religions, and any number of ethnic and linguistic groups. The fact that two countries are both Buddhist does not guarantee that they will be on friendly terms. Nor does the fact that they have different political systems necessarily mean confrontation between them.

Asia is several thousand kilometres from east to west, and the landscape is a mixture of islands, peninsulas, continents, mountains, deserts and oceans – with an immense climatic variety.

By contrast, Europe is far less diverse. Europe shares in the Christian tradition, and is geographically more compact. After World War II, Europe was sharply divided into East and West. The political and military divisions remain today sharp and deep, and offer no prospect of easy resolution. There are neutral and non-aligned countries in Europe, of course, and there are also important ethnic and religious differences. But I think the pattern is not so complex, nor the differences so great, as in Asia.

Asia's diversity is sustained by the historical differences, and the unique cultural traditions. Thus, it is not useful to paint things in clear brushstrokes of black and white. Rather, most people are willing to accept diversity as diversity, and to live and let live. I believe that Asian peoples tend to think and act in terms of peaceful co-existence within diversity, a willingness to talk things out in search of consensus, and an emphasis on the things that unite rather than divide.

When conflict does break out in Asia, it is necessary to respond flexibly and comprehensively, assessing the many historical, social, psychological, geopolitical, cultural, religious and other factors behind the conflict.

Does this mean East and West must remain forever inscrutable to each other? I do not think so at all. I believe that great progress in communications, the mass media and information exchange make it no longer possible to speak of any clear line of demarcation between Occident and Orient. Europe is no longer the Europe of the past; nor is Asia the Asia of the past. Both are searching for new identities.

Japan was profoundly influenced first by the ancient civilizations of India and China, later by Europe and, especially after World War II, the United States. We neither blindly accepted nor rejected foreign influences, but rather welcomed and assimilated the best of other civilizations. In the process, Japan created a distinctive culture of its own.

In Europe, more people are becoming interested in the Asia–Pacific region, and in learning from its cultural, spiritual and social traditions.

We are coming together. I believe we are entering a new era in world history – an era in which Japan and the countries of Western Europe will work together for world peace and for the creation of a new civilization. I am determined that Japan shall do its part.

The world we live in today is plagued by a variety of woes, hindrances and difficulties. But the truth is there exists only this one world and nations should behave as if the world were one entity.

This is what underlies Oriental philosophy and my belief. Thank you.

Image 1: **ISS–*Yomiuri*–JIIA Conference: The Institute for Strategic Studies (ISS) and Japan Institute of International Affairs (JIIA), in cooperation with the *Yomiuri Shimbun*, host the International Conference on Asian Security Problems in Nikko, Japan (April 1967)**

Source: IISS Archives; the *Yomiuri Shimbun*

Image 2: **ISS–*Yomiuri*–JIIA Conference: Co-founder and Director of the ISS Alastair Buchan (centre) visits a shrine in Nikko, Japan with Japanese and ISS delegates (April 1967)**

Source: IISS Archives; the *Yomiuri Shimbun*

Image 3: **ISS–*Yomiuri*–JIIA Conference: Co-founder and Director of the ISS Alastair Buchan (fourth from right) with Japanese colleagues in Nikko, Japan (April 1967)**

Source: IISS Archives; the *Yomiuri Shimbun*

Image 4: **Brigadier Kenneth Hunt (left), former Deputy Director of the International Institute for Strategic Studies (IISS), receives the Order of the Rising Sun, 3rd Class, from Ambassador of Japan to the UK Tsuyoshi Hirahara, at the Japanese Embassy in London (May 1984)**

Source: IISS Archives; Embassy of Japan to the UK

Image 5: **Japanese Prime Minister Nakasone Yasuhiro (right, seated) is introduced by Sir Michael Palliser GCMG, Chairman of the IISS Council (right, standing) before delivering the IISS Alastair Buchan Memorial Lecture (June 1984)**

Source: IISS Archives

Image 6: **(l–r) Dr Robert O'Neill, Director of the IISS, and Sir Michael Palliser GCMG, Chairman of the IISS Council, listen as Japanese Prime Minister Nakasone Yasuhiro delivers the IISS Alastair Buchan Memorial Lecture (June 1984)**

Source: IISS Archives

Image 7: **(l–r) Sir Michael Palliser GCMG, Chairman of the IISS Council, a Japanese aide, Japanese Prime Minister Nakasone Yasuhiro and former US Secretary of State Henry Kissinger engage in conversation (1984)**

Source: IISS Archives; Embassy of Japan to the UK

Image 8: **(l–r) Professor Nishihara Masashi, Professor Kosaka Masataka, Dr Robert O'Neill, Prime Minister Nakasone Yasuhiro, Sir Michael Palliser GCMG and Saeki Kiichi enjoy a conversation during the 28th IISS Annual Conference in Kyoto, Japan (September 1986)**

Source: With kind permission from Robert O'Neill and the Prime Minister's Office, Japan

Image 9: **(l–r) Professor Kosaka Masataka, Sir Michael Palliser GCMG, Professor Nishihara Masashi, Hasegawa Kazutoshi, Dr Robert O'Neill, Prime Minister Nakasone Yasuhiro and Saeki Kiichi raise a glass during the 28th IISS Annual Conference in Kyoto, Japan (September 1986)**

Source: With kind permission from Robert O'Neill and the Prime Minister's Office, Japan

Image 10: **(l–r) Director-General of the Defense Agency of Japan Ishiba Shigeru, a Japanese aide and IISS Director-General and Chief Executive Dr John Chipman converse at the 3rd IISS Shangri-La Dialogue (June 2004)**

Source: IISS Archives

Image 11: **(l–r) Nukaga Fukushiro, Minister of State for Defense, Japan; Dr John Chipman, Director-General and Chief Executive, IISS; Yoon Kwang-ung, Minister of National Defence, Republic of Korea and The Right Honourable Adam Ingram, Minister of State for the Armed Forces, UK, speak at a plenary session at the 5th IISS Shangri-La Dialogue (June 2006)**

Source: IISS Archives

Image 12: **(l–r) Former ambassador Yingfan Wang, Vice Chairman, Foreign Affairs Committee, National People's Congress, China, with Fleur de Villiers, Chairman of the IISS Trustees, and former ambassador Satoh Yukio, President, JIIA, at the IISS–JIIA Tokyo Conference (June 2008)**

Source: IISS Archives

Image 13: **Japanese Prime Minister Abe Shinzo delivers his keynote address to the 13th IISS Shangri-La Dialogue (May 2014)**

Source: IISS Archives

Image 14: **Ambassador of Japan to the UK Tsuruoka Koji and IISS Director-General and Chief Executive Dr John Chipman sign in the establishment of the IISS Japan Chair Programme (March 2019)**

Source: IISS Archives

Image 15: **Robert Ward, the inaugural IISS Japan Chair and Director of Geo-economics and Strategy, meets with former Japanese Defense Minister Kono Taro in Tokyo (December 2019)**

Source: Ministry of Defense website (https://www.mod.go.jp/j/profile/minister/kono/2019_12.html)

Image 16: **Japanese Prime Minister Kishida Fumio delivers his keynote address to the 19th IISS Shangri-La Dialogue (June 2022)**

Source: IISS Archives

Image 17: **After several years of delay due to the COVID-19 pandemic, the IISS Japan Chair Programme hosts its formal launch event at Arundel House in London: (l–r) Robert Ward, Japan Chair and Director of Geo-economics and Strategy, IISS; Bill Emmott, Chairman of the Trustees, IISS; Dr John Chipman, Chief Executive and Director-General, IISS; Yuka Koshino, Research Fellow for Security and Technology Policy, IISS (July 2022)**

Source: IISS Archives

Image 18: **Dr John Chipman, Director-General and Chief Executive, IISS, shakes hands with Japanese Prime Minister Kishida Fumio during a visit to London (January 2023)**

Source: Official Website of the Prime Minister of Japan and His Cabinet (https://www.kantei.go.jp/jp/101_kishida/actions/202301/11uk.html)

CHAPTER FOURTEEN

Japanese security policy: address by Mr Tadashi Kuranari, foreign minister of Japan, 8 September 1986 (excerpts)

Kuranari Tadashi

Survival 29-1, 1987

In the opening address to the twenty-eighth annual conference of the IISS in Kyoto, the Foreign Minister, Mr Tadashi Kuranari, described Japanese views on the nature of the Soviet SS-20 threat in Asia and the requirements for a credible American nuclear strategy and arms-control policy. Excerpts from this speech are reprinted below.

For a considerable period of time since the advent of the SS-20, the views on the impact that this weapon system would have on Western security were not necessarily identical in the United States, Canada, Western Europe and Japan and other Asia-Pacific countries. Differences appeared to be particularly marked between the perception held by NATO and the way we perceived the same weapon system in the context of the Asian strategic situation.

Given that NATO bases its strategy upon the concept of supplementing the inadequacies in conventional forces by the US and other nuclear forces, it was understandable that the Soviet deployment of the SS-20 gave rise to the concern that it might 'decouple' the defence of Western Europe from the US strategic nuclear weapon systems. And therefore it was also understandable that NATO decided as a response to this Soviet move to deploy in Europe *Pershing* II and cruise missiles. It was from this point of view that Prime Minister Nakasone expressed his support, at the Williamsburg Summit, for the policy of NATO on INF.

In the Asia-Pacific region, on the other hand, the reaction on the part of the free-world countries at the early stage of the SS-20 deployment was not as acute as in Western Europe. The main reason was that the Soviet deployment of this weapon system in this region was thought to have been initiated with China as the primary preoccupation. As you know, the Soviet claim that SS-20s are targeted against US naval and air power in this region is not very persuasive in a military sense. Further, given the transportability of this weapon system, we also thought the possibility could not be ruled out that part of the SS-20s deployed in Asia had the nature of being a strategic reserve force for the European theatre.

In relation to Japan's security, the deployment of the SS-20 does constitute an additional threat, if we do not take into consideration the functioning of the extended US nuclear deterrence. But, as we looked at the issue, taking into full account the effect of the extended US nuclear deterrence, frankly, we did not have much doubt as to whether the new weapon system would be a major added destabilizing factor for the mechanism of extended deterrence, particularly in contrast to the very powerful Soviet nuclear forces that had already existed in this region since before the introduction of the SS-20.

This was primarily because the prevailing perception in this country is that the mechanism of the US nuclear deterrence will function effectively in this region so far as the American nuclear forces in total remain balanced against the total Soviet nuclear power in the global context. In this context, it was generally believed that the SS-20 would not undercut greatly the effectiveness of the American nuclear deterrence.

Behind the prevailing tendency in Japan to look at the question of nuclear force balance in a global context rather than regional, there exists a perception that such an eventuality as a limited regional nuclear war between the United States and the

Soviet Union is most unlikely as a realistic possibility. Another reason for this line of thinking is that with the American military presence in the Western Pacific functioning as a major stabilizing element, and also with China pursuing an independent and autonomous foreign policy, there has been little recognition in this region, except in the case of the Korean Peninsula, that the West faces a disadvantage in the East–West balance of conventional forces. Accordingly, the concept of counting on US nuclear forces to supplement the inadequacy in conventional forces has generally not been underlined in Western strategy in this region. Furthermore, on the question of how to maintain a regional East–West nuclear balance, the deployment of American land-based weapons to counter the similar weapons on the Soviet side has not been a part of American strategy in this region because of the existence of the Pacific Ocean.

As for the question of the credibility of the US nuclear deterrence provided for Japan's security, too, the common view in Japan is that there should be basically no problem so long as the close Japan-US alliance relationship, based on the bilateral security arrangements, is maintained in good order across the entire spectrum of our bilateral political, economic and social relations.

Needless to say, Japan does not depend upon the extended American nuclear deterrence alone for its security. Rather, it is our thinking that to maintain the East–West conventional force balance in this region is indispensable for the stable functioning of the American nuclear deterrence, and from this perspective, we are greatly concerned about the Soviet military build-up in the Asia-Pacific region which has shown significant growth over the past ten years or so. Japan, therefore, has been making continuous efforts in recent years to strengthen its own self-defence forces with primary emphasis on naval and air capability, to facilitate further the operations of the Japan-US security arrangements and to promote

Japan-US defence co-operation. This is based on the judgment that Japan should, in response to the marked increase of Soviet military power in the region, exert as much effort as possible in the area of self-defence, and at the same time, see to it that yet smoother functioning of the Japan-US security arrangements is realized. We think that such efforts by Japan are required in order that the East–West balance in conventional forces in this region is not upset. We also think that such efforts on our part will contribute to the security interests of the West in a global context.

Against such a background, the Japanese Government has been demanding a global and total elimination of SS-20s primarily for the following three reasons. The first and foremost reason is that the weapon can easily reach Japan and therefore increases the potential threat against us. We also think that given the transportability of the weapon, the elimination of the SS-20 deployed in what they define as the Asian part of the Soviet Union would contribute to West European security as much as the elimination of the same weapons in Europe would contribute to Asian security.

Secondly, we suspect that the Soviet Union is attempting to use this weapon system as a lever to drive a political wedge between the United States and Western Europe, between the United States and its Asian allies, and between these Asian countries and Western Europe. Should this happen, damage would be done to the relationship of trust and mutual confidence between the Western allies, an important requirement for the functioning of the mechanism of deterrence. Precisely for this reason, we want at least to avoid the kind of agreement that would trigger off public criticism in Asia that 'the United States and Western Europe have given precedence to the security interests of Western Europe over those of Asia', even if the United States and the Soviet Union are to agree to interim measures pending the attainment of a global 'zero–zero option'.

The third reason for our demand for the total elimination of the SS-20 is our concern that the existence of such a system will work to push up the level of the East–West nuclear force balance in the global context and might end up in destabilizing the mechanism of deterrence.

In thinking about the tasks for Western security in the future, the issue of utmost importance is how best we can open a new prospect for the total abolition of nuclear weapons, the common ultimate goal for all Mankind, while maintaining the stability of the mechanism of mutual deterrence between the United States and the Soviet Union which is functioning now. To that end, it is a question of utmost urgency to bring down as low as possible the level of nuclear forces possessed by both East and West while maintaining the mutual balance. This also is the way to respond to the fears and concerns held by the citizens of each country as to nuclear weapons and nuclear strategy. Japan's strong support for the American efforts in the arms-control negotiations is based on such recognition.

CHAPTER FIFTEEN

East Asia, the Pacific and the West: strategic trends and implications: part II

Professor Masataka Kosaka

From Adelphi Paper 216, 1987

The decade after the fall of Saigon has turned out to be a peaceful and happy one for most East Asian countries, contrary to many forecasts. There was good reason for pessimism. The failure of the United States in Vietnam did great damage to US capability and will. American prestige was tarnished and the trust of Asian countries in the United States as their guarantor was severely diminished. The Soviet Union, on the other hand, was vigorously building up its forces in the Far East. The days of American dominance in the Pacific seemed to be coming to an end.

Such thinking was not entirely wrong. The United States did not recover its former strength. Its efforts at revitalization brought only limited success at considerable cost. The human rights diplomacy of the Carter Administration perplexed and annoyed allies and friends of the United States more than it reassured them. The efforts of President Reagan to reassert US leadership somehow lacked credibility, as they ran counter to the political and economic changes in the world.

Yet, despite these changes, international relations in East Asia and the Pacific remained peaceful, and even became more stable. Such an unexpected development was brought about because on the whole both the United States and Asian countries adapted themselves successfully to the altered circumstances, and a new structure of regional relations came into being. This Paper first looks at the reasons for this unanticipated peace and stability, which in turn throw light on the new structure. But any success is bound to be short-lived, and the problems that are emerging are then discussed.

Stability in East Asia

The basic reason for the stability was that the United States was militarily still far stronger in the region than the Soviet Union, though the overwhelming superiority of the 1950s and 1960s had been lost. The growth of Soviet military capability since 1965 has been real, and since 1978 striking. Ground force strength in the Far East, Siberia and Central Asia has risen in the last twenty years from about 17–20 divisions and 170,000 men to more than 50 divisions and nearly half a million men; new and more capable aircraft, such as MiG-27 *Flogger* and Su-24 *Fencer*, have been introduced; the Soviet Pacific Fleet has grown from about 50 vessels to 90, with remarkable qualitative improvements, such as a *Kiev*-class carrier and guided-missile anti-submarine warfare (ASW) cruisers; it has also acquired significant amphibious capability. Recently the Soviet Union has deployed long-range strike forces in the form of SS-20 intermediate range ballistic missiles (IRBM) and the *Backfire* bomber.

It is not unreasonable to say that the change is from a negligible Soviet force in the region to one which is a possible challenger to that of the United States. Soviet air and naval power now control Siberia and the adjacent seas, though beyond the Kurile Islands they are overshadowed by US forces. However, it should be noted that the increase of Soviet strength on land has been due largely to Sino-Soviet tensions.

As yet, the United States has not been really challenged in its sphere of influence – the Pacific Ocean.

The second important reason was a fundamental change in Sino-US relations. What can be called a diplomatic revolution took place when Henry Kissinger met Chou En-lai in Beijing in 1971 and the two countries began to move towards normalization of their relationship. It would be incorrect to say that the United States and China concluded a kind of alliance opposing Soviet 'social imperialism', but the US did cease to treat China as one of its main adversaries in league with the Soviet Union, and instead rather as a sovereign and great power with its own interests and own concerns about the growth of Soviet power. China, in the face of the confrontation with the Soviet Union and the growing Soviet threat, obviously wanted to improve its diplomatic position by normalizing its relations with the United States. The two countries clearly have a common interest in restraining the Soviet Union and this largely overshadowed the 'Taiwan problem'. This they agreed to shelve through the tactful formula of 'one China but not now'. As China was no longer an antagonist, the burden for the United States in the region became much lighter. These developments also relieved Asian countries, including Japan, of their psychological inse- curities. To them, the Soviet threat was largely a military one, to counter which US forces were both necessary and effective. But China represented a more complex influence in East Asia, and to try to cope with it by military means alone did not seem either necessary or likely to be effective.

Perhaps more important was the dramatic change in the orientation of China, which jettisoned its revolutionary foreign policy and radical domestic policy and instead adopted modernization as its main objective. This change may have started before 1971, but was clearly encouraged by the Sino-US normalization and had taken clear shape by 1978. To achieve its new goal, China now needed a calm and quiet international environment and the foreign capital and technology which could be best provided by the West. China seemed prepared to enter the regional family of nations instead of trying to upset it.

The third factor was a new US policy of asking its Asian allies to help themselves, which led to a more balanced relationship. This policy was set out in President Nixon's first Foreign Policy Report to Congress on 18 February 1970:

> Its central thesis is that the United States will partici-
> pate in the defense and development of allies and
> friends, but that America cannot – and will not –
> conceive all the plans, design all the programs, execute
> all the decisions and undertake all the defense of the
> free nations of the world. We will help where it makes
> a real difference and is considered in our interest.

President Nixon actually reduced the number of US troops in South Korea and asked Japan to play a more positive role in its own security and foreign policy. Such a move could easily be excessive – a pendulum can swing too far. In fact, President Carter committed himself during his election campaign to withdraw all US ground forces from South Korea, which, if it had been carried through, would have changed the structure of international relations in the region drastically and probably unfavourably. But South Korea and Japan made persistent efforts quietly to change the mind of President Carter and, with the help of a number of Americans, succeeded. The end result of the process was that one US division remains in South Korea and South Korea is stepping up its own security efforts.

Japan has been quite slow to do more in the field of security, but its achievements have not been negligible. More importantly, Japan and the United States have constructed a better working relationship since 1975, through better consultation on security policy, the conduct of joint exercises and the exchange of intelligence information, demonstrated on the occasion of the shooting down of the Korean Air Lines aircraft KAL 007 in September 1983. One scholar described this development as 're-Americanization', which followed a rather brief period of 'de-Americanization' in the early years of the 1970s. The Japanese were resentful of the abrupt change of US policy towards China in 1971 and of the fact that the change was made without any warning to Tokyo, but by 1975 they had re-discovered the importance of the US-Japan relationship.

The reasons for 're-Americanization' were multiple and are not dealt with at length here. It must be pointed out, however, that the change of US policy towards China was basically sound. After all, to have a normal relationship with China is better than being troubled by a hostile China. Moreover, 're-Americanization' had a solid foundation in that the image of the United States in the eyes of the average Japanese began to recover in 1976. Until about 1965, the United States had been the most popular country for Japanese, but friendly feelings began to decrease when the US intervened in Vietnam, reaching a low point in 1975.

Such changes in South Korea and Japan may not appear important if measured only by how much the security burden, previously shouldered by the US, was now shared by the two countries. The direct costs to the United States of ensuring the security of South Korea and Japan have never been very large – one division in South Korea does not cost all that much. And the United States does not deploy troops and aircraft in Japan, or send naval vessels there, exclusively to help Japan: it needs to control the North-west Pacific to ensure its own status as a super-power. To put it differently, the additional costs of helping Japan to maintain its own security are not high. Accepting Soviet control of the North-west Pacific would result in a completely different structure of international politics in the region. Similarly, the United States could not accept Soviet control over Western Europe. But the important difference is that the additional cost of containing the Soviet Union in Europe is high, whereas in the Pacific it is low.

Nevertheless, the defence effort being made by South Korea, even if not large enough to permit withdrawal of the US troops is important in political terms. Of course, the US troop presence is evidence of the American commitment to the security of South Korea. This is a powerful deterrent to the North and exercises a degree of control over the military activities of the South. Though US forces in Korea are not large in number, the US Air Force squadrons there provide significant backing to South Korean aircraft. Japan's willingness to increase security co-operation with the United States is also significant, even if its defence efforts are not large enough to provide for the security of Japan by themselves. It can be argued that Japan's support function is more important than its combat capability.

The fourth reason has been the impressive economic performance of many countries in Asia, South Korea being only the most spectacular example. Paradoxically, the US intervention in Vietnam, though a historic blunder in itself, can be considered to have played an important role in buying time for many Asian countries. In 1965, the situation in East Asia was bleak. Indonesia seemed on the verge of a Communist take-over; most of the South-east Asian countries were weak and lacked confidence; South Korea appeared in need of a permanent flow of aid from the United States to maintain its government in power. By 1975 economic growth had begun, under such authoritarian governments as that of President Park in South Korea, Prime Minister Lee Kuan Yew in Singapore and President Suharto in Indonesia. These countries managed to weather the two oil crises and the stagnation of the world economy that followed. The region has been developing more rapidly than anywhere else in the past fifteen years.

This economic development has been a fundamental cause of the region's relative domestic stability and has also made many countries militarily stronger, as witness South Korea. Without its economic miracle, South Korea could hardly have built up its military forces, and without this the US commitment to South Korea might have been difficult to maintain. With some 5–6% of GDP devoted to defence, South Korea has been able roughly to match the military forces of North Korea, which is believed to spend as much as 20% of its GDP on defence.

The impact on the global balance

The above trend, if it continues, will have a very strong impact on the global balance. First, the economic development of the past fifteen years will ensure that the region will have global importance. Of course, Europe and the Atlantic world have greater weight than the Asian-Pacific region and will continue to have in the foreseeable future, but the tempo of change in the Asian-Pacific region is faster. An area which changes more rapidly tends to influence things more. Although Europe constitutes the central and therefore important element of the East–West balance it is, by the same token, in something of a stalemate and seems unlikely to change much. In contrast, the Asian-Pacific region is changing rapidly and if an Asian-Pacific Community, in which the United States and Japan would occupy a central place, should come into being in some form or other, it could become a major creative force in the world.

Second, China is in transition and developments within the region are likely to exert considerable influence on its future. China should not be seen as merely providing a counterweight to Soviet military power, or treated simply as a 'China card'.

What is important about China is its basic orientation: the way it develops will, inevitably, influence the shape of a future world. If China continues on its present course of modernization, maintaining close contact with the West, it is likely to provide a new model for growth – neither a Soviet-style command economy nor a free-enterprise system. This itself constitutes a fundamental challenge to the Soviet Union, especially as the Soviet economy has begun to show marked signs of stagnation. Moreover, if China is successful, the Soviet Union will have to deal with a more powerful neighbour. Taken together, China and an Asian-Pacific region of vigorous economic growth will contribute to the containment of the Soviet Union.

It has often been pointed out that the Soviet Union has been largely unsuccessful in its diplomacy in the Asian-Pacific region. An important reason for this has been its heavy-handed approach, but this cannot be the sole explanation for its failure: the Soviet Union has been heavy-handed outside Asia and yet has had some diplomatic successes. It is more likely that it has failed diplomatically in Asia because it has been working from a position of weakness. It is militarily in an inferior position and cannot offer much in the field of economics. A growing Asian-Pacific region will not be much attracted by the Soviet Union.

Looming clouds

Every path has its pitfalls, and there are signs of difficulty ahead. Tensions are rising between China and Japan. There are growing anti-government movements in South Korea, and there is continuing political instability in the Philippines. Moreover, the cumulative psychological effect of the Soviet military build-up must not be neglected.

As to the military equation, it can be argued that this has not changed much and will not change further. The United States will maintain control of the Pacific: though the Soviet Union may cause problems and be a nuisance, it will not present a military challenge that cannot be met. In addition to its geographical handicaps, there are clear limits to Soviet power. Its economy has not been performing well, for fundamental structural reasons. Though it may be simplistic to believe that the Soviet Union will curb its military spending in order to revitalize its economy, the relatively poor economic performance is bound to affect military strength in the longer run.

Moreover, Soviet military advances have been achieved only at considerable cost. Although the Vietnamese invasion of Kampuchea and the subsequent Chinese punitive attack forced Vietnam into dependence on the Soviet Union and to concede a Soviet military foothold in Indochina, Soviet policy in South-east Asia will be handicapped as long as the present situation continues in Kampuchea. Soviet support of Vietnam is an important reason for the cool relations between the Soviet Union and China, and the Soviet invasion of Afghanistan weakened its diplomatic position in the Muslim countries of the Middle East – and more widely.

Yet there may be danger in an excessive or unwise reaction by the US to Soviet military power. The confidence of East Asian countries can and must be strengthened by adequate US guarantees, but it is important to note that very few countries in the region feel a direct and imminent Soviet threat. A general guarantee by the United States will continue therefore to satisfy most of them. Indeed, some already regard the US reaction as excessive, contributing to a super-power arms race in the region. Recent troubles between the United States and New Zealand seem to confirm such feelings.

The Soviet deployment of modern intermediate-range nuclear forces (INF) in East Asia must be met with great caution. The arrival of the missiles did not seem to alarm

East Asian and Pacific countries as much as it did the West Europeans perhaps because the geographical situations are different. Nuclear weapons must always be treated largely as political and psychological weapons, in East Asia and the Pacific in particular. The United States can match Soviet INF deployments with sea-borne systems, which are clearly more acceptable to its allies and friends. Furthermore, confidence in the United States can be strengthened by appropriate efforts towards arms control.

The most important cause of trouble and disturbances in the coming decade seems likely to lie in the process of economic modernization itself. This modernization has greatly benefited the region in the past decade, but is a very difficult process to direct and control and can so easily end in failure. Even if it goes smoothly on the whole, it can still require difficult societal adjustment, the failure of which may result in serious political crisis. Such internal developments can obviously influence the orientation of countries and lead to significant geopolitical changes.

The first of such concerns relates to China. China embarked on modernization in earnest in 1978, as collective farms were abandoned and a market mechanism introduced with spectacular results – a very rapid increase of agricultural output. Emboldened by this success, Deng Xiaoping went on to introduce reforms in industry in 1984 and to step up measures to open the Chinese economy to the outside world. Then several problems came to the surface: gaps between rich and poor appeared; there were undesirable traits, such as materialism and indiscipline; some Chinese seemed to have been charmed by foreign products and the hedonistic culture of the West to an undesirable degree; and the open trade with the outside world resulted in a sharp deterioration of China's trade balance, which went into serious deficit in 1985.

As a consequence, internal opposition to Deng began to appear in mid-1985, from those who are either convinced or moderate believers in a centrally-planned economy, or from bureaucrats and party members with vested interests. An important target and symbol of the opposition has been Japan, which invaded China militarily fifty years ago and is now only too eager to sell its products to China and make large profits through a kind of economic invasion. The official visit of Prime Minister Nakasone to the Yasukuni Shrine (where not only war dead but some war criminals are commemorated) and a text-book written by revisionist historians gave the opposition the opportunity to voice their dissatisfaction. Japan is in a natural position to provide China with goods, capital and technology, but can easily create enmity for well-known historical and psychological reasons. The attitude of China to Japan is bound to be ambivalent: the Chinese at once resent Japan and are attracted by it. Japan's recent economic behaviour makes things more difficult: exports to China increased by 72.9% in 1985, but imports from China went up by only 8.8%; the Japanese have been reluctant to invest in China. For these several reasons, it is not at all clear whether China will continue smoothly on the present course of modernization.

In addition, the Soviet Union may not repeat its past mistake of antagonizing China. It will learn from the errors of the past, or may judge that it can no longer afford bad relations with China, as Soviet power has ceased to grow so rapidly. There is thus some likelihood that Sino-Soviet relations will improve in the coming decade, which together with the difficulties of modernization or its failure, could change China's orientation, with serious geopolitical implications.

Another possibility is that South Korea, which since 1965 has recorded an extraordinarily high growth rate, will run into political instability. The standard of living has been greatly improved and the people have grown more sure of themselves. But every success brings its problems. An emerging middle class now wishes to have a greater say in the management of the country and greater political freedom to choose how it is governed. Economic growth has changed South Korea's social structure and value system. Moreover, the memories of the Korean War are now too distant to unify the country. The overall effect of these changes is that authoritarian rule, in force since President Syngman Rhee, is no longer an appropriate form of government for the country. But it is always difficult to change an authoritarian form of government. Change should be gradual, but there are many who regard gradual change as dangerous and who want only radical change. Whether South Korea can carry out the necessary political reforms and maintain political stability remains to be seen.

North Korea will, of course, be watching events. Aware that it is lagging seriously behind the South in the race for economic growth, it might try to use the opportunity provided by domestic turmoil there to act in some way against South Korea. Or Seoul might decide to pursue a populist but unwise foreign policy in the face of growing instability at home. As the structure in the Korean Peninsula is so delicate and subtle, and as it constitutes perhaps the most sensitive element for the stability of the whole region, such changes may have serious geopolitical repercussions.

China and South Korea are merely examples. Many other countries, such as the Philippines, Indonesia and Malaysia, are also in a difficult phase of modernization. In East Asia and the Pacific, change in the military balance itself may not be particularly significant but, when combined with political strains resulting from over-rapid modernization in countries which occupy important positions, geopolitical changes of great significance can result. That is what is of concern.

US-Japan relations

Another possible cause of turbulence lies in US-Japan relations, which have become a key factor in the region. They can be described as a 'special relationship', analogous to Anglo-US relations after the war.

Japan is now an important supporter of the United States, which is still a dominant power. A few facts reveal the story. Each has an important role in the management of the world economy. The US accounts for a little more than 20% of world output, and Japan for about 10%. Therefore jointly they produce one third of the world's wealth.

Though the industrial output of the European countries is twice that of Japan, the weight of the United States and Japan is plain. First, today Japan is the largest net creditor, with $100 billion of assets, making it a very important country in the financial world, as the meeting of the 'Group of Five' in the autumn of 1985 demonstrated. Second, the US and Japan enjoy a clear lead in the high-technology industries, at least in the field of microelectronics, seen by many as having a decisive influence on the total balance of forces in the world and to have considerable civilian implications as well. Though conducting different programmes, the United States and Japan happen to be developing similar technologies. Both the Strategic Defense Initiative (SDI) programme and the plan of MITI (Japan's Ministry of International Trade & Industry) emphasize fifth-generation computers, artificial intelligence, new materials, lasers and optical fibres as the technologies likely to be dominant in future. Third, the economies of the two countries are very closely linked, perhaps without precedent. The US market, which takes about 30% of Japanese exports, is clearly vital to the Japanese economy, and the Japanese market is also important to the United States, though it may not be indispensable. Japan has invested a large amount of money in the United States, which needs investments. It has also extended large loans.

Japanese firms have stakes of 50% or higher in some hundreds of American manufacturing concerns. Moreover, Japanese industry supplies a large variety of components to US firms. The US has been and still is the most important source of new technology for Japan. Clearly the two economies are very closely interlocked and gain strength from each other. It can be argued therefore that the US-Japan relationship is the driving force for the modernization of the economies of many of the regional countries.

In the field of security, Japan has still not played a very large role, but geography makes the US-Japan relationship the centrepiece of the security arrangements of the region. Japan is situated where it can guard against Soviet naval expansion into the Pacific. The Soviet Union is not completely blocked by Japan, as it faces the Sea of Okhotsk and has bases on the Kamchatka Peninsula, but the Soya Strait lies between Vladivostok and the Sea of Okhotsk and the passage through that Strait is not free, regardless of Japan's publicized intentions.

The main difficulty with the US-Japan relationship is that the benefits and costs for the two countries are not well balanced, at least in the ordinary way. First, Japan has benefited greatly from the US-Japan Security Treaty, and at very low cost. American nuclear forces provide Japan with the basis for its security, and the dominant sea and air power of the US in the Pacific has given Japan a very reliable security shield. The strength of the United States alone has been almost enough to provide Japan with its security. For the past twenty years or so, Japan has spent less than 1% of GNP on defence, one of the lowest percentages in the world. (If NATO criteria are used the figure goes up to nearly 1.5%, but this is still much less than the 3–4% of most NATO countries.) In contrast, the United States spent nearly 10% of GNP on defence until the end of the 1960s. The security burden for the United States and that for Japan bear no comparison.

The balance sheet of economic relations is, however, more complex. Economists have argued incessantly about the meaning of the US-Japanese trade balance. Some hold that a big surplus is bad while others doubt it. The political fact remains, however, that many Americans have criticized the Japanese trade surplus. They argue that the Japanese are eager to sell their products in the US market but are reluctant to buy from the United States in return. Therefore US-Japanese economic relations are not truly reciprocal. Such an argument lacks precision, and those who argue in this way tend to overlook the problems and weaknesses of the US economy, including the fact that the United States has not, until recently at least, been eager to export and therefore does not have the experience or the system to promote exports. Nevertheless, American criticism is not groundless and it does have political force. Fundamentally, a large US deficit on current account, in which Japan's trade surplus is an important factor, if it continues may cause serious disturbances in the world economy.

Though such trade and security imbalances must not be left uncorrected, trying to correct them in a direct and rash way will be counterproductive. For example, Japanese defence expenditures cannot be increased much beyond 1.5–2.0% of GNP without a negative impact on international – and especially regional – relations. Indeed, there could be an impact before such levels were reached. It may be thought that there would be no great difference between spending 1% and spending 1.5% of GNP. But the additional money would go on doubling the procurement of weapons and on base construction, possibly changing the regional balance to the considerable concern of Japan's neighbours. The trade imbalance will continue, though it can and should be somewhat reduced. Protectionist measures are not a remedy. Imaginative measures and a long-term view are required, but neither is easy to find.

CHAPTER SIXTEEN

The security of north-east Asia: part I

Professor Masashi Nishihara

From Adelphi Paper 218, 1987

Basic problems of Japanese security

In May 1983, when Prime Minister Nakasone signed a statement at the Williamsburg Summit that Western security is 'indivisible and must be approached on a global basis', it was indicative of the change in Japanese security concerns – from regional to international or global. Three factors have actively contributed to the change: the fast pace of Soviet military deployment, now able to challenge the United States in some fields; the growth of Japan's own economic strength, now some 10% of the world's GNP; and Prime Minister Nakasone's leadership.[1]

In the past, Japan's military security concerns have been primarily regional. The Korean Peninsula, for instance, has been a vital interest. By contrast its non-military security concerns have been global; Japan has traded with practically all the regions of the world and depended upon foreign sources for the supply of vital goods such as oil, iron and rare metals. Yet in the last few years, the Japanese people have gradually become conscious that their military security concerns are of a global, not just a regional nature. Tokyo has been forced to see the link between SS-20 intermediate-range nuclear missiles (IRBM) deployed in Europe and in Asia because of their transportability: a US–Soviet agreement on the reduction of IRBM in Europe could result in the transfer of these missiles to Asia. An aggravated Middle East situation could disrupt the international economic system. President Reagan's Strategic Defense Initiative (SDI) has to be dealt with on the basis of allied cohesion and stable East–West relations. If Japanese technology is to make a significant contribution to research, Japan must think of its own responsibility for the security of the West.

This new awareness must still, of course, take into account some basic security problems which Japan faces. First its serious vulnerability as a resource-poor nation. In 1983, 82.2% of its energy and 30% of its food came from abroad, making the political stability of its supplier countries, most of them in the Third World, vital for Japan. All of its sources of nuclear energy which provides 8% of its total energy requirements, were foreign as well. It is also imperative that its long world-wide sea-lanes should remain safe, making a favourable maritime balance of power indispensable. Second, Japan's geographic proximity to the potential adversary, the Soviet Union, makes for military vulnerability. The air distance between Tokyo and Vladivostok is only about 600 miles (960 km). Hokkaido, closest to Soviet territory, could easily be subject to Soviet attack. Third, Japan's domestic political constraints, symbolized by Article 9 of the Constitution and pacifist sentiment, limit the range of policy options such as the roles and missions and types of weapons of the Self- Defense Forces (SDF). Fourth, Asian apprehension about Japan's conventional build-up as a 'revival of Japanese militarism' serves as a restraint. The Japanese defence budget, just below 1% of GNP, was some US$ 12.0 bn in 1984, about equivalent to the combined defence budgets of the ASEAN nations ($7.6 bn) plus South

Korea ($4.5 bn).[2] Finally, the ties with the US are a vital source of security but also of fear, for too close an alliance may mean an unnecessary or unwilling involvement in US military activities.

How do these basic problems of Japan relate to its new awareness in terms of its military and non-military responses? This Paper attempts to identify and evaluate new military threats to Japan and responses to them.

New military threats

North Korea

Today, military threats in North-east Asia come from either the Soviet Union or North Korea or both. North Korean fire-power and armed forces have generally been considered to be stronger than those of South Korea, but a balance has nonetheless been maintained in various ways, notably by US military support for the South, strong Japanese and US economic ties with it, precariously normalized Sino-Soviet relations and friendly US-China relations. No external power sees another outbreak of armed conflict in the Korean Peninsula as in its interest, but despite some progress in a North-South dialogue, armed confrontation and tension continue there. For example, North Korea is known to maintain, just north of the demilitarized zone (DMZ), 80,000–100,000 commandos, the largest surprise-attack force in the world.[3] Three new elements have to be taken into account in assessing the threat from North Korea. First, the coupling of the high-growth South Korean economy with the succession issues in both Pyongyang and Seoul. Seventy-four-year-old President Kim II Sung has been in power in the North for 38 years. He has apparently been preparing the ground for his son, Kim Chong-il, to succeed him, but he may not be able to leave 'a glorious and prosperous' North Korea for his son, because by the late 1980s the North's military strength may be overtaken by the South, with its fast growing economy and a GNP over five times as large.[4] In addition, the success of the Olympic Games scheduled to be held in Seoul in 1988 would enhance the South's international prestige at the expense of the North. Out of desperation President Kim Il Sung just might start armed conflict across the DMZ before or during the Olympics. The short-term stability of North-South Korean relations would depend partly upon whether Moscow decides to take part in the Olympics. China is already committed, and if the Soviet Union should participate as well, it would no doubt press Pyongyang not to disrupt the Games through subversive activities or more open military operations.

The Soviet Union is currently strengthening military ties with the North. Since May 1985 it has supplied Pyongyang with some 25 MiG-23 fighter aircraft and obtained overflight rights in return. In August 1985 Soviet warships called at Wonsan, a large port facing the Sea of Japan, and a year later the North Korean Navy reciprocated by visiting Vladivostok. There is growing speculation that the Soviet Union has also acquired access to Nampo, a port near Pyongyang.

What is significant now is the apparently increased Soviet involvement in North Korea. This could imply that any conflict in the Peninsula might implicate the Soviet Union more directly than the Korean War of 1950 did, though conversely it could also mean that Moscow can exert more control over Pyongyang. Soviet-North Korean military ties could also suggest that the Soviet Union may use North Korea as a proxy against Japan and the US, which would quickly broaden any conflict in the region.

The Soviet Union

Soviet military capabilities in Asia are formidable. The Japanese Defense White Paper each year emphasizes the alarming nature of the Soviet deployment of modern arms in

Asia. The 1986 edition describes the Soviet Far East military presence as consisting in 1985, of 41 army divisions or 370,000 troops, 840 ships or 1,850,000 tons (835 ships or 1,780,000 tons in 1985) and 2,390 operational aircraft (2,200 in 1985), while SS-20 IRBM are now given as over 162 and *Backfire* bombers as over 85. The Pacific Fleet includes two aircraft carriers, 83 other principal surface combatants, 19 amphibious ships, 88 submarines, and other vessels.[5] Their naval bases at Vladivostok and Petropavlovsk are being enlarged, while those at Da Nang and Cam Ranh Bay in Vietnam are growing fast.

More specifically, where Japanese security is concerned, the Soviet Air Force has increased its flights near Japanese air space. Japanese interceptions (scrambles) of such flights went up from 305 in 1975 to 944 in 1984. The Soviet Union occupies the disputed Northern Territories off Hokkaido, where it deploys over one army division, about 40 MiG-23 fighters, some Mi-24 attack helicopters and ground-launched cruise missiles capable of carrying nuclear warheads.[6] In September 1985 Soviet forces conducted large-scale landing exercises on one of these islands, of a pattern which could be applicable to Hokkaido itself.[7] They involved the dispatch of three amphibious ships, including the *Ivan Rogov*, from Vladivostok through the Soya Strait to Sakhalin where the troops were embarked. *Backfire*, MiG-23 and MiG-27 aircraft participated in this exercise.

In addition to the increased Soviet-North Korean ties mentioned above, the Soviet-Vietnamese alliance, formed officially in November 1978, could also threaten Japanese security. The Soviet Union can do this by sponsoring subversive activities in the ASEAN region, thus weakening its economic viability and political stability, and by reinforcing its own military presence in Vietnam, which can challenge the US presence in the Philippines.

Soviet forces are now capable of conducting war against Japan on several scenarios, ranging from nuclear attack or blackmail to the armed occupation of Wakkanai, the northern tip of Hokkaido facing Sakhalin. According to the Defense Agency's estimates, the Soviet Union could allocate some eight divisions (five to six motor rifle, one airborne, and one naval infantry division) and four airborne brigades for an invasion of Japan, compared with just five divisions in 1976.[8] It is also estimated that if all landing ships were used, one and a half to two divisions could be landed in Japan in a short time.[9] Some Japanese officers consider that the USSR would seize part or the whole of Hokkaido in order to ensure safe sea passage between the Sea of Japan and the Sea of Okhotsk.[10] Soviet forces could also interdict Japanese sea-lanes in the Western Pacific, the South China Sea and the Indian Ocean.

However, despite the growing Soviet military strength in the Western Pacific, the general balance of power there still favours the US and its allies, Japan and South Korea. The maritime balance, for instance, is favourable to the US side, as the Pentagon admits.[11] A political coalition, though still loose, between America and China and between Japan and China isolates the Soviet Union, whose only friend is North Korea. Thus Soviet military power can perhaps be more effective for political intimidation in peacetime than for attack in war. Nevertheless, the fast pace of the Soviet build-up is alarming. Gorbachev's speech in Vladivostok in July 1986 seems to have been intended to end Soviet isolation and to claim its legitimacy as an Asian-Pacific power with its new military might.

Japanese military responses

In the face of these security threats, the Japanese government has made two forms of response, military and non-military. The development of these responses has shown that domestic political constraints on security policy are undergoing slow but notable change. The military responses that the government has made are of several kinds: increased defence expenditure; the purchase of more sophisticated weapons; more flexible interpretations of Article 9 of the Constitution to allow for a larger defence role; and closer defence co-operation with the US.

Increased defence expenditure

For 1982–6 the government has appropriated funds for the defence budget at an average annual increase of 6.9% nominal or 5.6% in real terms.[12] This percentage is higher than the 3.0% average annual rate of increase of the total budget, and this special treatment for defence (at a time when the huge government debts have required tight budgets) has naturally caused heated debates in the Diet but been accepted in the end. There would have been much opposition ten years ago, but the Soviet threat and the perceived need to maintain good relations with Washington have contributed to the opposition being tamed.

However, the annual defence expenditure is still just below 1% of GNP, following the policy adopted in 1976. This has been a point of strong political controversy in the Diet. Yet even this political barrier seems to be beginning to erode; the new Minister of State for Defence, Kurihara Yuko, stated in July 1986, in face of little opposition criticism, that policy priority is now concerned with how to complete the 1986–90 defence modernization programme rather than with how to remain within 1% of GNP. The 1% ceiling is likely to be revised under the leadership of Nakasone, after his landslide electoral victory.

In August 1985 the Nakasone Government decided to appropriate for the 5-year 1986–90 programme ¥18,400 bn or ¥3,680 bn per annum. This annual spending would have been equivalent to $16.0 bn under the then ruling exchange rate of $1=¥230, but it now equals $23.7 bn at the current rate of $1=¥155. While the annual figure is still roughly 1% of GNP, when expressed in US dollars it looks quite impressive. It is larger than were the 1984 defence budgets of France ($20.1 bn), or West Germany ($20.4 bn) and only slightly smaller than that of Britain ($22.0 bn) - calculated at the exchange rates ruling at that time.[13] These European budgets have admittedly risen since, as have the currencies against the US dollar, but the sharp increase in the value of the yen confuses the arguments as to which of the US allies contributes most towards the burden of Western security.

More sophisticated weapons

The Ground Self-Defense Force plans, for example, to strengthen the defence of Hokkaido by transferring some troops and tanks from other parts of the country and by deploying modern anti-tank helicopters. Its primary concern is to enhance readiness and sustainability. In July 1986 the three services undertook a large-scale joint exercise in which they transported 4,500 troops and 1,000 vehicles from Kyushu, the southern part of the country, to Hokkaido.[14]

In 1981 Prime Minister Suzuki stated that Japan would place its defence emphasis on air and naval power rather than on ground forces. To be able to defend long sea-lanes requires more sophisticated weapon systems. In 1982 the government decided to increase the number of P-3C anti-submarine patrol aircraft to be procured for the Maritime Self-Defense Force from 45 to 75, and then in 1985 to 100. Similarly, the number of F-15 interceptors to be procured for the Air Self-Defense Force was increased from 100 to 155 in 1982 and then to 187 in 1985.[15] It was also decided in 1982 to procure *Patriot* surface-to-air missiles (SAM) to replace the obsolete *Nike*. E-2C early-warning aircraft are soon to be deployed and the government is considering the purchase of an over-the-horizon (OTH) radar to be installed perhaps in Iwojima, 780 miles (1,250 km) south of Tokyo. Airborne warning and control system (AWACS) aircraft may also be on the agenda in the near future.

Relaxation of constitutional constraints

Article 9 of the 1946 Constitution renounces 'war . . . as a means of settling international disputes', and does not recognize the right of belligerency. This Article has been a fundamental point of controversy in post-war Japanese politics. It has been interpreted variously. The original view of the government was that Japan should have no armed forces at all. The interpretation was then relaxed to mean that Japan might have forces, but only for 'individual self-defence', and not for 'collective self-defence'. The definition of individual self-defence then became and still is a matter of repeated parliamentary debate.[16] Successive governments of a conservative persuasion have attempted to introduce flexible interpretations, and Nakasone has widened the concept by accepting that the grey area between individual and collective self-defence should be included in it. Since he took office in late 1982, he has advocated, among other things, the constitutionality of Japanese naval forces helping to protect US naval forces operating outside the 12-mile territorial waters in wartime when these US forces were on the way to defend Japan, something considered unconstitutional in the past. This new interpretation widens the area of joint operations that Japanese forces can conduct with US forces, a significant step towards Japan acting like a normal ally of the United States.

Closer defence co-operation with US forces

Another important response to the Soviet military threat has been to build closer defence ties with US forces. In recent years, there has been an increasing number of joint exercises between the forces of the two countries. In 1985 there were eight joint naval exercises, related to minesweeping, anti-submarine warfare, surface operations and command post practices, and ten joint air defence, air combat and rescue exercises. The ground forces conducted six joint manoeuvres in that year, two in Hokkaido. Since 1980 Japan has also participated in the multinational *Rimpac* (Rim of the Pacific) naval exercises with the US, Canada, Australia and New Zealand (which was replaced by Britain in 1986).

Since 1978 officers of the two nations have been engaged in joint studies of how to work together in emergencies which threaten the security of Japan, its sea-lanes and South Korea. The Defense Agency has also increased its expenditure for the maintenance of US bases and some 46,000 US troops in Japan. In 1985 ¥277.5 bn or $1.8 bn ($1=¥155) was appropriated, representing about $39,000 per US serviceman in Japan.[17] Japan has also agreed to the US deployment of 40 to 50 F-16 fighters at Misawa, a base just south of Hokkaido, and made a financial contribution to the cost of the facilities there. This meets both Japanese and US interests in balancing Soviet air power in the North-west Pacific.

In 1983 the Nakasone Government agreed to transfer Japanese defence technology to America. Japan has a policy of tight control on arms exports, including defence technology, but the transfer of such technology to the US was treated as an exceptional case, justified under the Japan-US Mutual Defence Assistance Agreement of 1954. This was again designed to strengthen ties with the US. In September 1986 the government also decided that Japan should participate in SDI research, something not discussed further here for lack of space.[18]

Japanese non-military responses: the 'Comprehensive Security' approach

Along with the military responses, the Japanese government has various non-military ones, mainly economic and diplomatic. When

Prime Minister Ohira introduced the concept of 'Comprehensive National Security' in 1979, the government explained that Japan's national security cannot be enhanced by defence efforts alone but that economic and diplomatic efforts were also needed. Japan has become more conscious of the impact of its economic power upon international relations. Japan would like to see China balancing the Soviet Union and to see South Korea functioning as a buffer state against North Korea. Its large yen loan to China ($1.3 bn for 1979–83 and $2.1 bn for 1984–90) and to South Korea ($1.8 bn for 1984–90) can be seen in this light.[19] There is no possibility in the foreseeable future, however, of a formal military alliance between Japan and South Korea or between Japan and China. Tokyo simply finds it politically most acceptable to seek close ties with them by non-military means.

Japan's basic concern is to help reduce tensions in the Northeast Asian region and to help to maintain a favourable balance of power. The region has three areas of potential rupture: the Korean Peninsula, Sino-Taiwan relations and the Sino-Soviet border. The region has not reached the stage of détente where states such as the two Koreas, and China and Taiwan recognize each other diplomatically. Neither of the Koreas is recognized by the countries linked with their opponents. Japan maintains non-diplomatic contacts with North Korea and Taiwan despite complaints from South Korea and China, respectively, and tries to help reduce tensions between the two Koreas and between China and Taiwan by simply keeping communications channels open with all parties.

However, Taiwan and North Korea cannot be treated in the same way. Compared with Japanese relations with North Korea those with Taiwan are far closer, notably in the economic and tourism fields. The political stability of Taiwan and the fairly stable relations between Beijing and Taipei favour the security of Japan's southern sea-lanes. Japan considers its relations with North Korea as contributing to the stability of the Peninsula.

The absence of a clear demarcation line in North-east Asia between the US and Soviet spheres of influence makes any discussion of the regional balance of power very difficult. A major difficulty is China, which claims to be an independent power and yet has fairly close relations with the US, including military ones. Japan's interest is to ensure China's political stability and its friendly posture towards the West.

Similarly, Japan tries to establish stable, not friendly, relations with the Soviet Union. Japan assumes that it can hardly improve relations with the USSR because of historical distrust, the territorial disputes and differences of ideology, but it hopes that such impaired relations can be stabilized through economic and cultural contacts. The relations are, in fact, asymmetrical in that three Japanese Prime Ministers have visited Moscow in the post-war years, while no Soviet equivalent has ever been to Tokyo. Prime Minister Nakasone apparently wishes to improve relations by his invitation to General Secretary Gorbachev to visit Tokyo. The current diplomatic issue from Tokyo's point of view is the territorial dispute, whereas Moscow's apparent interests are to weaken Japan-US relations and to gain access to Japan's economic and technological strengths to develop Siberia. Japan's limited military capabilities can be supplemented by its non-military options, in such a way as to influence Siberian development in a direction which will not reinforce Soviet military power.

Japanese dilemmas

A significant new aspect of these Japanese responses, military and non-military, is that they have been made with a sense of contribution to Western, not just North-east Asian security. The 1981 Defense White Paper writes, for instance, that 'Japan's defense capability constitutes an important factor in establishing a relationship of trust between Japan and other free nations which share the same values and which are interdependent'.[20] But the question is whether or not the Tokyo government is making sufficient defence efforts as a member of the West. Japan faces a few dilemmas.

Japanese efforts to strengthen preparedness, sustainability, command, control, communications and intelligence, and a framework for closer working relations with US forces certainly contribute to Japanese security. And the overall balance of power in the Western Pacific appears still favourable to the United States, upon which Japan depends. But if there were multi-regional conflicts such as Europe, the Middle East and North-east Asia, in which US forces were to be engaged, Washington might not be able to mobilize sufficient forces in the Western Pacific. In addition, Soviet forces might concurrently assault parts of Hokkaido and let North Korea start a conflict at the DMZ, thus making demands on the US forces designated for the defence of Japan and South Korea. Under such circumstances, some 60 destroyers, 16 submarines and 350 operational aircraft that Japan possesses would not be sufficient to defend the country.

Japan will soon be able to take on a reasonable level of patrolling over the international straits around Japan and the 1,000-mile sea-lanes. With OTH radar it could also take on early-warning functions. But to defend the sea-lanes remains a highly difficult task, calling for a faster force build-up. The Japanese government is, however, always restrained here by domestic opposition, including opposition from several factions of the ruling party itself. This is the first dilemma.

If Japan cannot build up its capabilities fast enough, it must depend upon the US, as it has in the past. Nakasone's strategy is to please Washington by taking a positive posture on defence; and this has so far worked very well. Yet it would be risky for Japan to assume that the two countries fully share strategic interests. The US might, for instance, open a second front in the Western Pacific in order to divert Soviet forces from the European front. Japan would almost automatically be involved, against its will, in such a US strategy of horizontal escalation. The United States might like to mine the Soya Straits, for instance, against Japanese opposition, which Japan would not like to see happen. And SS-20 missiles deployed in Soviet Asia may be intermediate-range nuclear forces for Washington, but they are strategic forces for Tokyo, because they can destroy it. Here is a second dilemma.

So far Japan has been concerned primarily only with a conventional build-up and has avoided an important question of how this might be linked to nuclear warfare, if Japan were to follow the US doctrine of flexible response. That Japan should have no nuclear weapons fits the anti-nuclear sentiment among the Japanese people, but Japan pursues a highly sophisticated, if not contradictory, policy of expecting US nuclear protection but not allowing the United States to bring nuclear weapons into its territory. This policy, popularly symbolized by its 'three non-nuclear principles' (not possessing, not producing and not introducing nuclear weapons), has worked successfully in peacetime. But there is an absence of debate about how Japan should meet the SS-20 threats.[21] Tokyo has certainly expressed concern about the SS-20 in Asia on many occasions, but has stuck to the three non-nuclear principles.

SS-20 missiles targeted on Europe have led European NATO members to request the US to balance them by deploying cruise missiles and *Pershing* II in Europe. Those same Soviet missiles in Asia have had a different impact upon Japan: the matter has been left to the US, which has made no visible response so far other than to equip some US ships, and submarines in the Pacific with *Tomahawk* cruise missiles. A handful of Japanese defence specialists argue that the country should exercise a nuclear option,[22] while a few others maintain that Japan should relax the principle of 'not introducing' or not allowing the introduction of nuclear arms from outside, by openly permitting US nuclear-armed ships to enter Japanese territorial waters and make port calls in Japan.[23] (Even if Japan should relax this principle, this alone would not really strengthen the Japanese and US positions *vis-à-vis* the SS-20.) Most specialists, however, think that Japan should take no action nor panic on the SS-20 issue, because the position has not basically changed since the time when SS-4 missiles were deployed with the capacity to destroy Tokyo by a nuclear strike, the SS-20 have merely replaced them.[24]

Strategic debates about Japanese security as coupled with the US policy of extended deterrence and flexible response, have hardly begun in Japan, primarily due to the nuclear allergy. This is not to advocate a Japanese nuclear option in any form, but to stress the need to discuss theoretical ways in which Japan can ensure its security against limited and less limited nuclear wars. One such way might be the deployment of a theatre SDI which could destroy SS-20 in the boost phase. But given the time needed for the research and development of such a defence, an alternative option would be a faster conventional build-up by Japan, which would keep the nuclear threshold higher.[25] For the reasons mentioned earlier, this would be difficult. This is a third dilemma for Japan.

In the meantime, with changes in the Japanese posture, supportive of closer defence ties with the US forces, the Japan-US Security Treaty assumes new implications for global security. The two Pacific powers, whose combined economic might represents about one-third of the world total, can play a vital role in promoting comprehensive international security through economic and political activities as well as through the effective use of high technology. Japan's role, in this sense, has gone beyond North-east Asian security and begins to assume new implications for global security.

NOTES

1 New attitudes discernible, for instance, in Nakasone's Peace Problems Study Group (Chairman: Masataka Kosaka), *Kokusai kokka Nihon no soogoo anzen hoshoo seisaku* ([Report on] Comprehensive security policy for an internationalist nation, Japan), December 1984, pp. 1–3. See also Chalmers Johnson, 'Reflections on the Dilemmas of Japanese Defense', *Asian Survey*, May 1986, pp. 557–72.

2 Calculated from the *The Military Balance 1985–1986*, (London: IISS, 1986).

3 *Sankei Shimbun*, 5 November 1985. See also Larry A. Niksch, 'The Military Balance on the Korean Peninsula', *Korea and World Affairs*, Summer 1986, p. 261.

4 *Tooyoo Keizai Nippoo*, 15 August 1986. In 1984 South Korea's GNP was estimated at $81.1 bn, and that of North Korea at $14.7 bn. *The Military Balance 1985–1986* gives $83 bn for South Korea's GDP and $40 bn for North Korea. (*op. cit.* in note 2) pp. 126–7.

5 Japan, Defense Agency, *Booei hakusho 1986* (Defense White Paper 1986), pp. 31–2; *The Military Balance 1985–1986*, p. 29.

6 The last item was revealed by US Secretary of Defense, Caspar Weinberger, in a press conference in Tokyo. See *Sankei Shimbun*, 7 September 1985, morning edition.

7 *Sankei Shimbun*, 7 September 1985, morning edition.

8 *Sankei Shimbun*, 9 August 1985, morning edition.

9 *Ibid.*

10 Shigeki Nishimura, 'Soren: senzaiteki kyooi no jittai' (The Soviet Union: the real state of its potential threat), *Voice*, November 1985, pp. 84–93.

11 See, for instance, US Department of Defense, *Annual Report to the Congress, Fiscal Year 1987*, pp. 66–7.

12 Calculated from *Defense of Japan 1985* (Tokyo: The Japan Times, 1985), *Asahi nenkan 1986* (Asahi Almanac 1986), p. 154; and *Sekai Shuuho*, August 12, 1986, p.72.

13 Based on the NATO definition of defence costs. See *The Military Balance, 1985–1986*, (*op. cit.* in note 2), pp. 40, 46 and 49.

14 *Asagumo Shimbun*, 10 July 1986.

15 Asagumo Shimbun Sha, *Booei handobokku 1986* (Handbook on Defense, 1986), p. 71.

16 Masashi Nishihara, 'Expanding Japan's Credible Defense Role', *International Security*, Winter 1983–4, pp. 180–205.

17 *Defense of Japan 1985*, p. 169.

18 For problems of Japanese participation in SDI research, see, for instance, Yasuto Fukushima, 'SDI to Nihon no sanka mondai' (SDI and problems of Japanese participation), *Sekai Shuuhoo*, 12 August 1986, pp. 12–17.

19 *Asian Security 1985*, (Tokyo: Research Institute for Peace and Security pp. 170–71.

20 *Defense of Japan 1981*, p. 120.

21 Tomohisa Sakanaka, 'Nihon no kaku senryaku ga towareru toki' (It's time that Japan's nuclear strategy was questioned), *Voice*, September 1985, pp. 232–43.

22 For views favouring a nuclear option for Japan, see, for instance, Ikutaro Shimizu, 'Nihon yo, kokka tare!' (Japan, be a state!), *Shokun*, July 1980, pp. 22–68; and Yatsuhiro Nakagawa, *Gendai kaku senryaku ron* (Contemporary nuclear strategies), *Hara Shoboo*, Tokyo, 1985, chapter 7.

23 For views favouring a slightly modified interpretation of the three non-nuclear principles, see, for instance, Masashi Nishihara, (*op. cit.*, in note 16), p. 198.

24 A typical view advocating no action against SS-20 may be found, for instance, in Ken'ichi Ito, 'SS-20 Kyokutoo haibi ni Nihon wa doo taioo subeki ka' (How should Japan cope with the SS-20 deployed in the Far East?), *Chuuoo Kooron*, special issue, July 1983, pp. 88–99.

25 Masataka Kosaka, 'Theater Nuclear Weapons and Japan's Defense Policy', in Richard Solomon and Masataka Kosaka, (eds) *The Soviet Far East Military Buildup: Nuclear Dilemmas and Asian Security*, (Dover, MA: Auburn House Publishing Co., 1986), pp. 123–140.

CHAPTER SEVENTEEN

Prospects for security co-operation between East Asia and the West

Ambassador Yoshio Okawara

From Adelphi Paper 218, 1987

Any discussion of security co-operation between East Asia and the West is bound to be more speculative than practical at the present stage of the evolution of the concept of Western security. For, given the differences between East Asian and Atlantic (North American and West European) security which this Paper tries to underline, a practical basis for such co-operation hardly exists, if, indeed, it exists at all.

The fundamental question lies in the concept of Western security itself. This has been developed by the United States through consultations primarily with its European allies, or it certainly seems so to many in East Asia, despite the fact that the US fought both of its two major post-World War II wars (Korea and Vietnam) in Asia. US allies in East Asia, let alone many non-allied nations in the region, have regarded the concept as designed primarily to serve American or Euro-American interests more than their own. Many free-world nations in East Asia, allied or non-allied, know that they benefit from the American or 'Western' strategy to deter Soviet military interference, but, rightly or wrongly, have seen the United States' strategy as more preoccupied with the security of North America and Western Europe than with their own. Despite the recent American and, to a lesser extent, Western European emphasis on the need for a global approach to Western security, countries in East Asia, with the exception of Japan and possibly South Korea, distinguish themselves from the so-called 'West'. Only within the last ten years has Japan come to act explicitly as a member of the West.

Looking towards the future, however, there appears to be a greater need for security co-operation between the countries of the Atlantic Alliance and the free-world nations in East Asia. The global expansion of Soviet military capability and the increased possibility of interaction between European and Asian security already underline the need for co-operation. The prospect that more East Asian nations will become 'industrialized democracies', if not specifically Western, suggests that co-operation might add to an element of convergence rather than divergence, between the traditional West and East Asia. This Paper tries to explore ways, if there are any, to seek such security co-operation.

Similarities

There are already similarities between the security circumstances of the NATO countries and those of certain East Asian nations: first, the Soviet Union is a primary source of military threat; second, alliance with the US is the mainstay of security; third, the regional stability of strategically important areas in the Third World is increasingly important; and fourth, public opinion has a great impact on the formation of security policies.

This is applicable particularly to Japan, and to Australia and New Zealand, which are inseparable from the security of East

Asia. It also applies with some qualifications to South Korea, and to a lesser extent to the Philippines. It could also apply to a degree, to some non-allied countries in East Asia, particularly those of ASEAN.

The first point, that the Soviet Union is a *primary* source of threat to both the NATO countries and those in East Asia, is one of the major reasons why the need for a global approach to security has come to be emphasized among the Western industrialized democracies in which Japan is included. Such security concerns as the Soviet Union's invasion of Afghanistan and its deployment of SS-20 intermediate-range ballistic missiles (IRBM) have made it increasingly evident in recent years that the US and its allies in both Western Europe and East Asia share common interests. Moreover, given that the Soviet military build-up in East Asia in the past ten years appears to be designed to affect the global East–West military balance as well as the regional one, it has become increasingly important for all Western nations, whether or not in East Asia, to be concerned with this.

With regard to the second point, alliance relationships with the United States, a growing American tendency to demand that its allies should bear a greater share of the burden of international security has been making the management of alliance politics a matter of common concern to US allies in both Western Europe and East Asia. Moreover, while political solidarity between the US and its allies becomes vital in coping with such questions as arms control and the transfer of high technology to the USSR, yet the problems involved in these areas are also working to awaken US allies in Western Europe and East Asia to interests which they might possibly share in their relations with the United States.

Third, the question of regional stability in the Third World has become a matter of common concern to the industrialized nations of the Atlantic Alliance and East Asia, as the growing interdependence, political and economic, between various parts of the world has become plain. The increased impact which Third-World conflicts could have on global security has given this greater emphasis, the Arab-Israeli wars and the Iran-Iraq war being cases in point.

The political and economic stability of the countries in East Asia is also important to Western security. The political stability of the Philippines is vital for the functioning of the American deterrent capability in the Western Pacific, which has significant implications for the protection of Western interests in the Indian Ocean and the Gulf. It is also obvious that ASEAN is important for the West as a whole. The economic difficulties of these nations, if not properly attended to by the Western industrialized democracies would provide a welcome opportunity to the Soviet Union for political, if not military, advances into the region. Western nations should similarly be alert to the recent Soviet moves in the South Pacific.

With regard to the fourth point noted above, public opinion, it hardly needs stressing that one of the most important common tasks is to respond to public fear and anxiety about nuclear weapons and about US, let alone Soviet, nuclear strategy. Modern communications and mass media allow such public concerns to spread between nations faster and more directly than ever before.

Differences

Despite all these similarities, there are some marked differences between the security conditions of the NATO countries and those of the free-world nations in East Asia.

The first is that there is a variety of threat perceptions in East Asia, which derive from different local circumstances. The existence of China particularly distinguishes East Asian security concerns from those of the Atlantic allies. Of course, the North American and Western European nations and many in East Asia share the common interest that China should maintain its independent foreign policy, particularly in its relations with the Soviet Union. But the implications of China for the regional military balance are more direct, and therefore more complex, in East Asia than in Western Europe. It should be noted here that for many in Asia such an eventuality, for example, a direct military conflict between the Soviet Union and China that might involve other neighbouring countries, is a source of serious concern. And the enhancement of Chinese military strength, with a possibility that this might pose a regional military threat, is a subject of anxious attention, particularly for countries in South-east Asia. It needs to be underlined in this regard that the Western industrialized nations should not take for granted the present Chinese posture towards the West. China pursues its independent foreign policy not only in its relations with the USSR but also in its approach towards the West. Efforts to keep China favourably disposed to the West therefore need to be sustained.

The second difference relates to alliance relationships with the US, which vary between Western Europe and East Asia. Most of the countries in Western Europe are in NATO, while only a few in East Asia are allied with the United States. In East Asia, to maintain close co-operation with non-allied free-world nations, such as many in ASEAN, is most important for Western security. However, all the American alliance systems functioning in East Asia – except for ANZUS in its original form – are bilateral ones. Furthermore, the pattern of alliance relations is also different. The relationships between Western Europe and Canada and America are based on historical, social and cultural bonds, whereas the alliances with the US in East Asia are set against varying political, economic, cultural and historical backgrounds. This results in differing patterns of alliance politics.

Most fundamentally, military strategy differs. While NATO needs American nuclear weapons as well as American ground forces to make up for a Western European weakness in relation to the Warsaw Pact in conventional forces, the alliance systems in East Asia, except in the case of South Korea, are not faced with such an obvious conventional imbalance, at least not so far. This is largely because the Pacific Ocean is the setting for the US military presence. The function of American nuclear forces is therefore far less conspicuous in East Asia.

South Korea alone is faced with a Communist adversary across the border, as is Western Europe. The presence of US armed forces there is vitally important for the security of South Korea, backed by the essential presence of US naval and air power in the Far East and the Western Pacific. The US-Japan and US-Philippines security arrangements are important for the effective functioning of American deterrence in the region, although their importance is of course far more extensive than this.

A third marked distinction between the security of East Asia and that of the NATO countries is the vital problem of regional domestic stability. Many countries in East Asia are still at the developing stage and remain fragile politically as well as economically. They are vulnerable to interference from outside. To ensure domestic stability is thus a premise for the security of the countries in East Asia. Although many of them in recent years have made dynamic economic progress, their economic and political structures are as yet weak and they are now facing an economic slowdown.

Concerning public opinion, there is little need to explain the differences of interests and preoccupations between Western European and East Asian publics, let alone the differences between US public opinion and those of its allies. To complicate matters further, the level of mutual understanding between the publics of Western Europe and East Asia remains, broadly speaking, low, despite a growing awareness among experts and professionals of the need to improve it. It is particularly worrying here that mutual recrimination between the Western European countries and Japan is rising over trade and economic issues.

The differences noted above are the major ones affecting the security of NATO and East Asia, as seen from a Japanese perspective. There are no doubt many other differences which should be taken into consideration if security co-operation between countries in NATO and in East Asia is to be sought. A conclusion that could possibly be drawn from these observations is that security co-operation between the free-world countries in the Atlantic Alliance and East Asia will not readily be forthcoming.

Japan's security policy

Japan stands unique among East Asian nations. Depending heavily upon the alliance with the US for its security, Japan's security policy has an overtone of being a member of the Western Alliance in a broader context of the word. First, Japan has been intensifying its efforts to strengthen its Self-Defense Forces (SDF), with a particular emphasis on air and naval capability. Although the operational responsibility of the SDF is strictly confined to the defence of Japanese territory and sea-lanes, strengthening the SDF's capability would help the United States allocate its resources to other areas so as to enhance the security of the region and, as a result, that of the West as a whole.

Secondly, Japan has also been intensifying its efforts to enhance the effectiveness of the Japan-US security arrangements. These efforts are in broad policy areas such as providing 120 facilities for the US forces; sharing part of the financial costs for the presence of US forces in Japan and facilitating the so-called 'home-porting' of a US aircraft carrier. The defence co-operation between the SDF and the US forces, which has been progressing rapidly in recent years, is serving the mutual interest in implementing better the security arrangements between the two countries.

As a third aspect of its security efforts, Japan conducts diplomatic activities aiming at the political and economic stability of the countries in the region. One such example is Japan's efforts to strengthen its political as well as economic support for South Korea. Japan was one of the first countries to extend support for the economic reconstruction of the Philippines. It is also the biggest donor to Thailand, which has been much troubled by the Vietnamese invasion of Kampuchea. The political and economic support of the ASEAN countries has been one of the major preoccupations of Japanese foreign policy. All these efforts are aimed at contributing to the peace and stability of East Asia. In the same vein, Japan extended financial support to Pakistan, Turkey, Egypt and Central American-Caribbean countries from the viewpoint of helping countries which are strategically important for regional stability. Japan's diplomatic efforts also include activities aiming at creating an environment which would facilitate a settlement of the Kampuchean question and the Iran-Iraq war.

Fourthly, Japan, with an increased awareness of the need to act as a member of the Western industrialized democracies, became a positive participant in the concerted Western efforts on such issues as the Soviet invasion of Afghanistan and the Poland crisis. Japan supported NATO's position on INF at the Williamsburg Summit. It is from the same viewpoint that

Japan started to participate in the process of consultations within the Western Alliance over arms control.

To act in international politics as a member of what might be called, in a broader context of the word, the Western Alliance, is now an important dimension of Japan's security policy.

Security co-operation

Yet, it is unrealistic to seek direct co-operation between NATO and the Japan-US security arrangements.

A more realistic approach to co-operative relationships between the NATO countries and Japan would be by way of closer consultations over questions of mutual concern. In this respect, it is a very welcome trend that the economic summits now pay attention to political and security questions. It is also encouraging to see that the bilateral consultations on security questions between Western European countries and Japan have increased at all levels, in addition to the already close US-Japan consultations. It is desirable that those consultations should help the countries concerned to understand each other's policy and thereby help to work out mutually productive co-operation in the spirit of partnership.

There is a timely subject for such consultations: how to co-ordinate policy towards the new Soviet approach towards Asia. The Soviet Union appears to have decided to re-emphasize its interests in East Asia, and the Gorbachev speech at Vladivostok in July 1986 was no doubt a part of this. Given the prospect that Soviet initiatives aiming at increasing influence in East Asia would have significant implications for Western security in the world as a whole, it is high time for the NATO countries and Japan to seek even closer co-operation in working out Western responses to these initiatives. One important such Western response is, of course, the efforts of the US and its allies to intensify defence efforts. To co-ordinate diplomatic responses is also vital. This is particularly true for Japan, which is seemingly one of the prime targets of the new Soviet policy towards East Asia.

Because of the characteristics of East Asia described earlier, the efforts to secure the political and economic stability of the countries in the region are important to Western security. For these nations are vulnerable to Soviet political, if not military interference. The North American and the Western European countries have already been exerting efforts with regard to the strategically important regions of Africa, the Middle East, South-west Asia and Latin America, and Japan has taken part in these concerted actions. In the same spirit, it is important to add the issue of regional stability in East Asia to the common agenda for Western security.

Looking towards the future, it is important for the Western nations, including Japan, to try to expand policy co-operation in the security field to include other East Asian nations, allied or non-allied. In the light of the importance of many non-allied nations in East Asia for Western security, it is too narrow to confine such co-operation to the one framed solely by the present alliance systems.

Such an attempt would obviously involve many difficulties. Yet, a combination of efforts designed for mutual benefit could be tried with the hope of improving the conditions surrounding relations between Western and many East Asian nations. It is plausible to expect in this regard that countries in East Asia might possibly come to seek closer co-operation with the Western industrialized democracies when they see Soviet attempts to increase its influence in East Asia. The prospect that not a few countries in this region are bound to become industrialized democracies could also work to create a favourable environment for closer co-operation between Western countries and those in East Asia.

A few approaches to this end are conceivable. First, the free-world countries in North America, Western Europe and East Asia could increase bilateral as well as multilateral opportunities to discuss security questions. They could also organize more systematic exchanges of information through a network of bilateral channels. Such information should include security policies and the analysis of international security conditions, particularly the assessment of threat. This is important to facilitate policy consultations.

Secondly, joint research and studies as well as dialogues on policy issues should be further strengthened at the private level among these nations. Needless to say, non-governmental dialogues could be much freer and therefore more creative in exploring avenues for security co-operation.

Thirdly, it is advisable to establish a forum for dialogue among the members of the legislatures of the free-world countries in North America, Western Europe and East Asia on security issues. It is encouraging to see that Japanese and Australian members have been attending the sessions of the North Atlantic Assembly for the past several years.

Dialogues among the elected officials of the countries concerned are important in order to reflect varying public security perceptions of the countries involved in debates exploring mutual security co-operation. Needless to say, public support is indispensable for any such co-operation. It is particularly so because in recent years the public opinion of democratic nations is the very target at which Soviet diplomatic strategy has been aiming.

These approaches would be painstakingly slow and they would in no way assure any positive result. After all, security co-operation has proved to be a difficult task even among the Western industrialized democracies, particularly in the absence of a common security perception. To expect any immediate result from these approaches would therefore be too ambitious. But dialogues along the lines described above would at least help the countries involved to understand each others' security perceptions as well as the different security conditions in which they find themselves. This could be the first step in the direction of seeking common ground for security co-operation, if there is any, between the West and the free-world nations in East Asia.

1990s

August 1990

Japan announces its contributions of funding to the UNSC-led coalition against Iraq, eventually amounting to US$13bn.

August 1990

Iraq invades Kuwait.

October 1990

Germany is reunified.

December 1990

The Nikkei Stock Market loses US$2trn in value over 12 months by December 1990.

January 1991

The First Gulf War begins.

April 1991

JSDF minesweepers are deployed to the Persian Gulf, the JSDF's first overseas dispatch.

June 1991

South Africa repeals apartheid legislation.

August 1991

An unsuccessful coup against Soviet leader Mikhail Gorbachev contributes to the collapse of the Soviet Union.

January 1992

Prime Minister Miyazawa Kiichi officially apologises to South Korea for the abduction of 'comfort women' during the Second World War.

May 1992

The Japan New Party is founded; it dissolves in 1994.

June 1992

Japan enacts the Act on Cooperation with United Nations Peacekeeping Operations and Other Operations.

September 1992

Approximately 600 JSDF personnel are deployed to Cambodia, marking the service's first support to a UN peacekeeping operation.

December 1992

The North America Free Trade Agreement (NAFTA) is signed by the leaders of Canada, Mexico and the US.

January 1993

The Strategic Arms Reduction Treaty (START) II is signed by the US and Russia, banning the use of multiple independently targetable re-entry vehicles (MIRVs) on intercontinental ballistic missiles (ICBMs).

July 1993

Japan hosts the 1993 G7 Summit in Tokyo.

August 1993

Hosokawa Morihiro of the Japan New Party is elected prime minister, leading a seven-party coalition. This is the first time since 1955 that a non-LDP government is formed.

October 1993

Japan hosts the first Tokyo International Conference on African Development (TICAD). In the same month, 75 Japanese police officers are deployed to Cambodia to participate in UN peacekeeping operations.

November 1993

The Maastricht Treaty enters into force, officially creating the EU.

 **DOMESTIC EVENTS**    **INTERNATIONAL ENGAGEMENT**    **KEY GLOBAL EVENTS**

June 1994

The Aum Shinrikyo cult carries out the deadly Sarin gas attack in Matsumoto, Nagano prefecture, killing eight people and injuring over 600.

December 1994

The First Chechen War begins, lasting until August 1996.

January 1995

The World Trade Organization (WTO) is created.

July 1995

China conducts missile tests near Taiwan. Aggressive military tactics continue until March 1996. This is known as the third Taiwan Strait crisis, the previous two being in 1954–55 and 1958.

November 1995

Japan hosts the APEC summit in Osaka.

April 1996

The US–Japan Joint Declaration on Security is announced, returning land occupied by the US Marine Corps' Futenma Air Station in Okinawa.

December 1996

As a direct response to the Okinawa rape incident, the US agrees to reduce the acreage of its bases in Okinawa prefecture by 21% by 2008.

July 1997

Hong Kong is returned to China.

September 1997

The Guidelines for US–Japan Defense Cooperation are revised to expand the alliance's role to maintain peace and stability in the region.

June 1998

The Financial Supervisory Agency is created, separate from the Ministry of Finance, to conduct detailed inspections of Japan's financial institutions. The FSA is merged with the Financial System Planning Bureau in 2000 to become the Financial Services Agency.

June 1994

The LDP returns to power in a coalition government, led by Murayama Tomiichi, Japan's first socialist prime minister since Katayama Tetsu in 1947–48.

January 1995

The Great Hanshin-Awaji Earthquake occurs, leaving approximately 6,434 dead, 43,792 injured and three missing.

March 1995

The Aum Shinrikyo cult carries out another deadly Sarin gas attack in the Tokyo subway, killing 13 and injuring over 6,000 people.

September 1995

Three US servicemen in Okinawa rape a 12-year-old Okinawan girl. The Okinawa rape incident triggers widespread debate over the presence of US forces in Okinawa.

March 1996

Lee Teng-hui becomes the first directly elected president of Taiwan, marking its transition to a democracy.

September 1996

The Democratic Party of Japan (DPJ) is formed from the merger of several opposition parties.

April 1997

The national consumption tax is raised from 3% to 5%.

July 1997

Thailand devalues its currency relative to the US dollar, triggering the Asian financial and economic crises of 1997–98.

May 1998

Pakistan successfully conducts its first nuclear-weapons test.

August 1998

North Korea test fires its *Taepodong*-1 ballistic missile.

 DOMESTIC EVENTS  **INTERNATIONAL ENGAGEMENT**  **KEY GLOBAL EVENTS**

October 1998

The Japan–Republic of Korea Joint Declaration is agreed following the state visit of South Korean President Kim Dae-jung to Japan. The agreement pledges improved bilateral relations.

January 1999

The euro is launched, first as an 'invisible currency' for accounting and electronic purposes.

May 1999

Japan's Emergency-at-Periphery Law is enacted, enabling it to respond to contingencies in nearby areas that could spread to Japan, and not just those within.

November 1998

The Japan–China Summit and Joint Declaration on Building a Partnership of Friendship and Cooperation outlines Japan–China relations for the 21st century.

February 1999

The Bank of Japan announces its zero interest-rate policy.

 **DOMESTIC EVENTS** **INTERNATIONAL ENGAGEMENT**  **KEY GLOBAL EVENTS**

CHAPTER EIGHTEEN

Japan's role in international affairs

Takashi Inoguchi

From Survival 34-2, 1992

A debate is under way – both in Japan and in capitals around the world – about the role Japan should play in international affairs. Some maintain that Japan should do more, given its position as one of the world's leading economic powers. Others worry that the emergence of an active, assertive Japan would alarm its neighbours and disrupt existing patterns of relations among the great powers. The worst-case scenario, according to some, is that an energetic Japan might become aggressive and militaristic.

In this article, the international and domestic factors that will shape the course of Japan's foreign and security policy in the near future are analysed. The article begins by examining the international and domestic pressures that are pushing Japan in the direction of a more activist role in international affairs. Next, the international and domestic impediments to a more active Japanese role are assessed. Finally, Japan's role in two issue areas of particular importance, international economic affairs and international security institutions, are examined.

The pressures on Japan to play a greater role in world affairs are beginning to overwhelm the countervailing obstacles. Japan, in short, will probably play a more active role internationally in the future than it has in the past. Moreover, this development should be encouraged, provided two conditions are met. First, Japan's policies must be in harmony with those of the international community as a whole. In practice, this means that Japan's actions should be linked to multilateral undertakings wherever possible. Second, Tokyo's initiatives need to be grounded by a solid domestic consensus about the broad course and content of Japan's foreign policy.

International pressures for a more active role in world affairs

A number of developments in the 1980s began to push Japan in the direction of a more active international role. In security affairs, the United States embarked on a systematic campaign to strengthen its military forces, both conventional and nuclear. The belief in Washington, at least during the first term of the Reagan administration, was that the Soviet Union had to be countered militarily if it was to be contained politically. With that in mind, the United States encouraged its allies, including Japan, to strengthen their own forces. Japanese Prime Minister Yasuhiro Nakasone supported this policy by increasing defence spending, increasing the amount of support provided to US troops stationed in Japan and entering into a number of joint technological ventures and wide-ranging joint military exercises with the United States. These exercises essentially overturned Japan's longstanding policy of restricting the activities of its Self-Defense Forces (SDF) to local venues.

At the same time, the economic fortunes of the United States and Japan began to go in opposite directions. By the mid-1980s, the United States was immersed in record budget deficits as a result of a severe recession, deep tax cuts and high levels of military spending. Its fiscal resources were limited, and its long-term economic competitiveness began to suffer. Japan's economy, on the other hand, was robust. Japan's industrial competitiveness, bolstered by favourable exchange rates, generated ever-higher levels of exports. This, in turn, embedded Japan even more deeply in the international economic system, giving it a wide range of international economic interests and making it highly interdependent with other countries.

By the time Yasuhiro Nakasone and Ronald Reagan left office in 1987 and 1988, respectively, the Cold War order was beginning to crumble. The US military build-up, combined with Soviet economic weaknesses and a commitment in Moscow to improve relations with the West, led to the signing of the Intermediate-range Nuclear Forces (INF) Treaty in December 1987. This treaty, the first to eliminate entire classes of nuclear weapons from the arsenals of the superpowers, marked an end to the most intense phase of the US–Soviet military competition and led many to conclude that further improvements in East–West relations were likely to be forthcoming. And, indeed, they were. The collapse of Soviet power in Eastern Europe in 1989, the Soviet decision to accept the reunification of Germany and the signing of the Conventional Armed Forces in Europe (CFE) Treaty in 1990 clearly indicated that the Cold War was over. The final chapter in the Cold War unfolded in December 1991, when the Soviet Union itself disintegrated.

These developments have had a tremendous impact on international relations as a whole and on Japan in particular. The old bipolar international order has collapsed, but a new order has not yet emerged in its place. What is clear, however, is that this new order will be multipolar in character and that all of the world's leading powers, including Japan, will have an important role in shaping it. Many world leaders would like to see Japan play a more active role in these deliberations.

Second, with the demise of the Soviet military threat, military power is not as important in international affairs as it once was. This is not to say that it has become unimportant, only that economic power has become increasingly significant. Many people around the world feel that Japan, with its immense financial, industrial and technological resources, should be more active in addressing international problem areas. The most pressing issues in the world today, many would argue, are not deterrence and defence, but economic reconstruction (in Eastern Europe and the former Soviet Union) and economic development (in the Third World). Few states are in a better position to deal with these economic problems than Japan. Policy-makers and analysts around the world are putting pressure on Japan to do more. Clearly, one of the driving forces behind Japan's growing role in world affairs has been the demand by the United States and others for Japan to assume more global responsibilities.

Other economic and political developments have also propelled Japan into a leading role in world affairs. Under President George Bush, the United States has maintained rigid tax and energy policies, and US industry, on the whole, has failed to become significantly more competitive internationally. As a result, the United States lacks significant financial or economic leverage in its international dealings. Second, a cascade of events in Europe – the liberation of Eastern Europe and the dissolution of the Warsaw Pact, German unification, the disintegration of Yugoslavia and the Soviet Union and the signing of the Maastricht Treaty on European economic and political union – has kept Europe preoccupied. Most of Europe's intellectual energy and economic resources are being devoted to local problems. Finally, other countries with large trade surpluses, such as Taiwan and some oil-exporting countries, are unwilling or unable to play a leading role in international affairs.

Thus, Japan with its high savings rates and large trade surplus has emerged as virtually the only country that can afford to underwrite large-scale international public policy actions.

Domestic pressures for a more active role in world affairs

'Occupying an honourable place in the international community' was an aspiration of Japanese people even before this phrase was written into the 1952 Constitution. Since 1952, Japan's desire to be accepted as a full-fledged member of the international community has been reflected in its membership in international institutions such as the United Nations Educational, Scientific and Cultural Organization (UNESCO), the General Agreement on Tariffs and Trade (GATT), the United Nations (UN), the Organization for Economic Co-operation and Development (OECD) and the Western Economic Summit.

More recently, Japan has begun to play a more influential role in institutions such as the International Monetary Fund (IMF) and the World Bank. This is not at all surprising, given Japan's position in the international economic hierarchy and the Japanese people's longstanding interest in multilateral organizations. In the World Bank, for example, Japan's capital share was 2.77% in 1952 when it obtained membership and 6.69% in 1987, second only to the United States. In the International Development Association, an arm of the World Bank, Japan's replenishment share was 4.44% in 1961 and 20.98% in 1990, again second only to the United States.[1]

Japan is also interested in attaining a prominent position on the UN Security Council and would like to establish closer ties to the North Atlantic Treaty Organization (NATO), the European Community (EC) and the Conference on Security and Co-operation in Europe (CSCE). If the international community encouraged and endorsed developments along these lines, Japan would not hesitate to pursue them. Japan's self-confidence in this regard is clearly growing.[2]

It is important to keep in mind, however, that there are internal debates in Japan on the international stance that country should take. For example, an inconclusive debate about the perennial US–Japan trade imbalance has been conducted between Japan's Economic Planning Agency and the Ministry of Finance. The US government has argued that Japan must eliminate structural barriers against imports to reduce Japan's trade surplus. In response, the Economic Planning Agency has argued that the root cause of the trade imbalance is macroeconomic: US savings rates must be raised, and the US fiscal deficit must be reduced. The Ministry of Finance, on the other hand, has argued that Japan needs to run a large trade surplus, given existing international demands for economic assistance and foreign direct investment. In addition, the Ministry worries that savings rates in Japan will decline as the population ages, and the country's capital resources will dwindle as a result. In short, the former is aggressive in calling for changes in an ally's savings and spending behaviour, while the latter is self-serving in its justification of the *status quo*.

Policy disputes also emerged in the internal deliberations leading up to the agreement reached between Japan and the EC in July 1991. According to the terms of this agreement, Japan and the EC are to hold regular consultative meetings on a wide range of issues, including security. The EC was reluctant to enter into discussions with Japan on security issues, especially European security issues; France, in particular, was adamantly opposed to this. Japan's Ministry of Foreign Affairs was anxious to move in this direction, but the Ministry of International Trade and Industry was apprehensive: it feared that pushing ahead in the security arena would create a backlash on trade issues, given that Japan had perennial trade surpluses *vis-à-vis* most EC members. In the end, Japan and the EC agreed that they would attempt to provide 'equitable access' to each other's market. The Ministry of International Trade and Industry is not unaware of the need to liberalize the Japanese economy in light of the fact that Japan is virtually the only country with a large trade surplus; criticism from abroad is likely to mount unless such efforts are vigorously undertaken by Japan.[3]

International impediments to a more active role in world affairs

Japanese misconduct in the 1930s and 1940s casts a long shadow over Japan's international activities even today.[4] It is important to recognize that Japan's actions in the 1930s and 1940s were indeed very cruel. Although most Japanese acknowledge this, many feel that Japan behaved no more brutally than other powers. In addition, abetted by the version of history propounded by the Allied occupation powers, most Japanese regard themselves as victims of a past engineered by the militarist cliques. As a result, Japan has not always done enough to atone for past misconduct.

Not surprisingly, many of Japan's neighbours – the two Koreas, China, the Philippines, Singapore, Malaysia and Hong Kong – are apprehensive about Japan's growing economic influence. The concern is that economic preponderance could transform at some point into military dominance. Although official protests to the Japanese government have been rare, unofficial murmurings are not uncommon. Various newspapers in the region expressed concern, for example, about Prime Minister Nakasone's visit in 1985 to the Yasukuni shrine for the war dead, including war criminals; about Japan's decision in 1986 to build an advanced jet fighter (the FSX) on a largely indigenous basis; about Japan's growing levels of defence spending (which surpassed 1% of gross national product in 1987); about Japan's decision to send mine-sweepers to the Persian Gulf in 1991; and about Japan's recent moves to pass legislation that would allow the SDF to be sent abroad.

Powers outside the region also have reservations about Japan's growing role in international affairs. The five victorious allies in World War II whose pre-eminent positions were institutionalized in the United Nations – the United States, Britain, France, China and (now) Russia – naturally do not want to give up their places of prominence. However, UN financial contributions of the vanquished powers of World War II – Germany and Japan, in particular – have been increasing at a faster rate than those of the victorious powers.[5] As a result, German and Japanese influence in UN debates has been growing. The funding issue is delicate, however, because although the victorious powers do not want to see the UN fall apart or their institutional positions deteriorate, they are not, by and large, able to increase their own contributions; the US Congress, for example, is adamant about any increase in US support for the United Nations. In addition, the five permanent members of the Security Council are reluctant to introduce the question of permanent membership for Germany and Japan.

Ironically, one of the main countries presenting a covert barrier to Japan's assumption of a greater role in world affairs is the United States, which has for many years publicly argued that Japan should assume more of the collective defence burden. As a recent US Defense Department memorandum indicates, there is a great deal of interest in some segments of the US policy establishment in maintaining a preeminent global military position. According to this memorandum, the United States should seek to maintain a military position that would enable it to dominate a unified Europe, a restructured Commonwealth of Independent States (CIS) or a more assertive Japan.[6] Thus, some in the United States would like to share the defence burden without relinquishing the pre-eminent military position the country now enjoys.

Two things work to moderate these impediments, however. First, those Pacific Asian countries with close economic ties to Japan – trade, investment, manufacturing and training – tend to have higher economic growth rates than countries that do not. Recognizing the increasing dependence on Japanese capital and technology for their own economic development, they have tended to moderate the otherwise harsh criticism of Japan. Japan's application of economic sanctions following the Tiananmen Square massacre in June 1989 is a good example of this.

Second, Japan's economic success has encouraged others to emulate the Japanese model – that is, the Japanese system of financing, manufacturing, distribution, education, health care and pollution control. Some South-east Asian countries have even adopted Japanese-style police and military institutions; others have attempted to hire Japanese forces to provide internal security at a time of rapid socioeconomic change.[7] This suggests that views in Asia are changing from what they were 30 or 40 years ago.

Domestic impediments to a more active role in world affairs

The increasing demands for Japan to assume more global responsibilities, in conjunction with the international and domestic opposition to such steps, has led Japanese policy to zigzag in a manner frequently characterized as 'two steps forward and one step backward'. In the words of Ichiro Ozawa, the former secretary-general of the ruling Liberal Democratic Party, it is 'the Japanese way of leaving everything in an ambiguous state and accumulating established facts through makeshift circumstantial judgments'.[8]

For example, Prime Minister Zenko Suzuki visited the United States in May 1982 to meet President Ronald Reagan; they subsequently issued a communiqué in which the word 'alliance' was used. In terms of shouldering more responsibilities, confirmation of an alliance relationship by a Japanese prime minister was 'two steps forward'. However, Suzuki reinterpreted the word 'alliance' and insisted that this did not refer to a military alliance – thus, 'one step backward'. This was later followed by Suzuki's abrupt resignation, Yasuhiro Nakasone's assumption of power and Nakasone's subsequent championing of legislation that paved the way for military co-operation with the United States. This move represented another 'two steps forward'.

Similarly, the Japanese government's response to the Gulf crisis in 1990–91 was also characterized by zigzagging.[9] The Japanese government introduced a bill in the Diet that would have allowed Japan to send Self-Defense Forces abroad for peace-keeping operations, but the bill was killed in late 1990 because of pacifist sentiments at home. Following the Gulf War's end in March 1991, the Japanese government, emboldened by apparent public support for the SDF's mine-sweeping operation in the Gulf, tabled a revised bill, potentially opening the way for the SDF to be sent abroad. However, by failing to accommodate the Democratic Socialist Party demand for a revision of the bill – which insisted that the Diet had to give prior approval before the SDF could be sent abroad – the bill was killed. In the spring 1992 session of the Diet, the government tried to advance its position by confining SDF missions to UN peace-keeping operations.

The reasons for such fluctuation in Japanese foreign policy lie in the domestic impediments to an activist policy. First, the pacifist tendencies that grew out of Japan's experiences in World War II are still strong. A particularly powerful domestic approach is known as 'pacifism in one country', which reasons that even if other states are aggressive, Japan should restrain itself from using force or participating in violent international conflicts.

Second, domestic vested interests oppose taking any steps that might undermine economic prosperity at home. Many believe that the preservation of Japan's economic dynamism is the key to overcoming global economic difficulties.

Third, decision-making in Japan is consensual, and it is undermined by a lack of strong political leadership. Consequently, it is difficult for the Japanese government to move quickly to shoulder new international responsibilities. Instead, the government tends to move incrementally. For example, it might attempt to develop a broader or more flexible interpretation of the Constitution. Thus, a consensus would be sought, which would seek to incorporate as many divergent positions as possible.

Net assessment

The pressures on Japan to assume a more active role in world affairs appear to outweigh the countervailing forces. Japan has the will, the need and the capacity to assume more global responsibilities. It is driven by a tenaciously held aspiration to occupy an honourable place in the world, increasingly dictated by the self-interested need to sustain international stability and economic prosperity. It is also likely to enjoy high savings rates and increasing technological accomplishment for some time. Thus, as long as Japan does not deviate substantially in its positions from the international community as a whole, the United States and other leading powers will, with but limited reservations, continue to prod Japan to do more. If the world economy avoids the beggar-thy-neighbour policies of the 1930s, economic interdependence will deepen. This, in turn, will strengthen Japan's overall international position.

Naturally, Japan's historical legacy, its weakly articulated vision of its international role and its feeble political leadership will prevent it from taking up some responsibilities with vigour. These, however, are constraints that Japan will have to live with for the foreseeable future.

Japan's role in international economic affairs

In examining Japan's role in international economic affairs, one has to consider both unilateral actions, such as economic aid, and multilateral activities in institutions such as the Group of Seven (G-7) and the World Bank.

The argument of 'yen for development' has been made by many and is fairly well accepted by Japan.[10] Acting within the financial constraints imposed by savings rates, energy and food needs, demographic structure and other factors, Japan's role in aiding development is bound to constitute a major pillar in its approach to shouldering global responsibilities.

Japan's financial contributions to Third World economic development, human and social needs and environmental protection are expected to be increasingly aimed towards Africa, South Asia and the Middle East, compared with previous support, which was largely concentrated on East and South-east Asia. Staggering amounts of debt accumulated by countries such as Brazil and Mexico have also drawn Japanese banking interests to Latin America. In the 1980s, Japanese banks increasingly helped compensate for the difficulties associated with bad debts. In the Pacific, Japan has been encouraging both recipient and donor countries alike to consider not only what is essential for manufacturing and infrastructure development, but also the needs associated with environmental protection and social and political stability. Thus, Japan's role has become much more complex and wide-ranging in the Asian Pacific.

The sudden disappearance of command economies in many Eurasian countries has also expanded Japan's role. Prime Minister Toshiki Kaifu's pledge to aid East European countries in January 1990 was the first of its kind. The Japanese government's recent emergency aid to Mongolia to facilitate the transition to a market economy is another. Most recently, emergency aid was given to the Commonwealth of

Independent States. In addition, a number of plans are being drawn up in Japan to help the CIS – especially the Russian Republic – move away from its tightly regulated economy. In light of the growing mood of reconciliation between the Russian Republic and Japan after the August 1991 abortive *coup d'état* in Moscow, these plans could become quite extensive, at least in the long term. Aiding the CIS has been made particularly attractive because of increasing needs by Japan for energy and other resources still to be exploited in Siberia, the Far East and Central Asia. In addition, there has been a steadily growing geographical division of labour among the European Community (Moscow and St Petersburg), the United States (the vast industrial area surrounding the Urals) and Japan (the vast Siberia, the Far East and Central Asia).[11]

The eagerness of North Korea to bring in Japanese capital and technology to make itself more competitive *vis-à-vis* South Korea has reinforced the expectation that Japan would help North Korea so that, should there be a sudden reunification of the two Koreas, South Korea would not be bankrupted by the heavy burden of absorbing North Korea.

Of course, Japan's contributions to the execution of the Gulf War included a large transfer of funds to the United States. Due in part to Japan's Gulf War contributions, the US current account deficit decreased from $92.1 billion in 1990 to $8.6 billion in 1991.[12]

Japan's unilateral actions increasingly include the dissemination of the 'Japanese development model'. Many would like to draw on this model and the Japanese development experience. The latest to import the Japanese model is Peru, under President Alberto Fujimori. Some of Japan's East and Southeast Asian neighbours (for example, China and Malaysia) and former socialist countries (such as Hungary) find it relevant to their own development.

Japan's role in multilateral economic activities is no less important. Japan's multilateral activities take place in such international institutions as the IMF, the World Bank, the Inter-American Development Bank, the Asian Development Bank, the OECD, the Bank for International Settlement (BIS), the G-7, the European Bank for Reconstruction and Development and the Post-Ministers' Conference of the Association of South-east Asian Nations (ASEAN). Japan makes a significant contribution in two areas of multilateral activities: surveillance and systems design.

In this context, surveillance is the monitoring of data pertaining to global management and to the improvement of indicators and measurement for such monitoring. Japan's surveillance activities involve wide-ranging policy areas, detailing economic, technological and social activities.[13] These contributions have been quite robust, and Japanese technical expertise has had considerable impact on organizations such as the OECD and Asian-Pacific Economic Co-operation (APEC). Befitting its status as an economic superpower, Japan has moved ahead steadily in consolidating economic surveillance, in part because organizations such as the IMF and World Bank have become less vigorous in this task.

Systems design includes envisioning, conceptualizing and institutionalizing devices and mechanisms for global management. Requests for such a role have been increasingly heard from within and outside Japan. The need for systems design covers virtually all major fields, including manufacturing (for example, the Intelligent Manufacturing System, a system of jointly constructing and utilizing manufacturing technologies), environmental protection (for example, a system of controlling carbon dioxide emissions around the globe), administrative institutions (for example, a system of recruiting and training bureaucrats) and economic development (for example, a system of state-led, yet market-based, economies, much like Japan's in the 1950s and 1960s).[14]

The latest Japanese development in systems design can be found in the way in which US-led World Bank lending strategies were called into question by World Bank Executive Director Masaki Shiratori, who pushed successfully for the publication of a controversial study on the industrial strategies of South Korea, Indonesia and India. The study argued that select government intervention can complement market mechanisms and thus promote economic development.[15] If World Bank lending policies change in the direction envisioned by Shiratori, then economic development policy of recipient countries will also change to an enormous extent.

Growing interdependence and finite financial resources force donors like Japan to weigh many different options before arriving at the best portfolio of contributions. This process requires donors to have a much more global outlook and a clearer sense of global citizenship. In other words, the Japanese need to depart from the all-too-often narrowly conceived calculations of national interest. Domestically, the Japanese must rectify and restructure their often opaque system to ensure that the Japanese entry into global systems design is more apparent and acceptable to the rest of the global community. Japan's role in envisioning, conceptualizing and designing global systems in the future is bound to grow when the Japanese are convinced of such needs.

Japan's role in international security institutions

Japan's role in international security is an area that creates controversy, as the attendant phrases 'cheque-book diplomacy' and 'revival of militarism' imply. However, Japan's role in international security has begun to take shape steadily, albeit slowly. Aside from bilateral regimes and devices such as the

Japan–US Security Treaty and the Japan–Republic of Korea Basic Treaty, which are not covered here, the five most important institutions for Japanese security are the UN, NATO, CSCE, the G-7 and the Post-Ministers' Conference of ASEAN. As long as Japan's role is to consolidate global peace and development, its role in relation to these five institutions must be discussed, even if one has difficulties envisioning how this might unfold. The Japanese government has several concerns regarding the United Nations: deletion of the 'enemies' clause in the UN Charter, accession to permanent membership on the Security Council, participation of Japan's SDF in the UN peace-keeping forces and monitoring of arms transfers. The Japanese government also wants to enhance its current 'observership' status in the CSCE and in NATO. The Japanese government wants to see the G-7 raise several global issues, including security, as part of their agenda for discussion and co-operation. Finally, the Japanese government would like to see the Post-Ministers' Conference of ASEAN take up regional security issues.

Japanese participation in the UN

The United Nations, an organization established by the major victors of World War II, originally excluded Japan as a defeated country. It was not until 1956 that Japan was able to become a member, and today Japan still lives with the 'enemies' article (Article 107) of the UN Charter. Although the three original 'enemies' of the UN – Japan, Germany and Italy – make financial contributions that together match that of the United States – some 25% – none of these countries is represented on a permanent basis on the Security Council. Italy has recently proposed that the 'enemies' clause be deleted from the UN Charter. Japanese Prime Minister Kiichi Miyazawa, too, has expressed Japan's long-term desire to enhance its representation, albeit in a characteristically vague expression in a speech at a UN Security Council meeting engineered by British Prime Minister John Major.

Because of the torrent of resistance likely to face Japan when it moves onto the world stage, especially in the political and military arenas, the Japanese government prefers to move slowly. Even though permanent membership on the Security Council is one of the Japanese government's goals, the time is not yet perceived to be ripe for both the current permanent members and non-members, particularly for Japan itself, to move boldly in this direction. Japan would have difficulties fully abiding by a number of key clauses of the UN Charter that pertain to political and military roles, particularly those that apply to permanent members. A still-influential interpretation of Japan's Constitution forbids Japan from using military force for the resolution of international disputes. However, the special deliberative council of the ruling party has recently put forward a document asserting that the SDF's participation in the UN forces (as distinguished from UN peacekeeping operations) is fully constitutional.

Two bills, which were not addressed in the autumn session of 1991, have much to do with this point. If the interpretation of the Cabinet Legislative Bureau is accepted, these bills would allow Japan's SDF to participate as part of UN peacekeeping forces and would allow Japanese emergency relief forces to work on world disasters. These would clearly be two steps forward.

In autumn 1991, the two bills met with fierce opposition by some in the ruling party (which opposed the SDF's participation in the UN peace-keeping forces, if not the UN peace-keeping operations) and by the small opposition party, the Democratic Socialist Party, which demanded the Diet's prior approval before sending the SDF to those missions. Perhaps recognizing the lack of wisdom in skirting the well-established practice of consensus formation, Foreign Minister Michio Watanabe has been hinting of late about a 'moderated' version of the two bills, clearly eyeing the spring 1992 Diet session.

Aside from the zigzagging domestic legislative process, reinforced by the scandals of the ruling Liberal Democratic Party (LDP), international policies have been steadily shaped in favour of greater Japanese contributions. Cambodia is one example. Yasushi Akashi has been made head of the UN Transitional Authority in Cambodia (UNTAC), and the UN High Commissioner for Refugees is Sadako Ogata; both appointments are widely regarded as conducive to greater Japanese financial (and other) contributions to the United Nations. Domestically, the latest changes in the SDF's officers' assignments suggest the SDF's preparedness to meet the likely contingency of being sent to join peace-keeping and other types of operations in Cambodia, and possibly elsewhere.[16]

Permanent membership on the Security Council will be no less difficult. Japan was not able to be elected as a non-permanent member in 1978, was barely able to get elected in 1986 and got elected with a handsome vote only in 1991. The permanent membership issue was raised in 1990 at a meeting between Mikhail Gorbachev and Helmut Kohl when the Treaty on German Reunification was concluded. At that meeting, Gorbachev suggested that Germany become a permanent member of the Security Council. Reacting to this conversation, Italian Foreign Minister Gianni de Michelis suggested that the two West European members – Britain and France – be replaced by the EC and Japan, with the EC participant rotating among the four major EC members: Germany, Britain, France and Italy. Although the Japanese government has not made any comment on these events, its position is in stark contrast to Germany's. Germany has repeatedly expressed a lack of interest in seeking permanent membership on the Security Council, if only for tactical reasons.

One positive step the Japanese government has taken in relation to UN participation is to propose that the UN pass a resolution whereby all member countries register all arms transfers with the United Nations. Although the proposal does not go very far, it reflects Japan's concern about arms proliferation and takes a positive step towards conflict management. Although arms control expertise in Japan needs further development, Japanese technical expertise in monitoring and surveillance argues favourably for such a role for Japan.[17]

Japan's relations with NATO

Japan's interest in improving its observership status in NATO is somewhat different from its interest in the UN. The steady development of the notion of international security or co-operative security, which has developed extensively in the context of US–Soviet disarmament negotiations, has been a major factor driving Japanese interests. This has two related components. One is that the United States and the former Soviet Union, the two major nuclear superpowers, have had a strong interest in promoting steady and stable arms reductions, along with joint research and development, manufacturing and monitoring of military weapons. Japan, a US ally, feels that it should be kept informed of developments in this area to a greater extent than has been the case in the past. Indeed, Japan feels that it should be kept abreast of developments to the extent to which NATO members are informed. The second component is that, as an ally of the United States, Japan feels that it cannot help but be part of the broader US-led international security coalition, which includes NATO and the Republic of Korea (ROK). Bilateral arrangements function well with respect to US–Japan and Japan-ROK security consultations. Regarding NATO, however, no such forum existed until 1991, when Japan's observership in NATO began. Today, Japan's participation is still nominal, and much remains to be done if Japan is to take up global security responsibilities in the future. Exposure to regular meetings of NATO and to NATO-sponsored seminars and conferences would provide an impetus for Japan to provide training for more personnel in the realm of international security – one precondition for Japan's ability to monitor arms transfers and arms control actions.

Japan's interest in CSCE

Japan's interest in the CSCE, although overlapping its interest in NATO, does have somewhat different origins. In Japan, there is apprehension that Europe may evolve independently, possibly leaving Japan outside its consideration. With the end of the Cold War, the notion of Europe has clearly changed. According to US Secretary of State James Baker, Europe now extends 'from Vancouver to Vladivostok'. This suggests that emphasis is being given to a 'greater Europe', particularly in regard to the CSCE, perhaps because of the tendency on the European continent to think more narrowly. Although Baker's statement did not arouse a strong negative reaction in Japan, the fact that Japan is the only major developed country excluded from the CSCE or from Baker's notion of a greater Europe is disturbing to some Japanese.

The recently concluded agreement between Japan and the European Community on establishing regular consultative mechanisms underlines the same sort of apprehension. In addition, the CSCE has introduced new criteria for judging societal behaviour. Human rights and arms control are two international relations criteria that have not been particularly familiar to the Japanese government; until recently, the government had favoured more traditional concepts of relations between sovereign states.

Japan and the G-7

Although having started as a loose organization through which advanced countries could consult and co-ordinate their policies on global, regional and national economic issues, by 1991, the G-7 had become a global custodian for many international security issues. Its 1991 declaration on arms control with respect to nuclear weapons, proliferation, arms production and trade is a major step forward, particularly for Japan, because the G-7 represents an international institution in which Japan has been anchored for some time. The Japanese government would like to see the G-7 continue its work in the security area.

Japan and ASEAN

Although ASEAN functions largely as a regional organization, the Post-Ministers' Conference of ASEAN includes non-members such as the United States, Japan, South Korea and Australia. Although started as an anti-communist alignment of Asian nations, since the demise of the Cold War, ASEAN has developed into a more all-encompassing institution, with emphasis given to free trade and regional security. The East Asian Economic Grouping proposal by Prime Minister Mahathir Mohamad of Malaysia has sought to develop an East Asian Free Trade Area. This then resulted in a pronouncement by the Post-Ministers' Conference about regional security. ASEAN has long been regarded largely as a mouthpiece, taking little significant action, and, since that pronouncement, ASEAN has manifested its fissiparity in developing jointly executable ideas on regional security. Yet, to Japan, which has long been concerned about regional security, as the United States steadily reduces its military presence in the region, ASEAN's initiatives present significant value as a local initiative. Japan cannot envisage regional security arrangements that are not driven by regional powers. Because of Japan's historical debts, its economic preponderance and the potential rivalry with the United States, it feels it must be deferential to regional preferences and pursue joint activities wherever possible.

Conclusion

In sum, as far as international security policy is concerned, more time is needed for the Japanese to articulate their thoughts, given the large-scale structural transition taking place around the globe and Japan's traditional piecemeal adaptation to change. At present, Japan's interests derive largely from its 'search for an honourable place in the world community', from its apprehension of being isolated and from its genuine desire to make positive contributions to international security.

Those who complain that Japan's international efforts have been half-hearted should keep in mind that Japan has been a global power for only two decades. Another constraint has been that many in Japan worry about the future: an aging population and declining savings rates could lead to a deterioration in Japan's international position some time after the turn of this century. It is not surprising, therefore, that Japanese policy has been tentative in the past. In some respects, this might well continue into the future.

Overall, though, Japan's readiness to play a more active role in international affairs is growing. This should be encouraged as long as Japan's policies are compatible with those of the international community and Japan's initiatives are, by and large, undertaken in conjunction with multilateral ventures. Japan appears to be ready, willing and quite able to shoulder more global responsibilities. In all probability, therefore, Japan's contributions will steadily rise in tandem with the increase in the global demand for them and the rise in Japan's own capacity to supply them. As time goes by, Japan's international role is certain to broaden and deepen.

NOTES

1   Sadako Ogata, 'Shifting power relations in the multilateral development banks', *Journal of International Studies*, no. 22, January 1989, pp. 1–25.

2   Kuriyama Takakazu, 'New directions for Japanese foreign policy in the changing world of the 1990s', *Gaiko Forum*, no. 20, May 1990, pp. 12–22.

3   See Ministry of Industrial Trade and Industry, *White Paper* (Tokyo: Government Printing Office, 1991).

4   See Barry Buzan, 'Japan's future: old history versus new roles', *International Affairs*, vol. 64, no. 4, Autumn 1988, pp. 557–73.

5   In 1946, 33.9% of the UN's budget came from the United States, 0% from Japan, 6.6% from France, 12% from Britain and 6.3% from China. In 1968, 31.6% came from the United States, 3.8% from Japan, 14.6% from the Soviet Union, 0% from West Germany, 6% from France, 6.6% from Britain and 4% from China. In 1989–90, 25% came from the United States, 11.4% from Japan, 10% from the Soviet Union, 8.1% from West Germany, 6.3% from France, 4.9% from Britain and 0.8% from China. See Ministry of Foreign Affairs, *The UN and Japan* (Tokyo: Government Printing Office, May 1990), p. 11.

6   Patrick E. Tyler, 'Pentagon's new world order: US to reign supreme', *International Herald Tribune*, 9 March 1992, pp. 1–2.

7   Personal Communication with Atsushi Shimokobe, president of the National Institute for Research Advancement, 24 September 1991.

8   Quoted in 'Ozawa heads new committee', *Liberal Star*, 15 June 1991, p. 2.

9   Takashi Inoguchi, 'Japan's response to the Gulf War: an analytic overview', *Journal of Japanese Studies*, vol. 17, no. 2, Summer 1991, pp. 257–73.

10 Shafiqul Islam, ed., *Yen for Development* (New York: Council on Foreign Relations, 1990).

11 The Japanese government is now thinking of providing official development assistance to the Central Asian republics.

12 'US current account deficit greatly improved to 8.6 billion dollars for 1991', *Mainichi shimbun* (evening edition), 18 March 1992, p. 1.

13 Included in Japan's surveillance are monetary policies, commodity prices, exchange rates, economic growth rates, unemployment figures, energy demand and supply rates, climatic changes, environmental deterioration, population and migration

statistics, details on criminals and terrorists, literacy rates, arms production and trade, telecommunications and airline networks, transportation data, depletable resources, health and hygiene, scientific and technological developments and income distribution. Thus far, Japan has not done much monitoring of civil liberties, political freedom or human rights.

14 See 'Training customs officials from Asian countries', *Nihon keizai shimbun*, 25 August 1991, p. 3; 'Japan extends co-operation in environmental protection', *Nihon keizai shimbun*, 23 September 1991, p. 9; Okita Saburo, 'Contributions should be based on Japanese experiences', *Asahi Shimbun* (evening edition), 19 August 1991, p. 3.

15 Steven Brull, 'Japan wants strings on aid', *International Herald Tribune*, 9 March 1992, pp. 9, 11; Susumu Awanohara, 'Question of faith', *Far Eastern Economic Review*, 12 March 1992, p. 49.

16 'SDF personnel changes', *Asahi shimbun* (evening edition), 10 March 1992, p. 2.

17 'Consolidating the pool of arms control experts', *Nihon keizai shimbun*, 1 October 1991, p. 31.

CHAPTER NINETEEN

What role for Europe in Asian affairs?

Fumiaki Takahashi

From Adelphi Paper 276, 1993

After the Second World War, Europe withdrew militarily from Asia.[1] In the political field as well, Europe's role in Asia has decreased and its political interest has waned, due partly to the presence there of the United States, which has taken the greatest responsibility for the region's security, and partly to the influence of the former USSR and China during the Cold War. In the economic field, however, Europe has remained interested in the region and, in spite of – perhaps even because of – progress in the economic integration of the European Community (EC) and the economic development of East Asian countries, has contributed to the region's prosperity.

East Asia now has the world's fastest-growing economy, and a dynamic one, and has become a region which can assert influence, at least in the economic field, on a global scale. This coincides with the end of the Cold War and the collapse of the Soviet Union which have affected international relationships in Asia, although not as dramatically as in Europe. But as this new situation is bound to bring about a fundamental change in the structure of international politics, this in turn will gradually induce new developments in the international situation in East Asia. In this context, how will the relationship between Europe and Asia develop from now onwards?

East Asia and western Europe: the present situation

East Asia is not only made up of countries with very varied geopolitical characteristics – including population size, geographical factors, political and social systems, the degree of economic development and military capability – but also the peoples themselves vary greatly in their ethnic, linguistic, religious, traditional and other cultural aspects. Given both the different colonial pasts of the European countries and their current interest in the region, the roles they play there vary accordingly. Thus generalizations about the relationship between the two continents are hard to make.

Economy

As a result of global economic growth in recent years, the economic ties between Europe and Asia, which generate 30% and 20% of world national income respectively, have steadily strengthened. East Asia is a region in which the countries' economic size and stage of development, together with their economic structures and systems, differ enormously. The degree of importance which Europe has attached to its relations with these countries is roughly proportional to the degree of economic activity of the particular country or group of countries. Thus Europe's most significant relationship is with Japan, the only industrialized democracy in the region, accounting for 70% of its economy. The other countries in the region are basically developing countries and, among them, Europe has important relations with those Asian newly industrialized economies (ANIEs) which are about to join the ranks of the industrialized countries, followed by the Association of South-East Asian Nations (ASEAN) countries which are promoting industrialization and pursuing the ANIEs. Europe's economic relations with China are no less impressive than its relations with the ASEAN countries, although its ties with Indochina and other non-ASEAN states are not yet as close.

The EC has recently and rapidly increased its trade with East Asia; the annual average increase in exports from 1986 to 1990 was 14%, and for imports it was 16%. This surpassed the growth rate of Europe's world trade in the same period. On the other hand, Europe's trade balance *vis-à-vis* Asia shows a deficit of approximately 10 billion ECU, even excluding Japan. Investment has also recently become more active, and the percentage of investment between the two regions over total world direct investment reached 6% in 1990. European private funds are contributing to the growth of developing countries in East Asia, although the amount of European investment in the region is smaller than that between North America and East Asia and that within East Asia. Also, the accumulated amount of European investment in Japan remains only 10% of Japanese investment in Europe over the past 40 years. European countries also extend financial assistance to low-income countries and technological assistance to East Asia, although its priority is higher in other regions.

Thus western European countries have participated in economic activity in East Asia and, while they have benefited from it through increased exports and other means, they have also contributed to the region's growing economic prosperity. Because of the many developing countries in East Asia, Europe's contribution to economic development also implies a contribution to the region's political stability. The recent remarkable economic performance of the ANIEs and the ASEAN countries has made their trade structure *vis-à-vis* Europe similar to that between industrialized countries. For example, 64% of ASEAN exports to the EC in 1988 were manufactured products. Electrical machinery, as well as textiles and clothing, are showing rapid growth replacing the traditional export of primary goods. Europe, through importing manufactured products from ASEAN and the ANIEs, can thus play a role in promoting their industrialization. Trade frictions between the two regions are likely to gain in importance, but such problems should be resolved by making adjustments both to the industrial structures of the developed countries, and within the framework of the General Agreement on Tariffs and Trade (GATT).

The EC's intraregional trade as a percentage of its world trade increased from 50% in 1980 to 60% in 1991. Intraregional trade in East Asia, however, remains only 30% of the total as of 1990, and East Asia depends greatly upon extraregional trade, including with Europe whose role is relatively small. The economic realities of East Asia may be grasped more adequately by placing it in the broader context of the Asia-Pacific region as a whole, which extends to North America and Australia. The role of the US market and capital is significant in that it supports high growth in Asia, and Japan and the United States still play a leading role in the region's trade and investment with Europe's contributions following them. Some countries in the region hope for a third competitor to alleviate their dependence upon Japan and the US, and there are those whose trade or investment *vis-à-vis* the EC is actually larger than *vis-à-vis* the US.

On the other hand, the relative importance for European countries of economic links with East Asia in relation to their global economic relationship is not so large. For instance, in 1991, the percentage of trade with Japan remained 3.2% and with ASEAN 1.6%. This would seem to be due to the fact that, in Europe, intraregional exchanges in the highly homogeneous economic space can yield profits quickly, and also that the EC countries have concentrated on promoting economic integration to strengthen their industry and economy. In contrast, the percentage of trade with the EC for Asian countries is generally large at around 10–20%.

Security

Security in Asia is guaranteed by the United States through its bilateral arrangements with Japan, Korea, the Philippines and other countries in the region, and through the forward deployment of its military forces. In the first half of the Cold War era, Europe gradually reduced its military presence in Asia and now only the UK, which has traditionally been interested in this region, stations modest forces in Hong Kong and Brunei. The UK, through the Five Power Defence Agreement (FPDA), also plays a role in the defence of Singapore and Malaysia. There are several reasons why Europe, despite its own economic and other interests in the region, has placed the military role in this region of high strategic importance in the Cold War era in the hands of the United States.

First, East Asia is geographically far from Europe. Conventional forces on a scale large enough to meet the security requirements of the region would be immensely expensive to deploy, and far in excess of the capabilities of western European countries. Moreover, in Northeast Asia – strategically the most important subregion and where the former Soviet Union and China, both nuclear powers, have had significant interests – the extension of nuclear deterrence has been indispensable. Second, as the colonies gained independence, the economic interests of the former European colonial powers diminished. Instead, it gradually became evident that, under the free trading system, substantial economic benefits could be gained in the region without the added weight of armed forces; indeed, the cost-effectiveness of military power has declined. Third, in terms of the degree of interest in East Asia, there has been a discrepancy between that of former suzerain states or major powers such as the UK, France and Germany, and that of other states. Fourth, the importance of the United States' presence, whose power has been something to be trusted in the eyes of Asian countries, cannot be underestimated. Fifth, the security interests of western Europe have been directed solely at dealing with the Soviet threat, in cooperation with the United States, on the European front.

While its security ties with East Asia are extremely weak, Europe has had important, if not vital, interests in this region, even if these have not always been recognized. First, it enjoyed the economic benefits summarized above. Second, as economic relationships are based on political stability, Europe was as interested in the domestic stability of East Asian countries based on a market economy system as it was in the overall peace and stability of the region. Third, should the former Soviet Union or 'World Communism' have succeeded in large-scale expansion in East Asia, given the region's economic vitality, the power balance would have tilted towards the Soviet Union, thus increasing the Soviet threat on the European front. This in turn could have meant the diversion to the Asian front of US military resources allocated to Europe, and the possibility of war as a result of the extreme tension between the superpowers. These are the scenarios which Europe has wanted to avoid more than anything else. Fourth, preventing isolationism from gathering strength in the United States has been indispensable for European defence. If the US were to reduce its commitment in East Asia due to indifference on the part of its allies, it would have unfavourable effects on the European front as well. On the other hand, such interests have probably not been recognized to the full extent. For instance, Europe was critical of US intervention in Vietnam for fear that this would jeopardize the North Atlantic Treaty Organization's ability to cope with the Soviet threat in Europe.

Politics

Although Europe's military presence in the region has been very limited, in the latter half of the Cold War era it has been showing some interest in the security of Asia as well as in the closely related regional and international political issues. And in many instances Europe has taken a common stand with the United States and Japan. A symbolic example of this is the US–Soviet intermediate-range nuclear forces (INF) negotiations. Japan, the US and Europe acknowledged the indivisibility of security and, as a result of these negotiations, succeeded in realizing a common position, recognizing that a situation which had temporarily improved the level of security in Europe – but at the same time adversely affected Asia – would in time have threatened European security. A common position, however, has not been reached easily. It is natural for countries to give greater priority to attainable aims nearer home rather than to situations in far-away regions. Moreover, in cases where the degree of interest is relatively low – for example, the Korean peninsula for Europe and the former Yugoslavia for Asia – the perception of whether an incident has global implications or not is less acute when viewed from outside the region concerned. For Europe, the East Asian region is a lower priority on its diplomatic agenda. In addition to its concern over European integration and its relations *vis-à-vis* the US, the EC is also currently devoting itself to its relations with eastern Europe and the former Soviet Union. Furthermore, Europe also has to look after its political interests in the Middle East, the Maghreb and Africa. In the past six years, the heads of state and foreign ministers of the Group of Seven (G-7) countries in Europe only visited Japan for political consultation once or twice each. The German Chancellor and the French President had not made any such visits in this period.

The relative weakness in the Euro-Asian political relationship, as compared to the economic one, is not without its reasons. First, just as Europe cannot provide Asia with security commitments, Asia is no more equipped for such provision *vis-à-vis* Europe. Second, Asia is neither sufficiently politically organized, lacking as it does in cohesiveness, nor in a position to speak with one voice with global influence. Third, in a situation in which the importance of Asia for European security is limited – and for the European economy relatively limited – Europe's sense of political solidarity towards those Asian countries which are perceived as economic 'threats' tends to be slight. Fourth, East Asia – apart from Japan – is basically a developing area, and its relationship with Europe over issues of international politics and economics has involved a conflict of interests between industrialized nations and non-aligned nations and, in some cases, emotional confrontations between an ex-suzerain state and an ex-colony. Moreover, socialist states contribute factors that complicate interests even in relations between western European states and free nations in East Asia when dealing with regional issues. Finally, partly due to their intensive exchanges in all fields with the US and Japan, the East Asian countries' interest in and understanding of western Europe is less than they exhibit towards the US and Japan. Their language, religion and culture are substantially different from those of Europe, and they tend to react against European experience and values when these are proposed as absolutes.

In spite of the above constraints, in recent years European countries have been supportive of the efforts of free nations in Asia in dealing with their international political problems. This reflects the expanding basis of interest shared by European and Asian countries. To cite some examples, European countries have been actively supporting South Korea's position in the international arena over the issue of North–South unification, its UN membership and North Korea's suspected nuclear development. The refugee problem in Indochina is an issue relevant to the stability of ASEAN and other neighbouring countries, as well as to the stability of the entire region, and western European countries have contributed by accepting refugees and providing assistance to the asylum countries. As for the Cambodian problem, France and some other European countries have been playing their part in its solution in cooperation with Indonesia and other countries in the region. Contributions have also been made by the Europeans in support of the Philippines, assistance for the democratization of Mongolia and support for regional efforts to fight against the drugs trade. On the other hand, when dealing with political issues involving cultural differences and antagonism against former suzerain states, rather than concern with common interests such as security and economic aspects, confrontation can occur. Human rights problems and environmental issues are typical cases in point. In contrast, seen from the European side, when political systems differ, even when certain economic ties exist, confrontation over political problems can easily spill over into the economic arena. Europe has traditionally deemed China more important than Japan as a large potential market and as a politically influential country. However, as was recently seen in the Tiananmen Square incident, political aspects – including human rights – can cool political relationships and shrink economic ties.

Euro-Japanese relations and Japan–US relations

Throughout the post-war era, the relationship with the United States has been the top priority for both Japan and Europe, their mutual relationship being limited to the economic field for a long time. When dealing with occasional economic frictions, the incentive for compromise has been relatively weak, while the limited nature of the overall relationship has proved beneficial in resolving problems according to economic logic, free from political considerations. Therefore, while Japan entertained the feeling that the EC applied discriminatory protectionist measures towards it on the one hand, the EC could easily have felt that Japan made concessions only to the US and shifted the strain to the EC. The EC tends particularly to feel that because Japan entrusts its security to the US, it yields to the US on economic markets, which is incorrect. As Japan's trade with the US is 1.6 times as large as that with the EC, and investment 2.4 times as large, Japan's relationship with the United States, even only in economic aspects, is so important that it cannot be replaced by that with the EC. (The Euro- American relationship is even closer; trade is double and investment is seven times as large as in the Euro-Japanese case.) It should also be noted that the concessions Japan makes to the US are automatically applied to the EC as well. On the other hand, the necessity for adjustments in economic relations tends to rise in proportion to the closeness of the bilateral relationship in general.

The EC does not have the close consultation and cooperation on international political problems with Japan as Japan does with the US. It is only in the past few years that western Europe has developed an interest in the political role of Japan, a member of the G-7, after Japan established its economic strength. The turmoil in Europe after 1989 has also contributed to this. It is not too much to say that until then how to cope with Japan's 'aggressive economic behaviour' was at the centre of the EC's approach to its relationship with Japan. It was as recently as July 1991 that the Japan–EC joint declaration giving priority to political relations was announced.

Japan may, at times, have been more or less neglectful of its political relations with Europe, but it played an important role in extending economic assistance to Turkey, a wing of NATO, in the 1980s, and recently, it has come to pay due consideration to European contributions to global security. For example, Japan provided the UK and France with a portion of the $11.4bn financial contribution to the coalition forces against Iraq during the Gulf War – although the bulk of this was designated to the US forces. The recent decision to establish a special relationship between the Conference on Security and Cooperation in Europe (CSCE) and Japan indicates recognition of the necessity to initiate greater cooperation on both sides.

As the Japan–US relationship gradually moves closer to that of the US and Europe, both countries should be able to solve peacefully those economic frictions which are bound to arise from time to time, and this should not adversely affect the Euro-Japanese relationship. Even so, it is still desirable as far as is possible to solve problems in multilateral frameworks in the post-Cold War era when trilateral coordination has become increasingly important. Thus the interests of Japan, the US and Europe should be balanced as much as possible and Japan and Europe must make conscious efforts in that direction.

East Asia after the Cold War

Examining the characteristics of the security environment in East Asia and how the end of the Cold War might change them provides a clue to how international relations in the region might turn out in the post-Cold War era.

First, since most countries in the region are developing countries, their policy priorities have been directed towards economic development rather than reducing military tension, and this tendency will continue with the end of the Cold War. The current trend towards a market economy in the socialist countries in Asia will flow into the main stream of East Asian economic development.

Second, there are a number of factors within the region, including the issue of China, which do not fall into a clear-cut

East–West dichotomy. Thus, the effect of the end of East–West confrontation on the enhancement of stability has been attenuated to a certain extent. The China factor still remains; Russian power is declining; the importance of the ANIEs is growing; and the process of multipolarization should progress. How to integrate Russia into the region has emerged as an important new question.

Third, in this region, the conflict of interests among nations is complex and their threat perceptions are diverse, thus making the overall security configuration extremely complicated. The sources of conflict created by the former Soviet Union's support of socialist states are no longer there now that Russia is aiming towards democratic status. On the other hand, the framework of the East–West relationship, which used to perform a certain function in preventing the occurrence or expansion of regional conflicts, is no longer available. This is relevant in cases where conflicts of interest between countries in the region become acute before their economic standards rise to the level at which there would be less incentive to resort to military means. It would therefore be wise to prepare for the probability of new regional conflicts occurring.

Fourth, among the unresolved disputes and conflicts which exist in the region, the Cambodian conflict is in its last stage of resolution as a result of the end of the Cold War. This has also had a favourable effect on the North–South confrontation in the Korean peninsula, but it is still uncertain whether or not North Korea will open up to the outside world. The Northern Territorial issue between Japan and Russia has not progressed towards a solution because Russia, influenced by the military and by nationalism, has not yet changed its Cold War attitude towards Asia. Only after resolving these issues can the calamity brought about by communism in Asia be fully eradicated.

Finally, this region has been pursuing economic interdependency based on political, social and cultural diversity among countries, while a move towards integration as seen in Europe has not been felt. The end of the Cold War seems unlikely to influence this fact immediately. There may be emerging movements that call for the organization of economic and political cooperation, but they are likely to be caused by factors inherent in this region, such as the requirements resulting from economic development and the necessity of adjusting various conflicts of interest.

In sum, the effects of the end of the Cold War and the collapse of the Soviet Union are less significant in Asia than in Europe. This implies two things: first, the tendency for economic logic to work free from political considerations was and is relatively strong in Asia; and second, the Soviet factor has been less important for the security of Asia as a whole, North-east Asia excepted, than it was in Europe.

Russia

The enormous military build-up in the far east of the former Soviet Union has had a marginal effect on Asia as a whole due to geostrategical factors. The former Soviet Union failed to translate this into political influence because of the US military counterbalance in the region. This, however, is not to deny that the Soviet military threat has been perceived as serious by its neighbouring countries. Although the emergence of Russia after the Cold War reduced the military threat, this has again had a less dramatic impact in Asia than in Europe. The disappearance of the Warsaw Treaty Organisation (WTO), the Soviet military withdrawal from Germany and eastern Europe, the emergence of a buffer zone comprising the three Baltic States, Ukraine and Byelarus in addition to eastern Europe, have all dramatically changed the geopolitical situation in Europe. Russia and its forces have receded far from the western European horizon and the lead-time for Russia to attack western Europe has increased greatly; it now seems almost impossible for Russia to win back eastern Europe. Nothing of the sort has taken place in North-east Asia. The Russian border and its forces have not receded an inch with the end of the Cold War. If more advanced military resources were to be deployed in the Far East because of their withdrawal from the European front, and if greater priority were given to the Far-East fleets because of constraints in the Baltics and the Black Sea, this would reverse the trend towards improving the situation. Also, Russia is trying to identify itself with western Europe culturally as well as politically, and therefore has been identifying less with Asia. Russia, as a Eurasian state, claims to be a bridge from Europe to Asia, but its foreign policy towards Asia has a low priority. Moreover, in the Far East, the military–industrial complex has a firm basis and remains conservative. If NATO now considers Russian instability and uncertainty a risk, it is not surprising that Asia should also be vigilant to the movements of far-eastern Russia, even by European standards. Furthermore, if one accepts that the reconstruction of an economy or of a military organization is far easier than the alteration of geopolitical realities, anxieties concerning Russia are far stronger in North-east Asia, where Russia maintains an enormous military capability that can be deployed, than they are in Europe. It is legitimate for Europe to wish for a democratic system to take root as soon as possible in Russia, and the West should do all it can to support this. And yet Europe must also remember that Russia has another face when seen from North-east Asia, as mentioned above, and that this has global implications.

If Russia wants to play its role in Asia as a country that shares common values with the West, it should first of all accept the West's position advocating the liquidation of Russia's Stalinist and Cold War heritage, and swiftly reduce its military forces which far surpass its requirements for self-defence in the Far

East. Through such moves, Russia's policy stance would move closer to that of the West, as has already been demonstrated in the Korean peninsula and Cambodia; and a way for Russia to participate in the economic development of East Asia would be opened. Russia, when it participates in consultations over Asian issues, should respect the ways of Asia and refrain from introducing new destabilizing factors in its security environment through such acts as the export of weapons. Western European countries can put pressure on Russia to adopt policies that take into consideration the wishes of Asian countries. They can also avoid advocating that Asia should emulate the European framework of regional security after the Cold War by understanding the characteristics of the Asian security environment.

Changes in the Western Europe–East Asia relationship

Will the end of the Cold War and the collapse of the Soviet Union change the conditions that prescribed the role of western Europe in East Asian affairs? If so, what might these changes be? The factors governing why Europe played so small a military role in Asia must now be examined. First, the limitation in Europe's capabilities, which is the most important point, is unlikely to change in the near future, and the effectiveness of military power will continue to decline. As to the presence of US forces, though some worry about their withdrawal, the author believes that, essentially, its forward deployment will be maintained. The discrepancies among European countries' interests in the region will diminish due to the progress in EC political integration and deepening interdependency in the post-Cold War era. Europe can also decrease its resource allocation for coping with uncertain security factors arising from the former Soviet Union. New developments are taking place in Europe which are forcing it to devote itself to European affairs, but these can be resolved in the long run.

As regards any change in European interests in East Asia, its economic interests should increase further as long as the free trading system and regional stability are maintained. Should confrontation over economic interests become acute and either of the parties take to protectionism, or should the common recognition of or snared interests in security be lost, the interest in political stability could also disappear. In the former case, an adjustment of interests would take place before such a stage were reached. As for the latter, the concept of the indivisibility of security that stood between Europe and East Asia via the Soviet (Russian) threat seems to have disappeared. On the other hand, it is unlikely that Europe's political interests, detached from its economic relations, are going to grow in East Asia. Therefore there is a risk that, unless the recognition of a common security interest is confirmed from a different perspective, the relationship between the two regions may either worsen or become remote. Europe can indirectly contribute to East Asian stability by keeping US forces in Europe thereby preventing the US from becoming isolationist. In sum, any increase in the interests of Europe in East Asia seems unlikely to go so far as to justify changes in the basic European policy concerning its security role in Asia.

Asia's political influence could increase in the long term, depending upon the degree of economic development and progress in regional cooperation in East Asia, which would help attenuate confrontational attitudes between industrialized and developing countries in Europe and Asia. But when shared security interests decrease, perceptions of political solidarity decrease even further. Besides, the cultural differences between the two regions are basically irrelevant to the Cold War, and should be overcome through unremitting efforts for mutual understanding by both regions. In total, as far as Asia is concerned, the end of the Cold War is unlikely to create new obstacles to the efforts made by both regions towards intensifying their political relations. On the other hand, there is a risk that Europe, which should have been endowed with a global view, may further concentrate purely on European affairs. Asian countries generally expect western Europe to play a role in neutralizing the influence of the US and Japan, and Japan also welcomes any European role that reassures its Asian partners. Thus, a western Europe interested in Asia serves the best interests of the region.

Interdependency and 'mutual engagement'

The collapse of the Soviet communist regime occurred because of its inability to adapt to the transnationalization of economic activities, progress in science and technology, and the evolution of an information society, all of which are contrary to the nature of a regime which suppresses individual initiatives and survives only in a closed society. This tide is, at the same time, rising and deepening interdependency among countries, and economic development in East Asia in recent years has been achieved by riding on this tide which is thus changing the component factors of power in international relations. These changes, in turn, are inducing a realignment of power relations among states. Thus, in the post-Cold War world, power is becoming dispersed, creating a multipolar structure in which each pole depends on the other. World peace and prosperity, therefore, cannot be secured without coordination and cooperation among major countries which share common objectives and values. This means that the bases on which the US, Europe and Japan share common interests and aims not only in the economic, but also in the security and political areas are expanding. It is therefore inaccurate to claim that the removal of the Soviet threat will lead to a worsening relationship among these three regional players as a result of bilateral economic frictions. On the other hand, as the new structure is multipolar and fragile, the participation of major countries in solving important transnational issues is even more necessary, and conscious efforts need to be made to achieve common goals. One such is the need to increase the intensity of consultations between Europe on the one hand, and Japan and other East Asian countries on the other. Creating new fora for this purpose is unrealistic for the time being, thus bilateral consultations and multilateral cooperation within existing frameworks, such as the ASEAN Post-Ministerial Conference (PMC), should be increased. Such issues as the improvement of the peacekeeping and conflict-prevention functions of the UN, nuclear non-proliferation, discipline in the export of weapons, human rights and the environment could be the subject of such a course of action. Furthermore, it is important to strengthen the G-7 – the forum for the trilateral cooperation among Japan, US and Europe – as a place not only for economic, but also for political consultation.

This growing interdependency is compatible neither with exclusive regionalism nor with regional blocs. It cannot be denied that recently, not only in the economic, but also in the political field, the concerns of each region were divided in such a way that the EC was interested in Europe and the former Soviet Union (as well as in the Middle East and Africa at times), the US was interested in the American continents, and Japan was interested in the Asia-Pacific region. The major countries should, while refraining from the temptation to establish spheres of influence, consciously endeavour both to promote cooperation with outside regions, and to engage in matters of important concern to different regions. This, in turn, would contribute to upgrading the recognition of shared benefits and responsibilities among different regions. Japan has recently been increasing its international responsibilities

by deepening its relationship with Europe, including its association with the CSCE, and, furthermore, by participating in
support for eastern Europe (G24), support for the former Soviet
Union (the Washington Process and others) and the multilateral conference for peace in the Middle East. Japan's bilateral
official development assistance (ODA) to Africa has increased
from 6.3% of the total ODA in 1977 to 15.3% in 1989. Europe,
for its part, is expected not only to continue with its engagement in East Asia, but also to strengthen it. Today, Europe
holds three of the permanent five (Perm 5), four of the G-7
and two-thirds of the Organisation for Economic Cooperation
and Development (OECD) seats, and thus enjoys a large representation, making its global responsibility accordingly large.
By the same token, just as European countries participate
in the United Nations Transitional Authority in Cambodia
(UNTAC), Japan should also be seeking to participate in the
peacekeeping operations in Yugoslavia and elsewhere where
European interests are at stake. APEC should accelerate its
work to consolidate its aims and methods of organization and
cooperation, and thereby forms of engagement with Europe
should appear on its agenda as soon as possible. East Asian
countries that promote global cooperation with Europe are no
longer limited to Japan; Korea is hoping to join the OECD in a
short while. Along with progress in economic development in
East Asia, the foundations and scope of cooperation between
Europe and East Asia should expand further. Now it is time to
start discussing how to expand mutual engagement between
the two regions.

NOTES

[1] In this paper, 'Europe' is understood as western Europe, comprised mainly of European Community and European Free Trade Association (EFTA) countries, unless stated otherwise. In view of the present diversified relationship between European countries and East Asia, Europe is sometimes represented by certain major countries such as the UK, France or Germany in the context of its relations with specific Asian countries or subregions. East Asia, comprising North-east and South-east Asia, includes Japan, the Korean peninsula, China, the Association of South-East Asian Nations (ASEAN) countries, Indochina and Myanmar; and far-eastern Russia is also taken into account. The Indian subcontinent is not discussed here.

CHAPTER TWENTY

Rethinking Japan–US relations: security issues

Kenichiro Sasae

From Adelphi Paper 292, 1994

Japan's strategic environment

The effects of the end of the Cold War on East Asia have been gradual and somewhat vague. When the Berlin wall fell, the Japanese government cautiously defined the situation as 'the beginning of the end of the Cold War'. The much-vaunted Soviet policies of perestroika and glasnost were essentially directed at Europe and the United States, and Asia–Pacific policies were given low priority. In both the Asia–Pacific and Japan–Russia contexts, the Cold War was not necessarily over. Although Soviet disintegration and the receding military threat in the region marked the end of the Cold War in the global East versus West sense, it could not completely change the historical relationships and geopolitical component in East Asia.

During the Cold War, the US military presence and its bilateral security ties with Japan, South Korea, Taiwan and the Philippines were designed to contain the power and ideology of the communist Soviet Union, China, North Korea and North Vietnam. However, there were other complicated and delicate relations between regional countries, which preceded the Cold

War confrontation. To Japan, the Soviet Union had been a difficult partner geopolitically since the days of the old Russian Empire. In contrast, Japan had enjoyed strong historical and cultural ties with China for more than a thousand years, while communist governance in China had existed for less than 50 years. China had a history of confrontation with neighbouring Russia and Vietnam well before communism took over in these three countries. The Korean peninsula had been the focus of competition between Russia, China and Japan long before the peninsula split into two hostile camps and Japan inflicted colonialism and war. Most importantly, Japan's encounter with the United States continued to spark Japanese domestic reform and the opening of the nation, and the status of the cooperation and rivalry between the US and Japan set the basic tone of Pacific peace.

Today, Japan's security perception is mostly conditioned by these historical and geopolitical factors. The Japanese tend to judge security threats intuitively rather than in terms of military capability. Long-term predictability and intentions are significant and are largely affected by Japan's relationship with other countries. The stability of relationships thus counts for as much in Japanese foreign relations as it does in domestic social and political life.

From Japan's perspective today, it is only with Russia and North Korea that it does not have a 'normal' relationship, and it is therefore these countries that are the source of instability and possible threat. Japan has normalised its relationship with China in parallel with the US move to do the same in the 1970s. Even though a future Chinese military build-up and domestic volatility is a potential worry for Japan, its lack of serious concern can be explained partly by this 'normalised' relationship. Japan's alliance with the US, however, could be affected by policy differences between their individual relationships with Russia, China and the Korean peninsula.

Russia

Japan's security perception of Russia is shaped by three factors: Russia's military capability and presence in the Far East; the stability of its evolving regime; and bilateral diplomatic relations. The situation is fluid in all these areas and Japan remains cautious.

On the first point, Japan's 1993 Defense White Paper states that 'the Russian military force constitutes an unstable factor for the security of this region', stressing 'the modernisation of forces including the transfer from Europe', while admitting 'the overall trend of quantitative force reduction and lower level of activities reflecting the serious domestic situation'. However, more striking in the short run as evidence of Russian political will is the deployment of Russian forces in the Northern Territories. In 1978 the Soviet Union began to build up its armed forces there, until they reached the estimated equivalent of one army division.[1] In May 1992, President Boris Yeltsin announced his readiness to withdraw Russian troops, except for border guards, from the islands in the near future. During his visit to Japan in October 1993, Yeltsin told Japanese Prime Minister Morihiro Hosokawa that half the troops had already been withdrawn and that the other half would definitely be leaving. Most of the 40 MiG-23 *Flogger* fighter aircraft that were once there seem now to have left, but uncertainty remains over future Russian actions.[2]

As for the stability of the Russian regime, Japan's view is more reserved. First, the Russian penchant for power and the clash between those committed to centralised and those committed to diffused control continue to exist throughout the wide political spectrum: the left wing and communists; the right-wing nationalists who want a dictatorship; and the conservative liberals working for a pluralist democracy. The pendulum could swing many times before a stable pluralistic model is reached. The impact of growing right-wing nationalism in the Russian parliament since the elections in December 1993 and the centrist repositioning of President Yeltsin is still speculative, but it signals the beginning of a long, oscillating process of political conversion. The transition from a socialist to a market economy, a precondition for political democracy, cannot be achieved quickly, even if Western support were to be extended on a much larger scale. The gradual evolution of a unique Russian market economy consistent with Russian culture and history would ensure more stability, but would take time. Equally, a sudden jump from a socialist to a market economy would invite confusion and instability, which would also take time to resolve.

Despite this reserved view, Japan has been an active participant in the G-7's concerted financial support to Russia. Japan's aid commitment for Russia, amounting to $4.4 billion, is now behind only that of Germany and the United States. Following President Yeltsin's visit to Japan in October 1993, a number of large economic projects were confirmed, and bank as well as trade credits are now in place.

Japan's dilemma is not over economic assistance itself, but rather over bilateral diplomatic relations. President Yeltsin's meeting with Prime Minister Hosokawa in 1993 opened the way for further negotiations on the return of the Northern Territories. They confirmed the fulfilment of past treaties and commitments, including the 1956 Japan–Soviet Joint Declaration. But Yeltsin implied that more economic and other assistance would be needed to settle the territorial issue, while also admitting that Russian public opinion was a problem. Over the Gorbachev and Yeltsin years, Japan's policy has gradually shifted from strict adherence to economic and political links with Russia, to a more positive, expanded equilibrium between them. But it is uncertain whether Russia can react to this process in a balanced manner and, if mishandled, the current situation could either deepen the mistrust of the Japanese public, or offend Russian nationalism and pride.

Against this background the Japanese continue to value the support of the United States and other G-7 nations. The failure of the US to give strong backing would create resentment in some quarters of the Japanese public. Although the territorial issue is fundamentally a bilateral one between Japan and Russia, how the US deals with Russia on this issue as US–Russia relations develop in the future is also seen as a yardstick of US commitment to its alliance with Japan.

China

Increasing attention has been paid in the West to China's recent trend towards a military build-up. Japan's reaction, however, has on the whole been modest and less anxious. Three factors explain this: Chinese military capability; Chinese policy priorities and the strategic environment; and the Japan-China relationship.

First, although Chinese forces have been undergoing modernisation for some time, it is generally believed in Japan that Chinese military technology is still 15–20 years behind that of Western nations.

Second, since the 1970s military modernisation has been given consistently lower priority among the 'four modernisations' (agriculture, industry, defence and science/technology). Although it has been stepped up in parallel with more open economic policies, especially since 1978, economic growth has always had top priority for resource allocation. The Chinese defence budget has certainly increased considerably every year since 1991, but this was a means of winning further support from the Chinese military for the government's policy on economic reform. The Chinese possession and testing of nuclear weapons is more political by nature. In the near future, the provision of military weapons and technology could be accelerated in step with the pace of China's economic development, although this could largely be defined as a catching-up process. In the longer run, Chinese military strength, especially its nuclear missiles, could become a matter of serious concern. But here again, more significant is the strategic environment, both domestic and international, in which China would maintain its military strength.

Will China sustain its current policy of modernisation focusing on economic development? Some in the West are cautious or pessimistic about the future stability of Chinese governance.[3] It is indeed debatable whether Chinese economic liberalisation and decentralisation of power would ensure democratisation and political stability. But Chinese domestic policies are also affected by the approach of the Western industrialised countries. To the extent that China sees its strategic environment as favourable and non-confrontational, especially as it relates to the US, Russia and Japan, there should be no strategic reason for China drastically to alter the course it has pursued so far, other than to make tactical adjustments to balance economic reform and domestic stability.

Third, Japan's links with China are developing much more predictably. China's criticism of the danger of Japanese militarism and right-wing trends, once vocal, has more or less subsided as China pursues more realistic policies, and as trade and investment between the two countries expands. In the defence field too, the process of confidence building has begun with a security dialogue between China and Japan. Although in both countries there is concern over the future hegemony of the other's economic and military potential, it remains rather theoretical.

Japan's relations with China, however, are only one side of the strategic triangle in which US–China relations play an equally vital role. Ideally for Japan, Japan–US relations should be excellent, Japan–China relations good, and US–China relations reasonably good. The strategic environment before the Second World War was the reverse: the US got on well with China and poorly with Japan. While Japan disapproves of apparent secret deals between the United States and China, it also regards US–China confrontation as a major source of strategic instability in East Asia. Japan therefore expressed serious concern over the Clinton administration's focus on Chinese democracy and human rights, which led to the downward spiral of the US–China relationship in the initial phase of the administration in 1993. However, the policy the United States then developed regarding China was more pragmatic, and the US–China summit meeting in Seattle in November 1993 opened the way for less dogmatic relations. In particular, the subsequent US decision to eliminate the link it had made between human rights and trade, granting China Most Favoured Nation (MFN) status, further solidified matters. It is now up to China to work to improve its human rights situation without any outside 'intervention'.

From Japan's perspective, the promotion of democracy and the protection of human rights in China are essential, but Chinese domestic equilibrium is just as important for regional stability. The status of democracy and human rights is largely governed by a long history of socio-political, economic and cultural evolution embedded in Chinese society as a whole. Japan recognises that forcibly linking trade and human rights is an inappropriate and coercive measure, which would endanger the possibility of self-generated, enduring reform in China. The opening up of the Chinese economy based on the free-market system will also influence Chinese socio-political evolution. Whether Chinese economic liberalisation can translate into political democracy remains to be seen. In any case, it is essential to Japan that China becomes more constructively engaged in such common regional and international issues as the North Korean nuclear-missile problem, nuclear proliferation and UN peacekeeping.

Korea

On the Korean peninsula, the North Korean nuclear issue is the immediate focus. In the longer term, strategic stability will be the concern, with the collaborative involvement of the US, Japan, China and Russia influencing the course of events.

Almost unchanged from the days of the Cold War are the military confrontation and tense political relationship between North and South Korea, with the basic objective continuing to be the deterrence of aggression from the North. North Korea's military capabilities, especially in ground forces, far exceed those of the South. The North's *Scud*-derived missiles now have an extended range – the latest being tested is able to cover most of Japan. If the North could fit this missile with a nuclear warhead, the implications for Japan's security would be very serious. South Korea has improved its military capability in recent years, especially in the maritime and air forces. The US military presence there has been an effective deterrent, maintaining equilibrium on the peninsula even under the suspended second phase of reductions of the Strategic Framework for the Asian Pacific Rim.

The most far-reaching impact of the end of the Cold War, however, has been that the changing relationships of South and North Korea with the surrounding major powers have altered the strategic environment for both. In the short term this has heightened tensions between them. South Korea, more confident of its economic progress and political democracy, established diplomatic relations with China in August 1992, and signed a treaty to govern its fundamental relationship with Russia in November 1992. The rigid Cold War power configuration between the two Koreas was thus half torn apart, with the strategic balance shifting in favour of the South. North Korea, beset by severe economic problems, waged an ideological campaign for mass control to safeguard the regime, thus minimising the impact of the Soviet dissolution and the Chinese evolutionary shift to a market economy.

North Korea has sought a nuclear capability, regarded as a less expensive instrument for national security, at least since the 1960s. However, its tough reaction to external pressure, including its declared withdrawal from the Nuclear Non-Proliferation Treaty (NPT) and its refusal to allow a special International Atomic Energy Agency (IAEA) inspection, reflected North Korea's sense of international isolation, its fear of being besieged and concern over the strength of its regime. In negotiations with the US, it has thus used the nuclear issue to obtain a comprehensive deal to assure the legitimacy of the regime, with full diplomatic recognition and security.

From Japan's perspective, strategic stability in the Korean peninsula can better be attained by encouraging the North to seek more moderate and open policies rather than its current isolationist and hardline ones. Leaving aside the requisite diplomacy, the resolution of the nuclear issue would benefit from cross-recognition between North and South, involving neighbouring great powers. Accordingly, any military action against the North when it refused IAEA inspection would have been undesirable, and any economic sanctions would have needed careful synchronisation with diplomatic talks. However, the real challenge for the Japan–US alliance would have occurred if deadlock invited American or UN military intervention. Supportive action by Japan would then have required specific definition within its constitutional framework, and the viability of Article 6 of the Security Treaty (the use of Japan's facilities for US operations in the Far East) would have been tested.

If resolution of the nuclear issue were successfully to bridge the next stage of North–South relations, it could be the beginning of the end of the Cold War on the Korean peninsula. Progress in North–South relations made possible by strategic stability could eventually lead to unification, but this step would have to be undertaken primarily by the Koreans themselves. At the same time, however, support as well as collaboration among the key surrounding powers (the US, Japan, China and Russia) is most important. Trilateral security discussions on nuclear and other concerns have been under way between the US, South Korea and Japan. Japan has also initiated security-policy talks with China and Russia. Should China and Russia participate jointly, the process could develop further into a subregional security network, although a rigid structure would not be appropriate given the still delicate relations between them.

In sum, Japan's territorial dispute with Russia, human rights and stability in China, and the instability of the Korean peninsula continue to be central to the credibility of policy coordination between Japan and the US, and the solution of each problem requires the democratic transformation of Russia, China and North Korea. External forces could help to provide a favourable strategic environment for such transformation, but such real and deep changes will take a long time to achieve. Can the Japan-US alliance sustain itself while this transition takes place?

Japan's security policy and alliance with the US

Given Japan's present strategic environment and the emergence of a rough consensus after many years of domestic ideological debate, it is unlikely that Japan will change its fundamental security policy of a minimum SDF coupled with security arrangements with the United States. Yet new currents are appearing in the domestic debates, concerning the size and role of the SDF in relation to the Constitution; the *raison d'être* of the security alliance with the US; and burden sharing as well as defence collaboration between them.

Japan's security-policy debates have peaked at roughly ten-year intervals: in the late 1950s over the constitutionality of the SDF and the decision to revise the original 1951 Japan–US security arrangements; in the late 1960s and early 1970s over the size and speed of Japan's defence build-up; in the late 1970s and early 1980s over the viability of Japan's greater defence capability at the climax of the Cold War arms competition; and, finally, in the late 1980s and early 1990s over the new role and mission of the SDF in the post-Cold War era.[4] Throughout these debates, the Japanese Constitution remained a central concern.

The pacifist group in Japan, associated with the political left and intellectuals, sought 'unarmed neutrality'; it was anti-military, anti-government and anti-American. Regarding the SDF as unconstitutional, the group sought to reduce its size and eventually to dissolve it. It saw the Japan–US security agreement as symbolic of Japan's subjugation to the US, which tried to draw Japan into dangerous adventures overseas. The pacifists therefore sought to abrogate the arrangements and replace them with a peace and friendship treaty.

The nationalist group, in turn, advocated Japan's independence; this group's basic orientation was pro-military and pro-government, but often anti-American. It saw military independence and rearmament as a matter of national pride, and the military forces of such countries as the former Soviet Union and China as dangerous. It regarded the treaty arrangements with the US as important, but believed that the two countries were not on an equal footing.

Adopting the middle ground between these two positions, the conservative and moderate mainstream of the Liberal Democratic

Party (LDP) and the establishment (foreign, defence and financial) have followed and developed the policy lines initially laid down by Prime Minister Shigeru Yoshida in the late 1950s. Under these policies, most of the nation's resources were directed towards economic reconstruction while the self-defence capacity was kept to a necessary minimum, with defence commitments guaranteed by the US. The Japanese government also interpreted the Constitution as defining the legitimacy as well as the limits of the SDF, but did not change the Constitution itself.[5]

In the context of the Japan–US relationship, it was mostly the level and slow pace of Japan's defence build-up that caused concern in the US Congress and administration during most of the Cold War, especially in the late 1970s and early 1980s. During this period the Japanese Diet also vigorously debated the credibility of the third of the three non-nuclear principles (not to possess nuclear weapons; not to produce them; and not to permit their introduction into Japan). Japanese resistance to nuclear weapons reflected deep-rooted anti-nuclear sentiment following the atomic bombs dropped on Japan towards the end of the Second World War. The notion of 'comprehensive security' was also debated, with its proponents claiming the importance of diplomatic and economic security.

Under the government of Prime Minister Yasuhiro Nakasone, formed in 1983, stronger defence efforts were initiated in conjunction with increased defence collaboration with the United States and HNS for its forces. As a result, the tensions of the preceding decade abated in the later 1980s, and 'quiet diplomacy' was said to be the most successful strategy for the post-war Japan–US security relationship. When the Bush administration announced that the West had won the Cold War in the early 1990s, and that it intended to reduce the US defence budget, Japan's defence spending was no longer a controversial issue to the United States.

During the 1980s, the Japanese domestic debate became less ideological, and left-wing opposition to government security policies lost its original cutting edge and public appeal. The Japan Social Democrat Party (JSDP) gradually shifted its position. After the JSDP had formed an essential core of the coalition government in mid-1993, Sadao Yamahana, Social Democrat Cabinet Minister for political reform, reportedly stated that the coalition government would sustain the policies of previous governments, although the JSDP still believed that the status of the SDF was unconstitutional.[6] The process of convergence seemed to have been completed when Social Democrat Prime Minister Tomiichi Murayama, in coalition with the long-time rival LDP and the New Pioneers Party, confirmed in mid-1994 that the existing national security policy would be maintained, including the constitutionality of the SDF.

While Japan's defence build-up had placed the left-wing opposition in a more realistic position, it also subdued the right-wing nationalists who had once advocated military independence. The receding Russian threat further diminished their persuasive power. Some nationalist views were, however, directed more towards the economic aspect of the relationship, criticising the US government for its unilateral approach and the Japanese government for a weak attitude.

The years of post-Second World War ideological debate and the split over Japan's fundamental security framework are coming to an end. Today, roughly two-thirds of the Japanese public support the combination of security arrangements with the US and the maintenance of the SDF.[7] Those supporting abrogation of the arrangements and the phasing out of the SDF, and, conversely, those in favour of military independence, poll fewer than 10% each.

Japan's post-Cold War security policy debates are now based on this national consensus. In January 1994, Prime

Minister Hosokawa announced his intention to review the National Defense Program Outline (NDPO), to adjust it to the worldwide trend of reducing military spending.[8] (The NDPO was formulated in 1976 to stipulate, *inter alia*, the level of defence to be reached and then maintained in peacetime.) The review would include a reduction of the Ground Self-Defense Force (GSDF); the definition of UN PKO as an essential component of the SDF's role and mission; the strengthening of theatre missile defence (TMD); and improvements in intelligence and communications.[9]

The official ceiling of the GSDF, currently 180,000 personnel, may reportedly be reduced to less than 150,000.[10] Given that the actual strength of the GSDF is only around 150,000 and that there are increasing recruitment difficulties, lowering the official ceiling is in line with the trend already developing. More importantly, the possible reduction would go hand in hand with force modernisation and the evolution of a role in UN peacekeeping.

Former Prime Minister Hosokawa was strongly in favour of a high-technology-oriented force modernisation.[11] The Japanese Defense Agency has thus begun to study the feasibility of introducing a reconnaissance satellite, a concept that would be affected by a number of factors. Domestically, there are several difficulties to be overcome: the attitude of the political left; the 1969 Diet resolution that limits development and use of space technology to peaceful purposes; and the high cost. Internationally, the reaction of surrounding Asian countries to the possible surveillance of their military installations, and US reaction to Japan developing such a high-technology military satellite, could pose problems.

The place of the SDF in UN peacekeeping was much debated when the PKO bill was passed through the Diet, and will be defined in the context of Japan's search for a new international role and its interest in greater responsibility in the UN. To the defence establishment, this is closely related to the reduction of the GSDF. A possible PKO force unit would need to be under the control of the Director General of the Defense Agency.[12] A PKO force independent of the SDF has been proposed by the JSDP on the one hand, and by such a key political figure as Ichiro Ozawa on the other, but for opposite reasons: the former stresses the non-military aspect of the PKO; the latter the military aspect of such a unit being under the control of the UN.

As for TMD, domestic debate has raised the issues of the relationship with collective defence forbidden by the Constitution; the Diet resolution banning the military use of space; the military effectiveness of the improved *Patriot* system; and the financial cost. The status of North Korea's missile development and Japan–US technology cooperation would have much to do with the persuasiveness and speed of such a study.

The above debates will continue to be bound by the basic thrust of the constitutional ideal and principles built up in the past decades. Today, about 40% of the Japanese believe that the fundamental reason for Japan's peace and stability since the Second World War is their peace constitution; 18% give the Japan–US security arrangements as the reason; while only 1% credit it to the existence of the SDF.[13] In December 1993, Keisuke Nakanishi, Director General of the Defense Agency, resigned over his public proposal to change the Constitution. He had also previously expressed his personal view that the use of the SDF under UN command was constitutional. A recent opinion poll of Japanese Diet members shows that two-thirds prefer not to change Article 9 of the Constitution (which renounces war), while one-quarter believe there is a need to debate it.[14] The argument for changing the Constitution itself is no longer taboo, but it is uncertain how far the debate will affect actual policy evolution in the coming years.

Security arrangements

Recent domestic debates on the meaning and merit of Japan's security arrangements with the US can be divided into three categories. One argues that the arrangements were necessary to meet the Soviet threat, but are no longer needed now that threat has gone. The second sees present-day challenges more in economic terms and plays down the role of military force both for shaping world order and for the Japan-US relationship. The third argues in terms of Japan's objective national-security requirements and the political role of the arrangements in managing its alliance with the US.

Why does the Japanese public seem to favour the status quo? First, Japan's view of Russia is still formed more by their difficult relationship than by the military dimension of the Russian threat. Although Soviet military expansion and adventurism in the late 1970s and 1980s had begun to be perceived as a threat by Japan, as it had long been by the US, Japan still saw its security arrangements with the US more as an instrument to manage bilateral relations than as protection against the Soviet Union. The recognition that the Russian military threat is now receding is thus not a major factor affecting the security arrangements with the US.

Second, the economic arguments are regarded as premature, one-sided and oversimplified, showing only one aspect of a world in which geo-economic factors should assume more importance. The Japanese public is not at all convinced that a military security alliance could be replaced by one based on economics, particularly as the economy is seen to be more of a problem in the US.

Third, the public finds the status quo comfortable after decades of fierce domestic ideological battles given the decreased pressure for Japanese defence expansion from the US. The majority supports the Japanese government's justification of its security alliance with the US: that it is an essential component of national security; a contribution to the stability of East Asia; the core of Japan–US relations; and the basis of Japan's international and regional diplomacy.[15]

Although national consensus is in favour of maintaining the security alliance, there are nevertheless some shifts of emphasis in the Japanese debates. A wider perspective seems to be given to political and economic objectives beyond military security (which is still the core of the alliance). The Japanese government seems to follow this trend, but the Japan–US Security Treaty could be more candidly viewed as a pledge of 'no war' between two countries determined not to repeat the mistakes of the Second World War.[16]

The alliance is also now seen more in the context of Northeast Asian security. Not only is American nuclear deterrence against a possible North Korean nuclear threat required, but the viability of Article 6 of the Security Treaty, concerned with the maintenance of peace and security in the Far East, could also be tested, should the need arise for American military operations in the Korean peninsula. As the US security concern shifts from East–West rivalry to regional conflicts, such as in the Gulf or the Korean peninsula, the priority role of the American military presence in Japan could also change. Some argue that Japan's HNS can be seen as a contribution to Asia–Pacific security as a whole, and not just as a sharing of costs for the defence of Japan.[17] Others argue that the axis of the arrangements has shifted and call for a new Asian security framework.[18]

But there are deeper movements in the area of burden sharing between the two nations. On the surface, burden sharing meant to the US that Japan should shoulder more of the cost of maintaining its own peace and security, and that of the Far East and the world, as befitted its economic status and power. From Japan's perspective, sharing was deemed to be necessary for the credibility of the Japan–US security arrangements; to maintain the American military presence in the Asia–Pacific region; and to help keep the United States internationally committed. Fundamentally, however, burden sharing meant competition and collaboration between two giant economic powers seeking or maintaining a technological lead in either the civil or military field, while taking advantage of the military or economic powers of the other, bilaterally and internationally.

From the American perspective today, financial support for US forces is only part of the overall burden sharing needed to achieve common security objectives through military, political and economic contributions, although the relative importance of Japan's financial share is accepted, given the constitutional constraints on its military contribution.[19] In policy terms, however, the United States has given a rather positive assessment of Japan's efforts in four broad areas: Japan's own defence build-up; host-nation support and official development assistance (ODA) to developing countries; Japan–US defence cooperation; and Japan's contribution to the Gulf War and UN peacekeeping.

As far as Japan's defence build-up is concerned, the current budget, although slightly less than 1% of gross national product (GNP), ranks fifth in absolute terms among major Western nations (measured in US dollars). Its real growth over the past decade exceeds the United States and North Atlantic Treaty Organisation (NATO) average. But, as has been said, the receding Russian threat and the reductions in US defence expenditure have removed Japan's defence budget from the list of bilateral issues, and it now carries less weight in America's assessment of allied contributions. However, as US defence policy emphasises the effective use of military resources for civil rebuilding and for the protection of a defence industrial base now that the major threat has diminished, US interest in Japan's defence build-up has become more specific, reflecting the particular interests of US industries.

American concern is also related to Japan's deficiencies in the areas of early warning, maritime air-defence and anti-missile defence. For example, Japanese debate over the introduction into its air defence of Airborne Warning and Control System (AWACS) aircraft, made by Boeing in the US, has wider implications for Japan's security policy.[20] First, it will become more controversial, politically and economically, to procure expensive high-technology systems at a time when the military threat is diminishing. Second, such an enhanced system will continue to be criticised by traditional left-wing and liberal circles as providing an offensive capability or as being threatening to neighbouring countries.[21] Third, lowered US domestic demand for defence products would increase the pressure from the US defence industry to export their products to Japan, particularly given the bilateral trade gap.

As an example of actual and visible burden sharing, however, Japan's host-nation support for American forces has played a significant role and will continue to do so throughout the 1990s and beyond. Although noise and other environmental problems involved in force training and housing construction have been a source of contention with local residents for many years, the most critical part of Japan's support has been financial, sharing labour costs for Japanese employees working on the bases of the USFJ. This has increased step by step since the late 1970s.[22] As a result, in 1994 the Japanese government added over $1bn to the $4.6bn in HNS in 1993, in effect bearing almost an equal (50%) share of the costs of maintaining US forces in Japan. If the salaries of the US forces themselves are excluded from the calculation, the share would be more than 70%.

This issue has bilateral, regional and international implications. Bilaterally, the Japanese government has defined
some of the HNS measures as 'provisional, exceptional and
limited'. Despite these qualifications, however, it has made an
exception to the original Agreement on the Status of Forces, to
advance the level of HNS through substantial special agreements. On the other hand, the constraints have also been a
safeguard against unlimited demands from the United States,
especially from Congress. Even after Japan took a major
initiative at the beginning of 1992, the US Congress called for
the entire costs to be covered, other than the salaries of the US
forces themselves, while the US administration pointed out
the inappropriateness of Japan paying the remaining costs on
the grounds that it would invite Japanese intervention in the
management of US forces.[23]

Regionally, US demand for increased burden sharing has
run in parallel with reductions in the level of its forward-
deployed forces in the Asia–Pacific region. The common
denominator is, of course, the reduction of the financial
burden on the US. Burden-sharing negotiations were also
initiated by the US with South Korea at the beginning of 1990,
and South Korea has agreed to bear one-third of the won-
denominated costs of the US Forces in Korea (USFK) in 1995.
Future Japanese HNS programmes, especially beyond 1995,
will also be affected by the status of the third phase of the US
force reductions beginning in 1995.

Internationally, from the perspective of the US Congress, the
increasing Japanese financial assistance in the 1990s contrasted
with that of the European NATO allies, which reduced the
budget for common defence. But the US administration sees the
Japanese financial contribution as a special case, not as a model
for NATO and the Korean peninsula. In the longer term, the
special character of Japanese burden sharing, which offsets its

lack of a military contribution with a larger financial one, could be the subject of debate in Japan in relation to its role in the world. Japan's major initiative for increasing HNS at the beginning of 1992 was in parallel with its financial contribution to the 1991 Gulf War operations, which amounted finally to more than US$13bn, including economic and refugee assistance.

In the meantime, Japan–US economic rivalry has entered a new dimension, focusing more on high-technology trade and questioning the fundamental economic structure of both countries. US revisionist views have invited Japan's nationalistic rebuttal. The deteriorating economic atmosphere has begun to erode the outer edge of the mutual trust on which the security alliance depends – as illustrated by the polemics over the FS-X project.[24]

The FS-X is a new support fighter aircraft for Japan's Air Self-Defense Force (ASDF) being jointly developed by the United States and Japan following agreements reached initially in 1988. The problems that arose in the development of this joint project had serious implications for the management of the Japan–US alliance, suggesting that the days when defence cooperation was a separate from economic competition were coming to an end. For those in the US Congress and administration who opposed the FS-X project, three economic concerns overrode the adverse impact on the security partnership:

- general concern over America's eroding industrial base and competitiveness that was being increasingly challenged by Japan, especially in high-technology (not least because Japan took advantage of the transfer of American technology);
- specific concern over the possible evolution of Japanese aircraft/ aerospace industries competing with US industries in future world markets as a result of transferring American aircraft technology to Japan; and

- short-term concern over the wide bilateral trade gap, which the export of existing F-16 aircraft, rather than co-development of the FS-X, could help to reduce.

When President Bush announced the final clarification of the agreement in April 1989, he said that the issue had been reviewed taking into account not only strategic and diplomatic considerations, but also America's trade, industry and technology policies.

The issue also revealed the increasing influence of the economic nationalists in US defence and security policy-making, at least in the Japan–US context. Within the US administration, the Departments of Defense and State and the National Security Council (NSC) fought in defence of the original FS-X agreements, with the combined forces of the Commerce Department, the US Trade Representative (USTR), the Labour Department and the Science and Technology office of the White House in opposition to them. Notably hardline on the issue was the Commerce Department. In Congress, the core opposition included Republican right-wingers, trade and economic hardliners against Japan, supporters of the strengthened Commerce Department and the development of US military industries, and protectors of Congressional power against the administration. Those who supported the advancement of the FS-X project from the perspective of the alliance warned of the danger of parochial nationalism in both the United States and Japan, but their influence in Congress dwindled.

More importantly, the FS-X debate highlighted once again the strategic implication of high-technology for alliance management. It involved differences of perception in Japan and the US about each other's technological capability and the impact of technological transfer on the aerospace, defence and civil industries in general. From the Japanese perspective, the spin-off effect of US military technology, if transferred to Japan, seemed to be overemphasised by the Americans. From the American perspective, the Japanese civil technology 'spin-on' for defence technology tended to be overestimated by the Japanese.

Those Americans who warned of the danger of US technology transfer pointed to Japanese industrial skills in developing and applying military technology for a wide range of civil products; close collaboration between the government and defence industries; *Keiretsu* (group-affiliated) relationships among industries themselves; and the lack of a clear division between civil and military business as seen in the US.[25] But objective American assessment also questions the possibility of strong Japanese defence and aircraft industries emerging in the future. The perceived difficulties are: the possible levelling off of Japanese defence procurement; the continuing export ban on military weapons and technology (except to the US government); the failure of the Ministry of Trade and Industry's (MITI) policy to develop indigenous aircraft industries; the lack of competition among defence industries; the limited scale that spin-off could have; Japanese political and bureaucratic concern over the financial costs; the viability of military alliance with the United States, including the lack of interoperability of weapons; and worsening economic conflicts between the two nations.[26] Yet, in the FS-X case, it was the political mood emerging from increased Japan–US competition over technology that finally dictated much of the American approach.

Japanese military technology depends heavily on civil dual technology. For those in the Japanese SDF and defence industries who initially sought the domestic development of the FS-X, it was an exciting dream to develop a Japanese-made aircraft using some of the best civil technology and engineering, which in their eyes was superior to that of the Americans.

Although the development of military aircraft requires militarily capable systems, this presented a worthy challenge. From the US perspective, the vast cost involved in undertaking such a project domestically did not make much sense in terms of Japan's defence needs and led to suspicion of Japan's motives – more for industrial and commercial than for security-policy reasons. And, of course, there were those who saw a dangerous nationalist current in Japan bidding for high-technology supremacy and independence: Japan's deterrent power today might work against the US in the future.

The FS-X issue was also influenced by a mutual distrust of each other's perceived behaviour. The sense of unfairness about Japan's 'closed' market and frustration over Japan's negotiating style and lack of results in trade and economic talks had much to do with the negative attitude of the US Commerce Department and other trade and economic agencies. When the rumour spread in the US Congress that Fuji Heavy Industries, a major Japanese FS-X contractor, and Mitsubishi might have been involved in the construction of Libyan chemical-weapon factories, the memory of Toshiba selling high-technology to Russia immediately sprang to mind. Even from the viewpoint of former US Secretary of Defense Dick Cheney, a traditional ally and supporter of the Japan–US security alliance, abrogation of the FS-X project could invite a more independent Japanese national-security policy.[27] From the Japanese perspective, however, the coercive and unilateral nature of the American trade negotiating style, coupled with a tendency to blame others for its own domestic economic problems, increased anti-American sentiment among the general public, in some parts of business and government departments. But there was still a wide consensus among Japanese policy-makers that it was not wise to shake the security alliance by economic confrontation. Once again, right-wing politicians in the LDP criticised the result of the FS-X arrangement as an example of an unequal treaty: the financial cost would be borne by Japan, and the US would have access to all the technology to be developed while Japan's access to American technology would be restricted.[28] But to the United States, the FS-X deal was a way to change the past imbalance of the one-way technology flow to Japan.[29]

As the FS-X issue has shown, trade and economic concerns in the US carry the most weight and those government agencies concerned with trade and the economy exert more influence over the fundamental tenor of the alliance. High-technology issues could dominate trade and security relationships; the strategic nature of high-technology industries, already much emphasised by the Clinton administration, will be an increasingly essential component of both national security and economic policies. The specific policy actions of the Clinton administration were seen in the initiative for greater scales of defence-technology cooperation in 1994, as well as increased interest in a civil industrial technology flow into the US within the continuing economic framework talks. Japan seems to be moving ahead gradually, conscious of the necessary price of alliance both in economic and security terms.

In sum, Japan will continue to debate the role of the SDF and the Constitution, but focusing more on its contribution to UN peacekeeping. These arguments will be conducted within the confines of the constitutional ideals for the foreseeable future. The Japan–US security alliance will also remain in place, unless the US preoccupation with economic concerns should cause it to misjudge its strategic priorities. Japan will continue to shoulder the burden of the US forces and step up technology transfer to the United States, as long as its major contributions as an ally remain economic.

Asia–Pacific security

Even if security relations between Japan and the US become manageable, their security collaboration requires much wider and deeper adjustment. This means not only avoiding conflicts of interest between them in wider Asia–Pacific settings, but also involves the more positive task of creating a new regionwide security order. For this, four objectives have to be pursued simultaneously: the maintenance of a US military presence and commitment as a balancing power; strategic stability between the US, Japan and China; confidence-building in politico-military relationships among the countries in the region; and management of economic conflict caused by increasing regional economic integration and interdependence. These goals are interrelated, and all four must be achieved to create and sustain a regional security order.

As to the US military presence, the three-phase reduction is now under way, based on the Strategic Framework for the Asian Pacific Rim announced by the Department of Defense in April 1990. The *Bottom-up Review* undertaken by the Clinton administration confirmed America's intention to maintain its military presence overseas, adopting the basic strategy of the Bush administration. It was the 'cooperative engagement strategy' that once again assured US commitment to the region through its 'adaptive forward presence'.[30]

Warnings against possible American isolationism and the plausibility of a power vacuum being created by a dramatic withdrawal of the US military from the region are, it must be said, more theoretical than practical. While a power vacuum is most unlikely, the candidates to fill it are either a revived Russian nationalist empire, an unstable militant China hostile to neighbouring countries, or a nationalistic Japan without much confidence in its future economic prosperity. None of these are welcome, and this is precisely why the American military presence is necessary for the region's security. Even if the Russian military threat were to be revived or Chinese military potential were to give cause for alarm in the future, a credible presence of US forward-deployed forces would be an effective counterbalance. From Japan's perspective, therefore, it is more meaningful to address the transparency of Chinese defence policy, to transmit concern about this bilaterally and to involve China in regional security dialogues rather than to argue about the future danger of China's military potential. Likewise, it is essential to pursue strategic stability between Japan, the US and China as a safety net against Russia's uncertain future.

Japan's military role would remain defensive and restrained, if combined with an American commitment that included nuclear deterrence under bilateral security arrangements. This has been described as 'keeping the cap on the bottle' – a fitting analogy in the sense that Japan would have to allocate more resources for defence if it had no strong military support from the US. But it is misleading if it suggests that the US military presence in Japan has put the lid on Japan's possible militarism. It is rather the strength of domestic feeling that has checked the revival of militarism, and a reluctance to believe in the effectiveness of such a Japanese democratic force could sow the seeds of distrust between the two nations.

Over the long term, however, Asia–Pacific security depends largely on trust and policy transparency among countries in the whole region, checking and confirming each other's intentions and capabilities, while pursuing a subregional solution to conflicts and confrontations. Japan's Asia–Pacific security policies are based on this, termed a 'two-track approach' by Prime Minister Kiichi Miyazawa in July 1992.[31] The first Japanese initiative was taken in July 1991, when Foreign Minister Taro Nakayama proposed political dialogue to 'increase the sense of security' to take place at the Association of South-East Asian

Nations (ASEAN) Post-Ministerial Conference (PMC), together with the establishment of the senior officials' meeting (SOM).

The initial reaction of ASEAN countries was reserved, and the United States was less than enthusiastic, but a consensus did gradually emerge. Following the agreement among the heads of states in January 1992 (the Singapore Declaration), the July ASEAN PMC officially addressed regional politico-security issues for the first time. In January 1993, the ASEAN SOM agreed and proposed that the other PMC partners should set up a PMC SOM for regional security discussions. In May 1993, the first round of PMC SOM was convened in Singapore, with subcabinet-level participation. The agenda addressed the approach for regional security, an analysis of the region's security status and necessary response, and cooperation with non-participants of the PMC SOM.

In July 1993, the ASEAN PMC further developed the process of discussions. On the ministerial level, it was decided to initiate the ASEAN Regional Forum (ARF) from 1993 in which five countries (China, Russia, Laos, Papua New Guinea and Vietnam) were invited to join the original 13 members of the ASEAN PMC for regional security talks. The Asia–Pacific security discussions are still evolving, and in the future will be characterised by diversity, gradualism and loose association. The multi-layered structure, in which the ASEAN ministerial core is encircled first by the ASEAN PMC and then by the outer ARF, reflects the reality of diverse interests and complicated security relationships, while preserving and encouraging ASEAN cohesion, autonomy and initiative. The gradual evolution reflects the Asian method of consensus-building in which the unilateral leadership of major powers needs to be carefully avoided in the longer Asian time span. The orientation for a loose gathering reflects Asian pragmatism, whereby improving relationships through dialogue creates a better environment for resolving conflicts than bringing national interests into collision in an attempt at a binding and quick resolution. The Asia–Pacific security framework is certainly unlike comprehensive European frameworks such as the Conference on Security and Cooperation in Europe (CSCE); Japan's Asia–Pacific approach seems to be more inclined to consensus-oriented, step-by-step undertakings.[32]

In the longer term, Asia–Pacific security needs to be addressed comprehensively, so that economic, political and diplomatic evolution are combined to create an harmonious and stable order. In this context geo-economic factors play an even more vital role in the region's future security. Mutually reinforcing economic reform and growth of the nations in the region, both developed and developing, is the precondition for socio-political evolution towards better democracy and demilitarisation. Japan and the United States are themselves important contributors to this process. Such a regionwide trend would support the reinforcement of nonhegemonic and cooperative diplomatic postures both in security and economic policies.

This national strategy has to co-exist with the realistic security frameworks already established in the region. Increasing economic links and interdependence among regional nations offers both the danger of conflicting economic interests and the opportunity for a new Pacific economic community. Strategic stability, for example, between Japan, US and China, will be largely affected by the degree to which the economic reform or development strategy of each nation is built into the dynamism of regionwide trade and economic growth, and the degree to which each nation establishes trust based on mutually reinforcing economic benefit.

The end of the Cold War heightened the value of this regional geo-economic collaboration. The strongest catalyst for its evolution came from the shift in the US policy priority. The increased emphasis on the domestic economic and social agenda and the economic security component of foreign and defence policies in the Clinton administration have accelerated the 'look West' orientation of American policies. The initial success of US foreign economic policies, as shown in the North American Free Trade Agreement (NAFTA), the Asia–Pacific Economic Cooperation (APEC) forum and the Uruguay Round of the General Agreement on Tariffs and Trade (GATT) talks in the latter half of 1993, was paralleled by its domestic economic recovery. The APEC summit of November 1993 symbolised the new American initiative to give priority to Asia–Pacific affairs. The US wanted to make the most of potential future economic growth in the Asia–Pacific to stimulate exports and employment.

Japan welcomes increasing US engagement and economic presence. Japan's link with the other countries of the Asia–Pacific region is well established in terms of the flow of trade, investment and economic assistance. Its economic link with the region's developing nations, especially ASEAN countries, has been guided more by business and market forces than by such European institutional arrangements as the Lome Conventions. US trade across the Pacific, now 1.5 times as great as the transatlantic trade, and flourishing investment in the region provide a substantive basis for US economic engagement there and a strong incentive for American security interest and commitment.

Economic integration in the region could also promote and preserve US confidence in its economic power and future, thwarting the sense of threat arising from competition with Japan and other Asian economies, and thus tempering the adverse impact of economic revisionist and protectionist forces.

Further, increasing the US role in the region's economic integration process, as represented by APEC, will promote a 'civilisational' experiment in the longer term. In pursuance of the Asia–Pacific Economic Community, where historical, political, cultural, ethnic and religious diversity is more evident than any commonality, APEC seeks to confound Samuel Huntington's theory that there will be civilisational conflict in the unique Asia–Pacific geo-economic setting.[33] Asian values and approaches and American (Western) ones could indeed collide, but nevertheless a common strategy for regional and global integration and unity should be possible. The successful marriage of the Asian values of fusion and harmony and Western values of confrontation and progress might even produce 'a new breed of cross-fertilised Asia–Pacific civilisation'.[34] In actual policy terms, integration faces two difficulties that are not necessarily insurmountable: a clash between Asian nationalism and American encroachment and the speed of regional trade liberalisation.

There has indeed been a collision between Asian nationalism, represented by the East Asia Economic Caucus (EAEC), and American economic encroachment, represented by the defensive and discriminatory management of NAFTA. When Prime Minister Mahathir of Malaysia first enunciated the EAEC, the Bush administration reacted rather emotionally, perceiving danger in an ethnic gathering that excluded the US. Although the Japanese government was well aware of inherent problems in the original concept of the EAEC, it was also concerned about the American attempt to kill the idea without sufficient understanding of the reasons for such an Asian initiative, which was itself a reaction to the American NAFTA undertaking and the evolution of the enlarged European Union.

From the Asian perspective, the US seemed to be adopting a double standard. The Japanese government, giving conditional support for NAFTA, also scented danger when the Deputy Assistant Secretary of the US Commerce Department referred to the possibility of the selective enlargement of NAFTA in the Asia–Pacific region, excluding Japan, although this was later denied by the US government as not being official policy. Japan was also concerned when the Clinton administration, for domestic reasons, pointed to the Japanese economic threat when seeking NAFTA's passage through Congress. To some Asian intellectuals, Asian regional fora, such as the EAEC, are an insurance against unpredictable American trade policies, including the future of NAFTA.[35]

Given this danger, however, APEC has begun to function as a central coordinating body for regional economic integration. In July 1993, the ASEAN foreign ministers decided to define the EAEC within the framework of APEC. Mexico, a member of NAFTA, joined APEC, and Chile also became a member in November 1994. Former Singaporean Prime Minister Lee Kuan Yew proposed that APEC should seek a regional free-trade arrangement, transforming NAFTA into PAFTA (Pacific–Asia Free Trade Agreement).[36]

The other issue involving a difference of ethos is the goal and speed of regional trade liberalisation and institutionalisation of the APEC regime. The informal APEC heads of state meeting in November 1993 defined regional trade liberalisation as a final goal, and agreed to set up a trade and investment committee to devise a specific work programme for trade liberalisation. Yet ASEAN countries expressed much concern over the 'hasty and binding nature' of the US proposals and leadership. As former Prime Minister Miyazawa of Japan put it, 'it is better not to try to take leadership when you go along with ASEAN people'.[37] However, the United States seems to be adjusting to the somewhat slow Asian pace of evolution.

US economic integration in the region would also help the transition of such socialist market economies as China and Vietnam into the Asia–Pacific free market. And it would act as a stepping-stone for the future integration of these countries into the international free-market system. From this viewpoint, the recent trend of increasing American investment in China and the decision to re-open trade and economic relations with Vietnam are both steps in the right direction. Political *rapprochement* is often preceded by economic warming-up.

Finally, there are global implications, especially for Europe. While ASEAN does not wish to be dominated by such a major power as the US, it is concerned by the defensive nature of the European market. Japan wants the Asia–Pacific community to be one of open regionalism, different from European economic integration based on a customs union. A united US–Europe front 'bashing' the Japanese market is a bad dream that would trigger narrow 'Asianism' in Japan. To the extent that APEC would pursue the goal of open and free regionalism, Japan seems to be more favourably disposed to European participation than are the US and some Asian countries. Europe's positive role in the Asia–Pacific, beyond the wish to be a part of the APEC evolution, would mean facilitating European openness and access to and from the Asia–Pacific region.

The titles of all Japanese publications cited were translated from the original Japanese by the author of this paper.

NOTES

1   *Defense of Japan* (Tokyo: Defense Agency of Japan, 1993), p. 55.
2   *Ibid.*, p. 57.
3   For example, Gerald Segal, *China Changes Shape: Regionalism and Foreign Policy*, Adelphi Paper 287 (London: Brassey's for the IISS, 1994).
4   For an historical review of Japan's post-Second World War security policy, see Yukio Satoh, *The Evolution of Japanese Security Policy*, Adelphi Paper 178 (London: IISS, 1982). For recent discussions on the subject, see Francis Fukuyama and Kongdan Oh, *The US–Japan Security Relationship After the End of the Cold War* (Santa Monica, CA: RAND, 1993); Norman D. Levin, Mark Sorell and Arthur Alexander, *The Wary Warriors: Future Directions in Japanese Security Policies* (Santa Monica, CA: RAND, 1993).
5   For the view of the Japanese government on the SDF and the Constitution, see *Defense of Japan*, pp. 86–89.
6   *Asahi Shinbun*, 30 November 1993.
7   *Defense of Japan*, p. 376.
8   *Yomiuri Shinbun*, 5 January 1994.
9   *Nihon Keizai Shinbun*, 5 January 1994.
10 *Asahi Shinbun*, 4 January 1994.
11 *Nihon Keizai Shinbun*, 16 January 1994.
12 *Asahi Shinbun*, 10 December 1993.
13 Public Relations Office, Prime Minister's Secretariat, 'Public Opinion Survey on Japan's Peace and Security', *Asagumo Shinbun*, Defense Handbook, 1994, p. 539.
14 *Asahi Shinbun*, 14 June 1994.
15 *Defense of Japan*, pp. 94–96.
16 Ichiro Ozawa, *Blueprint for a New Japan* (Tokyo: Kodansha, 1993), pp. 117–18.
17 See, for example, Kan Nakanishi, 'Japan–US Security Relations after the End of the Cold War', *Gaiko Forum*, no. 65, February 1994.
18 *Asahi Shinbun*, editorial, 8 April 1994.
19 US Department of Defense, *Report on the Allied Contribution to Common Defense*, October 1993.
20 For a factual analysis of the AW ACS issue, see Kensuke Ebata, 'What is AW ACS?', *Sekai Shuho*, 20 October 1992.
21 For example, see Hirohito Sano, 'AWACS Questioning Japan's Defense Policy', *Asahi Shinbun*, 29 October 1993.
22 *Defense of Japan*, pp. 103–5.
23 Testimony by Richard Solomon, US Assistant Secretary of State, before the East Asia and Pacific Sub- Committee, Senate Foreign Relations Committee, 17 May 1991.
24 For a vivid account of the FS-X issue, see Ryuichi Teshima, *Strike at Japan FS-X* (Tokyo: Shinchosa, 1991).
25 American revisionist views tend to emphasise the danger of technology outflow from the US. See, for example, Fukuyama and Oh, *The US–Japan Security Relationship*, pp. 53–66.
26 Levin, Sorell and Alexander, *The Wary Warriors*, pp. 78–87.
27 Statement by Dick Cheney, US Secretary of Defense, before

the House of Foreign Relations Committee, 3 May 1989.

28 Teshima, *Strike at Japan FS-X*, pp. 191–93.

29 Statement by Dick Cheney, 3 May 1989.

30 Testimony by Charles R. Lason, Commander-in-Chief, US Pacific Command, before the Senate Armed Services Committee, 21 April 1993.

31 Address by Prime Minister Miyazawa at the National Press Club, Washington DC, 2 July 1992.

32 For Japan's perspective on Asia–Pacific security, see, for example, Yukio Satoh, 'Towards the Watershed of 1995: Asia–Pacific Security', *Gaiko Forum,* no. 64, January 1994.

33 See Samuel P. Huntington, 'The Clash of Civilizations', *Foreign Affairs,* vol. 72, no. 3, Summer 1993.

34 Yoichi Funabashi, 'The Asianisation of Asia', *Foreign Affairs,* vol. 72, no. 5, November/ December 1993.

35 See, for example, the debates in 'Let's Speak From an Asian Perspective', *Gaiko Forum,* no. 64, January 1994.

36 Former Prime Minister Lee's keynote speech at the symposium sponsored by the Committee for Japan of the 21st Century, reprinted in *Asahi Shinbun,* 1 November 1993.

37 Former Prime Minister Miyazawa's speech, reprinted in *ibid.*

CHAPTER TWENTY-ONE

Identities and security in East Asia

Koro Bessho

From Adelphi Paper 325, 1999

Introduction

While East Asia has its share of flash-points, from the Korean Peninsula to the South China Sea, the region has been relatively free from large-scale combat in the 1990s. Under these circumstances, two opposing views of the future of East Asian security relations have emerged. Optimists argue that increased interdependence and the development of international fora will lead to a sense of community in the region, which will in turn facilitate cooperative security relations. Advocates of this view cite developments in the Asia-Pacific Economic Cooperation (APEC) forum and the Association of South-East Asian Nations (ASEAN) Regional Forum (ARF) as sure signs that East Asia is moving towards this benign future.[1] Others, however, forecast more volatile conditions characterised by balance-of-power politics reminiscent of nineteenth-century Europe. Proponents of this view predict either the re-emergence of old conflicts that lay dormant during the Cold War, or the onset of new problems such as energy and food scarcity. Without the institutional frameworks to deal effectively with these difficulties, competition between nations will increase.[2]

Whichever view prevails, China and Japan, given their size, power and status in the international community, are likely to bear much of the responsibility for maintaining East Asia's stability. However, both countries have been reluctant to adopt a leadership role, while China has itself often been seen as a source of instability. By contrast, South-east Asia, through ASEAN, has been willing to take the initiative outside of its sub-region, and has shown how unity can be forged from diversity. However, South-east Asia does not have the resources or the authority to lead the whole of East Asia, especially after the financial crisis of 1997–98.

The states of East Asia seem still to be in the process of adjusting to the greater unpredictability of post-Cold War international relations. In this new environment, issues of identity can be as crucial as questions of national interest. The influences shaping a nation's sense of itself include not only relatively static elements like religion and ethnicity, but also more malleable factors such as national pride and past history. These ingredients can change in response to changing circumstances, notably alterations in relations with other states. This paper analyses the way in which these senses of identity have affected the actions of the key players in East Asia, and assesses future challenges and possibilities in the search for regional security.

Chapter One: Japan: reluctant leader?

Japan is often seen as caught between two conflicting identities: Asian and Western. The country seems to have succeeded in becoming a modern, industrialised nation without losing its distinct heritage or personality. At the same time, its sense of self seems torn between Asia and the West. In the more practical world of politics and security, both Japanese and non-Japanese alike have complained that the country has neither assumed the leadership role in Asia that it should, nor been a prominent advocate of Asian points of view on the world stage: an economic giant, but a political lightweight. Conversely, concern over the ramifications of a greater Japanese involvement in security affairs persists, both at home and abroad. For Yoshibumi Wakamiya, 'Japan's political outlook on Asia is a mixture of feelings of superiority and indebtedness, and of affinity and alienation'.[3]

This ambivalence in the way in which Japan sees itself, and is seen by its neighbours, stems not from any 'cultural' or 'civilisational' characteristics, but from the history of the country's dealings with Asians and Westerners. Japan's identity has been profoundly shaped by the international environment, and has undergone important changes at turning-points in the country's history such as the Meiji Restoration of 1868 and defeat in the Second World War. The rise of East Asia's economies and the end of the Cold War, together with the prolonged stagnation of the Japanese economy, have significantly affected Japan's identity, and may in turn alter the country's relations, both with Asia and with the wider world.

Japan's dilemma

Since the mid-nineteenth century, two competing schools of thought have dominated Japanese views of the outside world: the 'Asianist', and the 'Euro-Americanist'. After the Meiji Restoration, which abolished Japan's traditional feudal structure, the belief that the country should 'leave Asia to enter Europe' became predominant within the political elite.[4] The *samurai* (warriors) who brought down the isolationist regime of the Tokugawa *shogunate* (military government) did so under the slogan *son-no jo-i* ('worship the emperor, and fight off foreigners'). However, the Restoration leaders quickly concluded that to resist US and European pressure was futile, abandoned their stated isolationism and instead decided to learn from the West. Under the banner *wakon yosai* ('Japanese spirit, Western technology'), the country absorbed European technology and, to an extent, adopted its lifestyle and political system. These changes were essentially pragmatic, far-reaching in form rather than in spirit: the aim was to build 'a rich nation and a strong army' (*fukoku kyohei*) to gain the West's respect.

By contrast, Asianism in Japan up to the mid-twentieth century was more an idealistic than pragmatic response to Western encroachment. When Sun Yat-sen, the leader of the Chinese revolution of 1911, addressed a Japanese audience in 1924, his appeal for a 'great Asia', through which the region could achieve equality with the West and liberation from colonialism, met with a receptive response, although it was not clear how these aims might be achieved. Asianism became the ideological justification for Japan's claim to dominance in East Asia. The idea of a united 'Asia for Asians' was used to legitimise Japanese imperialism to secure and monopolise Asia's resources and markets under the Greater East Asia Co-Prosperity Sphere, first announced in 1938. Japan had 'left' Asia only to 'return' in the guise of the Western colonial states that it tried to supplant. Although Japan's post-war identity problems are of a different nature, the bitter experiences of Japanese militarism before 1945 continue to shape the country's outlook, both to the rest of Asia and to the world at large.

The Second World War destroyed Japan's military machine and its economy, and rid the country of its ambitions to dominate Asia; after the conflict, its isolation was complete. The country's immediate task was to re-establish its sense of orientation, rebuild its economy and find its way back into the international community. The Constitutional Law introduced by the Allied occupation authorities in November 1946 embodied principles of liberal democracy, pacifism and egalitarianism. Although for the Allies the Constitution was designed primarily to prevent Japan from again posing a military threat, its provisions were welcomed by the Japanese public as a fresh start after the country's experience of totalitarian militarism. Unlike Japan's earlier encounter with Western ideas under the Meiji Restoration, after the Second World War these values were accepted in themselves, rather than as a means to a pragmatic end. As a result, Japan identified itself as one of the industrialised democracies of the West, and reconciled itself with the US. Washington helped Japan to re-enter the international community, with membership of the General Agreement on Tariffs and Trade (GATT) in 1955, of the UN in 1956 and of the Organisation for Economic Cooperation and Development (OECD) in 1964.

Despite the consensus in favour of the values embodied in the country's post-war Constitution, some, notably pacifism, caused problems. While the concept itself, as the opposite of the country's catastrophic militarism, won widespread support, there was disagreement over what it meant in practice. The question of how to promote the values of liberal democracy in East Asia, particularly human rights, also posed problems. These dilemmas often led Japan to eschew a leadership role in the region.

Pacificism

Under Article 9 of the Japanese Constitution, the 'Japanese people forever renounce war ... and the threat or use of force as a means of settling international disputes ... in order to accomplish this aim ... land, sea, and air forces, as well as other war potential, will never be maintained'.[5] This unprecedented article has caused debate since it came into effect in 1947. The interpretation developed by Japan's post-war governments forbids the country from sending troops overseas for the purpose of using force, but allows it to maintain a military for self-defence.

As the Cold War deepened, the US reversed its policy towards Japan's military capability and urged Tokyo to revise its 'Peace Constitution' and remilitarise. Under Prime Minister Shigeru Yoshida, Japan refused, although it did accede to US pressure to sign Second World War peace treaties only with states allied to Washington. In return, the US–Japan Security Treaty, initially agreed in 1951, ensured US protection.

Article 9's interpretation was long protested by the country's main post-war opposition party, the Social Democratic Party of Japan (JSDP), which argued that self-defence forces and participation in peacekeeping operations were unconstitutional, and that the US–Japan Security Treaty should be abolished. (The JSDP reversed its position when it came to power in 1994.) The JSDP was in effect advocating neutrality without armament – a type of isolationism sometimes referred to as 'one-country pacifism'. Any mention of using Japan's Self-Defense Forces (SDF) outside the country, or of Japan intervening in international conflicts, prompted strong opposition, both from the JSDP and from 'progressive' intellectuals.

These two incompatible views divided the country, allowing no common ground for a meaningful debate on national security. The taboo on discussing military issues was broken only in the early 1980s, when Yasuhiro Nakasone became Prime Minister and initiated a debate on these matters.[6] In 1990, during the Gulf crisis, Japan's policy of not exporting weapons led to debate over whether it was acceptable to send gas-masks to Japanese Embassy staff in the region. No serious public discussion of how the SDF should cooperate with US forces in the event of a crisis took place until the 'Japan–US Joint Declaration on Security', which was issued during President Bill Clinton's visit to Japan in April 1996.

Internationally, the turning-point in Japan's role came when the country joined the West in imposing sanctions against the Soviet Union in response to its invasion of Afghanistan in 1979.

Although primarily economic, Japan's involvement also meant participation in a joint political action, thus marking a break with post-war practice. The build-up of Soviet forces in the Far East and the deployment of SS20 intermediate-range ballistic missiles (IRBMs) in the early 1980s compelled Japan to stress the need for the Western bloc to act together to deal with the Soviet Union in Asia. Specifically, Japan cautioned that Western Europe could not be content with securing the removal of SS20s from Europe if Moscow simply transferred them to Asia. These concerns led the Group of Seven (G-7) industrial nations to declare the indivisibility of Western security in a Political Statement issued at the Williamsburg Summit in 1983.[7] Japan's insistence on being included in debates over Western security was seen at the time as a bold step forward by both the political left and the right in Japan.

Nonetheless, Japan's reluctance to become involved in matters requiring discussion of military-related affairs persisted. Despite its strong economic position in South-east Asia, the country played a relatively limited role during the Cambodian war of the 1980s. Apart from putting forward general ideas, Tokyo for the most part simply stated its support for ASEAN, and pledged that it would contribute to Indochina's reconstruction once the conflict was resolved. This approach may have been partly the result of Tokyo's desire not to upset the ASEAN states. During a visit to ASEAN members in 1974, Prime Minister Kakuei Tanaka was greeted by violent protests against Japan's perceived economic 'invasion' of the region. But Tokyo's reluctance to become too deeply involved in an issue with military implications also shaped its approach. Only in the 1990s did Japan begin to send peacekeeping personnel to Cambodia.

Liberal democracy and human rights

Liberal concepts such as freedom, democracy and human rights were not controversial in post-war Japan, but the country generally lacked the missionary zeal of Americans or Europeans in propagating these ideas overseas. Until South Korea's democratisation began in the late 1980s, Japan had no close neighbour sharing the same key values. Pushing for human rights overseas could therefore have risked further alienation in East Asia. Successive governments were also wary of charges of hypocrisy stemming from the country's colonial conduct. Finally, there was concern that direct coercion, sanctions for example, might make targeted countries more, rather than less, intransigent over human-rights issues. Japan stressed this view to its G-7 partners following the Tiananmen Square incident in China in 1989. Although Tokyo did not oppose economic measures against China, it argued at the G-7 Summit in Houston in 1990 that Beijing should be encouraged to continue reform, and stated that Japan would eventually resume soft loans. With East Asian states becoming more vocal in expressing their own views on human rights, and economic sanctions in many cases not having the desired result, this issue has remained a difficult one for Japan.

Relations with East Asia

Japan's identification of itself with the Western bloc, both politically and in terms of its values, generally meant that it viewed its relations with East Asia in the context of US strategic priorities. According to Kazuo Ogura:

> Japan's Asia policy is based on cold calculation and a strategy that takes into consideration the overall international situation and global order ... The Asia strategy that the United States (and, in turn, Japan) has followed – economic prosperity and democratisation in Asia and maintenance of American influence in the region – is gradually bearing fruit ... And by helping to implement this strategy, Japan is sharing in Asia's peace and prosperity.[8]

Although this perceived 'subordination' to Washington prompted continued criticism, particularly from liberals and the left, the general perception of Japan as *in* Asia, but not necessarily *of* Asia, meant that the country's relationship with the US enjoyed basic support.

Despite this confidence in the merits of alliance with the US and of Japan's broader identification with the West, there was a widely shared feeling that the Japanese should be more understanding of, and sympathetic to, East Asia than either Europeans or Americans. In a revision to the late-nineteenth century view that Japan should be a link between Asia and the West, many in post-war Japan felt that the country should 'build a bridge' from the West to Asia. Within the industrialised West, Japan claimed that it best understood Asia and Asian ways, and that it represented the region's interests. Before each annual G-7 summit, Japan sent envoys to its neighbours to gather their views and wishes; after each meeting, it sent representatives to brief them on the discussions that had taken place. This practice strengthened cooperative relations between Japan and its neighbours, while at the same time adding weight to its views in the G-7.

A maturing identity?

The 1990s have seen the end of the Cold War, the Gulf conflict of 1990–91 and the fiftieth anniversary of the end of the Second World War. While the basic framework of Japan's approach to the outside world has not changed, these developments appear to have made the country's key dilemmas less acute, and allowed it to adopt a less ambivalent position. The Japan–US security relationship, the cornerstone of Japan's foreign policy since the Second World War, lost its original *raison d'être* with the Soviet Union's demise. However, developments in Japan's security thinking triggered by instability on the

Korean Peninsula, together with reduced economic tensions with the US in the mid-1980s, have allowed Washington and Tokyo to reaffirm the importance of their relationship. The Cold War's end also affected Japan's relations with the rest of East Asia by requiring the country to clarify its position regarding liberal values such as human rights, and also its stance towards its own past. Japan's efforts to meet these challenges, while neither fully satisfying its neighbours nor resolving its identity dilemmas, may nonetheless help the country to develop a more confident foreign-policy style.

Reconfirming the Japan–US alliance

The end of the Cold War brought controversial US–Japan issues such as trade to the fore, and raised fundamental questions about the continued utility of the security alliance between the two countries. Japanese confidence, bordering on arrogance, in the country's economic strength and management style aggravated US frustration with the bilateral trade imbalance, leading to calls for greater unilateralism and trade sanctions. Literature in both Japan and the US fed resentment on both sides. Some US commentators argued that, with the end of communism, Japan had become America's major adversary; some in Japan held that it was time to 'leave America to enter Asia'. In a related, albeit uncontroversial, move, the Japanese Foreign Ministry was reorganised in August 1993, when the Foreign Policy Bureau was created as a coordinating body. The stated purpose of the reform was to respond to domestic criticism of the poor coordination between Foreign Ministry bureaux that had made it difficult for the ministry to respond effectively to the Gulf crisis. However, the Japanese media and outside observers saw the move as reflecting the post-Cold War decline in the importance of the North American Bureau.[9]

By the mid-1990s, relations between Japan and the US had improved. The conclusion of GATT's Uruguay Round and the establishment of the World Trade Organisation (WTO) in January 1995 gave both countries a stronger dispute-settlement mechanism. The trade imbalance declined, while the bursting of Japan's 'bubble economy' combined with vigorous growth in the US to transform American perceptions. Far from being a larger-than-life threat, Japan now seemed an ailing and ageing society facing major problems.

More fundamental to the reaffirmation of the Japan–US alliance was the realisation on both sides that the continued presence of the US in East Asia, for which the alliance provided the basis, was critical to the region's stability and prosperity. During a visit to Singapore in January 1997, Prime Minister Ryutaro Hashimoto made an important speech in which he argued that 'the presence of the United States, a country of unrivalled power and founded upon principles such as democracy, [the] market mechanism, and respect for creativity, is essential'; the Japan–US security treaty was 'a sort of infrastructure for stability and economic prosperity in the Asia Pacific ... Japan will continue to do its utmost to maintain confidence in the arrangements'.[10] Japan's decision to maintain its US link was taken not simply out of habit, nor was it based purely on US strategic aims. Rather, Japan had reconsidered its own security and the stability of East Asia as a whole after the Cold War, and had concluded that the alliance remained vital. The importance of the Japan–US alliance notwithstanding, the relationship has not been trouble-free. The issue of US bases on Okinawa, triggered by the rape of a schoolgirl by US servicemen in 1995, persists, while trade problems can occasionally flare up. But the relationship has survived its immediate post-Cold War test.

New foreign-policy guidelines

Japan's pacifism and liberal democracy, combined with its reluctance to be seen as 'dominating' or 'leading' East Asia, meant that during the Cold War it did not play an international political role commensurate with its economic weight. In this it was assisted by the Cold War's bipolarity, which tended to subordinate individual countries' actions to the needs of alliance. By the early 1990s, however:

> one of the responsibilities of Japan, which has become capable of influencing the construction of an international order, is to articulate the philosophy of [its] foreign policy and to make clear constantly to the international community the ideals and objectives which Japan pursues internationally.[11]

In an effort to achieve this clarity, the country took three specific measures. First, it formulated new guidelines governing the provision of overseas aid. Under the Overseas Development Assistance (ODA) Charter, announced in June 1992, aid became dependent on a variety of factors, including a potential recipient's environmental record, levels of military expenditure and arms exports and stance on the non-proliferation of weapons of mass destruction (WMD). Positions on democracy and human rights were also to be taken into account.[12] The Charter signalled Japan's new-found willingness to use aid to promote its preferred values and ideas, although the country has been cautious in applying specific measures.

Secondly, Japan altered the guidelines governing its military posture in the light of the 1990–91 Gulf crisis and North Korea's suspected nuclear-weapons programme, which made clear the extent to which Japan was unprepared for security developments in the Asia-Pacific. Throughout the Gulf crisis, the Japanese public was adamantly against sending SDF forces abroad for combat. At the same time, however, it seemed that the country would be more willing to support a contribution to international peace and stability that went beyond the merely financial. Since the Gulf conflict, SDF personnel have participated in mine-sweeping operations in the Gulf, and have been deployed as peacekeepers in Angola, Cambodia, El Salvador and Mozambique, and as part of the UN Disengagement Observer Force (UNDOF) on the Golan Heights. They have also taken part in humanitarian missions for Rwandan refugees in Zaire (now the Democratic Republic of Congo). In November 1995, Japan's National Defense Programme Outline was revised for the first time in 19 years. Under the new Outline, 'defense capability is to be expanded to encompass not only national defense ... but also response to large-scale disasters ... as well as contribute to the creation of a more stable security environment'.[13] The 'Japan–US Joint Declaration on Security' announced in April 1996 initiated a review of the Japan–US Defence Cooperation Guidelines established in 1978, the results of which were announced in September 1997. The new Guidelines stipulated the nature of US–Japanese cooperation 'under normal circumstances'; in 'actions in response to an armed attack against Japan'; and in 'cooperation in situations in areas surrounding Japan that will have an important influence on Japan's peace and security'.[14] The Annex to the Guidelines identified several fields of permissible SDF activity outside Japan, including relief operations and dealing with refugees; search and rescue; and non-combatant evacuation. The review met with a mixed response from Japan's neighbours. Most neighbouring governments cautiously welcomed it, with the proviso that they wanted continued transparency, while China remained sceptical at best. In making clear to its neighbours what its armed forces would do in a crisis, Japan

Table 1: **Top ten recipients of Japanese overseas development assistance, 1997**

(US$m net)

China	576.86
Indonesia	496.86
India	491.80
Thailand	468.26
Philippines	318.98
Vietnam	232.48
Jordan	139.63
Sri Lanka	134.56
Bangladesh	129.98
Egypt	125.40
Sub-total	**3,114.82**
Total ODA	**6,612.59**

Source: *Japan's Official Development Assistance Annual Report, 1998* (Tokyo: Ministry of Foreign Affairs, 1998), p. 119

sought to provide the clarity that it felt would ease fears of its possible rise to military power. One major purpose of issuing the new Guidelines was therefore to provide the transparency that Japan's neighbours, as well as its own people, sought.[15]

Japan's possible candidacy for Permanent Membership of the UN Security Council has played an important role in the pacifism debate. Some in Japan, Shusei Tanaka, Special Assistant to Prime Minister Morihiro Hosokawa, for example, argued against membership on the grounds that it would entail military activity on a par with that undertaken by the existing Permanent Members.[16] In his statement at the fiftieth session of the UN General Assembly in September 1995, Foreign Minister Yohei Kono declared Japan ready to discharge the responsibilities of Permanent Membership of the Security Council. At the same time, however, Kono made clear that this would not include modifying the provisions of Japan's 'Peace Constitution'. Debate between those keen to see Japan become a 'normal' country with a 'normal' role for its military, and those who argue that it should remain a 'civilian power', persists.[17] Conservatives in the US may still complain that Japan is not doing enough in security affairs. However, the nervous response of Japan's neighbours to the new Guidelines for security cooperation suggests that both Tokyo and Washington should remain cautious in their approach to military issues.

The third step that Japan took in reshaping its foreign policy was to address its pre-1945 record. On 15 August 1995, the fiftieth anniversary of the end of the Second World War, Prime Minister Tomiichi Murayama issued a statement acknowledging that Japan, 'through its colonial rule and aggression', caused 'tremendous damage and suffering to the people of many countries', and expressing 'feelings of deep remorse'.[18] Japanese leaders had made similar statements before. Murayama's apology was not, however, that of an individual politician, but had been officially approved by the Cabinet, and signed by Murayama (a Social Democrat), the conservative Liberal Democratic Party (LDP) leader and Foreign Minister Kono and by Hashimoto, who succeeded Murayama as Prime Minister in January 1996. The Joint Declaration issued during South Korean President Kim Dae Jung's visit to Japan in 1998 expressed 'deep remorse and heartfelt apology' for the 'damage and suffering' Japan had caused the Korean people during 'a certain period in the past'.[19]

Future challenges

During the 1990s, Japan increasingly felt that, through economic development and democratisation, notably in South Korea, its neighbours were moving closer to its values and principles. East Asian countries were no longer simply the objects of a policy implemented in coordination with the US, but had become 'dialogue partners' to whom Japan tried to explain its policy and the importance of its US alliance; to clarify its stance on key values like democracy, human rights and pacifism; and to more convincingly atone for its past. Japan has become far more active in these areas than before, but, by virtue of its history and affinity with its neighbours, has taken positions that differ from those of the other Western powers.

Japan's identity dilemma is becoming less acute, and the country may become better able to assume a leading role in shaping the international environment. This outcome is not, however, guaranteed. It presupposes that East Asia's progress towards broadly Western values is inevitable, but a vocal school of thought argues that, far from converging, the region should carve out a distinct 'Asian way'. If so, East Asia's economic development may not bring it as close to Japan as expected. Second, it is debatable whether Japan's easing identity dilemma will automatically lead the country to assume a greater leadership role in East Asia. Since the Second World War, Japan has sought to emulate the West, rather than setting its own standards or introducing new ideas. Japan's efforts to bridge the gap between the West and Asia have sometimes been criticised as taking the middle ground, rather than expressing a firm position of its own.[20] If the country is to take on a greater leadership role in East Asia, it needs original policies based on its long-term national interests.

East Asia's financial crisis of 1997–98 exacerbated some of the problems that had arisen earlier in the decade by denting Japan's self-confidence. In the short term, the country needs to recognise that whatever influence and respect it may enjoy has stemmed largely from its ability to lead the East Asian economies, and thus to contribute to regional stability. Allowing the region's economies to disintegrate will undermine decades of effort, both by Japan and by the US. Japan needs to reform its own economy and lead the way out of the gloom. In the longer term, with regained confidence the country will need to carry forward the development begun in the early 1990s to stimulate original thinking and a more active leadership role, both in its relations with its neighbours and with the wider world.

Chapter Two: China: future leader?

Like Japan, China has shown little willingness to lead in East Asia. This reluctance is partly the result of domestic political and economic preoccupations, but, again like Japan, also stems from identity problems. China during the 1990s has presented two very different faces to the world. The Tiananmen Square incident in 1989, nuclear tests in 1995 and 1996, and tension in the Taiwan Straits have created an image of China as a resentful, disruptive nation willing, at times, to be at loggerheads with the international community. On the other hand, Beijing's diplomatic actions in 1997 and 1998 suggest that China is aspiring to be seen as a responsible world power working for stability.

Following China's smooth handling of two key events in 1997 – the reversion of Hong Kong and the leadership transition in the wake of paramount leader Deng Xiaoping's death – conventional wisdom has it that the country will, at least for some years yet, continue the reform and opening process begun by Deng. Hence, it will seek to maintain the stable international environment conducive to such internal change. As Singapore's Senior Minister, Lee Kuan Yew, put it in late 1997, the leadership of Deng's successor, President Jiang Zemin, 'will thrive best in an atmosphere of stability and growth'.[21] However, the country faces a series of challenges which could threaten the reform process, including tackling its ailing state-owned enterprises, reducing corruption and strengthening the rule of law, and coping with the repercussions of decentralisation and unrest among non-Han ethnic groups. China's future, and its relations with the outside world, will also be shaped by the more complex question of the country's dual identity.

Stability above all?

Memories of Tiananmen, nuclear tests and tension in the Taiwan Straits have fostered the perception in the West that China is a disruptive nation outside the international community's mainstream. However, China's diplomacy in 1997 and 1998 suggests that the country is aspiring to be seen as a responsible power working for a stable international environment. Jiang's state visit to the US in October 1997 was an important early move for Chinese post-Deng diplomacy. Beijing's insistence that the trip be treated as a state visit by a world leader suggests that it was, at least in part, designed to consolidate Jiang's position within the Chinese Communist Party (CCP). At the same time, however, the trip can be seen as an attempt by Beijing to portray China as America's equal; the joint statement issued after the meeting, for example, declared that 'the two Presidents are determined to build towards a constructive strategic partnership'.[22] China appeared genuinely interested in improving relations with Washington: it declared its intention to increase efforts to reduce nuclear proliferation and pledged significant tariff reductions by 2005. The US reciprocated by lifting its ban on sales of nuclear items to China. Although Beijing made clear its views on human rights, several weeks after the trip China freed one of its better-known dissidents, Wei Jingsheng, possibly reflecting a wish to live up to its own self-image as 'firm on principle but pragmatic'. Clinton's return visit to China in June–July 1998 seems to have consolidated the progress made the previous year by formalising the emerging partnership between the two countries.

China also made progress with other powers. It reached a milestone in its relations with Russia in November 1997, when the two countries resolved their long-standing border dispute. The move was part of efforts to elevate their relationship from 'constructive cooperation' to 'strategic partnership'. While this change may be more symbolic than real, the use of the word 'strategic' is important given China's aspirations for a 'strategic partnership' with the US. China's relations with Japan were strained in 1995–96, partly because of the question of past experiences, and partly because of China's nuclear tests, which prompted Japan to suspend grant aid. However, the atmosphere improved with Prime Minister Hashimoto's visit in September 1997, which was returned by Chinese Premier Li Peng two months later. In February 1998, Chinese Defence Minister Chi Haotian travelled to Japan, the first such visit for 14 years. During the trip, both countries agreed to increase exchanges between their armed forces, including reciprocal visits by their chiefs of staff and, possibly, by their navies. Together with Jiang's visit to India in December 1996, the first ever by a Chinese head of state, these initiatives indicate the application with which China has sought to present itself as an important and responsible member of the world community, on a par with the major powers.

Beijing has also tried to play a responsible role in some of East Asia's potentially most destabilising issues. China has made constructive contributions to the Four Party Talks over the Korean Peninsula, pointing out that it is the only participant enjoying diplomatic relations with the other three (the US and the two Koreas). At a meeting with ASEAN leaders in December 1997, Jiang stated that China would 'never seek hegemony', but would 'forever be a good neighbour, a good partner and a good friend with ASEAN countries'. Less predictably, he was reported to have proposed that unresolved disputes with several ASEAN nations over the sovereignty of islands in the South China Sea be 'shelved temporarily' to prevent them from impeding the development of good relations.[23] At the news conference following the meeting, Chinese Foreign Minister Qian Qichen claimed that there was 'no tension in the South China Sea', and described the sovereignty disputes as a 'historic legacy'.[24] From late 1997, China also called upon Taiwan to resume cross-Straits talks, which it did in 1998.

Mutual distrust

Despite these developments, Western analysts continue to voice concerns about China's possible future behaviour as its economy expands. Abundant Western literature in the 1990s has warned of a coming conflict between China and the US.[25] Even those who take a more sanguine view still sound a note of caution. While arguing that China 'will neither have the will nor the capability to exercise hegemony over Asia in the decades to come', David Shambaugh also believes that the US and China will 'become competitive rivals and possibly strategic adversaries'.[26] The relevant question for Western experts, as it was in Cold War debates over the Soviet Union, remains whether China should be engaged, or contained.[27] However frequently Chinese leaders claim not to seek hegemony, Western experts continue to discuss the possibility, turning to past patterns to suggest future trends. While Alastair Johnston argues that 'China's decision-makers and strategists have displayed a consistently *real politik* world view since 1949', Tomoyuki Kojima contends that 'the average life cycle of a given national policy has been from five to ten years: the eighteen year duration of Deng's reform policies was a notable exception'; 'signs of fatigue are obvious', suggesting a policy change in the near future.[28] Analysts have also noted China's tendency to resort to coercion, rather than persevere with diplomacy, to achieve its aims.

From China's perspective, these Western views presuppose that the country is, if not an adversary, at least an outsider. 'Engagement' seems a Western ploy to become involved in the country's affairs in order to bring about the peaceful collapse of the regime from within. Deng ended open debate on this point in 1992, when he strongly reaffirmed his intention to open up to the West. Nonetheless, many in China undoubtedly believe that the country is not viewed with the respect and trust worthy of a 'strategic partner'. The revision of the guidelines for Japan–US security cooperation seems an aggressive act of containment, rather than an attempt to clarify and consolidate cooperation between Tokyo and Washington. However, Chinese policy-makers must understand that the West's mistrust stems not from a sinister hidden motive or from any cynicism inherent in Western culture, but from the confusing message China sends to the world. On the one hand, the country wishes to see itself as a world power, and to be treated as such; on the other, it believes itself to be a weak developing nation still seeking redress for past injustices. These contradictory views co-exist and, although both are in some ways justified, their combination confuses assessments both by outsiders, and by the Chinese themselves.

China's dual identity

A world power

China has never officially taken the position that it is a super-power, or that it is destined to become one. On the contrary, it has consistently claimed to be a champion of developing countries. It was a co-sponsor of the Asian–African Conference at Bandung, Indonesia, in 1955, the first international meeting of what became the nonaligned states. Under its conception of the three-world theory, China stood, not with the First World, but with the Third World of developing nations. This position became difficult to sustain following China's strategic alliance with the US against the Soviet Union in the 1970s. The multipolar post-Cold War world sought by China seems to remain based on an 'inner core' of itself, the US and Russia, both of which it has identified as 'strategic partners'. Although its military capability and economic strength do not allow it a global reach similar to that of the US, China has acted politically as a world power.

Several factors inform China's self-image as a global power, including its size, huge population and significant resources. The country's long and illustrious imperial history is also important. To its contemporaries, the Middle Kingdom was not simply Asia's largest state, but was the world itself, ruled by an Emperor mandated by Heaven. In theory, there were no boundaries between the Empire and neighbouring nations, which were seen as little more than 'barbarian' lands owing differing levels of allegiance to the Emperor. Thus, China is not part of Asia; Asia is China's periphery. Given this history, the belief in modern China as a world power comes naturally, while partnership with other Asian states does not. China does not yet appear to have found a comfortable way of dealing with its regional neighbours.

A developing nation
The contrasting – and more formally expressed – identity is of China as a weak and victimised developing nation. The reversion of Hong Kong to Chinese rule in July 1997 was celebrated with gusto in China, where it was seen as a symbolic event 'washing away one hundred years of national shame'. Jiang began his political report to the fifteenth CCP National Congress in September 1997 with a reference to China's humiliation in 1900, when eight foreign powers occupied Beijing, and narrated the country's twentieth-century history in terms of an effort to win national liberation.[29] Since 1993, China's Constitution has declared becoming 'wealthy and strong' (*fu qiang*) a national goal, indicating the lingering perception of the country as poor, weak and backward.

The slogan 'wealthy and strong' is reminiscent of that used in nineteenth-century Japan. Although it would be far-fetched to suggest that China, seeking to counter perceived 'imperialist pressure', could follow Japan's pre-war course, its conjunction of economic strength and military power has given its neighbours and the West pause for thought. Although Beijing may be interested in the South-east Asian model of development, the country's goals go beyond those of the 'development dictatorships', and will not be met until China has a 'strong army'. According to its self-image, China may be acting as a weak and victimised nation trying to put things right; its neighbours, on the other hand, may see it as a great power preparing to be more assertive. China's challenge is to recognise this perception, and to convince its neighbours that it has no intention of bullying them, even after it becomes economically stronger.

This is easier said than done. For example, China sees the Taiwan issue as a domestic matter, and therefore feels justified in using or threatening force in a bid to resolve it. Many South-east Asians outwardly agree that Taiwan is a domestic issue, and therefore no concern of theirs. Nevertheless, Chinese shows of force, and declarations that using force is the ultimate solution to a problem, make its neighbours uneasy. Although developments such as Hong Kong's return may weaken China's self-identification as a victim, the conventional view in the West is that the CCP will continue to promote this image because it will increasingly have to rely on nationalism to maintain its legitimacy given the general collapse of communism elsewhere. The problem of China's dual identity is thus likely to persist.

Sino-Japanese rivalry?

How do the implications of China's dual identity affect the most important bilateral relationship in East Asia: the one between itself and Japan? Analysts such as Denny Roy have argued that 'an economically powerful China may provoke a military build-up by Japan' leading to a new 'cold war'. A 'burgeoning China' therefore poses 'a long-term danger to Asia-Pacific security'.[30] According to Singaporean Senior Minister Lee, the region 'has never at the same time experienced both a strong China and a strong Japan. Some tensions may be inevitable'.[31]

The nature of the Sino-Japanese relationship is, however, more complex. While relations between the two countries since the end of the Second World War have not been trouble-free, they have also not primarily been adversarial. Despite China's strong verbal attacks on Japan in the 1960s over its past imperialism and militarism, both countries had unofficial channels of communication before relations were normalised in 1972. Soon afterwards, China became one of the top recipients of Japanese overseas assistance, and bilateral trade links grew significantly. Despite difficulties over their shared past, China's nuclear tests and disputes over the Senkaku (Diaoyu) Islands, Japan has tended to advise the international community against isolating Beijing.

Future relations between the two countries will depend on three main factors: national sentiment, which appears to have hardened on both sides in the 1990s; China's military build-up and reactions to it in Japan; and possible competition for leadership in East Asia. China's resentment of its past treatment by Japan, coupled with Tokyo's more assertive approach to democracy and human rights in the region in the 1990s, suggest a possible clash. Up until the 1980s, Japanese sentiment towards China had been marked by a mix of warmth and guilt. Immediately after the end of the Second World War, Nationalist leader Chiang Kai-shek allowed many Japanese to return home, while, as it normalised relations with Japan in the 1970s, the People's Republic declared that it would not seek war reparations. In response, Tokyo provided large amounts of official aid and other assistance. To many in Japan, China's post-war magnanimity suggested that, as it grew wealthier, the country would become a benevolent world power.

The suppression of students in Tiananmen Square in 1989 and China's nuclear tests in the mid-1990s fundamentally challenged this belief, and led Japan to suspend grant aid. The blasts – justified on the grounds that, compared with the other nuclear powers, China had conducted relatively few tests – touched a raw nerve in Japan, the only country ever to have suffered nuclear attack. Claims by Chinese officials that Japanese aid was in lieu of war reparations, and therefore that Tokyo had no right to suspend it, compounded the situation and undercut the goodwill that the earlier generation of Chinese leaders had cultivated. From China's point of view, continued insensitive remarks about the past by conservative Japanese politicians cancelled out expressions of remorse or apology made by the country's Prime Ministers. To coincide with the fiftieth anniversary of the end of the Second World War, Beijing launched a vigorous media campaign concerning Japan's actions during the conflict, thereby fuelling popular anti-Japanese feeling.

Although both China and Japan clearly need to make a determined effort to improve popular perceptions of each other, there are moderating forces on both sides. Fuelling nationalism may be useful to the CCP in its efforts to unite the nation and retain legitimacy, but the Party must be careful that it does not grow to the point where it comes to challenge the established order. When tensions rose over the sovereignty of the Senkaku (Diaoyu) Islands in 1996, prompting anti-Japanese demonstrations in Hong Kong and Taiwan, both Beijing and Tokyo were careful to prevent the situation from developing into a serious confrontation. In Japan, the 'romantic' view of a beneficent China may have faded, but policymakers still appear overwhelmingly to believe that supporting Beijing's reform process is crucial if the country is to become a responsible world power.

China's military build-up is the second key issue affecting future Sino-Japanese relations. Chinese analysts are said to 'seem incredulous that Japan, given its history of aggression towards China dating back to the 1890s, could sincerely view China as a threat and alter its defense policy accordingly'.[32] This can be seen as a typical case of 'victimised-nation' thinking: turning a blind eye to the possibility that military expansion by a power of China's potential may be viewed with unease by its neighbours. It would, however, be wrong to assume that this military development will inevitably prompt an arms race between China and Japan. The presence of US forces in East Asia makes any over-reaction in response to Chinese modernisation unlikely. Even if the US presence declined, Japanese attitudes towards militarism would make domestic military expansion unacceptable. Japan did not greatly increase

Table 2: **Chinese military expenditure, 1985–1998**

	GDP (1997 US$bn)	Official defence budget (1997 US$m)	Estimated real military expenditure (1997 US$m)
1985	421	9,178	28,276
1986	423	8,008	21,879
1987	422	7,512	16,120
1988	456	7,519	16,211
1989	454	8,231	22,537
1990	452	7,101	25,166
1991	456	7,013	25,698
1992	512	7,564	27,030
1993	562	8,575	29,909
1994	578	6,788	30,412
1995	584	7,902	34,345
1996	629	8,768	36,176
1997	639	9,719	36,551
1998	689	10,775	36,268

Source: IISS

its military capability in the face of the Soviet build-up of forces in the Far East in the 1970s and 1980s, even though it was encouraged to do so by Beijing. In April 1980, Premier Hua Guofeng reportedly told Diet member Yasuhiro Nakasone that Japan should increase its defence spending; the Deputy Chief of General Staff of the People's Liberation Army (PLA) claimed that Japan need not keep to its self-imposed expenditure ceiling of 1% of gross national product (GNP).[33] However, the highest percentage reached in the following two decades was 1.013%, in 1988.

Finally, it appears unlikely that Japan and China will compete for leadership in East Asia in the foreseeable future since neither has shown itself willing to assume such a role. When they act as global players, they do so on different stages: China in the UN Security Council, and Japan in the G-8 forum. For China, its position as a Permanent Member sits well with its self-image as a world power; for Japan, G-8 status accords with its wish to be identified with the industrialised West. Both countries seem to insist on playing a lead role through these fora, but neither wants the burden of leadership, and neither is at present keen to usurp the other's place.

The question is not how to prevent rivalry developing over this issue, but how to bring the two countries together in a multilateral forum to work for East Asian stability. China may not welcome Japan's admission to Permanent Membership of the Security Council, while both countries have not worked as closely together as may have been hoped for in APEC or the ARF. China's response to a Japanese and US idea for a trilateral government-level meeting on security affairs, developed in 1997, has been that it 'has merit, but we should study this idea between academics for the time being'.[34] The first of such 'non-government' trilateral meetings took place in July 1998, with high-level participation from all three countries.

This may lead to consultations at government level following agreement that officials could in the future participate in a personal capacity.[35]

A hegemon to be?

Western analysts continue to ask whether China will become a hegemonic power in the twenty-first century. This question may be necessary but, for the states of East Asia, it is insufficient. China's aspirations to fulfil its great potential cannot be denied. The question is thus what *kind* of world power it will become. Chinese leaders have repeatedly declared that they do not intend their country to be a 'hegemon' but, while these statements should not necessarily be met with scepticism, they do not fully answer the question.

The world, and East Asia in particular, needs China's active participation as a responsible power in specific security issues such as those pertaining to the Korean Peninsula, and in wider areas like energy and food security.[36] Following Asia's financial crisis in 1997–98, China was important to the recovery of the region's economies by not devaluating the *yuan* despite its lost competitiveness. China has thus come to be treated as a significant factor in financial affairs, as well as in trade issues. The prominent and favourable attention the country received in the wake of the crisis seems to have encouraged Chinese self-confidence and responsible behaviour. The challenge for the international community is to integrate this new economic power into the rule-based international system and, more specifically, into the WTO. This does not necessarily mean giving up preferential treatment as a developing nation: the benefits of further concessions from China must be weighed against the potential costs of China's perception of ill-treatment in this area, as long as the system's regulations and transparency are preserved.

After its show of force across the Taiwan Straits and its

nuclear tests in 1995 and 1996, China seems to have changed its approach to that of a responsible power seeking stable relations in a multipolar world. Does this shift reflect a fundamental change in the way that China sees itself in the international community? Has the smooth handover of Hong Kong, for example, weakened China's self-image as a victimised nation, or is this new, moderate tone a tactical move designed to maintain stability while the country grows richer and stronger? China has failed to reassure the international community of its motives. The way in which it governs Hong Kong will be important in shaping international perceptions, but mutual distrust and the problem of China's dual identity will persist unless a stable and durable situation is established *vis-à-vis* Taiwan. In the meantime, Beijing can demonstrate its willingness to take a leading role without bullying its neighbours, by playing an active part as an equal partner in multilateral institutions. The international community should encourage and assist China to do so.

NOTES

1   See, for example, C. Fred Bergsten, 'A Strategic Architecture for the Pacific', in Michael N. Bellows (ed.), *Asia in the Twenty- First Century: Evolving Strategic Priorities* (Washington DC: National Defense University (NDU), 1994), p. 258; Jose T. Almonte, 'Ensuring Security the "ASEAN Way"', *Survival*, vol. 39, no. 4, Winter 1997–98, pp. 80–92; and Yoichi Funabashi, *Asia Pacific Fusion - Japan's Role in APEC* (Tokyo: Chuo Koronsha, 1995).

2   See, for example, Kent E. Calder, *Pacific Defense – Arms, Energy, and America's Future in Asia* (Tokyo: Nihon Keizai Shimbun, 1996); Barry Buzan and Gerry Segal, 'Rethinking East Asian Security', *Survival*, vol. 36, no. 2, Summer 1994, pp. 3–21; and Samuel P. Huntington, *The Clash of Civilizations and the Remaking of World Order* (New York: Simon & Schuster, 1996).

3   Yoshibumi Wakamiya, 'Asianism in Japan's Postwar Polities', in Tadashi Yamamoto and Charles E. Morrison (eds), *Japan and the United States in Asia Pacific: The Challenge for Japan in Asia* (Tokyo: Japan Centre for International Exchange, 1995), p. 16.

4   See Naoki Tanaka, *Ajia no Jidai* (Tokyo: Toyo Keizai Shinpo-sha, 1996), chapter 2.

5   'The Constitution of Japan, Chapter II', www.ntt.co.jp/japan/constitution.

6   For an overview of Japan's 82 *Koro Bessho* security dilemma up to the early 1980s, see Yukio Sato, 'The

Evolution of Japanese Security Policy', in Robert O'Neill (ed.), *Security in East Asia* (Aldershot, Hants: Gower Publishers for the IISS, 1984), pp. 19–61.

7   See 'Statement at Williamsburg', www.library.utoronto.ca/www/g7/83secur.htm.

8   Kazuo Ogura, 'Japan's Asia Policy, Past and Future', *Japan Review of International Affairs*, vol. 10, no. 4, Winter 1996, pp. 1–15. When he wrote this article, Ogura was Japan's Deputy Minister for Foreign Affairs.

9   See Mike M. Mochizuki, 'Japanese Security Policy', in Michael J. Green and Mike M. Mochizuki, *The US–Japan Security Alliance in the Twenty-First Century* (New York: Council on Foreign Relations (CFR), 1998), pp. 25–52.

10 Mie Kawashima, 'Hashimoto Calls on Nations "To Build Trust" with Beijing', *Kyodo News*, Tokyo, 14 January 1997, in Foreign Broadcast Information Service (FBIS), *Daily Report*, EAS-97-009,15 January 1997.

11 1992 *Diplomatic Blue Book: Japan's Diplomatic Activities* (Tokyo: Ministry of Foreign Affairs (MOFA), 1991), p. 21.

12 The four principles governing Japan's Overseas Development Assistance (ODA) are: '1) Environmental conservation and development should be pursued in tandem. 2) Any use of ODA for military purposes or for aggravation of international conflicts should be avoided. 3) Full attention should be paid

to trends in recipient countries' military expenditures, their development and production of mass destruction weapons and missiles, their export and import of arms, etc., so as to maintain and strengthen international peace and stability, and from the viewpoint that developing countries should place appropriate priorities in the allocation of their resources on their own economic and social development. 4) Full attention should be paid to efforts for promoting democratization and introduction of a market-orientated economy, and the situation regarding the securing of basic human rights and freedoms in the recipient countries.' See *Japan's Official Development Assistance, Annual Report 1996* (Tokyo: MOFA, 1997), p. 211.

13 'New National Defense Program Outline', www.jda.go.jp/policy/ f_work/jndp/l_2_e.html.

14 'Completion of the Review of the Guidelines for US-Japan Defense Cooperation', www.jda.go.jp/ policy /f_work/sis in4_.htm.

15 Hitoshi Tanaka, '"Pacifist Japan" Reconsidered', *Caiko Forum*, no. 107, July 1997, pp. 35–40. Also see Tanaka, 'An Inside Look at the Defense Guidelines Review', interview with Hisayoshi Ina, *Japan Echo*, vol. 24, no. 5, December 1997, pp. 30–33.

16 On this debate, see Kenichiro Sasae, *Rethinking Japan-US Relations*, Adelphi Paper 292 (London: Brassey's for the IISS, 1994), p. 55.

17 Mochizuki, 'Japanese Security Policy'.

18 Statement by Prime Minister Tomiichi Murayama (15 August 1995)', www.mofa.go.jp/ announce/press/pm/murayama/ 9508.html.

19 'Japan–Republic of Korea Joint Declaration: A New Japan– Republic of Korea Partnership towards the Twenty-First Century, October 1998', www.mofa.go.jp.

20 In this context, see Funabashi, *Asia Pacific Fusion*, especially chapter 13.

21 Michael Richardson, 'Beijing Plays Key Role as East Asians Improve Ties', *International Herald Tribune*, 24 November 1997, p. 8.

22 'Sino-US Joint Statement October 29,1997', *Beijing Review*, 17–23 November 1997.

23 Lee Kim Chew, 'S-E Asia Gets East Asia's Vote of Confidence', *Straits Times*, 17 December 1997, p. 1.

24 'Jiang Vows China Will Be Good Neighbor to ASEAN', *International Herald Tribune*, 17 December 1997, p. 4.

25 See, for example, Caspar Weinberger and Peter Schweizer, *The Next War* (Washington DC: Regnery Publishing, 1997); and Richard Bernstein and Ross H. Munro, *The Coming Conflict with China* (New York: Knopf, 1997).

26 David Shambaugh, 'Chinese Hegemony over East Asia by 2015?', *Korean Journal of Defense Analysis*, vol. 9, no. 1, Summer 1997, p. 28.

27 Joseph S. Nye, 'China's Re-emergence and the Future of the Asia-Pacific', *Survival*, vol. 39, no. 4, Winter 1997–98, pp. 65–79. Nye, a strong proponent of engagement, shaped the Clinton administration's

China policy as Assistant Secretary of Defense for International Security Affairs in 1994–95. For a variation on the containment theme, see Gerald Segal, 'East Asia and the "Constrainment" of China', *International Security*, vol. 20, no. 4, Spring 1996, pp. 107–35.

28 Alastair Iain Johnston, 'China's New "Old Thinking"', *International Security*, vol. 20, no. 3, Winter 1995–96, pp. 5–42; Tomoyuki Kojima, 'China's Present Condition and Future Outlook', *Asia-Pacific Review*, vol. 4, no. 2, Autumn/ Winter 1997, p. 106.

29 'Kiyoshi Tanaka, '20 Seiki - Don'na; Idai Datta No Ka', *Yomiuri Shimbun*, 8 February 1998, p. 6.

30 Denny Roy, 'Hegemon on the Horizon?', *International Security*, vol. 19, no. 1, Summer 1994, pp. 149–68.

31 Lee Kuan Yew, Keynote Address, IISS Conference, Singapore, September 1997.

32 Thomas J. Christensen, 'Chinese Realpolitik', *Foreign Affairs*, vol. 75, no. 5, September–October 1996, p. 44. Also see Denny Roy, 'The Foreign Policy of Great-Power China', *Contemporary South-East Asia*, vol. 19, no. 2, September 1997, especially pp. 125–27.

33 '"Economic Power has the Right to be a Military Power", Says the Chinese Deputy Chief of Staff', *Nihon Keizai Shimbun*, 30 April 1980, p. 2.

34 Then Chinese Vice-Foreign Minister Tang Jixuan in discussion with Japanese Ambassador to China Yoshiyasu Sato. See 'Sino-Japanese Relations in the Twenty-First Century', *Gaiko Forum*, no. 110, September 1997, p. 32.

35 'Security Dialogue Between Japan, US and China Begins', *Asahi Shimbun*, 16 July 1998, p. 2.

36 Calder, *Pacific Defense.*

TIMELINE OF EVENTS

2000–2020s

June 2000

The first Inter-Korean summit takes place between President Kim Dae-jung of South Korea and Supreme Leader of North Korea Kim Jong-il.

July 2000

Japan hosts the 2000 G8 Summit in Okinawa.

August 2000

Japanese Prime Minister Mori Yoshiro makes a landmark visit to India to establish the Japan–India 'Global Partnership in the 21st Century'.

May 2001

Prime Minister Koizumi Junichiro delivers his inaugural speech to the Diet, promising reforms to revitalise the stagnant Japanese economy. These reforms included the privatisation of Japan Post.

September 2001

The 9/11 attacks on the US take place.

October 2001

Japan enacts the Anti-Terrorism Special Measures Law, allowing the JSDF to undertake refuelling missions in the Indian Ocean.

November 2001

The JMSDF and JASDF are deployed to the Indian Ocean, based on the Anti-Terrorism Special Measures Law.

December 2001

China accedes to the WTO.

May 2002

The Strategic Offensive Reductions Treaty (SORT) between the US and Russia is signed by Presidents George W. Bush and Vladimir Putin in Moscow.

June 2002

The IISS hosts the first Asia Security Summit in Singapore, later known as the Shangri-La Dialogue.

September 2002

Prime Minister Koizumi Junichiro becomes the first Japanese leader to visit North Korea since the Second World War. Both leaders sign the Japan–DPRK Pyongyang Declaration. Five Japanese abductees are brought home to Japan after the visit.

March 2003

An international coalition led by the US invades Iraq.

July 2003

Japan enacts the Law Concerning Special Measures on Humanitarian and Reconstruction Assistance in Iraq, allowing the JSDF to undertake humanitarian and reconstruction assistance missions in Iraq.

October 2003

The Japanese Aerospace Exploration Agency (JAXA) is established.

December 2003

The JGSDF is deployed to Iraq based on the Law Concerning Special Measures on Humanitarian and Reconstruction Assistance in Iraq.

January 2004

A small contingent of JSDF soldiers is deployed to Iraq.

 **DOMESTIC EVENTS**    **INTERNATIONAL ENGAGEMENT**    **KEY GLOBAL EVENTS**

December 2004

The Indian Ocean tsunami devastates several countries in South and Southeast Asia. The death toll is estimated to exceed 225,000, making it one of the deadliest natural disasters in history.

December 2004

Australia, India, Japan and the US form a partnership to deliver aid following the deadly Indian Ocean tsunami. This would mark the beginning of the 'Quadrilateral Security Dialogue', more commonly known as the Quad.

September 2005

The fourth round of the six-party talks on North Korean disarmament achieves a first breakthrough and issues a joint statement.

September 2006

Abe Shinzo succeeds Koizumi Junichiro as prime minister but resigns a year later owing to ill health.

October 2006

North Korea successfully conducts its first nuclear-weapons test.

January 2007

The Japanese Defense Agency is upgraded to ministry status.

May 2007

The first Quad working-level meeting is held in Manila. Momentum stalls in 2008 owing in part to Australian reluctance to antagonise China.

August 2007

Prime Minister Abe Shinzo delivers his 'Confluence of the Two Seas' speech in New Delhi, India.

April 2008

The Japanese high court rules the JSDF dispatch in Iraq to be unconstitutional.

July 2008

Japan hosts the 2008 G8 Summit in Hokkaido.

September 2008

The Lehman Brothers investment bank collapses, triggering the 2008 global financial crisis.

March 2009

Two JMSDF destroyers sail for Somalia to patrol for pirates, the first overseas mission of its kind.

March 2009

Japan's lower house approves a ¥2trn stimulus plan, including cash handouts, to support the economy after the 2008 financial crash.

August 2009

The DPJ wins a landslide victory in the lower-house election.

April 2010

Okada Katsuya is the first Japanese foreign minister to chair a UNSC meeting on peacebuilding in post-conflict countries.

July 2010

China overtakes Japan as the world's second-largest economy.

September 2010

Japan and Australia found the ministerial-level Non-Proliferation and Disarmament Initiative (NPDI).

September 2010

Japan detains a Chinese fishing-trawler captain after his boat collides with Japanese Coast Guard vessels near the Japan-administered Senkaku/Diaoyu Islands. In retaliation, China halts the export of certain rare earth elements to Japan.

December 2010

Pro-democracy demonstrations in Tunisia mark the start of the Arab Spring.

 DOMESTIC EVENTS  INTERNATIONAL ENGAGEMENT  KEY GLOBAL EVENTS

March 2011

The Tohoku earthquake and tsunami ravage Japan's northeast, triggering the Fukushima nuclear disaster.

December 2011

Kim Jong-un becomes the leader of North Korea following the death of his father Kim Jong-il.

October 2012

Japan becomes the first party to the Anti-Counterfeiting Trade Agreement (ACTA), an international legal framework for enforcing the protection of property rights.

September 2013

China's President Xi Jinping launches the One Belt, One Road Initiative (later the Belt and Road Initiative–BRI) during a speech in Kazakhstan.

February 2014

Russia invades the Ukrainian territory of Crimea and annexes it a month later.

April 2014

The consumption tax is raised from 5% to 8%.

July 2014

Japan's cabinet approves a landmark change to the Japanese constitution, paving the way for Japanese forces to engage in 'collective self-defence' abroad to defend allies.

January 2015

The first Japan–UK foreign and defence ministers' meeting is held.

April 2015

The Convention on Supplementary Compensation for Nuclear Damage (CSC) enters into force, with help from Japan's signing of it in January 2015.

December 2015

196 countries adopt the Paris Agreement, a legally binding treaty on climate change.

March 2011

Anti-government protesters are shot dead in several Syrian cities, marking the start of Syria's civil war.

April 2012

The Liberal Democratic Party (LDP) announces a new draft constitution for Japan.

December 2012

The LDP wins back power in the lower-house election and Abe Shinzo becomes prime minister for the second time. He introduces 'Abenomics', an economic strategy designed to stimulate the economy through ultra-loose monetary policy, flexible fiscal policy and structural reforms.

December 2013

The Japanese government creates its National Security Council and adopts its first ever National Security Strategy.

April 2014

The Japanese government outlines 'The Three Principles on Transfer of Defense Equipment and Technology'.

June 2014

Prime Minister Abe Shinzo delivers the keynote address at the 13th IISS Shangri-La Dialogue.

December 2014

The LDP wins a comfortable victory in the lower-house election, confirming Prime Minister Abe Shinzo in power.

April 2015

The Guidelines for US–Japan Defense Cooperation are revised, increasing cooperation and inter-operability and expanding Japan's responsibilities in mutual defence.

September 2015

The National Diet passes the Legislation for Peace and Security, allowing Japan to engage in limited use of collective self-defence abroad.

 **DOMESTIC EVENTS**    **INTERNATIONAL ENGAGEMENT**    **KEY GLOBAL EVENTS**

May 2016

Japan hosts the 2016 G7 Summit in Ise-Shima.

June 2016

The UK votes to leave the EU in its Brexit referendum.

August 2016

Prime Minister Abe Shinzo announces Japan's 'Free and Open Indo-Pacific' (FOIP) concept at the TICAD VI in Kenya.

November 2016

After several years of construction, China's militarised artificial islands in the Spratly Islands area of the South China Sea expand to over 3,000 acres.

December 2016

Prime Minister Abe Shinzo delivers a speech at Pearl Harbor and becomes the first sitting Japanese leader to visit the USS *Arizona* Memorial.

April 2017

Japan signals that it will revive the Trans-Pacific Partnership after US withdrawal earlier this year.

July 2017

North Korea test-fires its first intercontinental ballistic missile (ICBM), the *Hwasong*-14.

August 2017

The Rohingya Refugee Crisis: hundreds of thousands of Rohingya flee armed attacks in Myanmar.

August 2017

Prime Minister Abe Shinzo hosts British Prime Minister Theresa May for a three-day summit in Japan, culminating in multiple joint declarations including the UK–Japan Joint Vision Statement.

October 2017

Prime Minister Abe Shinzo becomes the first Japanese premier since 1953 to win three consecutive lower-house elections.

November 2017

The Quad is revived by Prime Minister Abe Shinzo, with its first working-level meeting since 2007.

January 2018

US President Trump imposes tariffs on Chinese products, marking the beginning of the US–China trade war.

April 2019

Japan's Emperor Akihito abdicates, the first such abdication in over 200 years, ending the Heisei era. He is succeeded by his son, Naruhito, ushering in the Reiwa era.

July 2019

Amid deteriorating bilateral relations with Seoul, Japan announces trade restrictions on products to South Korea, citing national-security concerns.

October 2019

The consumption tax is raised from 8% to 10%.

January 2020

China imposes a lockdown on the city of Wuhan to contain the COVID-19 outbreak, which spreads globally by March 2020.

August 2020

Abe Shinzo resigns as prime minister owing to ill health. He is succeeded as prime minister in September by his Chief Cabinet Secretary, Suga Yoshihide.

September 2020

Japan and India sign an Acquisition and Cross-Services Agreement (ACSA), Japan's fifth ACSA.

 **DOMESTIC EVENTS**    **INTERNATIONAL ENGAGEMENT**    **KEY GLOBAL EVENTS**

September 2021

Prime Minister Suga Yoshihide launches Japan's Digital Agency to accelerate the digitalisation of the government. Suga pursued efforts to boost Japan's overall productivity and digitalise the nation.

September 2021

The first in-person Quad Leaders' Summit is held in Washington DC.

January 2022

Japan and Australia sign a Reciprocal Access Agreement (RAA) to facilitate cooperation between the JSDF and Australian defence forces.

February 2022

Japan announces the first of its sanctions against Russia.

June 2022

Prime Minister Kishida Fumio attends NATO's Madrid Summit, becoming the first Japanese prime minister to attend a NATO summit.

August 2022

Five ballistic missiles from China's People's Liberation Army fall into Japan's Exclusive Economic Zone after US House Speaker Nancy Pelosi's visit to Taiwan.

December 2022

The Japanese government releases its second National Security Strategy, first National Defense Strategy and the Defense Buildup Plan, pledging to increase defence spending to 2% of GDP by 2027.

January 2023

Japan and the UK sign an RAA.

May 2023

Japan hosts the 2023 G7 Summit in Hiroshima.

September 2021

Kishida Fumio replaces Suga Yoshihide as prime minister and the LDP comfortably wins the lower-house election in October.

September 2021

The last US troops pull out of Afghanistan after 20 years in the country.

February 2022

Russia invades Ukraine.

June 2022

Prime Minister Kishida Fumio delivers the keynote speech at the 19th IISS Shangri-La Dialogue.

July 2022

Former Japanese prime minister Abe Shinzo is assassinated during a campaign rally in Japan's western city of Nara.

October 2022

Prime Minister Kishida Fumio signs a joint security declaration with his Australian counterpart Anthony Albanese, substantially increasing defence cooperation between the two countries.

December 2022

Italy, Japan and the UK officially announce cooperation on developing a next-generation combat air fighter jet through the Global Combat Air Programme (GCAP), marking the first time Japan will cooperate with a partner other than the US on developing a military platform.

March 2023

Prime Minister Kishida Fumio visits Kyiv, Ukraine, the first post-war Japanese prime minister to visit an active war zone.

July 2023

Prime Minister Kishida Fumio attends NATO's Vilnius Summit.

 **DOMESTIC EVENTS**  **INTERNATIONAL ENGAGEMENT**  **KEY GLOBAL EVENTS**

CHAPTER TWENTY-TWO

China debates missile defence

Kori Urayama

Survival 46-2, 2004

Since the Bush administration's decision to withdraw from the Anti-Ballistic Missile (ABM) Treaty in December 2001, the US has embarked on aggressive plans for ballistic-missile defence (BMD). The Bush administration has also diminished the distinction between national missile defence (NMD) and theatre missile defence (TMD), effectively reorganising them into one conceptual framework.[1] In December 2002, President George W. Bush announced that US national missile defence (NMD) deployment would begin in 2004. While the initial deployment would be limited, the administration has indicated that the capability will subsequently be expanded and improved. Unlike the limited NMD system planned under Clinton, the Bush administration's layered NMD architecture envisions multiple-basing BMD systems capable of intercepting incoming ballistic missiles during their boost-phase, mid-course and terminal phase. Japan too has been making progress in its plans for BMD, and has decided to deploy a two-phase, layered theatre-missile defence (TMD) system by 2007. Based on US technology, this will involve a lower-tier *Patriot*

(PAC-3) surface-to-air missile capability designed to intercept cruise and ballistic missiles close to the terminal stage of their flight trajectories, and an upper-tier, exo-atmospheric defence involving Standard Missile-3 (SM-3) boosters mounted on *Aegis*-equipped destroyers.

The Japan Defense Agency (JDA) plans to deploy one of its four *Aegis* destroyers equipped with SM-3 by the end of 2007 and expand this provision to the rest of the *Aegis* destroyers by 2011. The JDA budget announced in December 2003 has set aside approximately ¥100bn ($930m) for BMD procurement and technological upgrades for the first year of the programme. An additional ¥500bn ($4.67bn) will be spent over the course of the next four years, with the total costs expected to reach at least ¥1 trillion ($9.26bn).[2]

China's reactions to these moves have thus far been muted. On 15 December 2001, the day after the US decision to withdraw from the ABM Treaty, the Chinese Foreign Ministry responded by calling for multilateral talks on the issue.[3] The official Chinese media was also measured in its response, calling the move 'unwise'.[4] In December 2002, the Foreign Ministry commented that the 'development of the missile defense system should not undermine international and regional security'.[5] Beijing's response to Japan's TMD decision has also been subdued, particularly considering its vociferous criticism of anti-missile defences in the late 1990s. In September 2003, during a meeting with visiting JDA Director General Shigeru Ishiba, Chinese Defence Minister Cao Gangchuan noted that Japan's defence policy, including its missile-defence plans, 'could undermine the region's military balance and trigger a new arms race'.[6] In December 2002, the Chinese Foreign Ministry reported that China was 'worried' about US–Japanese TMD cooperation, and urged that 'countries involved act cautiously'.[7]

With China's surprisingly measured response, a number of American and Japanese observers have begun to argue that Beijing's past anti-BMD campaign was merely rhetorical.[8] As one senior Japanese analyst puts it, 'It is important not to overreact to Chinese opposition to BMD; the more you react, the more they will exaggerate their anti-BMD claims'.[9] This article argues that China has made a conscious effort to prioritise stable relations with the US and Japan over its long-term concerns about BMD. Many Chinese analysts, backed by sober technological assessments of the prospects for BMD deployment, have concluded that time is on China's side. But this does not imply that China's opposition to missile defences has ceased to exist. Beijing remains wary of US and Japanese intentions, and believes that BMD is aimed at China's containment. The Chinese debate on BMD is complex, and involves a variety of motivations, concerns, calculations and assessments. It is not sound policy to dismiss its opposition as merely rhetorical. While some arguments are indeed illogical, contradictory and out of proportion to the issue at hand, there are some serious questions at the root of Chinese concerns.

China's views on missile defence

Chinese opposition to missile defence is not new. Beijing voiced concerns about US missile-defence efforts in the 1980s, when the Reagan administration announced its Strategic Defense Initiative (SDI), and again in the 1990s, when Washington decided to focus its research and development efforts on TMD over NMD. US–Japanese negotiations over TMD in the 1990s fuelled concerns in China that a system would be deployed in its neighbourhood.

Most Chinese experts reject the notion that missile defence is a defensive system. Combined with superior offensive capability, they argue, missile defence has the potential to become a strategically offensive weapons system. Chinese experts have also questioned the American and Japanese reasons for moving forward with missile defence against countries of concern such as North Korea. Some have argued that the US and Japanese depictions of North Korea's ballistic-missile threat are intentionally exaggerated to justify missile defence. In 1999, Sha Zukang, then-director of the Arms Control and Disarmament Department of the Chinese Foreign Ministry, was quoted as saying that Japan's 'perception' of a North Korea threat was 'just a pretext'.[10]

China has employed an array of arguments in support of its position. Five basic ones have developed over time: that missile defence undermines the Chinese nuclear deterrent; that it could affect the Taiwan dispute; that it will consolidate US hegemony; that it undermines arms-control processes; and that it encourages Japanese remilitarisation.[11]

BMD's impact on the Chinese nuclear deterrent

The first argument is that NMD poses a direct threat to the viability of China's nuclear deterrent. Given that China is estimated to have only two dozen or so strategic missiles, NMD could neutralise China's nuclear deterrent in its entirety.[12] Most Chinese experts do not believe US assurances that NMD is not targeted at China, and regard BMD as yet another US plan to consolidate its military advantage.

Although not as widely discussed as NMD, some Chinese analysts argue that TMD, too, could potentially negate China's nuclear deterrent. Although the declared goal of TMD is to defend against attacks by missiles with ranges of less than 3,500km, some argue that upper-tier systems such as the sea-based mid-course missile defence programme (SMD), which the US and Japan are co-developing, could theoretically defend a much larger area, and could be used to 'supplement' NMD.[13]

Concerns over Taiwan

Secondly, Beijing is concerned that BMD could be used to undermine Chinese efforts to reunify the mainland with Taiwan.[14] China worries that an effective NMD system could make the US more likely to intervene in the event of a military conflict in the Taiwan Strait. China has always considered the US to be the 'key obstacle to its eventual national unification'.[15] Moreover, the potential for conflict between the US and China over Taiwan – dormant since the 1950s – re-emerged in the 1990s, as illustrated by the 1995–96 Taiwan Strait crisis.[16]

There is similar concern that Japan's TMD programme is linked to potential Japanese involvement in any military conflict in the Taiwan Strait. This concern has been exacerbated since the revision of the US–Japan defence guidelines in 1997.[17] The guidelines outline the forms of support Japan will provide the US military during emergencies involving military attacks against Japan as well as in 'areas surrounding Japan'. Tokyo and Washington have both made conscious efforts to assure Beijing that the revised guidelines are not aimed at China but Beijing has interpreted them as Tokyo's increased commitment to support potential US intervention if a military conflict were to erupt in the Taiwan Strait.

There are two Chinese views on Japanese TMD and Taiwan. One contends that, since the US and Japanese command structures would need to be closely integrated for a TMD system to be effective, this would make Japan vulnerable to Washington's demands in times of military conflict. In the worst case, this could see Japan being dragged into a Taiwan Strait conflict. The other view is that Tokyo's real intention in acquiring TMD is precisely to enable intervention in a crisis in the Strait; Japan wants to protect Taiwan in order to boost Japan's military and political standing in East Asia. The crux of this concern is whether Japan's TMD-equipped *Aegis* ships would ever be deployed to the Taiwan Strait to protect Taipei from Chinese missile attacks. Chinese concerns over Japan's fielding of a lower-tier system such as PAC-3 is close to nil, as the system is immobile and its footprint limited. Some analysts claim not be concerned with Japan's TMD – including an upper-tier system – as long as it is not extended to cover Taiwan.[18]

As far as Taiwanese involvement in TMD is concerned, China would regard the US transfer of a system, particularly an upper-tier system, as a gross violation of Chinese sovereignty and as interference in China's internal affairs. As then premier Zhu Rongji put it: 'We … are firmly and particularly opposed to including Taiwan in the TMD because [it] not only violates international missile agreements but also interferes in China's internal affairs and encroaches on China's sovereignty and territorial integrity'.[19] China is concerned not so much about the strategic implications of the transfer of TMD technology to Taiwan – many analysts acknowledge that an upper-tier system would be ineffective against short-range ballistic missiles – but rather the political impact: it could integrate Taiwan into a US-led joint command system, which would be tantamount to the creation of a de facto military alliance.[20]

BMD as an element of 'Imperial America'

The Chinese believe that NMD will consolidate US hegemony.[21] Beijing tends to view NMD as part of a grand strategy for American domination, exacerbating the US inclination towards unilateralism and further strengthening America's willingness to pursue a pre-emptive strategy.[22]

Not surprisingly, the Chinese had a very negative reaction to the Nuclear Posture Review (NPR), leaked to the press in early 2002, which indicated that US concerns about China's military modernisation and about the possibility of a military confrontation over the status of Taiwan could affect US requirements and how Washington sizes its nuclear force. China sees the US world view being presented in the NPR as a dangerous one and interprets it as a continued demonstration by the Bush administration that it is committed to attaining 'absolute security' via unilateralist measures.[23]

Beijing also fears that a robust TMD system would help the United States to redefine power relations in East Asia. Depending on the architecture of the system, it would require the integration of Japan (and possibly other US allies in Asia such as Australia and South Korea) into the US-led command structure. TMD is thus seen as a 'magnet' drawing the US and its allies ever closer in order to counter those outside such a network.[24] Consequently, China sees US-led TMD initiatives in East Asia as an implicit expression of a policy of containment aimed at preventing China's emergence as the predominant regional power.

BMD and its impact on arms control

Fourth, China argues that BMD undermines international arms-control and disarmament regimes. China has long opposed BMD on the grounds that it violates the ABM Treaty, and has voiced its concerns regarding US proposals to revise or abrogate the Treaty. According to Chinese President Jiang Zemin, 'revision of … the existing disarmament treaties would inevitably exert a negative impact on international security and stability, triggering new arms races and obstructing disarmament and non-proliferation efforts'.[25]

China has also consistently opposed BMD on the basis that it would lead to weaponisation of space. Beijing has thus been campaigning for a UN treaty banning weapons from space, most recently in July 2003, along with Russia. As Chinese Ambassador Hu Xiaodi noted, 'The world is witnessing space weapons-related technology advance by leaps and bounds.

The risk of weaponisation of outer space is mounting'.[26] China has also argued that TMD violates the Missile Technology Control Regime (MTCR)[27] because any US sale of missile-defence technology to Japan would constitute an act of missile proliferation. The MTCR prohibits the transfer of technology for missiles with a range of over 300km, carrying a payload of 500kg.[28] One expert has estimated that an NTW interceptor with a 500kg payload would have a range of over 260km. With a possible upgrade of the propulsion system, such a system could potentially violate the MTCR.

TMD and Japan

Lastly, China is concerned about how BMD could affect Japan. Many Chinese analysts have argued that US–Japan TMD cooperation could provide the technical and political basis for eventual Japanese remilitarisation. Behind such suspicion is the belief that a stronger, more assertive Japan could weaken China's political power in the region. Beijing's distrust of Japan's 'real' intentions and ambitions is a lingering legacy of the Second World War.[29]

After 11 September: sources of change

So why has Chinese rhetoric on BMD been so muted? Broadly speaking, the answer involves four factors: the failure to estab-lish a Russian–Chinese united front against BMD; downbeat technological assessments of the system and a better under-standing of the issues; a greater priority on maintaining stable Sino-American relations; and tactical changes in Chinese policy towards Japan. China seems to have accepted – albeit grudgingly – that BMD deployment is inevitable, and that the US will go ahead with some form of NMD, and Japan with TMD, regardless of what Beijing has to say. This does not mean that fundamental Chinese concerns have ceased to exist. But

China has chosen to focus on domestic problems and adjust its foreign policy behaviour accordingly – for now.

The failure of Russian–Chinese collaboration

During the late 1990s and into early 2000, Beijing was keen to consolidate a Sino-Russian front in opposition to BMD. When the US Department of Defense announced in January 1999 its decision to allocate more funds to BMD research, one of Beijing's first responses was to step up talks with Moscow on a joint approach. In April 1999, China and Russia released a joint communiqué that expressed their anxiety over the issue, and declared that they would continue to consult each other. Russia and China introduced a resolution at the UN First Committee on Disarmament and International Security in October 1999, demanding that US programmes comply with the ABM Treaty.[30] China also succeeded in securing a joint statement with Russia, Tajikistan, Kazakhstan and Kyrgyzstan opposing the deployment of TMD in the Asia-Pacific.[31]

This united front collapsed when the US announced its decision to unilaterally abrogate the ABM Treaty on 14 December 2001. Moscow's reaction was reserved; Russian President Vladimir Putin stated that Russia considered the move a 'mistake', and Defence Minister Sergei Ivanov expressed Russia's willingness to press ahead with plans to cut nuclear arsenals. For some Chinese analysts, Russia's actions came as no surprise. One such analyst, from a government think-tank, noted: 'I doubt whether Russia is at all concerned about TMD, or even NMD for that matter, as calculations would indicate the target of these systems to be China, not Russia'. It is argued that Bush assured Putin that the system was not directed against Moscow, and that the US did not wish to neutralise Russia's nuclear deterrent.[32] The US and Russia have engaged in dialogue on missile-defence cooperation, and there have been attempts to step up a decade-old joint effort to permit the early detection of missile launches.[33] Such extensive assurances have never been offered to China, which fuels the belief in Beijing that BMD is targeted at China.

Technological assessments

It also seems that China has concluded that, from a technological point of view, systems still have a long way to go before they are actually deployed; some doubt that NMD can really be deployed by the end of 2004, as Bush has promised. Chinese experts are now well-informed about the technical aspects of BMD and, while some remain concerned about the system's negative implications in the long term, there is a view that its technical effectiveness has been overstated.[34] The current US plan for 20 interceptor missiles, one Chinese arms-control expert notes, does not call for an urgent Chinese response;[35] another believes that 'China will be able to live with BMD' while the current architecture remains limited.[36] In the long run, analysts are confident that China will be able to counter BMD: 'Assuming that Chinese economic growth continues for some time to come, China can easily produce 600 ICBMs [intercontinental ballistic missiles] by 2020 – a figure no BMD can ever deter'.[37] Based on current rates of increase, China's defence budget could double by 2005.[38] In July 2002, the Pentagon forecast that Chinese annual military spending could increase three- or four-fold in real terms by 2020.[39] There is a view that, in any confrontation between offensive ICBMs and BMD, offence is always going to be much cheaper and less technologically demanding than defence. Given the expense of the BMD project, some in China may even see it as distorting military budgets and so weakening, rather than strengthening, those countries that choose to pursue it.

Maintaining stable US–China relations

Since 11 September, the Bush administration has taken important steps to engage with China, with more regular consultations, including talks in Beijing on strategic security, multilateral arms control and non-proliferation. The administration has also resumed bilateral Defense Consultation Talks (DCT) high-level meetings that formalise a schedule of military-to-military exchanges.[40] Although difficult issues remain, for instance, over trade relations and export control, Beijing has opted to try to stabilise bilateral ties rather than focusing on particular areas of dispute.[41] For China, the key priority is domestic economic development, and so the country's foreign policy has been geared towards fostering the stable relations conducive to further growth.[42] Moreover, as one Chinese security expert has noted, 'after 9/11, China realized that the US was too strong to oppose in all senses – politically, militarily, economically'.[43]

The primacy of stable Sino-American relations can also be attributed to a desire to be an effective mediator in the unfolding crisis on the Korean Peninsula, which touches very directly on China's security interests. The collapse of the Kim Jong Il regime in North Korea could bring US troops based in South Korea right up to the China–Korea border; chaos stemming from massive economic dislocation could see a flood of North Korean refugees into China; and the political–military balance in northeast Asia could shift.[44] There are thus concerns in China that a North Korean collapse would be detrimental to the country's security.[45] As such, it seems that the Chinese have little choice but to take a low-key approach even on political issues where they may be at a disadvantage. Even on the issue of BMD, where Chinese suspicions are strong and alive, Beijing seems unwilling to alter the more cooperative posture it adopted vis-à-vis Washington after 11 September.

China's Japan policy

There has also been a marked shift in China's Japan policy. It appears that the Chinese leadership has learned that being 'tough' on the history question is more likely to provoke anti-China feelings than apologies among the Japanese public. Such was the case when Jiang Zemin's visited Tokyo in the fall of 1998. China toned down its rhetoric when Zhu Rongji visited Japan in 1999. As with its relations with the US, the source of this shift lies in China's willingness – albeit temporarily – to set aside some lingering problems for the sake of maintaining a stable bilateral relationship conducive to China's economic development. As long as China is concentrating on its economy, it seems likely that it will continue to push for broader bilateral cooperation, and avoid conflict.[46] Yang Bojing, an analyst for the Chinese government think-tank CICIR (China Institute for Contemporary International Relations), argues that there is a need for 'new thinking' on Sino-Japanese relations; a genuine improvement in bilateral ties and deeper bilateral cooperation would have 'profound strategic value, not limited to the significance of materialistic practical benefits such as economic and technical cooperation'.[47]

Another source for this shift in policy seems to lie in China's growing confidence more broadly. As Medeiros and Taylor note, there is a growing perception in China that the time has come to exchange the country's longheld 'victim mentality' with a 'great power mentality'.[48] Others have argued that China ought to adopt a more relaxed approach in dealing with some persistent problems in Sino-Japanese relations – including TMD – because 'after all, Japan is bound to decline relative to China in the longrun'.[49] Feng Zhaokui, a professor at the Chinese Academy of Social Sciences, has argued that 'the feeling of the majority of Japanese people toward China could be summed up as fear of a strong, rising China. Chinese economic development coupled with

Japan's economic standstill helped to spread the pathological China Threat among the Japanese'.[50] In particular, analysts note a possible decline in Japan's defence capability should Japanese economic paralysis continue, and contend that China need not make too much out of Japanese security programmes such as TMD.[51] Since 'Japan is bound to decline not only economically but also militarily', argues one analyst, 'is it really prudent for Japan to be diverting its resources into a technologically questionable system like TMD? If Japan really is concerned about its defense, there are so many other ways to strengthen its capability in much more credible ways'.[52]

While Chinese rhetoric on BMD has subsided, some Chinese analysts note that this does not mean that Chinese concerns over the system have disappeared entirely. They argue that, at the fundamental level, there really is no change, and China continues to view BMD as an irreconcilable problem between itself and the US and Japan. In particular, they contend that NMD represents the US desire to deny China its nuclear deterrent (and Japanese willingness to assist such containment efforts by joining the US-led TMD initiative in Asia).[53] Within this, there seems to be an inherent desire for China to be taken seriously by the US as a rising power: 'By 2020, Sino-American strategic parity will be achieved, and that is when the US, for the first time, will truly respect China and step aside on such security questions as the Taiwan unification'.[54]

Possible Chinese responses

There is no clear consensus within the Chinese security policy community on how to respond to missile defence. While some analysts are advocating a 'wait and see' approach, others are pushing for an aggressive action. It seems that the Chinese themselves are unsure about how to address this issue in the light of the country's varying diplomatic, security and domestic political interests. But the range of responses under discussion in the security community include a speed-up of strategic modernisation, back-tracking on arms-control commitments, and revisions to Chinese nuclear doctrine and posture.

Accelerating the strategic modernisation process

There is a clear consensus that, while BMD is not the direct reason for China's strategic military modernisation (the process began in the 1980s, long before BMD became an issue), there is now a correlation between the two. As such, China's future strategic modernisation efforts are likely to continue to reflect concerns over US BMD plans, both quantitatively and qualitatively. Quantitatively, there is a consensus that NMD will shape the ultimate size of the Chinese nuclear arsenal. The rate of increase is still subject to heated debate, however. In 2003, the US Defense Department estimated that China's arsenal of ICBMs capable of striking the US could increase from 20 to around 30 by 2005, and could reach 60 by 2010.[55] It appears that the pace of increase will depend on how the Chinese leadership judges the effectiveness of NMD. Dingli Shen argues that

> China may be forced to make a worst-case assumption – that the system could achieve an unbelievably high interception rate of 90%. In that event, it would be easy to respond by simply increasing the Chinese arsenal by nine times. That would retain the same level of deterrence and cost the equivalent of about a few billion dollars over a span of 10–20 years. It would not be difficult for China's economy to absorb that cost, if it has to do so.[56]

Chinese experts such as Shen argue that this is an issue that needs to be considered over the long term. These analysts make the point that China will be forced to respond aggressively should it conclude that NMD will neutralise its nuclear force. Some even contend that China will be able to deploy up to 600 ICBMs by 2020 should it continue to grow economically and militarily. As Chu Shulong, then a researcher at CICIR, put it in 2000: 'There's no problem for China to increase its arsenal by 100 missiles a year, even with today's budget constraints. These missiles are cheap to produce'.[57] Should that be the case, it is argued, NMD will have no chance of neutralising China's nuclear deterrent. China is also improving its operational capabilities for contingencies in East Asia. Currently, China has an arsenal of approximately 450 short-range ballistic missiles (SRBMs) that can strike Taiwan. The US Defense Department argues that this number will grow substantially over the next few years.[58]

Significant qualitative enhancements are also expected. The Pentagon's report to Congress in July 2002 stated that China

> likely will take measures to improve its ability to defeat the [BMD] system in order to preserve its strategic deterrent ... The measures likely will include improved penetration packages for its ICBMs, an increase in the number of deployed ICBMs, and perhaps development of a multiple-warhead system for an ICBM, most likely for the CSS-4'.[59]

Other possible enhancements, according to a 1999 US National Intelligence Council (NIC) report, include improvements in mobility, solid fuel, command and control and accuracy. Pentagon reports to Congress have consistently warned that China is working to improve its command-and-control capabilities, as well as employing global-positioning technology (GPS) to make significant improvements in missile accuracy. China may also be embarking on anti-satellite (ASAT) systems. The

July 2003 Pentagon report noted that China may already have acquired 'a variety of foreign technologies which could be used to develop an active Chinese ASAT capability'.[60] Some argue that China's development of manned spacecraft may also have significant military implications, including the possible deployment of manoeuvrable re-entry vehicles (MARVs). China has reportedly begun researching advanced military capabilities as part of an 'exo-atmospheric deterrent force' after its successful manned space launch on 14 October 2003. Chinese officials noted that Beijing is now working on both lasers and missiles capable of destroying satellites.[61]

It appears that certain responses to BMD, such as increasing the number of ICBMs, are technologically and financially manageable for Beijing. Others would require significant investment.[62] 'MARVing' is one example, and it is questionable whether China can aggressively develop this capability. Some Chinese analysts argue that, although MARV is a doubtful and costly technology, the defence industry is pushing the idea in order to procure more defence funding, just as the Chinese military establishment is using BMD as a pretext to secure greater budget allocations.[63]

China also seems to be working on various countermeasures to defeat TMD by improving its intermediate-range ballistic missile (IRBM) force. The *Washington Times* reported in July 2002 that China had test-fired a medium-range missile (the CSS-5 or *Dong Feng*-21) containing dummy warheads designed to defeat BMD. China has been upgrading its aging CSS-2 intermediate-range missile force since the late 1990s with the more advanced CSS-5, which is capable of carrying a nuclear warhead. As noted by a 1997 report by the US Air Force National Air Intelligence Center, the CSS-5 is being deployed near China's borders to provide target coverage of Russia, India and Japan.[64]

Backtracking on arms-control commitments

Some argue that China will reverse its arms control and non-proliferation commitments as a response to BMD: for example, delaying the ratification of the Comprehensive Test Ban Treaty (CTBT).[65] As one Chinese analyst has commented, 'Should China view its security environment to be hostile and perceive its national security interests at stake, it will certainly consider reversing its arms control commitment such as CTBT to preserve its security interests'.[66] Indeed, as noted in a 2003 report from the Henry L. Stimson Center, the Chinese leadership seems to be under considerable pressure to resume nuclear testing in part due to the perception that NMD poses a threat to its deterrent capability. China also has a history of attempting to link missile defence to multilateral arms control negotiations, as in its linkage of BMD to the UN discussion on fissile material control treaty (FMCT). The discussion has remained effectively paralysed, as China has refused to pursue further FMCT negotiations unless a 1981 UN General Assembly resolution called PAROS (Prevention of an Arms Race in Outer Space) would be discussed simultaneously.[67] Others, however, argue that Chinese policymakers are now too reluctant to cause a US–China schism over BMD.

Beijing's increased emphasis on its international image as a 'responsible great power' has also led China to de-link BMD from China's obligations in arms control and non-proliferation. They cite China's increased efforts to improve its export-control regimes (such as the promulgation of export-control regulations) as evidence for this.[68] China also remains wary regarding the Moscow Treaty of May 2002, in which the US and Russia have agreed to reduce their nuclear stockpiles to between 1,700 and 2,200 warheads. The Bush administration has reportedly told the Russians they could MIRV (multiple independent re-entry vehicle) their missiles should they feel uncomfortable with US BMD plans, and, accordingly, the Russians have effectively revoked START-II (Strategic Arms Limitation Treaty) in June 2002 to allow them to place multiple warheads on their strategic missiles.[69] The treaty has no reference to verification or inspection, and the US avoided any real cuts in its arsenal by including only operationally deployed' warheads in the reductions.[70] As a result, China does not see the Moscow Treaty as a roadmap to real reduction of nuclear stockpiles but merely as a rearrangement in which it would give both Washington and Moscow a free hand in maintaining their nuclear superiority, which, in turn, would increase Beijing's strategic inferiority.

Reconsidering China's nuclear doctrine and posture

At the moment, China's nuclear doctrine of minimum deterrence is comprised of a declaratory policy of 'no first use' and projected uncertainty regarding the actual size and composition of its nuclear forces. The question is whether NMD, which has the potential of neutralising China's nuclear deterrence, would prompt Beijing to alter its nuclear doctrine. Chinese nuclear experts have argued since the 1980s that minimum deterrence will not provide adequate security for China. Such concern is likely to be amplified with the deployment of NMD, provoking further internal pressure within Beijing for nuclear doctrinal change. Options for doctrinal change includes a shift towards limited nuclear deterrence (LND), in which China would be able to – at least theoretically – respond to all levels of attack.[71]

Should China decide to reformulate its nuclear doctrine, it would require Beijing to make substantial quantitative and qualitative changes to its military force. Such a move would provoke external suspicions that China was adopting an aggressive, offensive military strategy to challenge the status quo in Asia, making China's claim that its nuclear forces are 'defensive' in nature difficult to maintain. These technological, financial, and political costs might be considered too high.[72] Thus, Beijing may opt instead for more temporary measures – simple quantitative and modest qualitative force improvements – but also keep other options open.[73]

There is also a possibility that China would attempt to alter its nuclear posture in response to NMD by strengthening its theatre deterrent. This is an unsettling possibility for Tokyo.[74] China has already effectively targeted Japan and the US forces based there with theatre forces consisting of solid-fuel intermediate-range ballistic missiles (IRBMs).

The 2003 Pentagon report has argued that 'there are indications that some [Chinese] strategists are reconsidering the conditions under which Beijing would employ theater nuclear weapons against US forces in the [East Asian] region'.[75] Although this issue is not widely discussed by Chinese analysts, some argue that such a shift in the strategic theatre balance as a result of NMD deployment is possible.[76] Others, however, argue that openly targeting Japan would be a major strategic decision for China, as Beijing has every reason not to overly antagonise Tokyo – China is more interested in driving a wedge between the US and Japan than in pushing Japan closer to America.[77]

The Korea factor

In October 2002, North Korea admitted that it had resumed its nuclear-weapons development based on its covert uranium-enrichment programme. The following month, Pyongyang unilaterally left the NPT and the International Atomic Energy Agency (IAEA) nuclear-inspection arrangements. Since then, North Korea has threatened to increase its weapons proliferation and to abrogate its ballistic-missile testing moratorium should Washington refuse to meet Pyongyang's demands, which include a non-aggression pact from the US.[78]

China has taken an active part in attempts to defuse the crisis. It has formed the Leading Group on the North Korean Crisis, headed by President Hu Jintao,[79] and is said to be in frequent contact with North Korea 'at all levels'.[80] At one point, Chinese Vice-Foreign Minister Wang Yi told North Korean Foreign Minister Paek Nam Sun in Beijing to 'stop playing with fire'.[81] Chinese envoys also reportedly warned Pyongyang that any attack on the US, on US forces or on US allies in the region would be likely to prompt an overwhelming US response, and that Beijing would not come to Pyongyang's assistance.[82] The oil pipeline between China and North Korea reportedly experienced 'technical difficulties' and was shut down for three days in February 2003, in a move which analysts say sent a powerful signal to Pyongyang, and helped to persuade North Korea to join trilateral talks in Beijing in April 2003.[83]

Although the Bush administration's 'Sino-centric' diplomacy to resolve the nuclear crisis is not necessarily welcome in Beijing,[84] the April 2003 talks should be seen as a major shift in China's traditionally passive and reactive foreign policy. This shift coincided with the formation of a new government led by Hu Jintao, as well as the growing Chinese realisation that Beijing could lose its regional influence unless it makes a greater effort to resolve the crisis.[85] There is also speculation that China may increase its political leverage with the US and Japan if it played a larger role in defusing the North Korean crisis. Persuading Pyongyang not only to give up its nuclear ambitions but also to relinquish its ballistic-missile programmes would boost China's political standing in East Asia. In particular, a reduction in the North Korean missile threat would enable China to make the case that the US and – especially – Japan would no longer need TMD.[86]

The North Korea problem poses a significant challenge for China because, depending on how the situation unfolds, it could lead to situations unfavourable to Chinese security interests. China itself may be able to live with a nuclear North Korea, but it is unclear how such a situation would affect Japanese security policy, and the country's BMD policy. Whether pretext or justified cause, the fact remains that the direct impetus for Japan's move towards TMD is North Korea's missile threat. If the situation remains as it is, China will be unable to object to Japan's TMD. Some Chinese analysts recognise this, and argue that China will be unable to present a credible anti-TMD case unless the North Korea question is resolved so as to address Japan's missile concerns, as well the nuclear issue.[87]

BMD without tears?

China's response to BMD has been muted. This does not mean that the issue is settled, or that Chinese concerns have faded away. Depending on what the system looks like, BMD will have the potential to neutralise China's nuclear deterrent. Although there are various ways for China to react, an all-out aggressive response could have negative ramifications for Beijing, given its current emphasis on the domestic economy. An overtly aggressive policy response would also call Chinese intentions into question, as China would be perceived as attempting to change the status quo in Asia, which could destabilise regional security. Some Chinese analysts express the hope that the Chinese government will refrain from 'overreacting' as the US government continues with its BMD deployment.[88]

The Chinese have certainly thought long and hard about BMD. Is it fundamentally destabilising for East Asia, or is it nothing more than a modern Maginot Line – an expensive, grandiose project that can never achieve its objectives? While some warn that NMD is fundamentally a US attempt to attain 'absolute security' for itself, others note that 11 September has shown that, even for a superpower like the US, it is impossible to protect against threats at all levels. The Chinese have studied these debates carefully over the years, and are likely to continue their discussions on BMD and its ramifications for East Asian security. At this point, they seem to have acquiesced in the US suggestion that BMD deployment need not be destabilising – at least for now, given that most of the systems currently under development will not be ready for deployment for at least several years, and that even if they are fielded, their limited capability should not pose a direct threat to China's nuclear deterrent.[89]

Because the deployment of expanded BMD systems – assuming it occurs as advocated by the Bush administration – is still some years away, the US, Japan, and China still have time to shape events to avoid the worst-case scenario. Increasing numbers of Chinese analysts have expressed their hopes for improved US–Japan–China relations. One Chinese analyst argues that 'The US, Japan, and China ought to create an informal trilateral coalition to address such imminent security concerns as North Korea, and gradually develop it into a new channel of trilateral communication to discuss other security issues such as BMD and its implications for East Asian security'.[90] Comments like this seem to indicate that there is room for constructive discussion on East Asian security between the US, Japan and China. Before setting in motion a chain of events propelled by worst-case thinking, all parties should carefully examine their intentions, capabilities and policy options, and engage in further dialogue and exchange so as to do away with some unnecessary speculations and suspicions. The United States and Japan, as they implement long-term plans for missile defence, should be aware that the latent Chinese opposition will be an enduring factor.

Acknowledgements

The author is indebted to Yoichi Funabashi for all the guidance he provided her throughout the course of her research on the topic. She is also grateful to Peter Van Ness, Thomas Berger, Shen Dingli, Peter Almquist, Reinhard Drifte, Zhu Mingquan, Sijin Cheng, Kim Beng Phar, Lisa Sansoucy and Shinju Fujihira for their comments on the initial draft, as well as to James Malvenon, David Finkelstein, Evan Medeiros, Robert Sutter, Zhu Feng, Iain Johnston, James Przystup, Banning Garrett, Richard Nelson, Wayne Fujito, Yoshihisa Komori, John Newhouse, Kate Walsh, Kazuyasu Akashi, Joseph Fewsmith, William Grimes and countless other Chinese, American and Japanese specialists for their input and feedback on the project as a whole.

NOTES

1   The Bush administration has reorganised ballistic-missile defence (BMD) by merging national missile defence (NMD) and theatre missile defence (TMD) into one conceptual framework. Given that both US and Japanese involvement in BMD will be addressed in this paper, for clarity's sake US homeland defence will be referred to as NMD, and Japanese BMD as TMD (the Japanese government officially refers to its missile defence programme as BMD).

2   'Japan's Push for Missile Defence: Benefits, Costs, Prospects', *Strategic Comments*, vol. 9, no. 8, October 2003; Gary Schaefer, 'Japan To Spend Billions on US-Designed Missile Shield in Defense Rethink', *Associated Press*, 19 December 2003.

3   'Russia Ready To Negotiate Nuclear Arms Cuts, Despite US Withdrawal from ABM Treaty', *ibid.*, 18 December 2001.

4   'Unwise Move', *Renmin Jibao*, 18 December 2001.

5   'Foreign Ministry spokesman on US missile defence plans', Xinhua News Agency, 19 December 2002.

6   'China Concerned about Japan's Missile Defense, Poison Gas', *Japan Economic Newswire*, 3 September 2003.

7   'US–Japan Missile Defense Cooperation Worries China', *Xinhua News Agency*, 19 December 2002.

8   Brad Roberts, 'China and Ballistic Missile Defense: 1955 to 2002

to Beyond', report published September 2003 by the Institute for Defense Analyses, Alexandria, VA.

9   Interview with a Japanese BMD expert. Other experts, including government officials affiliated with the Foreign Ministry and Japan Defense Agency, have expressed similar views. Author interviews in Tokyo, 2000–2001.

10 'China Condemns US Missile Plans', *Associated Press*, 25 November 1999.

11 For Chinese views on missile defence, see: Jing-Dong Yuan, 'Chinese Responses to US Missile Defenses: Implications for Arms Control and Regional Security', *The Nonproliferation Review*, vol. 10, no. 1, Spring 2003; Dingli Shen, 'What Missile Defense Says to China', *Bulletin of the Atomic Scientists*, vol. 56, no. 4, July–August 2000; Yan Xuetong, 'Theater Missile Defense and Northeast Asian Security', *Nonproliferation Review*, vol. 6, no. 3, Spring/Summer 1999; Thomas Christensen, 'China, the US– Japan Alliance, and the Security Dilemma in East Asia', *International Security*, vol. 23, no. 4, Spring 1999; Kori Urayama, 'Chinese Perspectives on Theater Missile Defense (TMD): Policy Implications for Japan', *Asian Survey*, vol. 40, no. 4, July– August 2000.

12 Joanne Tompkins, 'Influences on Chinese Nuclear Planning', a report for the Stimson Fellowship in China, Summer 2002, p. 21.

13 Li Bin, 'The Impact of US NMD on Chinese Nuclear Modernization', paper prepared for the Pugwash Conference, April 2001.

14 Yan Xuetong, 'Theater Missile

Defense and Northeast Asian Security', p. 70. Also see Shen, 'What Missile Defense Says to China'.

15 Shen, 'What Missile Defense Says to China'.

16 Michael McDevitt, 'Missile Defense: Beijing's Bind', *Washington Quarterly*, vol. 23, no. 3, summer 2000, p. 179.

17 Yan, 'Theater Missile Defense and Northeast Asian Security', p. 71.

18 Interviews in China, 1999–2001.

19 'Chinese Premier's Press Conference, Full Text', *BBC Worldwide Monitoring*, 16 March 1999.

20 Interviews in Beijing and Shanghai, 1999–2001.

21 This is not a uniquely Chinese view. A number of Japanese government officials have expressed concerns that BMD (especially NMD) implies the consolidation of US hegemony and unilateralism, and that this could pose diplomatic and security dangers, globally as well as regionally. These comments were made before the US debate on the invasion of Iraq. Author's private communications with Japanese diplomats, 2000–2002.

22 For Chinese views on U.S. pursuit of 'unilateralist absolute security', see Xu Weidi, 'Unilateral Security? U.S. Arms Control Policy and Asian-Pacific Security', *The Nonproliferation Review*, vol. 9, no. 2, summer 2002; Tian Jingmei, 'The Bush Administration's Nuclear Strategy and Its Implications for China's Security', CISAC Working Paper, March 2003; and Yong Deng, 'Hegemon on the Offensive: Chinese Perspectives

on U.S. Global Strategy', *Political Science Quarterly*, vol. 116, no. 3, fall 2001.

23 Joanne Tompkins, 'Influences on Chinese Nuclear Planning', a Report on the Stimson Center Fellowship in China, Summer 2002, p. 15, http://www.stimson.org/inchina/pdf/InfCNPTompkins.pdf

24 You Ji, 'The Dark Cold War Clouds Over the Asia-Pacific Region', paper prepared for the IISS annual conference, 'The Powers in Asia, Manila, 14–17 September 2000.

25 Jiang Zemin, 'The Way To Get On With Nuclear Disarmament', *International Herald Tribune*, 16 June 1999.

26 'Russia, China say arms threat to outer space is growing', Associated Press, 31 July 2003.

27 China is not a formal member of the MTCR, though it has made a pledge (in the US–China bilateral context) to abide by it.

28 Li Bin, 'Ballistic Missile Defense (BMD) and the Missile Technology Control Regime', paper prepared for 'East Asian Regional Security Futures: Theater Missile Defence Implications', conference organised by the Nautilus Institute, Tokyo, 24–25 June 2000, http://www.nautilus.org/nukepolicy/tmd-conference/libinpaper.html

29 Interviews in Beijing and Shanghai, 1999–2001.

30 'Sino-Russian Anti-Ballistic Missile Treaty Communiqué Issued', *Xinhua News Agency*, 16 April 1999.

31 'Shanghai Five Nations Stress Unconditional Respect for ABM Treaty', *ibid.*, 6 July 2000.

32 Ted Carpenter, 'Bush Tries To Drive a Wedge Between Russia and China', *Cato Daily Commentary*, 3 August 2001.

33 'US–Russia Defense Cooperation Seen', *CDI Russia Weekly*, no. 211, 20 June 2002. Russia does not have much to spend on the project, and thus plans for US–Russian missile-defence cooperation remain tentative.

34 Shen, 'What Missile Defense Says to China'.

35 Interview with Chinese arms-control expert, November 2003. A similar view was expressed by a Chinese security expert in February 2004.

36 Author interview with Chinese arms-control expert, February 2003.

37 Interview with a Chinese security expert, November 2003.

38 Yuan, 'Chinese Responses to US Missile Defenses', p. 76.

39 *The Military Power of the People's Republic of China*, DoD report to Congress, 12 July 2002. This states that, in March 2002, 'China announced a 17.6% or $3 billion increase in spending, bringing the publicly reported total to $20 billion', but that the 'total spending is closer to $65 billion'.

40 Yuan, 'Chinese Responses to US Missile Defenses', p. 87.

41 Interviews with China experts, Washington DC, Summer 2003.

42 Yoichi Funabashi, 'China's Long-Term Strategy: Peaceful Ascendancy', *Asahi Shimbun*, 2 December 2003; Tadashi Itoh, 'Sekai no shijou wo buki ni shita chuugoku gaikou no hikari to kage', *Foresight*, September 2003, p. 20.

43 Author's private communication with a Chinese security expert, November 2003.

44 According to Narushige Michishita, an analyst for NIDS, a Japanese government think-tank, some Chinese analysts have begun to argue that it would be 'acceptable' for China even if US forces were deployed up to the northern part of a unified Korea, provided that the US continues to play a 'constructive' role in the region. Author's private communication, January 2004.

45 Bonnie Glaser, 'Beijing Ponders How Hard To Press North Korea,' *PacNet Newsletter*, 23 December 2002.

46 Robert Sutter, 'China and Japan: Trouble Ahead?', *Washington Quarterly*, vol. 25, no. 4, Autumn 2002, p. 47.

47 Yang Bojiang, 'Sino-Japanese Relations Entering a New Stage', *Kokusai Mondai*, January 2003.

48 Evan S. Medeiros and M. Taylor, 'China's New Diplomacy', *Foreign Affairs*, vol. 82, no. 6, November–December 2003.

49 Interview with a Chinese security expert, November 2003.

50 Feng Zhaokui, 'Factors Shaping Sino- Japanese Relations', *Contemporary International Relations*, September 2001.

51 Interview with Chinese security experts, February and November 2003.

52 *Ibid.*

53 *Ibid.*

54 Interview with a Chinese security expert, November 2003.

55 Department of Defense, *Annual Report on the Military Power of the People's Republic of China*, July 2003, p. 31.

56 Shen, 'What Missile Defense Says to China'.

57 Quoted in Jim Mann, 'China Snarls Against a "Paper Tiger"', *Los Angeles Times*, 19 January 2000.

58 Department of Defense, *Annual Report on the Military Power of the People's Republic of China*, July 2003, p. 48.

59 Department of Defense, *Annual Report on the Military Power of the People's Republic of China*, July 2002.

60 Department of Defense, *Annual Report on the Military Power of the People's Republic of China*, July 2003, p. 36.

61 *Deutsche Press-Agentur*, 20 October 2003.

62 Roberts, 'China and Ballistic Missile Defense'. A similar point has been made by a number of Chinese arms-control experts.

63 Interviews in Beijing, 2000.

64 Bill Gertz, 'China Tests Arms Designed To Fool Defense Systems', *Washington Times*, 23 July 2002.

65 Malik Mohan, 'China and the Nuclear Nonproliferation Regime', *Contemporary Southeast Asia*, 1 December 2000.

66 Interview with Chinese security expert, November 2003.

67 'China proposes a treaty to prevent arms race in space for TMD containment at Geneva CD' (Japanese), *Yomiuri Shimbun*, 18 Feburary 2000.

68 Yuan, 'Chinese Responses to US Missile Defenses', p. 87

69 Kenneth Timmerman, 'Rumsfeld Demands China Reciprocity', *Insight*, 15 July 2002.

70 Christopher Paine, 'Moscow

Treaty: Making Matters Worse', *Bulletin of the Atomic Scientists,* November/December 2002.

71 Paul Godwin, 'Potential Chinese Responses to US Ballistic Missile Defense', in Romberg and McDevitt (eds), *China and Missile Defense,* pp. 61–71.

72 *Ibid.,* p. 68.

73 Romberg and McDevitt (eds), *China and Missile Defense,* p. 26.

74 Interviews in Tokyo, 2000–2001.

75 Department of Defense, *Annual Report on the Military Power of the People's Republic of China,* July 2003, p. 31.

76 Interviews in Beijing, 1999–2001.

77 Thanks to Iain Johnston for raising this point.

78 See Jonathan Pollack, 'The United States, North Korea, and the End of the Agreed Framework', *Naval War College Review,* Summer 2003.

79 Willy Wo-Lap Lam, 'China Looks Ahead to Korea Crisis', *CNN World News,* 18 March 2003.

80 'Wary China Ups Diplomatic Pressure', *Reuters,* 7 July 2003. See also *Meeting the North Korean Nuclear Challenge,* Report of an Independent Task Force sponsored by the Council on Foreign Relations, May 2003.

81 John Pomfret, 'China Urges North Korea Dialogue', *Washington Post,* 4 April 2003.

82 Lam, 'China Looks Ahead'.

83 'Wary China Ups Diplomatic Pressure'.

84 *Meeting the North Korean Nuclear Challenge,* p. 9.

85 Karen D. Young and Doug Struck, 'Beijing's Help Led to Talks', *Washington Post,* 17 April 2003.

86 Interviews in Washington DC, Summer 2003.

87 Interviews in Washington DC, Summer 2003.

88 Author's private communication with a Chinese security expert, January 2004.

89 W. Slocombe, M. Carns, J. Gansler, R. Nelson (eds.), *Missile Defense in Asia,* (Washington DC: The Atlantic Council, June 2003), p. vii.

90 Interview with a Chinese arms-control expert, November 2003.

CHAPTER TWENTY-THREE

Great-power relations in Asia: a Japanese perspective

Yukio Okamoto

Survival 51-6, 2009–10

Japan, the United States and China will need to cooperate to secure the peace, stability and prosperity of the Asia-Pacific and indeed the wider world. The three countries must work together to address such problems as climate change, threats to energy security, pandemic diseases, poverty and other urgent problems. With the inclusion of other countries from Europe and Asia in this framework, positive results can be expected.

The alignment of each country's national interests is complicated, however, by differing views about human rights and other basic values, differences that, particularly in the case of China, can be fundamental. One such difference can be found in the field of national security. Japan and the United States wish to maintain the political status quo in Asia; China aims to challenge that status quo. In such cases there is a risk that the defenders of the status quo and its challengers will become trapped in a dangerous and counterproductive competition.

Sea change

Of particular concern to Japan is China's expansionary strategy and its efforts to develop a powerful blue-water navy. Beijing has claimed the greater part of the South China Sea as its territorial waters. It has sought the means of controlling the waters east of what China calls the 'First Island Chain' linking Kyushu, one of the main islands of Japan; the islands of Okinawa; Taiwan; and the Philippines. Recently, five Chinese ships harassed a US Navy surveillance vessel in international waters, while in late 2007 a new city was established to exercise administrative control over a district encompassing the Paracels, the Spratlys and the Macclesfield Bank. It is as though the East China Sea, the Taiwan Straits and the South China Sea have become China's internal waters.

China will soon possess aircraft carriers. It already possesses a formidable 62-vessel submarine fleet. Its strategic nuclear submarines are stacked with nuclear missiles. The country has demonstrated the ability to destroy satellites, and to sneak up on a US carrier strike group. All this suggests that China is equipping itself with the capabilities to go westward beyond the First Island Chain and project power into the western Pacific. China also has a determined policy of denying the US Navy access, during times of contingency, to the Pacific west of the Second Island Chain, stretching from Yokosuka to the Ogasawara/Bonin Islands to Guam and the Marianas. Indeed, many analysts agree that by the year 2030 China will possess such a capability.[1] China's strategy is to prevent US forces from coming to the aid of Taiwan within the waters between the First and Second Island Chains. This would mean that the US and Japanese fleets could no longer operate freely in the West Pacific.

The problem of history

Another destabilising problem is the fact that Japan has still not achieved reconciliation with China over historical grievances.

Indeed, the gap between the feelings of the citizens of both countries has widened, not shrunk, in the 60 years since the end of the Second World War. Since 1945, there has been a strong sense of remorse in Japan for having started the Pacific War, which resulted in the total devastation of the Japanese homeland and parts of East Asia. But the Japanese people tend to forget that the original war – the Sino-Japanese War – started in 1931 in Manchuria, ten years before the attack on Pearl Harbor. Japan was the aggressor in the Pacific War, but the country's sense of guilt over this conflict is considerably offset by the terrible price Japan had to pay, with 3 million Japanese victims, including those lost in Hiroshima and Nagasaki. In the case of the Sino-Japanese War, however, there is no way of finding psychological equivalence. Japan was the unequivocal aggressor; China was the unequivocal victim. This is something many Japanese forget. Japan must make great efforts to teach its children about their country's undeniable history of invading China. On the other hand, China must stop using the actions of the Imperial Army of Japan as the foundation for a patriotic education that nurtures antipathy, if not outright hatred, toward Japan among Chinese young people.

Given the gap separating Chinese and Japanese feelings about the war, it will probably be a long time before Japan and China achieve final reconciliation. It may be necessary to establish a framework for reconciliation in East Asia similar to the one established in Europe to achieve reconciliation with Germany. This framework eventually expanded to become the European Union, in which nations that were once enemies – particularly France and Germany – are now able to work together cooperatively. Students in France and Germany today learn history from shared textbooks. I am unsure whether Japan and China could go quite so far on their own. For scholars to craft a joint textbook, there has to be complete freedom of expression and thought among those taking part in the exercise. When one side is not allowed to deviate from the official party line, such an undertaking is unlikely to succeed.

The problem of nuclear proliferation

The actions of North Korea have added a further complicating factor to relations among the Asia-Pacific powers. Pyongyang tested a ballistic missile on 5 April 2009 and a nuclear device on 25 May. It would seem these tests were not attempts to strengthen the North's bargaining position in negotiations or to draw the attention of the United States, but rather were part of a determined plan to eventually acquire nuclear inter-continental ballistic missiles (ICBMs) capable of reaching the western shores of the United States.

The North Koreans are probably not seeking nuclear ICBMs in order to actually launch them against someone. Instead, they seem primarily interested in demonstrating a power-projection capability. Once North Korea has such missiles in hand, it will no longer have to beg the United States for security guarantees. North Korean leaders must also believe that the possession of such weapons will give them an advantage in future nego-tiations over the unification of the Korean Peninsula. In the interim, the country will be able to sell its nuclear and missile technologies for much-needed hard currency.

There is a tendency, particularly among Americans, to understate the significance of North Korea's actions because its missile and nuclear capabilities are still at a primi-tive stage of development. But these tests are a sign that the global nuclear non-proliferation system is failing. It is clear that merely extending the Nuclear Non-proliferation Treaty (NPT) will not be enough to keep the world safe from nuclear weapons. India, Pakistan and Israel all obtained nuclear weapons outside the framework of the treaty. North

Korea, once an NPT member, is now a primitive nuclear-weapons state. Iran will likely follow suit. President Barack Obama has presented an optimistic and uplifting vision of a world without nuclear weapons, but getting to that point over the long term will be no simple task. The difficult issues of process and procedures should not be underemphasised. Japan welcomes Obama's initiative; however, the country cannot allow itself to be carried away by euphoria based upon a manifesto.

If the further nuclear armament of North Korea is to be restrained even a little, it will be due to pressure from China, rather than the United States. North Korea is dependent on China for food and energy. China, however, is not likely to pressure Pyongyang for fear of triggering the regime's collapse, which could result in the creation of a unified, pro-America Korea facing China across the Yalu River. The United States should recognise that it needs to negotiate with China more than with North Korea. Before China can agree to work with the United States, however, Beijing will need a guarantee that, in the event of Korea's reunification, China's worries will not come true.

Both China and the United States need to take on the task of reducing nuclear weapons in East Asia in a serious way. The international community, including Japan, have registered their protests at the illegality of North Korea's acquisition of nuclear weapons. For Japan, however, once North Korea's possession of nuclear weapons becomes a fait accompli, the threat will not lie in whether the acquisition process was legal but rather in the capabilities and policy intentions of the countries that possess nuclear weapons.

Of these, the intentions of China are of no less interest than those of North Korea. China has deployed over 170 missiles fitted with nuclear warheads. In 1998 the Chinese government announced that China would de-target its missiles pointed at the United States. The question being asked in Tokyo is where those missiles are being aimed now, besides Taiwan.

* * *

Japan chose to enter an alliance with the United States as a means of maintaining its security after the Second World War. This was the country's only real option, as a constitutional ban on the possession of offensive weapons precluded the option of 'armed neutrality'. This alliance has served Japan well, enabling it to enjoy peace and stability for more than half a century. At the time the alliance was concluded, however, the current dynamism and growing importance of China was not foreseen. While Japan has to steadfastly maintain its alliance with the United States, the new geopolitical situation in East Asia and the need for a cooperative relationship with China must be included in the equation.

In China in 1990, only 1% of the population had incomes of over $6,000 a year. Today the proportion is 35%. By 2020, that proportion will double again.[2] As China grows in affluence and its relations with other countries mature, tripartite cooperation among Beijing, Washington and Tokyo offers the best way to secure the future stability and prosperity of the Asia-Pacific region. The advent of the government of Yukio Hatoyama has raised hopes of improvement in Japan–Asia relations. With Asia projected to produce half of the world's GDP in the year 2030,[3] Asian countries need to be responsible in managing their relations and must strive to develop a cohesive relationship. Improvement in the Japan–Asia relationship, however, should not come at the cost of the close Japan–US relationship. The two are perfectly compatible.

NOTES

1   US Department of Defense, *Military Power of the People's Republic of China 2009* (Washington DC: Government Printing Office, 2009), p. 18.

2   Dominic Wilson and Raluca Dragusanu, 'The Expanding Middle: The Exploding World Middle Class and Falling Global Inequality', Goldman Sachs Economics Papers No. 170, 7 July 2008, p. 10, http://www2.goldmansachs.com/ideas/global-economic-outlook/expandingmiddle.pdf.

3   Angus Maddison, 'Shares of the Rich and the Rest of the World in the World Economy: Income Divergence Between Nations, 1820–2030', *Asian Economic Policy Review*, 2008, p. 8, http://www2.warwick.ac.uk/fac/soc/economics/news/forums/conferences/econchange/programme/maddison.pdf.

CHAPTER TWENTY-FOUR

The 13th IISS Asia Security Summit – the Shangri-La Dialogue: keynote address

Shinzo Abe, Prime Minister of Japan

Friday 30 May 2014

As delivered

Your Excellency, Mr Lee Hsien Loong, Director-General Dr John Chipman, ladies and gentlemen, 'Peace and prosperity in Asia, for evermore'.

In order to make that a reality, what should Japan do and how should Japan contribute? That's what I am standing here to speak about. I think all of us in the room here share a common mission. The mission is one of pursuing better living standards and economic prosperity. It's a mission of bringing into full bloom the latent potential of this great growth centre and the people living there, stretching from Asia and the Pacific to the Indian Ocean. We must build and then hand over to the next generation a stage on which each and every individual can prosper still more and certainly benefit from the fruits of growth.

'Asia' is a synonym for 'growth' and another name for 'achievement'. Take TPP. The Trans-Pacific Partnership will surely bring an overwhelming economy of scale to the Asia-Pacific economies. Just as a rocket picks up even greater acceleration in its second and third stages, the RCEP [Regional Comprehensive Economic Partnership] and the FTAAP [Free

Trade Area of the Asia Pacific] as it were, the momentum sparked by the TPP will expand our free and creative economic sphere, enabling us to soar even higher. Asia and the Pacific will continue to propel the world economy forward.

And just for Japan to seek a win-win synergy with the growing Asia–Pacific region, my economic policy is now advancing at full throttle. If you imagine how vast the Pacific and Indian oceans are, our potential is exactly like the oceans, i.e., limitless, isn't it? In order to have the generations of our children and our children's children share in this bounty, it's absolutely imperative that we make peace and stability something absolutely rock solid.

To achieve this, all countries must observe international law. Japan will offer its utmost support for the efforts of the countries of ASEAN as they work to ensure the security of the seas and the skies, and thoroughly maintain freedom of navigation and freedom of overflight. Japan intends to play an even greater and more proactive role than it has until now in making peace in Asia and the world something more certain. As for Japan's new banner of 'Proactive Contribution to Peace', Japan already enjoys the explicit and enthusiastic support of the leaders of our allies and other friendly nations, including every leader of ASEAN member countries as well as the leaders of the United States, Australia, India, the UK, France and others. So let me just repeat: Japan for the rule of law, Asia for the rule of law, and the rule of law for all of us. Peace and prosperity in Asia, for evermore. That's what I wish to state to you today.

May I now tell you firstly how I perceive the situation? This region has achieved tremendous growth in the span of a single generation. However, a large and relatively disproportionate amount of the fruits of that growth is being allocated to military expansion and arms trading. To me, this is extremely regrettable. We also find ourselves facing the threat of weapons of mass destruction and attempts to change the status quo through force or coercion. Clearly there exist elements that spawn instability.

And yet nowhere do we find a need to be pessimistic. That's my approach. Recently, President Barack Obama of the United States and I mutually reaffirmed that the US–Japan alliance is the cornerstone for regional peace and security. President Obama and I also mutually confirmed that the United States and Japan are strengthening trilateral cooperation with like-minded partners to promote peace and economic prosperity in Asia and the Pacific and around the globe. When Australian Prime Minister Tony Abbott visited Japan at the beginning of April, we reaffirmed this exact stance, namely that in security affairs, we will further the trilateral cooperation among Japan, the US, and Australia. We clearly articulated to people both at home and abroad our intention to elevate the strategic partnership between Japan and Australia to a new special relationship. In India, Mr Narendra Modi has become prime minister through another free and fair election. I am absolutely certain that when I welcome Prime Minister Modi to Tokyo, we will successfully confirm that Japan–India cooperation, as well as trilateral cooperation including our two countries, will make the 'confluence of the two seas', that is the Pacific and Indian oceans, peaceful and more prosperous.

Last year, I visited all ten ASEAN member countries, and my determination grew increasingly firm with each country I visited. This is because these visits taught me that we share common groundwork regarding our commitment to valuing the rule of law, and that we enjoy a consensus in our respect for freedom of navigation and freedom of overflight. Indeed, in most of the countries of the region, economic growth has steadily brought freedom of thought and religion and checks and balances to the political systems, even though the speed of these changes varies from country to country. The sheer idea of the rule of law, which is one great pillar for human rights, has taken deeper root. Freedom, democracy, and the rule of law, which undergirds these two, form the Asia–Pacific's rich basso continuo that supports the melody played in a bright and cheery key. I find myself newly gripped by that sound day after day.

I have now shared with you how I perceive the circumstances that surround us. Now, my first central point for today is that we must observe international law. International law prescribes the order governing the seas. Its history is long indeed, stretching back to the days of ancient Greece, we are told. By Roman times, the seas were already kept open to all, with personal possession and partitioning of the sea prohibited. Ever since what is known as the Age of Exploration, large numbers of people have come together by crossing the seas, and marine-based commerce has connected the globe. The principle of freedom on the high seas came to be established, and the seas became the foundation for human prosperity.

As history moved on, the wisdom and practical experiences of a great many people involved with the sea, who were at times literally caught up in rough and raging waves, accumulated into common rules. This is what we now know as the international law of the seas. This law was not created by any particular country or countries, nor was it the product of some sort of group. Instead, it is the product of our own wisdom, cultivated over a great many years for the well-being and the prosperity of all humankind.

Today, the benefits for each of us lie in the seas from the Pacific to the Indian oceans being made thoroughly open, as a place of freedom and peace. All of us should find one common benefit in keeping our oceans and skies as global commons, where the rule of law is respected throughout, to the merit of the world and humankind.

Now, when we say 'the rule of law at sea' – what exactly do we mean in concrete terms? If we take the fundamental spirit that we have infused into international law over the ages and reformulate it into three principles, we find the rule of law at sea is actually a matter of common sense. The first principle is that states shall make and clarify their claims based on international law. The second is that states shall not use force or coercion in trying to drive their claims. The third principle is that states shall seek to settle disputes by peaceful means. So, to reiterate this, it means making claims that are faithful in light of international law, not resorting to force or coercion, and resolving all disputes through peaceful means.

So that is all about common sense, pure and simple. And yet these very natural things must be emphasised. I urge all of us who live in Asia and the Pacific to each individually uphold these three principles exhaustively.

Take a look at Indonesia and the Philippines. They have peacefully reached agreement of late on the delimitation of their overlapping EEZs [exclusive economic zones]. I welcome this as an excellent case in point that truly embodies the rule of law. My government strongly supports the efforts by the Philippines calling for a resolution to the dispute in the South China Sea that is truly consistent with these three principles. We likewise support Vietnam in its efforts to resolve issues through dialogue. Movement to consolidate changes to the status quo by aggregating one fait accompli after another can only be strongly condemned as something that contravenes the spirit of these three principles.

Would you not agree that now is the time to make a firm pledge to return to the spirit and the provisions of the 2002 Declaration on the Conduct of Parties in the South China Sea that all concerned countries in the Sea agreed to, and not to undertake unilateral actions associated with a permanent physical change? The time to devote our wisdom to restoring peaceful seas is now.

What the world eagerly awaits is for our seas and our skies to be places governed by rules, laws, and established dispute-resolution procedures. The least desirable state of affairs is having to fear that coercion and threats will take the place of rules and laws and that unexpected situations will arise at arbitrary times and places. I strongly hope that a truly effective Code of Conduct can be established in the South China Sea between ASEAN and China and that it can be achieved swiftly. Japan and China have an agreement concluded in 2007 between then-premier Wen Jiabao and myself, when I was serving as prime minister. That was a commitment we made to create a maritime and air communication mechanism in order to prevent unexpected situations between Japan and China. Unfortunately, this has not led to the actual operation of such a mechanism. We do not welcome dangerous encounters by fighter aircraft and vessels at sea. What we must exchange are words. Should we not meet at the table, first exchanging smiles as we sit down to have discussion? It is my firm belief that commencing the operation of this agreement between our two countries will lead to peace and stability of the region as a whole.

Be that as it may, in my view, the time has come to place emphasis on the East Asia Summit. The ARF [ASEAN Regional Forum] is a meeting held at the foreign-minister level, while the ADMM-Plus [ASEAN Defence Ministers' Meeting Plus] is a meeting at the defence-minister level. There is no stage that outshines the East Asia Summit as a venue for heads of state and government to come together and discuss the order that is desirable. Keeping military expansion in check and making military budgets transparent, as well as enlarging the number of countries that conclude the Arms Trade Treaty and improving mutual understanding between authorities in charge of national defence – there is no lack of issues those of us national leaders ought to take up, applying peer pressure on each other.

I urge the further enhancement of the East Asia Summit, as the premier forum taking up regional politics and security. Next year marks the tenth anniversary of the launch of the EAS. I propose that we first create a permanent committee comprised of permanent representatives to ASEAN from the member countries and then prepare a road map to bring renewed vitality to the Summit itself, while also making the Summit along with the ARF and the ADMM-Plus function in a multilayered fashion. The first thing we should discuss is the principle of disclosure. We have all heard the saying that 'sunshine is the best disinfectant'. From now, Asia will continue to play the leading role in pulling the prosperity of the world forward. Military expansion is not merely ill-matched, but also inherently unworthy of such a place as this. The fruits of prosperity should instead be reinvested into even greater prosperity and improving people's lives. I believe that a framework under which we publicly disclose our military budgets step by step, that enables us to cross-check each other, is a system that we should seek to establish as we extend the scope of the East Asia Summit.

Japan will offer its utmost support for efforts by ASEAN member countries to ensure the security of the seas and skies and rigorously maintain freedom of navigation and overflight. Then what will Japan actually support, and how? We have decided to provide ten new patrol vessels to the Philippine Coast Guard. We have already provided three brand new patrol vessels to Indonesia through grant-aid cooperation. And we are moving forward with the necessary survey to enable us to provide such vessels to Vietnam as well. No less important, when hard assets are sent out from Japan, experts also follow, together with instruction in the relevant technical skills. By doing so, the bonds between the people on Japan and the recipient's sides invariably become stronger. We also convey to the partners our sense of pride in committing ourselves to our duties. By cultivating a high degree of morale and proficiency and sharing our stringent training, buds of lasting friendship emerge.

Even if we look only at the three countries of the Philippines, Indonesia, and Malaysia, the number of people easily surpasses 250 who have learned from Japan about how coast guard operations should be conducted. In 2012, when we invited to Japan higher-ranking officials within the agencies enforcing maritime law in each of the five major ASEAN countries, all throughout the month-long training period, three members of the Japan Coast Guard were assigned to each person receiving training, with all of them living, eating, and sleeping together under the same roof. I understand that one participant from Malaysia said, 'In Japan, the technical aspects of course, but also the high level of morale of each individual is superb. What I wish to take back home with me is this spirit.' I feel that this trainee really understood what we were actually trying to convey.

Here in Singapore representatives of member nations of ReCAAP [Regional Cooperation Agreement on Combating Piracy and Armed Robbery against Ships in Asia], which was created eight years ago, are on high alert 24 hours a day spotting piracy. Heading the Information Centre at present is a Japanese ReCAAP representative.

Recently, Japan has formulated new principles governing the cases in which defence equipment can be transferred to other countries. We are now able to send out Japan's superb defence equipment, such as for rescue, transportation, vigilance, surveillance, and minesweeping, in cases in which appropriate control can be ensured, on the basis of a strict examination. Japan and the recipient country are first to forge a written agreement, and then to move the whole process forward, bearing in mind that each is strictly examined and aptitude is checked by supervision.

Japan will combine various options within its assistance menu, including ODA, capacity-building by the Self-Defense Forces, and defence-equipment and technology cooperation, to support seamlessly the capacity of ASEAN countries in safeguarding the seas. I have stated all that as a pledge to you.

I will now talk about my final topic for today, and that is about the new banner Japan has chosen to raise. We are in an era in which it is no longer possible for any one nation to secure its own peace only by itself. This is a view shared throughout the world. That is exactly why it is incumbent upon us in Japan to reconstruct the legal basis pertinent to the right of collective self-defence and to international cooperation, including the United Nations peacekeeping operations.

On my watch, discussion is under way in Japan. Japan's Self-Defense Forces are at this very moment working hard to foster peace in South Sudan, only recently independent, under the flag of the United Nations mission there. Units from such countries as Cambodia, Mongolia, Bangladesh, India, Nepal, the Republic of Korea, and China are participating in this same mission. There are also a great many civilian UN staffers as well as members of NGOs from various countries. They are all partners with us in the sense that they are all assisting in South Sudan's nation building. Imagine now that civilians or NGO workers there, powerless to defend themselves, came under sudden attack by armed elements. Under the approach that the Japanese government has taken to date, Japan's Self-Defense Forces are unable to go rescue these civilians enduring the attack. Is this an appropriate response into the future? My government is thinking hard about it, and a close consultation is under way within the ruling coalition parties. It is precisely because Japan is a country that depends a great deal on the peace and stability of the international community that Japan wishes to work even more proactively for world peace, and wishes to raise the banner of 'Proactive Contributor to Peace'.

Japan has for multiple generations walked a single path, loving freedom and human rights, valuing law and order, abhorring war, and earnestly and determinedly pursuing peace, never wavering in the least. We will continue to walk this same path, unchanged, for generations upon generations to come. I would like all of you gathered here today to understand that point in a way that is absolutely clear. Over what is almost now a year and a half, I have worked to the very best of my ability to remake the Japanese economy into an economy that once more grows robustly, abundant with innovations. People call this 'Abenomics' and classify it as a type of economic policy. But for me, it is a mission that goes far beyond economic policy. It is nothing less than an undertaking to foster 'new Japanese' who will shoulder the responsibilities of the coming years.

And what are these 'new Japanese' about? They are Japanese who have lost none of the good qualities of the Japanese of days gone by. Japanese who loathe poverty and believe that universal values are found in the joy of hard work have, since the days when Asia was still said to be synonymous with being impoverished, continued to contribute untiringly to the construction of Asia's economies, in the belief that there is no reason why other Asian countries would be unable to accomplish what the Japanese themselves achieved. The 'new Japanese' are not different in the least from their fathers and grandfathers in the sense of rejoicing at each and every one of these selfless and unselfish contributions. If anything has changed, it is that women will be both the target recipients of, and the people responsible for, Japan's support and cooperation with increasing frequency.

Bear in mind that all three of the Japanese who helped create the civil code and the code of civil procedure in Cambodia were young female judges and public prosecutors. It was in August 2011 that President Benigno Aquino III of the Philippines and Chairman Murad Ebrahim of the Moro Islamic Liberation Front held their top-level meeting in Narita, Japan. It was March of this year that a comprehensive peace agreement was finally reached between the two sides. Two years from now, the Bansamoro local government will finally let out its first cry as a newborn. Now, to help support the locals, in what areas is the Japanese assistance team concentrating their investment? One area is having women gain enough ability to make a living. In Mindanao, Japan built a vocational training centre for women. What now echoes through Mindanao, where the sounds of gunshots and angry cries have disappeared, is the light whir of sewing machines women are operating.

Given the fact that at the end of the day, the growth engine continues to be human beings and are likely to be women placed in an unfair and disadvantaged position, as has been the case until now, the 'new Japanese' are people who spare no effort to improve the abilities of these people. The 'new Japanese' are Japanese who are delighted at the prosperity of Asia and the Pacific as their own personal source of joy and who discover values and a reason for living in making Japan a place of hopes and dreams for aspiring young people in the region. They are Japanese that could go beyond their national borders and have a broad-minded sense of self-identity.

Dozens of high school students come each year to Japan from China. They spread out all over the Japanese archipelago, spanning the nation north to south, and share their daily lives and their studies with Japanese high school students for a full year. Without exception, these young men and women are moved by the friendships they have made with their Japanese schoolmates, and go back to their home country shedding tears at the affection they have received from their host families. They head back calling Japan their second home. I want the 'new Japanese' to place even greater importance on that spirit of welcoming non-Japanese with such deep affection.

These 'new Japanese' are Japanese who are determined ultimately to take on the peace, order, and stability of this region as their own responsibility. They are people who possess the drive to shoulder the responsibilities of peace and order in the Asia-Pacific region, working together with our regional partners with whom we share the values of human rights and freedom. 'Proactive Contribution to Peace' – the new banner for such 'new Japanese' – is nothing other than an expression of Japan's determination to spare no effort or trouble for the sake of the peace, security, and prosperity of Asia and the Pacific, at even greater levels than before. We will do this together with our regional colleagues, our partners who share our motivations and values. Taking our alliance with the United States as the foundation and respecting our partnership with ASEAN, Japan will spare no effort to make regional stability, peace, and prosperity into something rock solid. In our future, the highway to peace and prosperity rolls out wide before us. Our responsibility to the next generation is to bring this region's potential for growth into full bloom. So once again. Japan for the rule of law. Asia for the rule of law. And the rule of law for all of us. Peace and prosperity in Asia, for evermore. Thank you for your attention. Thank you very much.

CHAPTER TWENTY-FIVE

'We are all small countries now': IISS 2019 Alastair Buchan Lecture

Yoichi Funabashi, Chairman, Asia Pacific Initiative

Ladies and gentlemen, it is a great privilege to be addressing such a learned and distinguished group of scholars and practitioners. I am truly honoured to have been given the opportunity to share some of my thoughts and observations with you, and to be granted this platform to speak to you by the International Institute for Strategic Studies. I must express my deep gratitude to John [Chipman] for extending his warm invitation for me to deliver the Alastair Buchan Lecture, which, as with IISS, possesses an extraordinarily rich history.

Before I continue, I must also congratulate John and the Institute on the establishment of the IISS Japan Chair. Asia Pacific Initiative is incredibly humbled to be a part of this ambitious venture, and I am delighted to say that our institute will be sending a researcher to serve at IISS in the role of Research Fellow for Japanese Security and Defence Policy. It is my belief and hope that our cooperation on this fellowship will plant the seeds for further collaboration between our institutions.

The collapse of the LIO and its enormous impact on Japan

At this point in history, we are confronted with a harsh reality, that the rise and fall of nations in this period are determined by the state of the international order. Japan, which has perhaps gained more than any country from the liberal international order helmed by the United States, is a prime example of this, and would experience serious consequences if the US allowed for the regional order it has led in the Asia Pacific to collapse entirely.

The liberal international order in Northeast Asia already faces salient threats from China and North Korea. But in an unfortunate turn of events, this order now faces a serious threat by none other than the United States, the supposed guarantor of this system and, of course, Japan's closest ally. In the most tragic example of its abandonment of this order, the Trump administration withdrew from the Trans-Pacific Partnership a mere three days after the president's inauguration. We do not know yet how detrimental America's departure from this pact will be in the coming years, particularly in our competition with China.

To give this instance better framing, suppose the US had abandoned NATO just a year after its founding. What would have happened to our containment policy toward the Soviet Union? Would we have won the Cold War?

Even the alliance system, which has been the anchor of the liberal international order, has been challenged by the United States. Mr Trump is the first US president in post-war history to openly question the values of alliances. His view toward such relationships, including the US–Japan alliance, is transactional, zero-sum, and short-term. In June 2018 in Singapore, the president came close to trading the dissolution of US Forces Korea for a denuclearisation pledge from Kim Jong-un, and unilaterally cancelled a US–South Korea military exercise without even consulting his own secretary of defense. Earlier this year, Mr Trump criticised the US–Japan security treaty for favouring Japan too heavily by complaining that the Japanese are not obligated to help defend the United States, and could simply 'watch on a Sony television' if America were attacked.

Japan is of course not the only US ally in Asia that has felt Mr Trump's wrath. The president has demanded South Korea accept a five-fold increase in the amount of money Seoul pays in host nation support. He will likely pressure Tokyo to do the same, even though Abe has reportedly argued to Trump that Japan in fact pays 74% of what it costs to host US forces there. Trump's approach casts the US as a mere renter of resources, and its armed forces as a band of mercenaries. He shows no hesitation in linking trade and security issues, often seeking to reap trade benefits even at the expense of security interests.

Despite Trump's actions, Prime Minister Abe has done an admirable job in stabilising the US–Japan relationship, even if it means he's had to beg for certain things from the president. As a matter of fact, the Abe administration has two very different, but equally intense, feelings toward Trump. On one hand, Japan feels assured that the threat perception gap between Tokyo and Washington towards Beijing has narrowed to almost zero. Indeed, the Trump administration has taken a tough position against China that stands in stark contrast to the Obama administration's ambiguous stance toward the country. There is broad consensus in Tokyo that Trump is justified in publicly shaming China for its massive cyber theft, economic statecraft, predatory trade policy, civil–military fusion of industrial policy, and export of censorship.

At the same time, however, Japan has in no way granted Trump its full confidence. The administration's sheer lack of focus, along with the president's impulsive tweeting, poor policy coordination, and apparent 'death wish' for the alliance, as Edward Luce argued in his column in the *Financial Times*, all make Tokyo increasingly nervous. And then there is the troubling possibility that Trump's America First policy could continue uninterrupted, or even intensify, if he is re-elected, as he will most likely grow more uninhibited if left in office. Under such a scenario, Japan would suffer under either a profound fear of entrapment, if US–China relations slide toward confrontation, or a profound fear of abandonment, if the US turns even more inward-looking and abdicates its leadership role in the Asia-Pacific.

Trump's potential re-election is of course far from the only foreign-policy issue that Tokyo must concern itself with in the coming year. Japan already feels exposed to numerous mounting challenges, particularly from China, but also from the Korean Peninsula and the wider Eurasian region. Geopolitics, which John Foster Dulles declared was 'transcended' after the San Francisco Peace Treaty, is vengefully back in the Asia-Pacific. Ironically, it is the United States that unleashed its return by eroding the rules-based international order.

China's illiberal innovation

China has contributed equally to the rise of geopolitics in Asia by aggressively employing economic statecraft. We can trace this approach back nearly ten years, to September 2010, when a Chinese ship captain rammed through two Japanese Coast Guard vessels as his ship intruded near the Senkaku Islands. Japan detained the captain, leading China to retaliate with a de facto export ban of rare earths to Japan.

Such economic statecraft must be placed in the wider context of China's geopolitical ambitions. Speaking to the foreign ministers of the ASEAN countries at the organisation's Regional Forum in Hanoi in the summer of 2010, Chinese Foreign Minister Yang Jiechi declared, 'China is a big country and you are small countries, and that's just a fact.' The remark was eerily reminiscent of Thucydides's immortalised Melian Dialogue: 'The strong do what they will and the weak suffer what they must.' Well, only with Chinese characteristics. China's economic statecraft towards neighbours such as Taiwan, the Philippines, Singapore, South Korea, Australia and now Canada, is brutal and vindictive.

China's presence is now felt in a variety of areas, ranging from the South China Sea and Indian Ocean to the North Pole and now South Pacific. The country is rapidly becoming a revisionist power rather than being co-opted into existing institutions under the current rules of the game, as the West would prefer. Instead, China is operating on its own terms, and seeks to co-opt other countries into the system of rules it wishes to dictate. But China's grand projects are not without weaknesses. Its Belt and Road Initiative, dubbed 'One Belt, One Road, One Cloud', is already overstretched, and questions abound regarding its sustainability as China's economy slows. Despite this, however, China has already enshrined the Belt and Road Initiative in the constitution of the Chinese Communist Party, and it should therefore be seen as a long-term, perhaps 30-year, project.

China has embraced what Premier Li Keqiang has called 'mass entrepreneurship and mass innovation'. China's market and social implementation of technologies is both rapid and dynamic. The country also has the advantage of being able to harness big data on a massive scale, with the state providing such data for free to Chinese platformers while sidestepping property rights and the privacy of citizens. China's authoritarian political system is naturally aligned with the age of Dataism. In fact, data is a perfect weapon for China.

So, while some scholars may argue that China is more adept at deploying technology rather than developing it, and while others still posit that Chinese technological advancements are driven only by theft, we must avoid underestimating China's technological prowess. We also need to be cautious of this innovation despite whether it is liberal or, as I argue it is, illiberal. To fully understand my caution, one must view the future of Chinese technology from a Schumpeterian point of view, and focus on the connections between the technology and the market, and particularly the critical mass of customers who consume it. It is the customer that acts as the primary driver of technological innovation, and in China's case, such advancement is backed by the full weight of one, massive consumer: the Chinese Communist Party, whose survival depends on the state's strategic use of certain technologies, such as AI and big data, and the government's strengthening of social surveillance and political control.

And if this kind of illiberal innovation that Beijing supports is truly sustainable, then mounting a response to it will be all the more difficult. We will be unable to simply contain China and prevent it from further advancing its technologies. Instead, the lesson from President Kennedy's undelivered Dallas Trade Mart speech, that 'a nation can be no stronger abroad than she is at home', should guide our approach. We must develop our own technologies and foster innovation among our own societies.

Japan as a rule-shaper and proactive stabiliser

Japan's diplomatic efforts to conclude TPP11 following US abandonment of the pact and complete an Economic Partnership Agreement with the EU are truly remarkable in the sense that the country managed to emerge from these experiences as a rule-shaper and proactive stabiliser in the Asia-Pacific and beyond. Indeed, through these actions, Japan expressed a genuine desire and aspiration to uphold the liberal international order.

However, its leadership with respect to TPP has revealed Japan's keen sense of vulnerability and insecurity as the world witnesses the rise of crude power games among major states, particularly between the US and China, with their looming tech giants, among nuclear states on Japan's periphery, and amongst the emerging demographic giants of Asia, including China, India, Pakistan and Indonesia. Climate change, and the geopolitical conditions it is creating worldwide, has already heightened feelings of anxiety in Japan and elsewhere, as well. Japan of course still boasts the world's third-largest economy, and maintains the status of a major player on the international stage. But as the world becomes a mega-geoeconomic battleground, where rule-making is replaced by power-grabbing and economic interdependence is weaponised, Japan will find itself even more nakedly exposed, and feel smaller and smaller.

In his seminal 1979 work, *Japan as Number One*, Ezra Vogel outlined his own vision for how the Japanese could play a significant role on the global stage. Forty years later, Japan holds the same potential and now more than ever has the opportunity to leave its mark on the world as a 'rules-shaper' among other small countries. For, except for the US and China, 'we are all small countries now', connected through the same sense of vulnerability. Indeed, by connecting ourselves through our shared vulnerability, small countries can cooperate with one another and work to strengthen a rules-based order in which we may thrive.

In his famous January 1907 memorandum, Eyre Crowe asserted that Britain was the so-called 'natural protector of the weaker communities', and through its open-market policy, 'she undoubtedly strengthens her hold on the interested friendship of other nations'. E.H. Carr, citing this paragraph in *The Twenty Years' Crisis, 1919–1939*, stated 'this advantage made it natural for Great Britain to appear as a champion of the political independence of small nations'. Japan, together with like-minded nations, and particularly the countries of the European Union, must strive to become such a promoter of the rule-based liberal international order, particularly in the age of mega-geoeconomics.

CHAPTER TWENTY-SIX

The 19th Regional Security Summit – the Shangri-La Dialogue: keynote address

Kishida Fumio, Prime Minister, Japan

Friday 10 June 2022

As delivered

Dr John Chipman, Director-General and Chief Executive, IISS

Welcome to the 19th IISS Shangri-La Dialogue. It is a delight for me personally and for our hosts, the government of Singapore, to be convening this Asia Security Summit after a two-year hiatus. Prime Minister Lee, the IISS is proud that we have again been able to bring together the national-security establishments of so many different states here this weekend, and we thank you for your support and the hospitality that this country so warmly provides.

The IISS has had two strong years since we last met here, growing by more than 25%, generating more data and analysis for governments in the private sector on geopolitical and geo-economic trends. We are pleased to have established a major new IISS–Europe office in Berlin, Germany, with staff drawn from a dozen different nationalities. I expect that IISS–Asia, based here in Singapore, and IISS–Europe in Berlin will have a good deal of intellectual exchange and practical cooperation.

In both 2020 and 2021, we managed to hold in-person IISS Manama Dialogues in the Kingdom of Bahrain, where our

Middle East office is headquartered, and we look forward to the 18th Manama Dialogue on 18 to 20 November this year.

The strategic dynamic in the Indo-Pacific region has developed in ways that have naturally shaped our agenda for this weekend. The strategies of the US and China in this region remain central, as do the perspectives of Southeast Asian states on current geopolitical trends. The growth in number and importance of minilateral security arrangements in groups of three, four or five, plus or minus one or two, is dazzling even the most astute observers of diplomatic practice.

Military modernisation continues apace. Exercises at sea and in the air often bring operators dangerously close to each other as each stick to their national scripts on where freedom to operate begins or ends. The internal conflict in Myanmar has stressed the institution of ASEAN (Association of Southeast Asian Nations). Korean intercontinental ballistic missile (ICBM) tests multiply. Technological competition accelerates. The challenges of climate change and the requirement for developing green defence doctrines are pressing and urgent. All these issues are treated in depth in the IISS *Asia-Pacific Regional Security Assessment 2022*, released this week.

It is impossible, however, to pass by the fact that we convene as a major war is occurring and a geopolitical earthquake exploding in Europe that affects the globe. Russia's unprovoked and illegal war against Ukraine started as a war for regime change and occupation and has morphed into one of annihilation and destruction. The military tactics displayed by the Russians have little connection to sane political objectives.

The Western response has moved from noting that Ukraine was not in NATO but would be supported, to the determination to provide defensive weapons but avoid escalation, to the view that Russia's strategic failure must be assured, to the position that Ukraine can and must win, to the assertion that

Russia's conventional power must be so reduced that it can never threaten a neighbour again.

Personally, I don't feel it's necessary to underscore that NATO countries have no NATO Article 5 obligation to come to the defence of Ukraine. I prefer to emphasise that Ukraine has a UN Article 51 right of self-defence and any other UN member state has the right under the same Article 51 on the request of the defending state to give it all the military support it may seek for its self-defence and in the service of collective security.

The only similar case arose in August 1990 when Saddam Hussein invaded Kuwait with the clear intent fully to occupy it and with the possible subsequent ability to pose a direct threat to the Kingdom of Saudi Arabia. Then, the Middle East security order was hugely at stake. Today, it is the European security order and the largest country in Europe that has been attacked. It was already attacked in 2014. This time, Mr Putin has said that Ukraine is not a nation and has developed maximalist aims for his campaign.

To use a phrase commonly heard in Asia, the European security order is a core interest of the West. It is essential for the West to prevail in this contest, for Russia strategically to fail and for Ukraine to be able to dictate peace terms that can have the support of its people. To get there, it is essential to repeat that defence is not escalation. The paradox is that even though NATO has no formal obligation to Ukraine, the reputation of NATO is at least partly at stake in this war. That reputation has been strengthened by a broad show of unity and by the applications of Sweden and Finland to join.

Germany has pledged an additional €100 billion to defence and has said it would move at pace to spend 2% of GDP on defence. It will still take some time for Germany to adapt its strategic culture to this cash infusion. As NATO moves towards its summit in Madrid later this month, the Russian war will require thinking afresh the principles of pre-emptive action, flexible response, escalation dominance and intra-war deterrence that must underpin a revised NATO strategic concept.

Given the nature of contemporary warfare, the relationship between Articles 4 and 5 of the NATO Treaty might also require reassessment. For many countries in Asia and the Middle East, this war has raised questions about their alignments and hedging strategies. It is natural that countries engage in strategic hedging. There are few truly cast-iron guarantees in security. Some independence and autonomy of action is preferred by most states. Strategic self-determination may mean that interests do not always align with the same security partner. It is better to have many friends than only a few. Multi-alignment has its attractions.

But strategic hedging, rather like its financial equivalent, requires active portfolio management. Russia's strategic currency is now in free fall. It is perhaps not prudent to be too long Russia again, to use the financial-markets term. Indeed, being overweight Russia right now, including for those countries that have traditionally had Russia as a major arms supplier, may prove costly in the medium and perhaps rather soon. Rebalancing might become necessary.

What this war has additionally shown is that the Euro-Atlantic and wider Indo-Pacific strategic theatres are co-dependent. The largest importer of Ukrainian wheat is Egypt, the second largest Indonesia. The impact of this war in Europe is felt internationally. For North Americans and Europeans, who this weekend will be pledging their commitments to the Indo-Pacific region, success in Europe is vital to success in Asia.

It is not simply a question of time commitment but one of credibility. Put bluntly, how can one speak about helping to support a free and open Indo-Pacific, when so far it has not proven possible to ensure a free and open Black Sea? Negotiations are unlikely to be enough. It will require some risk-taking to get the traffic moving again from the Black Sea to the rest of the world. We are proud that, considering the global impact of Russia's invasion of Ukraine, President Zelenskyy has agreed to speak to us from Kyiv tomorrow at exactly 16.00 Singapore time, and I know that most of you assembled here will wish to be in this hall at that time.

Against that background, it is a great honour to introduce the keynote speaker for the 19th Shangri-La Dialogue. We have someone who can speak with unique authority on the links between European and Asian security. Prime Minister Kishida of Japan became head of government having had a long period of success as Japan's foreign minister. He represents in the diet a Hiroshima constituency, whose history naturally shapes his appreciation of the horrors of nuclear war. Hiroshima will play host to the 2023 G7 summit that Japan will chair.

As Prime Minister, he has developed his ideas on new capitalism and has been especially active on questions of international relations and strategy. He created a new cabinet position, Minister for Economic Security, which signalled the importance of economic statecraft and contemporary diplomacy, as well as a need to anticipate vulnerabilities caused by the various stresses on the global economic order. The Kishida administration will also be crafting a new national security strategy this year, the first update since 2013.

Some in his party have suggested that Japan move toward the NATO standard of 2% of GDP expenditure on defence, a level that would put Japan as the third-biggest defence spender in the world, behind only the US and China.

Prime Minister Kishida, everyone in the audience and across the world will be fascinated to hear your thoughts on global security and Japan's contribution to it. It is an honour and a privilege to have you at the Shangri-La Dialogue. Prime Minister, the floor and this podium is yours.

Kishida Fumio, Prime Minister, Japan

Prime Minister Lee Hsien Loong, Dr John Chipman, distinguished guests, it is my great honour to deliver this keynote address at the Shangri-La Dialogue, a conference of long history held in high esteem. I would like to share with all the participants gathered here today how I perceive the current severe situation facing the international community and look ahead to the future we should all aspire to.

There is no better place than this Shangri-La Dialogue to deepen such discussions. This is because Asia is indeed the centre of gravity of the ever-expanding global economy, accounting for nearly 35% of it, and because the region continues to enjoy growth characterised by diversity and inclusiveness, with ASEAN upholding unity and centrality at its core.

With the very foundations of the international order being shaken by Russia's aggression against Ukraine, the international community now stands at a historic crossroads. The last time the world faced such a major turning point was some 30 years ago. That was around the time of the Cold War, a period when the world was divided into two camps, and people were afraid that the two sides' cold antagonism might heat up again.

The Cold War came to an end and the post-Cold War era began. In an address to the Japanese diet, the Prime Minister Kiichi Miyazawa, who went before me as both a fellow legislator from Hiroshima and the leader of the Kochikai, the policy group I belong to, characterised the post-Cold War era as the start of an era of building a new order for global peace in his speech to the Japanese parliament, squarely addressing the reality that Japan was called upon to play a greater international role in the security arena.

Miyazawa, after an extensive debate in Japan, managed to get the Peacekeeping Operations Cooperation Act passed, and he deployed Japan's Self-Defense Forces to Cambodia based on this Act. With some 30 years having passed since Miyazawa's time, in what kind of era are we now living? Since the pandemic broke out, the world has become even more uncertain. Amidst continuing economic disruption, we have come to recognise the importance of reliable and secure supply chains.

Then, as the world was still recovering from the pandemic, Russia's aggression against Ukraine occurred. No country or region in the world can shrug this off as someone else's problem. It is a situation that shakes the very foundations of the international order, which every country and individual gathered here today should regard as their own affair.

In the South China Sea, are the rules really being honoured? Neither international law, in particular the United Nations Convention on the Law of the Sea, to which all relevant countries agreed after years of dialogue and efforts, nor the award rendered by the arbitral tribunal under this convention is being complied with. In the East China Sea, where Japan is located, unilateral attempts to change the status quo by force in violation of international law are continuing.

Japan is taking a firm stand against such attempts. Peace and stability across the Taiwan Strait, which is located between these two seas, is also of extreme importance. Unfortunately, much activity not respecting people's diversity, free will and human rights is also taking place in this region.

Furthermore, since the beginning of this year, North Korea has repeatedly launched ballistic missiles, including a new type of ICBM, with unprecedented frequency and in new ways. As such, North Korea is strengthening its nuclear and missile activities in violation of UN Security Council resolutions, posing a clear and serious challenge to the international community. It is deeply regrettable that the recently proposed Security Council resolution was not adopted as a result of the exercise of the veto.

The abductions issue, which is a top priority for my administration, is also a serious violation of human rights. At the root of all these problems is a situation in which confidence in the universal rules that govern international relations is being shaken. This is the essential and most serious underlying problem.

Can the rule-based international order we have built through hard work, dialogue and consensus be upheld? And the march of peace and prosperity continue? Or will we return to a lawless world, where rules are ignored and broken, where unilateral changes to the status quo by force are unchallenged and accepted, and where the strong coerce the weak militarily or economically? That is the choice we have to make today.

Japan is the world's third-largest economy and has consistently sought to bring about peace and prosperity in the region since the end of the Second World War, making contributions mainly in the economic field. Accordingly, the responsibility Japan must fulfil is heavy. With that understanding, what role should Japan play in realising peace and prosperity as we face this crossroads in history? While focusing on universal values that everyone should respect and defend, we must firmly hold aloft the banner of our ideals for the future, such as a world without nuclear weapons, while also responding astutely and decisively as the situation demands.

I am committed to realism diplomacy for a new era that adheres to this kind of thorough pragmatism. In the midst of all this, Japan will not lose its humility, flexibility in valuing diversity or tolerance that respects the individuality of others. However, we will be more proactive than ever in tackling the challenges and crises that face Japan, Asia and the world.

Taking that perspective in order to maintain and strengthen the peaceful order in this region, I will advance the Kishida vision for peace and boost Japan's diplomatic and security role in the region by promoting the following five pillars of initiatives.

The first is maintaining and strengthening the rules-based free and open international order. In particular, we will press forward in bringing new developments towards the free and open Indo- Pacific. The second is enhancing security. We will advance the fundamental reinforcement of Japan's defence capabilities in tandem with reinforcing the Japan–US alliance and strengthening our security cooperation with other like-minded countries. The third is promoting realistic efforts to bring about a world without nuclear weapons. The fourth is strengthening the functions of the United Nations, including UN Security Council reform. The fifth is strengthening international cooperation in new policy areas such as economic security.

In order to bring peace to the international community, it is imperative that we first press forward in maintaining and strengthening the rules-based free and open international order. The rule of law serves as the foundation supporting this kind of international order. Alongside it are the peaceful resolution of disputes, the non-use of force and respect for sovereignty. On the sea, it is freedom of navigation. And in the economy, free trade.

Needless to say, respect for human rights is also critical, as is a democratic political system that reflects people's free will and diversity. These are common and universal principles developed by all people worldwide who, longing for world peace, have amassed collective wisdom. It goes without saying that the rules and principles I have just mentioned are also consistent with the purposes and principles of the United Nations

Charter. Rules must be respected. Even if they become inconvenient, one cannot be allowed to act as if they did not exist, nor can one be allowed to unilaterally change them.

If one wants to change them, a new consensus must be made. Japan has been promoting a free and open Indo-Pacific with a view to maintaining and strengthening the rules-based free and open international order in this region. And the vision we have advocated has come to gain broad support in the international community. Japan has consistently and vigorously supported the ASEAN outlook on the Indo-Pacific, which ASEAN has developed as its own basic policy.

Looking around the world, a variety of actors, including the United States, Australia, India, the United Kingdom, France, Germany, Italy, the Netherlands and the European Union have all laid out visions for the Indo-Pacific, sharing a common grand vision. Like-minded partners are each taking action on their own initiative, not at the behest of others. This is the very concept of a free and open Indo-Pacific, which is based on inclusiveness, the so-called FOIP concept. In particular, here in the Indo-Pacific region collaboration with ASEAN is absolutely essential.

After assuming the post of Prime Minister, I first visited Cambodia, which holds this year's ASEAN chairmanship. Later, I visited Indonesia, Vietnam and Thailand. And today, I am here in Singapore. I have also held meetings with the leaders of ASEAN countries. The history of Japan and Southeast Asia is underpinned by a long history of goodwill and friendship. After the war, Japan supported the development of Southeast Asia. And Southeast Asian countries extended a helping hand to Japan in our recovery from the unprecedented earthquake and tsunami disaster.

I would like to continue to work hand in hand with the leaders of ASEAN countries to deepen discussions on ways to ensure peace and prosperity in the region. Along with ASEAN countries, Pacific Island countries are also important partners for the realisation of FOIP. We will contribute to strengthening the foundation for their sustainable and resilient economic development, including addressing the existential challenge of climate change.

We have provided timely assistance in response to recent changes in the security environment such as laying an undersea cable in East Micronesia in partnership with Australia and the United States, and we will work together with our Pacific Island partners to ensure a rules-based, sustainable maritime order. Cooperation based on FOIP is cooperation built upon long-standing trust. It is not limited to hardware, such as infrastructure construction, but instead also focuses on supporting the development of local human resources, promoting autonomous and inclusive development and fostering the industry through public and private initiatives.

As potential investment partners, we have also supported efforts to strengthen ASEAN's connectivity. It is also necessary for like-minded countries to work together to increase the investment of resources in this region. In addition to the ASEAN and Pacific Island countries that I mentioned earlier, Japan, Australia, India and the United States, also known as the Quad, are playing an important role in promoting a free and open Indo-Pacific.

At the recent Quad leaders' meeting in Tokyo, we confirmed that the Quad will seek to extend more than US$50 billion of further infrastructure assistance and investment in the Indo-Pacific over the next five years, which will be essential in promoting productivity and prosperity in this region. I will further accelerate these efforts. We intend to enhance existing free and open Indo-Pacific cooperation by beefing up our diplomatic efforts, including by expanding our official development assistance (ODA) while engaging in an optimised, efficient and strategic use of international cooperation through ODA.

I will lay out a free and open Indo-Pacific plan for peace by next spring, which will strengthen Japan's efforts to further promote the vision of a free and open Indo-Pacific with an emphasis on providing patrol vessels and enhancing maritime law-enforcement capabilities, as well as cyber security, digital and green initiatives and economic security.

In recent years, Japan has particularly been strengthening its maritime-security efforts while utilising advanced technologies, such as satellites, artificial intelligence and unmanned aerial vehicles, and we will continue to share its knowledge and experience with other countries. From this perspective, over the next three years, we will make use of technical cooperation, training and other means conducive to strengthening the maritime law-enforcement capabilities of at least 20 countries to promote efforts to train at least 800 maritime-security personnel and strengthen their human-resources networks.

In addition, we will provide at least approximately US$2bn in assistance such as the provision of maritime-security equipment, including patrol vessels and development of maritime-transportation infrastructure in Indo-Pacific countries over the next three years. We will strengthen our support in the Pacific countries, utilising cooperation of Quad and frameworks of international organisations.

In addition, in order to maintain and strengthen the international order based on rules and universal values, such as the rule of law, we will strengthen connections and networks among countries and peoples. To this end, we will train more than 1,500 personnel in the fields of the rule of law and governance over the next three years.

Second, I would like to talk about the role Japan should play in the realm of security. In light of Russia's aggression against

Ukraine, countries' perceptions on security have drastically changed around the world. Germany has announced that it will shift its security policy and raise its defence budget to 2% of its GDP. Finland and Sweden, Russia's neighbours, have changed their historical policy of neutrality and announced they have applied for NATO membership.

I myself have a strong sense of urgency that Ukraine today may be East Asia tomorrow. Japan has also made the decision to shift our policy towards Russia and is united with the international community in our efforts to impose strong sanctions against Russia and support Ukraine. As the Prime Minister of the peace-loving nation Japan, I have a responsibility to protect the lives and assets of the Japanese people and to contribute to a peaceful order in the region.

I will seek to build a stable international order through dialogue, not confrontation. At the same time, however, we must be prepared for the emergence of an entity that tramples on the peace and security of other countries by force or threat without honouring the rules. As a means of preventing such a situation and protecting ourselves, we need to enhance our deterrence and response capabilities. This will be absolutely essential if Japan is to learn to survive in the new era and keep speaking out as a standard bearer of peace.

As the security environment surrounding Japan becomes increasingly severe, we will set out a new national-security strategy by the end of this year. I am determined to fundamentally reinforce Japan's defence capabilities within the next five years and secure a substantial increase of Japan's defence budget needed to effect such reinforcement. In doing so, we will not rule out any options, including the so-called counter-strike capabilities, and will realistically consider what is necessary to protect the lives and livelihoods of our people.

To all of you, I stress that Japan's posture as a peace-loving nation will remain unchanged. Our efforts will proceed within the scope of our constitution and in compliance with international law in a manner that does not alter the basic roles and missions shared between Japan and the United States under our alliance. We will continue to explain our approach to other countries in a transparent and thorough manner.

No country can ensure its security entirely on its own. That is why I will promote multi-layered security cooperation with like-minded countries that share universal values, positioning the Japan–US alliance as the linchpin. In my meeting with US President Biden, during his recent visit to Japan, he strongly supported my determination regarding Japan's defence capabilities.

We were also in full agreement on expanding and deepening Japan–US security and defence cooperation. We will further reinforce the deterrence and response capabilities of the Japan–US alliance, which has become the cornerstone of peace and stability in not only the Indo-Pacific but also the entire world. At the same time, we will actively promote security cooperation with Australia and other likeminded countries.

Prime Minister Lee Hsien Loong, I am extremely pleased to begin negotiations with Singapore to conclude a defence-equipment and -technology transfer agreement. We will continue to promote our efforts to conclude such defence-equipment and -technology transfer agreements with ASEAN countries and materialise specific cooperation projects, according to their needs.

Regarding Reciprocal Access Agreements, or RAAs, following the signing of an agreement with Australia in January, we have recently reached an agreement in principle with the United Kingdom. Japan will work closely with like-minded partners in Europe and Asia towards the conclusion of these agreements. In addition, in order to contribute to the realisation of a free and open maritime order, Japan will dispatch a Maritime Self-Defense Force unit, led by the destroyer *Izumo*, to the Indo-Pacific from 13 June and conduct joint exercises with countries in the region, including Southeast Asia and the Pacific.

Third, we will do our utmost towards achieving a world without nuclear weapons. Amid the crisis in Ukraine, the use of nuclear weapons by Russia is being discussed as a real possibility. We must not repeat the scourge of nuclear weapons. The threat of nuclear weapons, let alone the use of them, should never be tolerated. As the Prime Minister of the only country that has suffered the devastation of atomic bombings, I strongly appeal for this.

The ramifications of Russia's threat to use nuclear weapons are not limited to the threat itself. The threat may have already caused serious damage to the nuclear non-proliferation regime. It may have already made it even more difficult for countries seeking to develop nuclear weapons to abandon their plans. Moves to develop and possess nuclear weapons might even spread further to other countries. These are among the various concerns that have been voiced.

Even before the Ukraine crisis, North Korea frequently and repeatedly launched ballistic missiles, including ICBM-class missiles, and we have great concerns that yet another nuclear test is imminent. The non-transparent build-up of military capacity, including nuclear arsenals that can be seen in the vicinity of Japan, has become a serious regional security concern.

The return to compliance with the Iran nuclear agreement has not yet been realised. I must admit that the path to a world without nuclear weapons has become even more challenging. It is, however, precisely because of this extremely difficult situation that I, Prime Minister with roots in Hiroshima, where an atomic bomb was dropped, have decided to speak out, work tirelessly to reverse the current situation and contribute to any scale of improvement towards achieving a world without nuclear weapons.

There is no contradiction between ensuring Japan's national security, while squarely facing the reality of the harsh security environment surrounding Japan, and at the same time advancing towards the ideal of a world without nuclear weapons. Based on the relationship of trust we enjoy with the United States, our sole ally, Japan will present a road map that will take us from the reality to our ideal and press forward with realistic nuclear-disarmament efforts.

Greater transparency of nuclear forces is what underpins such efforts. It serves as the first step in supporting the irreversibility and verifiability of nuclear disarmament and in building trust among nuclear-weapon states, as well as between nuclear-weapon states and non-nuclear-weapon states. Mindful of the non-transparent manner in which some countries have been increasing their nuclear capabilities, we call for all nuclear-weapon states to disclose information regarding their nuclear forces.

Together with countries concerned, we will encourage the United States and China to engage in bilateral dialogue on nuclear disarmament and arms control. In addition, it is also key to bring back discussions on the Comprehensive Test Ban Treaty (CTBT) and Fissile Material Cut-Off Treaty (FMCT), which have recently become nearly forgotten.

More than ever, we need to maintain and strengthen the Non-Proliferation Treaty (NPT), the very cornerstone of the international nuclear-disarmament and non-proliferation regime. We will do everything to ensure that the NPT Review Conference in August, in which both nuclear-weapon states and non-nuclear-weapon states will participate, achieves a meaningful outcome.

With the use of nuclear weapons now becoming a real possibility, reminding the world once again about the scourge and inhumanity of the use of nuclear weapons is vital. As the only country to have suffered the devastation of atomic bombings, Japan will seize every opportunity, including the upcoming Conference on the Humanitarian Impact of Nuclear Weapons, to convey the stark realities of atomic bombings to the world.

With a view to further bolstering discussions taken by the Group of Eminent Persons for Substantive Advancement of Nuclear Disarmament, which I established when I served as Foreign Minister, and to rekindle the momentum for international nuclear disarmament, we will establish the International Group of Eminent Persons for a World Without Nuclear Weapons. This group will enjoy the involvement of incumbent and former political leaders of various countries, and our plan is to hold its first meeting in Hiroshima this year.

With regard to North Korea, working towards the complete denuclearisation of North Korea in accordance with the UN Security Council resolutions, Japan, the United States and the Republic of Korea will work closely together in the areas of regional security, deliberations at the United Nations and diplomatic efforts. And Japan will further act in cooperation with the international community as a whole. Through each and every concrete effort, we will strive to move step by step towards a world without nuclear weapons.

Fourth, no time can be lost in reforming the UN, which should serve as the guardian of peace. Russia, a permanent member of the UN Security Council, a body having primary responsibility for maintaining international peace and security, has engaged in an outrageous act that has shaken the very foundation of the international order, causing the UN to face a time of trial. Japan's stance of attaching importance to the United Nations remains unchanged.

Since my time as Foreign Minister, I have been actively working towards the reform of the UN. Now, having assumed office as Prime Minister, I have taken advantage of summit-level diplomatic opportunities to hold discussions with leaders of various countries on ways to strengthen the functions of the United Nations.

UN reform is not an easy task given the complexity of the intertwined interests of various countries. But Japan, as a peace-loving nation, will lead discussions to strengthen the functions of the United Nations, including the reform of the Security Council. Japan will join the UN Security Council starting next year, and in the Security Council, too, we will work tirelessly. At the same time, we will also seek a way forward for global governance that responds to the new challenges in the international community.

Finally, I would like to discuss international cooperation in new policy areas such as economic security. In the midst of an unprecedented pandemic, the vulnerabilities of the global supply chain have come to the fore. Exerting unjustifiable economic pressure on other countries to impose unilateral claims or intentionally disseminating disinformation can also never be accepted.

The aggression against Ukraine has made us even more aware of the clear and urgent need to make our own economy more resilient as it directly affects our everyday lives. Taking into account that the economy is directly linked to national security and that areas such as cyber security and digitalisation are becoming increasingly important for national security, we will promote economic-security initiatives to ensure the security of the nation and our people from an economic perspective.

In Japan, to address this challenge, the Economic Security Promotion legislation was enacted under my leadership. However, Japan cannot go at this alone. International cooperation is essential, including within frameworks of like-minded countries such as the G7. Japan and ASEAN have long been building multi-layered supply chains. It is crucial that our public and private sectors continue to invest in maintaining and strengthening these supply chains. To this end, Japan will support more than 100 supply-chain resilience projects over the next five years.

In addition, once a country's status in the international community, including its economic development, has been elevated, that country should not only enjoy the benefits, but more importantly it should also fulfil the responsibilities and obligations commensurate with that status. Economic cooperation and financing must be characterised by transparency and they should lead to the long-term welfare of the people of the recipient country.

We will continue to promote economic cooperation based on the idea of human security, respecting the ownership of each country and the interests of its nationals. To achieve prosperity in these difficult times, ASEAN and the Indo-Pacific region must remain the growth engine of the world. Japan will contribute to building resilient nations that can overcome any great or difficult challenges they may face.

Ladies and gentlemen, I ask you to contemplate our future. The vision I have shared with you today, the vision of a rules-based free and open international order, is one in which we all work together. We will elevate a free and open Indo-Pacific to the next stage.

I firmly believe that if we do so, a future of peace and prosperity will surely await us, a bright and glorious world full of hope, where there is trust and empathy shared amongst us.

Thank you for your kind attention.

INDEX

9/11 *479*, 492, 495, 506

A

Abe Shinzo 24, 25, 28–29, 70–71, 308, 480–483, 521–532, 535
  Free and Open Indo-Pacific (FOIP) 29, 70, *482*, 550–552, 559
Abramowitz, Morton 222
Afghanistan *167*, 272, 283, 294, 325, 352, 358, 452, *483*
Albanese, Anthony *483*
Anti-Ballistic Missile (ABM) Treaty 485–487, 491, 493
Asanuma Inejiro 89
Asia and Pacific Council (ASPAC) 120
Asia-Pacific Economic Cooperation (APEC) 28, *261*, *364*, 380, 440–442, 447, 474
Asian-Pacific Economic Sphere 120
Asian Development Bank (ADB) 37–38, 380
Association of Southeast Asian Nations (ASEAN) 23, 28, 66–67, *80*, *166*, 203–204, 219, 265, 278–281, 293, 300, 334–335, 337, 352, 354–355, 358, 380, 382, 387, 392–394, 399, 408, 437–438, 442–443, 447–448, 453, 465, 522–523, 526–529, 532, 542, 546, 550–551, 554, 559
  Post-Ministerial Conference (PMC) 438
  Regional Forum (ARF) 438, 447, 473, 526–527, 536–537
Australia 28, 45, 62–63, 64, 112, 120, 121, 142, 251–252, 255, *259*, 281, 293, 342, 352, 361, *480*, *483*, 523, 554
Australia–New Zealand–United States (ANZUS) pact 251, 355

B

Bandung Asian–African Conference (1955) 40, 91, 111, 467
Bertram, Christopher 55, 58, 56
Biden, Joe 554
Bretton Woods 171, 206–207, 291
Brezhnev, Leonid 232, 267
Brookings Institution 56, 221
Brown, Harold 282
Brzezinski, Zbigniew 179, 191
Buchan, Alastair *303*
Bush, George H.W. *260*, 370, 422, 432, 436, 441
Bush, George W. 485, 491, 493–495, 501, 504, 506

C

Cambodia *167*, 279–280, 325, 358, *363*, 384, 399, 402, 409, 453, 531, 547, 550
Canada 342, 355
Carr, E.H. 539–540
Carter, Jimmy 265, 277, 282, 317, 320
Cheney, Dick 434
Chiang Kai-shek 470
China 22, 25–26, 28–29, 32, 43–44, 54, 57, 65, 71, *79–80*, 83–96, 97, 99, 101, 105–107, 109, 114, 117, 118, 121–125, 127–130, 133–140, 155, 163, *165–167*, 169, 170–172, 175–178, 185–188, 191–192, 193, 199, 201–203, 209, 216–222, 224–226, 232, 236–238, 247–248, 249–251, 254–255, 265–270, 276, 279–282, 294, 300, 313, 318–321, 323–324, 326–327, 335–336, 343–344, 354–355, *364–365*, 373, 393, 395, 401–402, 411–412, 415–418, 420, 436–438, 443, 448, 454, *460*, 463–475, *472*, *479–483*, 486–506, 513–515, 517–518, 526, 531–532, 534–539, 542

China Institute for Contemporary International Relations (CICIR) 496, 499
Chipman, Sir John 55–56, 66–68, *307–308*, *310*, 521, 533, 541, 546
Chun Doo-hwan *259*
Clinton, Bill 417, 435, 440–442, 452, 464
Cold War 27, 37–48, 53, 57, 64–65, 71, *79*, 101–102, 113, 128–129, 132, 139–140, 151– 152, *165–167*, 184, 245–258, *261*, 263–287, 295–296, 301, 317–331, 351–362, 368–369, 391, 396–397, 401–403, 406–407, 411–412, 418, 421–422, 439–440, 452–453, 455–456, 458, 467, 546
    detente 136, 141–142, *167*, 209–210, 212, 221–225, 232, 264
Commonwealth of Independent States (CIS) 374, 378–379
Communist Party (Japan) 101, 103, 115, 123, 125, 134
Comprehensive and Progressive Agreement for Trans-Pacific Partnership (CPTPP) 29, *482*, 521, 534, 438
Comprehensive Test Ban Treaty (CTBT) 501, 556
Conference on Security and Co-operation in Europe (CSCE) 371, 382, 386–387, 400, 409, 439
COVID-19 pandemic *310*, *482*, 558
Cuban Missile Crisis *80*, 132, 139

D
Democratic Party of Japan (DPJ) 364, *380*
Deng Xiaoping *167*, 269, 326–327, 463, 466–467
Doi Takako *260*
Dulles, John Foster 102, 122, 536

E
East Asia Economic Caucus (EAEC) 441–442
East Asia Summit 526–527
East Asian financial crisis (1997–98) 448, 462, 474
East China Sea 70, 248, 249–250, 514, 547
Egypt *166*, 358, *460*, 544
Emmott, Bill 71, *310*
Ethiopia 264
Eto Shinkichi 186
Euratom 154, 158, 160–161
European Community (EC) 191–192, 215, 294, *363*, 370–372, 384, 391, 393–394, 397, 400

F
Finland 543, 553
First Gulf War 23–24, 64, *363*, 373, 376, 379, 428, 431, 452, 455–456, 458–459, 543
Ford, Gerald *166*, 240
France *80*, 94, 102, 108, 200, 340, 384, 397, 399, 401, 515
FS-X project 431–435
Fujisaki Ichiro 67
Fukuda Takeo 22, *166*, 279
Fukushima nuclear disaster *481*
Funabashi Yoichi 70

G
G6 *166*
G7 27, 46, *167*, *260*, 290, 292, 298–300, 311, 333, 358, 378, 380, 382, 387, 397, 400, 408, 414–415, 452, 454–455, *482–483*, 544, 559
G8 473, *479–480*
General Agreement on Tariffs and Trade (GATT) *79*, 297, 371, 394, 440, 451, 457
Germany 94, 102, 114, 126, 153–154, 215, 222, 340, *363*, 370, 374, 382, 384–385, 397, 515, 543, 553
Gorbachev, Mikhail 22, *259*, 344, 359, *363*, 384, 414
Greece 102
Gulf, the 241, 267–268, 271–275, 284, 297, 354, *363*

H
Hashimoto Ryutaro 24, 31, 457, 462, 465
Hatoyama Ichiro 38–39, 40
Hatoyama Yukio 518
Ho Chi Minh 140
Hokkaido 334, 337–340, 342
Hong Kong 127, *363*, 373, 395, 463, 468, 475
Hosokawa Morihiro *363*, 414, 424, 460
Hotta Toshie 87–88
Hu Jintao 504
Hua Guofeng 473
Hungary uprising (1956) 111
Hunt, Kenneth (Brig.) 55, 59–60, *304*
Huntington, Samuel 28, 441

I
Ikeda Hayato *80*, 84, 95, 105–106, 118–119
India 126, 142, 220, *259*, 300, 381, *460*, 465, *479–480*, *482*, 500, 523, 539
Indian Ocean 241–242, 264–265, *266*, 267, 271, 284, 354, 521–523, 537
Indonesia 142, 246–247, 249, 255, 322, 381, *460*, 525, 527–528, 539, 544, 550
Inoki Masamichi 59–60 *see also* Research Institute for Peace and Security (RIPS)
intercontinental ballistic missiles (ICBMs) 135, 138–139, *363*, *482*, 494, 498–500, 516, 542, 547, 555
intermediate-range ballistic missiles (IRBMs) 318, 334, 337, 353, 453, 500, 503
International Institute for Strategic Studies (IISS) 44–45, 53–73, *259–260*, *303–310*, 533, 541–542
    Adelphi Papers 54, 55, 57, 58, 61, 66, 111–145, 169–188, 205–226, 229–243, 245–258, 263– 288, 317–331, 333–347, 351–362, 391–409, 411–444, 447–475
    Asia-Pacific Regional Security Assessment 542
    Manama Dialogue 68, 70, 541–542
    Shangri-La Dialogue (SLD) 68–70, *481*, *483*, 521–532, 541–559
    Strategic Survey 59–60
    Survival (journal) 54, 57, 61, 83–109, 149–164, 191–204, 311–315, 367–389, 485–507, 513–518

International Monetary Fund (IMF) *79–80*, 297, 371, 380
Iran *167*, 272, 274, 517, 555
Iran–Iraq War *259*, 272–273, 296–297, 354, 358
Iraq War (2003–11) *479–480*
Ishiba Shigeru 486
Ishibashi Tanzan 90, 92
Israel 54, *166*, 229–230, 232–233, 273, 354
Italy 94, 382, 384, *483*

J
Japan
  Air Self-Defense Force (JASDF) 253, 340, 357, 431, *479*
  constitution 22, 57, *79*, 101, 107, 113, 115, 116–117, 149, 177, 256, 283, 290, 334, 339, 341, 371, 377, 383, 421–425, 428, 435, 450–452, *481*, 518
  Defence Agency 59, 107, 116–117, 339, 424–425, *480*, 486
  Host-Nation Support (HNS) 422, 427, 429–431
  Maritime Self-Defense Force (JMSDF) 31, *79*, 275, 340–342, 357, *363*, *479*, 555
  Ministry of Finance 116, 372
  Ministry of Foreign Affairs (MOFA) 55–56, 59, 61–62, 66–68, 71, 120, 129, 456
  Ministry of International Trade and Industry (MITI) 234, 329, 433
  National Defense Program Guidelines (NDPG) 45, 47, *166*, 424
  overseas development assistance (ODA) 41, 237, *260–261*, 409, 428, 458, *460*, 470, 529, 552
  Self-Defense Forces (SDF) 31, *79*, 107, 108, 115–117, *165*, 283, 290, 334, 340, 357–358, *363*, 368, 373, 376, 382–384, 420–425, 433, 435, 452, 459, *479*, 529, 547
Japan Institute of International Affairs (JIIA) 54, 55, 59
Japan New Party *363*
Jiang Zemin 463–465, 468, 491, 496
Johnson, Lyndon B. 25, 83, 130, 140, 154

K
Kahn, Herman 191
Kaifu Toshiki 378
Kaya Okinori 92
Keidanren 56, 64
Kennedy, John F. 84, 132, 538
Kim Dae-Jung 278, *365*, 462, *479*
Kim Il Sung 335–336
Kim Jong-il *479–481*
Kim Jong-un *480*, 534
Kishi Nobusuke 21, 40–43, 92, 104, 118–119
  Basic Policy on National Defense 41–42
  Three Basic Principles 40–41
Kishida Fumio 30, 31, 49, 70, *309–310*, *483*, 544–559
Kissinger, Henry 22, 62–63, 181–182, *260*, *305*, 319
Kohl, Helmut 384
Koizumi Junichiro 24, 31, *479–480*

Komeito *80*, 118, 125
Kono Taro 70, *309*
Kono Yohei 461–462
Korean War 102, 113, 114, 115, 132
Kosaka Masataka 32, 43–46, 57–58, 60, *260*
Koshino, Yuka 71, *310*
Kosygin, Alexei 154, 219
Kuranari Tadashi 63, *260*, 311–315

L
Laird, Melvin 231
Lebanon 297
Lee Hsien Loong 521, 546, 554
Lee Kuan Yew 251–252, 322, 442, 463, 470, 541
Li Keqiang 537
Liao Chengzhi 123
Liberal Democratic Party (LDP) 21–22, 23, *80*, 91–92, 95–96, 98–99, 114–116, 118, 122–124, 144, *259*, *363–364*, 375, 383–384, 421–423, 435, 461, *481–483*

M
MacArthur, General Douglas 115–116, 248
Mackinder, Halford 245, 258
Mahan, Alfred Thayer 245
Malacca Strait 241, 249, 279
Malaysia 219, 373, 387, 395, 441, 528
Manila Conference (1966) 120
manoeuvrable re-entry vehicles (MARVs) 500
Mao Zedong *79*, 129, 133
Matsumura Kenzo 90–93
McNamara, Robert 130, 131–132, 136, 138–139
MiG fighters 336–337, 413
Miki Takeo 60, 120–121, 130, *166*
Missile Technology Control Regime (MTCR) 492
Miyazawa Kiichi *260*, *363*, 382, 437, 442, 546–547
Mongolia 378, 399
Mori Yoshiro *479*
Moscow Treaty (2002) 501–502
Murayama Tomiichi 423, 461
Myanmar 542

N
Nakasone Yasuhiro 23, 31, 46–48, 61–63, *259*, 289–303, *304–306*, 311–312, 327, 333, 339, 341–345, 368–369, 373, 375–376, 422, 452, 473
Nakayama Taro 437
NATO 29–30, 263–264, 274, 284, 287, 311–312, 330, 346, 354–361, 371, 385–386, 396, 400, 404, 428, 430, *483*, 534, 542–545
New Zealand 120, 251–252, 293, 325, 342, 352
Nixon, Richard 22, *80*, *165–166*, 169–174, 179, 180–182, 191–192, 200, 231–232, 239, 320
Nixon Doctrine 57, *81*, 169–174, 196, 265
Nixon Shocks 22, *165*, 171, 182, 208, 235, 282
Noda Eijiro 56
North America Free Trade Agreement (NAFTA) *363*, 440–442

North Korea 26, *79*, 127, *165–166*, 175–176,
  202–203, 209–210, 221–226, 251–252, 254,
  276–278, 297, 313, 323, 328, 335–337, 343–345,
  364, 373, 379, 398–399, 402, 411–412, 418–420,
  425, 427, 458, 465, *479–482*, 488, 495, 503–506,
  516–517, 534, 542, 547–548, 555, 557
nuclear weapons 22, 26–27, 54, 62–63, *79–80*,
  89–90, 93, 100–102, 107–108, 113, 117,
  126–129, 134–139, 141, 144, 149–164,
  191–204, 226, 232, 256–257, 285–288, 292,
  295–296, 311–315, 325–326, 330, 346–347,
  364, 369, 395, 398–399, 418, 427, 437, 458,
  464–465, 471, 474–475, *480–482*, 488,
  490–491, 493, 497–498, 502–505, 515–518,
  544, 549, 555–557
  Intermediate Range Nuclear Forces (INF)
    Treaty 63, *260*, 296, 358, 369, 397
  International Atomic Energy Agency (IAEA)
    127, 153–154, 160–161, 419, 503
  Treaty on the Non-Proliferation of Nuclear
    Weapons (NPT) 54, *80*, 149–164, *165*, 419,
    422, 516, 556–557

O

O'Neill, Dr Robert 57, 61–63, *305–306*
Obama, Barack 517, 523, 535
October War 229–230, 232–234, 240
Ogura Kazuo 454
Ohara Soichiro 88
Ohira Masayoshi 23, 44, 60, 283, 343
oil crisis (1973) 229–243, 273, 291
Okawara Yoshio 64, *260*
Okazaki Kaheita 94
Okinawa 25, *80*, 89, 97–98, 104–105, 127, 150,
  165, 213, *364*, 457, 514
Organization for Economic Co-operation and
  Development (OECD) *80*, 119, *165*, 295,
  371, 380, 409, 451
Organization for Security and Cooperation in
  Europe (OSCE) 30
Organization of Petroleum Exporting Countries
  (OPEC) *80*, *166*, 273
Ozawa Ichiro 375

P

Pacific Ocean 242, 250, 265–267, 313, 319,
  321–322, 330, 342, 345–347, 354, 356, 514,
  521–523, 537
Pakistan 300, 358, *364*, 539
Palliser, Sir Michael *304–306*
Paracel Islands 248
Park Chung Hee 276, 322
Pelosi, Nancy *483*
Persian Gulf *see* Gulf, the
Peru 379
Philippines 121, 127, 176, 246–247, 249, 251,
  255, 268, 324, 337, 352, 354, 356, 358, 373,
  395, 399, 411, *460*, 514, 525, 527–528, 531
Plaza Accord *259*
Putin, Vladimir *479*, 493, 543

Q

Quadrilateral Security Dialogue (Quad) *480*,
  482–483, 551–552

R

Reagan, Ronald 47, *259*, 267, 277, 283, 284, 317,
  334, 368–369, 375, 487
Research Institute for Peace and Security (RIPS)
  59–60 *see also* Inoki Masamichi
Russia 29, 49, 71, 379, 402–406, 412–415,
  418, 420, 423, 426, 436–438, 464, 467, *481*,
  483, 491–494, 500–501, 542–544, 546–547,
  552–553, 555, 557
Russo-Japanese War (1904–05) 90, 100
Ryukyu Islands 127–128

S

Saeki Kiichi 54–55, 58, 64, *306*
Sakamoto Yoshikazu 90
Sakata Michita 59
Sasae Kenichiro 66
Sato Eisaku 23, 24–25, 27, *80*, 83–84, 92, 95, 106,
  119, 123, 171
  Three Non-Nuclear Principles 27
Satoh Yukio 57, 59–60, 63, 65, 69
Schlesinger, James 248
Sea of Japan (East Sea) 249
Sea of Okhotsk 330
Second World War 39, *79*, 85–88, 100–102, 119,
  290, 373–374, 376, 422, 427, 450, 452, 461,
  470–471, 492, 515
Senkaku/Diaoyu Islands 26, 28–29, 225,
  247–248, 470–471, *480*, 536
Shigemitsu Mamoru 37, 39–40, 48,
Singapore 67, 251–252, 255, 322, 373, 395, 442,
  528, 541, 550
Socialist Party (Japan) 89–90, 94, 96, 99, 103,
  108, 114–115, 123–125, 144, 423, 452, 461
  Democratic Socialist Party (DSP) 118, 125,
    376, 383
South China Sea 28, 70, 226, 249, 447, 465–466,
  482, 514, 525–526, 537, 547
South-East Asia Treaty Organization (SEATO) 251
South Korea *79–80*, 121, 127, 142–143, 175–176,
  202–203, 206, 209–210, 221–226, 246–248,
  250, 252, 254, 256, *259–260*, 268, 276–278,
  297, 300, *307*, 313, 320–324, 327–328, 335,
  338, 343, 345, 351–352, 356, 358, *363*, *365*,
  373, 379, 381–382, 385–386, 395, 398–399,
  409, 411, 418–420, 430, 462, 465, *482*, 495,
  534–535, 557
South Sudan 529
Soviet Union 22, 23, 32, 38, 47–48, 57, 62, 63,
  79–80, 93, 109, 114, 121, 123, 127, 132, 133,
  136, 138–142, 151–154, 161, *165*, *167*, 169–
  172, 176, 178, 185–188, 191–193, 197–200,
  203, 216–222, 224–225, 236–238, 241–242,
  250–253, 255–256, *259–260*, 263–287, 294,
  295–296 , 311–315, 317–319, 322, 324–327,
  330, 333–338, 344, 351–362, *363*, 368–370,

385, 391, 395–397, 403, 406–407, 411–412,
426, 452–453
Soya Strait 330, 337, 346
SS-20 missiles 31, 63, *259*, 264, 267, 287,
311–315, 334, 346, 352
Strategic Arms Limitation Talks (SALT) *165*,
193, 198–199
Strategic Arms Reduction Treaties (START)
296, *363*, 502
Suga Yoshihide *482–483*
Suharto 322
Sun Yat-sen 450
Suzuki Kazuo 94
Suzuki Zenko 31, *259*, 280, 283, 340, 375–376
Sweden 126, 223, 258, 543, 553
Switzerland 258
Syngman Rhee 328

T

Taiwan 26, 89–90, 92, 93, 95–96, 121, 122,
143–144, *165*, 175, 187, 209, 246–248, 251,
254–255, 267, 269, 319, 343–344, *364*, 370,
411, 466, 468, 474–475, *483*, 488–491, 497,
499, 514, 518
Taiwan Strait 241, 252, *364*, 463–464, 474–475,
489–490, 514, 547
Takasaki Tatsunosuke 90–91, 122–123
Takeshima 248
Takeshita Noboru *260*
Takeuchi Yoshimi 90
Tanaka Kakuei 23, *165*, 187, *259*, 453
Thailand 99, 121, 127, 279, 358, *364*, *460*, 550
Thatcher, Margaret 46–47, 454
Tiananmen Square massacre *261*, 375, 399, 454,
463–464, 471
Toshiba–Kongsberg scandal *260*, 434
Trans-Pacific Partnership (TPP) *see*
Comprehensive and Progressive Agreement
for Trans-Pacific Partnership (CPTPP)
Treaty on the Denuclearization of Central and
South America 200–203
Trump, Donald 29, *482*, 534–536
Tsushima Straits 249
Turkiye 358, 400

U

Ukraine 29–30, 49, 71, *481*, *483*, 542–544,
546–547, 552–553, 555, 558
Ullman, Richard 200–201
United Kingdom 29, 32, 46, 54, 55, *79*, 94, 102,
108, 114, 154, 200, 202, *259*, *307*, 340, 374,
384, 395, 401, *481–482*, 539–540, 554
United Nations 37–40, 42, *80*, 99, 101, 122, 125,
150, 154, *165*, 200–202, 222, 248, *363*, 381,
374, 376, 382–385, 398–399, 409, 418–419,
424, 459–460, 473, *480*, 491, 493, 501,
547–549, 557–558
  Conference of Non-Nuclear Weapon States
  (1968) 153–154, 157, 161
  Eighteen-Nation Disarmament Committee

150–151, 204
  Law of the Sea Convention 249–251, *259*,
  524–525, 547
  peacekeeping forces *363*, 376, 382–384, 408–
  409, 418, 423–425, 428, 435, 459, *480*, 529
  Security Council 70, *80*, 371, 374, 382–385,
  460, 473, 547–549, 557–558
United States 21–28, 31, 37–38, 40–44, 47–48,
54, 57–58, 63–64, *79–80*, 83–85, 88–91, 93–95,
97–109, 113–115, 119, 121, 125–133, 136–143,
151–154, 161, *165–167*, 169–176, 178–179,
181–186, 188, 191–193, 196–204, 205–210,
212–214, 216–219, 221–222, 229–243, 248,
251–257, *259–261*, 263–278, 281–284, 285–
287, 289, 293, 295–296, 311–315, 317–331,
333, 338–342, 345–347, 351–359, *363–364*,
368–372, 374, 379, 385–388, 394–400, 405–
408, 411–412, 415–422, 426–443, 450–462,
464–467, 473, *479–483*, 485–506, 514,
516–518, 523, 532, 534–536, 542, 554, 556
  Arms Control and Disarmament Agency 221
  Congress 154, 179, 231, 240, *259*, 284, 320,
  374, 422, 430–431, 434, 400
  Guidelines for US–Japan Defense Cooperation
  167, *364*, 459–461, 467, *481*, 489
  Nuclear Posture Review 490–491
United States–Japan Security Treaty (1951) 21,
24, 43, *79–80*, 91, 97–98, 103–105, 107–108,
114–115, 124, *165*, 179, 181–183, 186, 188,
196, 214, 230–231, 274, 290, 330, 347,
381–382, 419, 421, 427, 452, 457
Utsunomiya Tokuma 92–93

V

Vietnam 22, 24–25, 57, 97–100, 105, 106, 109,
120, 123–124, 127–132, 134–135, 137, 140, 142,
165–166, 248, 253, 255, 263–264, 268, 279–280,
291, 317, 321, 322, 325, 337, 351, 358, 396,
411–412, 438, 443, *460*, 525, 527, 550
  Cam Ranh Bay 253, 279, 337
Vogel, Ezra 539

W

Wakamiya Yoshibumi 449
war on terror 31
Ward, Robert 71, *309–310*
Warsaw Pact 356, 370, 403
Weinberger, Caspar 283
Wen Jiabao 526
World Bank *79*, 371, 378, 380–381
World Trade Organization (WTO) 28, 457,
474, *479*

X

Xi Jinping *481*

Y

Yamahana Sadao 423
Yellow Sea 249

Yeltsin, Boris 413–414
Yemen 264
Yom Kippur War *see* October War
Yomiuri Shimbun 54, 56, *303*
Yoshida Shigeru 38–39, 44, 45, *79*, 84, 102, 103,
    115, 206, 422, 452
  Yoshida Doctrine 21–22, 31, 38

Yugoslavia 370, 397, 409

Z

Zelenskyy, Volodymyr 544
Zhou Enlai 90, 319
Zhu Rongji 490, 496

Six *Adelphi* numbers are published each year by Routledge Journals, an imprint of Taylor & Francis, 4 Park Square, Milton Park, Abingdon, Oxfordshire OX14 4RN, UK.

A subscription to the institution print edition, ISSN 1944-5571, includes free access for any number of concurrent users across a local area network to the online edition, ISSN 1944-558X. Taylor & Francis has a flexible approach to subscriptions enabling us to match individual libraries' requirements. This journal is available via a traditional institutional subscription (either print with free online access, or online-only at a discount) or as part of our libraries, subject collections or archives. For more information on our sales packages please visit www.tandfonline.com/page/librarians.

2023 Annual *Adelphi* Subscription Rates			
Institution	£973	US$1,707	€1,439
Individual	£333	US$571	€457
Online only	£827	US$1,451	€1,223

Dollar rates apply to subscribers outside Europe. Euro rates apply to all subscribers in Europe except the UK and the Republic of Ireland where the pound sterling price applies. All subscriptions are payable in advance and all rates include postage. Journals are sent by air to the USA, Canada, Mexico, India, Japan and Australasia. Subscriptions are entered on an annual basis, i.e., January to December. Payment may be made by sterling cheque, dollar cheque, international money order, National Giro, or credit card (Amex, Visa, Mastercard).

For a complete and up-to-date guide to Taylor & Francis journals and books publishing programmes, and details of advertising in our journals, visit our website: **http://www.tandfonline.com**.

Ordering information:
USA/Canada: Taylor & Francis Inc., Journals Department, 530 Walnut Street, Suite 850, Philadelphia, PA 19106, USA. **UK/Europe/Rest of World:** Routledge Journals, T&F Customer Services, T&F Informa UK Ltd., Sheepen Place, Colchester, Essex, CO3 3LP, UK.

Advertising enquiries to:
USA/Canada: The Advertising Manager, Taylor & Francis Inc., 530 Walnut Street, Suite 850, Philadelphia, PA 19106, USA. Tel: +1 (800) 354 1420. Fax: +1 (215) 207 0050. **UK/Europe/Rest of World**: The Advertising Manager, Routledge Journals, Taylor & Francis, 4 Park Square, Milton Park, Abingdon, Oxfordshire OX14 4RN, UK. Tel: +44 (0) 20 7017 6000. Fax: +44 (0) 20 7017 6336.